Mastering AWS Cloud

Cloud adoption using the AWS cloud computing ecosystem

Paulo H. Leocadio

bpb

www.bpbonline.com

First Edition 2026

Copyright © BPB Publications, India

ISBN: 978-93-65890-617

LIMITS OF LIABILITY AND DISCLAIMER OF WARRANTY

To View Complete
BPB Publications Catalogue
Scan the QR Code:

Dedicated to

My beloved wife Lucy

Our five children and Lily

the next generation

About the Author

Paulo H. Leocadio is a seasoned technologist, author, and international advisor with over four decades of experience spanning software engineering, cloud infrastructure, **artificial intelligence** (**AI**), and enterprise architecture. A Microsoft alumnus with a legacy of leading global transformation projects, Paulo has designed and delivered digital infrastructure strategies across 30+ countries, working with governments, multinationals, and startups alike.

Paulo holds a foundational degree in electronic and computer science engineering, postgraduate qualifications in solid state physics and data science, and a master's in international business. His work reflects a rare blend of theoretical expertise with practical application—from co-authoring public sector cloud modernization blueprints to developing AI-powered cybersecurity frameworks using Hugging Face Diffusers and AWS.

Beyond his consulting and engineering work, Paulo is a prolific academic contributor and peer reviewer for international AI journals. His published works reflect a commitment to bridging frontier science with real-world implementation, often grounded in speculative and philosophical views on the future of intelligent systems.

Currently, he leads Zinnia AI software engineering and digital design—a research-driven enterprise under Zinnia holdings—and mentors emerging AI professionals worldwide. Mastering AWS Cloud is his key contribution to the cloud-native community: a thorough, structured, and highly technical reference for professionals building the next generation of intelligent, scalable systems.

About the Reviewer

Baron Ntambwe is a Canadian professional software engineer. Most of his work focuses on AI, big data, and distributed systems. He holds a bachelor of engineering in computer systems, a bachelor of technology in software engineering, and a master of science degree in AI. With a strong educational foundation, Baron embarked on a successful career in software engineering. He has held various leadership roles, including engineering manager III at Amazon AWS and senior engineering manager at Walmart Global Tech, based in Silicon Valley, San Francisco. His professional journey is marked by a commitment to excellence and a drive to push the boundaries of technological advancements. Beyond his professional accomplishments, Baron is a member of the Baha'i Faith, whose principles of the Oneness of Mankind have prompted him to dedicate himself to giving back to his community. He actively participates in community-building activities initiated by his local Baha'i community, spending most of his weekends engaged in service and youth empowerment work. Through his endeavors, Baron strives to make a positive impact in the world around him.

Acknowledgement

I am grateful to BPB Publications for the invitation that developed into a meaningful partnership. Their editorial trust, accuracy, and support helped shape the scope and direction of this volume from its earliest drafts.

I extend my deepest gratitude to Dr. Rebecca "Becky" Smethurst, researcher at the department of astrophysics, Oxford University. Her rare ability to distill complexity without diluting depth, to inspire without exaggeration, and to teach without condescension has left a lasting mark on this work. During a time of significant personal and professional change, her example—communicated not only through her influential works but also through her demeanor, openness, and unwavering intellectual clarity—offered more than just insight. It provided guidance.

Finally, I dedicate this work to my family. In their constant presence, I found stability; in their patience, the rhythm; and in their belief, the strength to cross the invisible line between knowing and starting anew.

Preface

This book is motivated by a long-standing commitment to understanding how complex systems operate, from information theory and distributed infrastructure to human learning and scientific research. It reflects years of experience in both academic and practical aspects of computing, aiming to synthesize a deep, organized, and technically rigorous understanding of cloud computing from the perspective of **Amazon Web Services (AWS)**.

At its core, the motivation for this work is twofold: to provide meaningful insights into the scientific literature on cloud architecture and operations, and to serve as a practical guide for those navigating the rapidly expanding AWS ecosystem. Cloud computing is no longer a niche tool; it has become the foundation of contemporary innovation. This book aims to frame that transformation with both technical accuracy and clear teaching.

Chapter 1: AWS Architecture- Introduces the core concepts of AWS, including its worldwide data center network, Availability Zones, and service regions. It gives readers a basic understanding of how AWS functions globally and prepares them to explore services built on this solid infrastructure.

Chapter 2: Compute- Explores AWS **Identity and Access Management (IAM)**, service control policies, permission boundaries, and governance strategies. The chapter outlines best practices for securely managing users, roles, and resources on scale.

Chapter 3: Storage- Covers **Elastic Compute Cloud (EC2)** and AWS Lambda, comparing traditional and serverless compute models. Readers will gain insight into provisioning, configuring, and managing compute resources for various use cases.

Chapter 4: Content Delivery Network- Explores AWS container services, such as Amazon ECS, EKS, and AWS Fargate. The chapter emphasizes container deployment, orchestration, and infrastructure abstraction for modern microservices architectures.

Chapter 5: Security, Identity, and Compliance- Details AWS storage options such as S3, EBS, EFS, and Glacier. This chapter explains storage classes, performance optimization, lifecycle policies, and how they integrate into distributed application workflows.

Chapter 6: Database- Explores the **Virtual Private Cloud (VPC)** model, including subnets, routing, gateways, NAT, peering, and security groups. Readers learn how to design secure and scalable network environments.

Chapter 7: Developer Tools and DevOps: Part 1- Introduces managed database services such as RDS, DynamoDB, Aurora, and Redshift, along with analytics tools like Athena and Glue. Readers explore use cases and configurations for both real-time and batch processing.

Chapter 8: Developer Tools and DevOps: Part 2- Focuses on decoupling services and integrating them via SNS, SQS, EventBridge, and Step Functions. The chapter emphasizes designing loosely coupled architecture and event-driven workflows.

Chapter 9: End-user, Front-end, and Mobile- Covers security tools like AWS Shield, WAF, Config, and Inspector, along with observability solutions such as CloudWatch, CloudTrail, and X-Ray to ensure system resilience and auditability.

Chapter 10: Applications for Business- Guides readers through infrastructure automation using AWS CloudFormation, CDK, and the integration of CI/CD pipelines with CodePipeline, CodeBuild, and GitOps practices.

Chapter 11: Analytics and Machine Learning- Introduces AWS AI/ML services including SageMaker, Comprehend, Rekognition, and the broader ML stack. Readers learn how to integrate intelligent services into cloud-native applications.

Chapter 12: Management and Governance- Covers AWS Greengrass, IoT Core, and hybrid environments, including Outposts and Snowball. This chapter helps readers connect cloud and edge deployments for low-latency applications.

Chapter 13: Migration and Transfer- Focuses on AWS Budgets, Cost Explorer, Savings Plans, and governance policies for cost management. The chapter teaches how to align financial accountability with scalable cloud expansion.

Chapter 14: AWS Well-Architected Framework- Concludes with advanced architectural patterns, Well-Architected Framework pillars, and compliance considerations. This final chapter prepares readers to design resilient, secure, and regulation-compliant workloads.

Coloured Images

Please follow the link to download the
Coloured Images of the book:

https://rebrand.ly/644417

We have code bundles from our rich catalogue of books and videos available at https://github.com/bpbpublications. Check them out!

Errata

We take immense pride in our work at BPB Publications and follow best practices to ensure the accuracy of our content to provide an indulging reading experience to our subscribers. Our readers are our mirrors, and we use their inputs to reflect and improve upon human errors, if any, that may have occurred during the publishing processes involved. To let us maintain the quality and help us reach out to any readers who might be having difficulties due to any unforeseen errors, please write to us at:

errata@bpbonline.com

Your support, suggestions and feedback are highly appreciated by the BPB Publications' Family.

At www.bpbonline.com, you can also read a collection of free technical articles, sign up for a range of free newsletters, and receive exclusive discounts and offers on BPB books and eBooks. You can check our social media handles below:

Instagram

Facebook

Linkedin

YouTube

Get in touch with us at: business@bpbonline.com for more details.

Piracy

If you come across any illegal copies of our works in any form on the internet, we would be grateful if you would provide us with the location address or website name. Please contact us at business@bpbonline.com with a link to the material.

If you are interested in becoming an author

If there is a topic that you have expertise in, and you are interested in either writing or contributing to a book, please visit www.bpbonline.com. We have worked with thousands of developers and tech professionals, just like you, to help them share their insights with the global tech community. You can make a general application, apply for a specific hot topic that we are recruiting an author for, or submit your own idea.

Reviews

Please leave a review. Once you have read and used this book, why not leave a review on the site that you purchased it from? Potential readers can then see and use your unbiased opinion to make purchase decisions. We at BPB can understand what you think about our products, and our authors can see your feedback on their book. Thank you!

For more information about BPB, please visit www.bpbonline.com.

Join our Discord space

Join our Discord workspace for latest updates, offers, tech happenings around the world, new releases, and sessions with the authors:

https://discord.bpbonline.com

Table of Contents

Wrap up 285

AWS Cost and Usage Report 285

Key features 286

Benefits 286

Use cases 286

Best practices 287

Wrap up 287

AWS Cost Explorer 287

Key features 287

Benefits 288

Use cases 288

Best practices 288

Wrap up 289

Reserved Instance Reporting 289

Key features and benefits 289

Use cases 289

Best practices 290

Wrap up 290

AWS Savings Plans 290

Key features 290

Advantages 291

Managing AWS Savings Plans 291

Best practices 292

Use cases 292

Wrap up 293

Media services... 293

Amazon Elastic Transcoder... 294

Key features 294

Use cases of Amazon Elastic Transcoder 294

Best practices for effective usage 295

Wrap up 295

Amazon Interactive Video Service 295

Key features 295

Use cases of Amazon IVS... 296

Best practices for implementation 296

Prologue

In the architecture of a cloud system, the silent elegance lies not in any one service or script, but in the orchestration of parts—how communication, computation, and control converge in reproducible patterns that scale. It is, in many ways, the modern blueprint of systems thinking, echoing disciplines far beyond computer science.

However, behind every system lies a human system: intent, constraint, error, and learning. This book does not merely describe services; it follows the arc of decisions—technical and otherwise—that define how digital infrastructures evolve. It speaks to the engineer, the scientist, and the architect not as discrete identities, but as converging roles in the present technological epoch.

The impetus for writing this volume was not born in a vacuum of abstraction but shaped over decades of lived technical work. From navigating enterprise architecture in the corridors of global corporations to revisiting first principles under a different kind of light—one shaped by inquiry rather than delivery—cloud systems came to be viewed not as tools, but as environments in which reasoning, optimization, and resilience become visible.

And it was in that crossing—from execution to inquiry, from systems of deployment to systems of explanation—that this book began to take form.

Join our Discord space

Join our Discord workspace for latest updates, offers, tech happenings around the world, new releases, and sessions with the authors:

https://discord.bpbonline.com

CHAPTER 1
AWS Architecture

Introduction

In the constantly changing world of cloud computing, **Amazon Web Services** (**AWS**) remains a leading symbol of innovation and change. As we begin our exploration of AWS architecture in the first chapter of this book, we enter a space where cloud technology transforms what is possible. Founded by Amazon.com in 2006, AWS has grown into the world's most extensive and widely used cloud platform, supporting millions of customers worldwide [1]. This chapter acts as our guide to understanding the essential architectural foundations that support this digital giant.

Structure

In this chapter, we will discuss the following topics:

- Introduction to AWS
- Global Infrastructure
- Regions and Availability Zones
- Amazon Web Services
- Compute services

- Storage services

- Networking in AWS

- Security and identity

- Scalability and elasticity

- AWS Well-Architected Framework

- Cost optimization

Objectives

By the end of this chapter, you will gain a basic understanding of AWS's architectural principles and its role as a catalyst for digital innovation. These principles will form the foundation for a deeper exploration of AWS in the upcoming chapters of the book.

Introduction to AWS

In the vast landscape of cloud computing, AWS stands as a formidable titan, shaping the digital evolution of businesses and individuals alike. To embark on our journey into AWS architecture in this book chapter, it is crucial to contextualize its emergence and ascendancy. Founded by **Amazon.com** in 2006, AWS swiftly transcended its initial identity as a humble cloud computing experiment to become the unrivaled leader in cloud technology [2]. Its meteoric rise was propelled by the visionary leadership of Amazon's CEO *Jeff Bezos*, who recognized the potential for providing businesses with scalable computing resources, transforming IT infrastructure into a utility accessible to anyone, anywhere [3].

AWS's influence is worldwide, with a strong presence on multiple continents. Its infrastructure is a feat of engineering, comprising a network of data centers carefully placed across regions and **Availability Zones (AZs)**. This extensive reach not only offers low-latency service access but also ensures redundancy and fault-tolrance, which are essential in today's digital world [4]. With a customer base that includes startups, enterprises, governments, and individuals, AWS has made access to cutting-edge technology widely available. It serves as the foundation for many innovations, from web startups to scientific research, demonstrating its flexibility across a wide range of use cases [2].

Understanding AWS's historical development and the vast scale of its customer base and infrastructure is crucial when examining AWS architecture. These fundamental elements lay the groundwork for grasping the technical details and architectural principles discussed in later sections of this chapter.

Global Infrastructure

In the ever-expanding world of cloud computing, the foundation on which a cloud provider's services are built is critical. AWS, in its effort to provide unmatched performance, resilience, and scalability, has carefully designed a Global Infrastructure that exemplifies technological innovation. In this section, we explore the details of AWS Global Infrastructure, highlighting the strategic placement of data centers around the world, the concept of regions and AZs, and the significant impact this architecture has on ensuring reliability and low-latency access vital in today's digital age.

AWS's Global Infrastructure forms the backbone of its service offerings, carefully designed to meet customers' various needs worldwide. Key to this infrastructure are AWS Regions, geographic areas made up of multiple AZs. Each region is built to be isolated from others, ensuring redundancy and failover capabilities. This geographic distribution helps reduce the risk of service disruptions caused by natural disasters or other unexpected events. Within each region, there are several AZs, which are essentially data centers with independent power, cooling, and network connectivity. These AZs are connected through low-latency, high-throughput links, enabling synchronous data replication and high availability. This setup is vital for providing the resiliency and fault-tolrance necessary for modern applications [4]. Refer to the following figure:

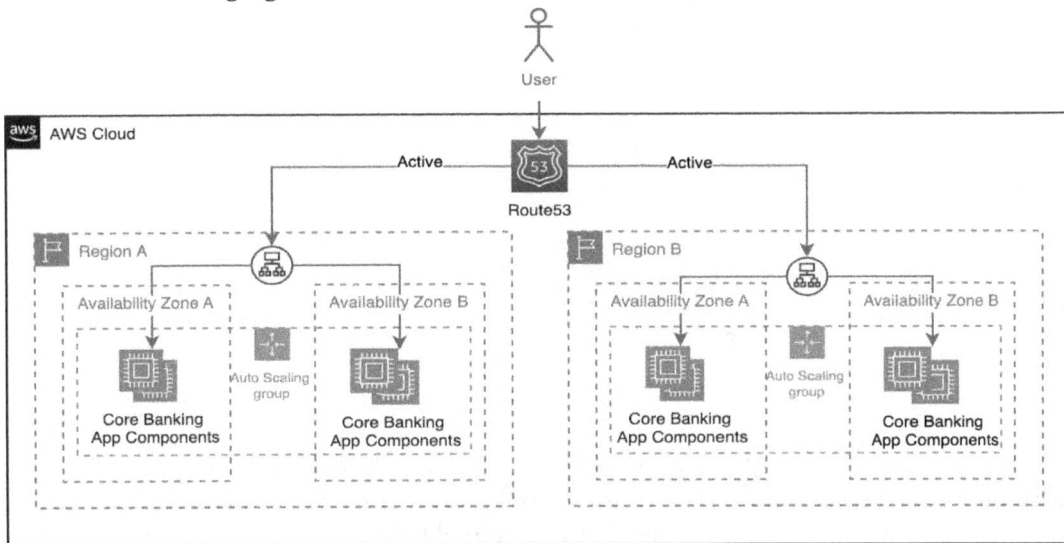

Figure 1.1: AWS commitment to resiliency, multi-region active-active pattern (P5)

Furthermore, AWS's careful approach includes selecting data center locations. These centers are strategically positioned across various regions worldwide to serve a global customer base. By providing regions across multiple continents, AWS ensures that users can deploy their applications and services near their end-users, thereby reducing latency and enhancing the user experience. This strategic placement of data centers is not just about proximity but also about regulatory compliance. It helps organizations meet data sovereignty requirements by keeping data within specific geographic boundaries. Whether you are a startup targeting local markets or a multinational corporation with a global reach, AWS's Global Infrastructure supports reliability, scalability, and low-latency access, making it a key part of modern cloud architecture [5].

Regions and Availability Zones

In the intricately woven tapestry of AWS architecture, the concepts of regions and AZs are essential threads, crucial for creating high availability and fault-tolrance. In this section, we thoroughly examine these fundamental building blocks that support AWS's infrastructure. By the end, you will understand their importance and how they form the foundation of AWS's commitment to keeping your applications and data resilient, available, and high performing. Refer to the following figure:

Figure 1.2: AWS Regions and AZs

AWS defines a region as a geographically distinct area with available AWS resources. Each region operates independently [5], encompassing multiple data centers, which makes it highly resistant to regional disruptions. For example, the AWS US East (*N. Virginia*) region is separate from the AWS EU (*Ireland*) region. These regions are strategically located around the world, allowing AWS users to deploy resources close to their target audience or to meet data residency and compliance requirements. This geographical diversity enables organizations to design their systems for redundancy, failover, and low-latency access, all while leveraging AWS's extensive global network infrastructure [4].

Within each AWS Region, the concept of AZs comes into play. It is essentially a data center, but AWS goes the extra mile by ensuring that these AZs are isolated from one another. They have power, cooling, and network connectivity, minimizing the risk of correlated failures. These AZs are interconnected through a network designed for low-latency, high-throughput communication, allowing for synchronous data replication and providing the foundation for high availability. By distributing resources across multiple AZs, AWS users can architect their applications and systems to withstand failures, ensuring that services remain available even in the face of unexpected events and data remains secure. The combination of regions and AZs exemplifies AWS's commitment to delivering robust and resilient cloud infrastructure [5]. Refer to the following figure:

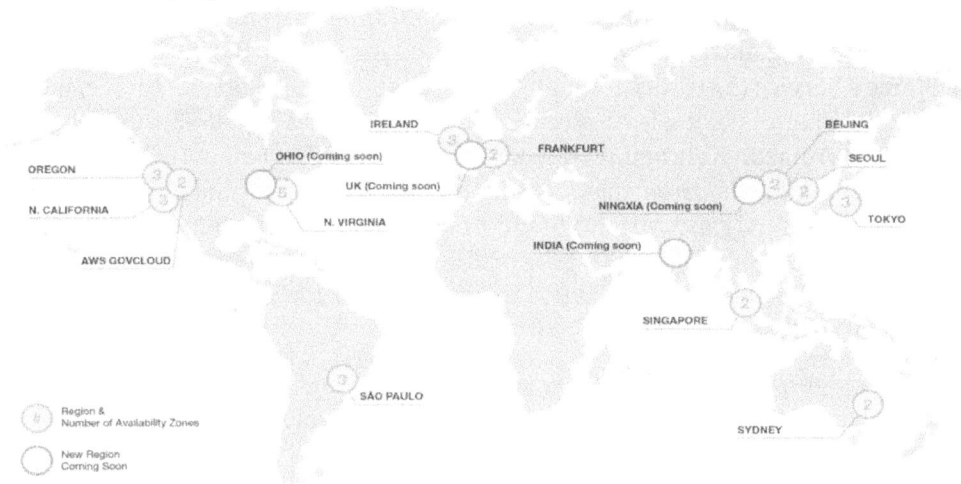

Figure 1.3: Map of AWS AZs

Amazon Web Services

AWS stands as a true titan in the cloud computing landscape, not just for its infrastructure but also for its extensive suite of services that address virtually every computing need imaginable. In this section, we take a journey through the rich landscape of AWS services, exploring their variety and depth and understanding how they together enable organizations to innovate, grow, and transform. Refer to the following figure:

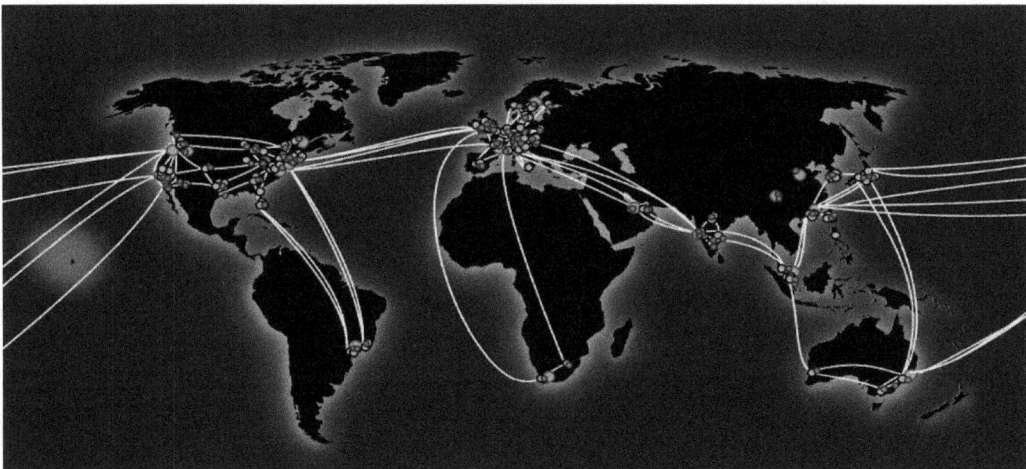

Figure 1.4: A map of the AWS Global Infrastructure network

At the heart of AWS's allure is its extensive portfolio of services, designed to address a broad spectrum of customer requirements. These services can be categorized into several key domains, including computing, storage, databases, **machine learning** (**ML**), and the **Internet of Things** (**IoT**) [7], and more. AWS offers **Elastic Compute Cloud** (**EC2**) for scalable virtual servers, Lambda for serverless computing, and **Elastic Container Service** (**ECS**) for containerized applications, ensuring flexibility for diverse workloads [8]. In the realm of storage, AWS **Simple Storage Service** (**S3**) provides highly durable and scalable object storage, while **Elastic Block Store** (**EBS**) offers block-level storage for EC2 instances [9]. AWS's managed database services, such as Amazon **Relational Database Service** (**RDS**), DynamoDB, and Aurora, cater to diverse database needs, from relational to NoSQL [9]. For organizations venturing into **artificial intelligence** (**AI**) and ML, AWS offers SageMaker, which streamlines model training and deployment, and Rekognition, a powerful image and video analysis service [10]. With AWS IoT Core [7], businesses can harness the potential of the IoT, managing and analyzing data from connected devices [5].

This extensive range of AWS services showcases innovation and addresses the changing needs of businesses and developers. AWS's dedication to offering scalable, secure, and versatile solutions is clear in the wide scope of its service options. As we explore this chapter and subsequent parts of the book, we will examine these services in more detail, highlighting their potential and illustrating how they can be strategically used to build strong, scalable cloud solutions.

Compute services

In the fast-changing world of cloud computing, AWS's strength is truly evident in its wide range of compute services, each designed to serve as a fundamental part of various applications and workloads. This chapter provides a detailed look at AWS's compute services. It offers a clear understanding of their unique features and emphasizes their crucial role in creating scalable and flexible cloud-based applications.

EC2 stands as one of the cornerstones of AWS's compute offerings. It provides resizable virtual servers, known as **instances**, allowing users to scale up or down based on their computing needs quickly. With EC2, organizations can deploy applications, host websites, and manage workloads precisely and flexibly. EC2 instances come in various configurations, including compute-optimized, memory-optimized, and storage-optimized, catering to a wide range of computational requirements [11]. Furthermore, AWS Lambda, a serverless computing service, represents a paradigm shift in application development. Lambda enables developers to run code responding to events without managing servers, automatically scaling based on incoming requests. This serverless approach simplifies application development, reduces operational overhead, and accelerates time to market [12]. In addition, the ECS empowers organizations to manage and orchestrate containerized applications effortlessly. Whether using Docker containers or AWS Fargate for serverless containers, ECS streamlines the deployment and scaling of containerized workloads, making it an ideal choice for modern application architectures [13]. Refer to the following figure:

Instance Types

The following table list the specifications for aach Amazon EC2 Instance Type:

Instance Family	Instance Type	Architecture	vCPU	ECU	Memory (GIB)	Instance Storage (GB)	EBS-optimized Bandwidth	# IP	Network Performance
General purpose	m1.amall	32-bit or 64-bit	1	1	1.7	1 x 160	-	8	Low
General purpose	m1.medium	32-bit or 64-bit	1	2	3.75	1 x 410	-	12	Moderate
General purpose	m1.large	64-bit	2	4	7.5	2 x 420	500 Mbps	30	Moderate
General purpose	m2.xlarge	64-bit	4	8	15	2 x 840	1000 Mbps	60	High
General purpose	m1.xlarge	64-bit	4	13	15	0 - EBS only	500 Mbps	30	Moderate
General purpose	m3.2xlarge	64-bit	8	26	30	0 - EBS only	1000 Mbps	120	High
Compute optimized	c1.medium	32-bit or 64-bit	2	5	1.7	1 x 350	-	12	Moderate
Compute optimized	c1.xlarge	64-bit	8	20	7	4 x 420	1000 Mbps	60	High
Compute optimized	cc1.4xlarge	64-bit	16	33.5	22.5	2 x 420	-	1	10 Gigabt [5]
Compute optimized	cc3.8xlarge	64-bit	32 [1]	88	60.5	4 x 840	-	240	10 Gigabt [5]
Memory optimized	m2.xlarge	64-bit	2	6.5	17.1	1 x 420	-	60	Moderate
Memory optimized	cc2.2xlarge	64-bit	4	13	34.2	1 x 850	500 Mbps	120	Moderate

Figure 1.5: EC2 instance types table

AWS's compute services go beyond simple tools; they enable innovation and boost efficiency. As we explore this chapter and future ones, we will reveal the detailed aspects of these services, including their use cases, best practices, and how they contribute to creating resilient, scalable, and high-performing cloud applications. Whether building a web app, analyzing data, or deploying ML models, AWS's compute services offer the flexibility and power needed to turn your ideas into reality.

Storage services

In the digital age, where data is the lifeblood of organizations, AWS provides a range of storage services that form the backbone of numerous applications and businesses worldwide. This chapter section takes a deep dive into AWS's storage services, specifically focusing on two key offerings: S3 and EBS [13]; [14]. We will delve into the intricacies of these services, examine their diverse use cases, and discuss how they enable organizations to manage, store, and retrieve data efficiently.

S3 represents the bedrock of AWS's storage solutions. It is an object storage service that provides highly durable and scalable storage for many use cases. S3's versatility extends from serving as a secure repository for backups and archives to acting as a foundation for web applications, mobile apps, and big data analytics. With its global reach and low-latency access, S3 enables organizations to store and retrieve data with ease, while its robust security features, such as data encryption and access control, ensure data remains protected [15]. On the other hand, EBS caters to block-level storage needs, primarily for use with Amazon EC2 instances. EBS offers a range of volume types, including general-purpose SSDs, high-performance SSDs, and magnetic volumes, allowing organizations to tailor their storage solutions to specific performance requirements. EBS volumes can be attached to EC2 instances, providing reliable and low-latency storage for applications, databases, and more [14].

The role of storage in the cloud ecosystem is crucial and cannot be overstated. AWS's S3 and EBS services exemplify the company's dedication to providing flexible, durable, and high-performance storage solutions. As we continue our exploration, we will examine these storage services in more detail, exploring advanced features, best practices, and real-world use cases that demonstrate how AWS's storage solutions are essential for building reliable and scalable cloud-based applications.

Networking in AWS

In the vast expanse of AWS, a robust and well-architected network infrastructure serves as the circulatory system, ensuring the seamless flow of data and resources. This section delves into the intricate world of AWS networking features, exploring key components such as **Virtual Private Clouds** (**VPCs**), Direct Connect, and Amazon Route 53. These elements form the vital connective tissue that underpins secure, scalable, and interconnected cloud environments.

At the core of AWS networking is the concept of VPC. It is a logically isolated section of the AWS cloud where you can launch AWS resources in a defined virtual network. It lets you define your IP address range, create subnets, configure route tables, and control traffic flows with security groups and **network access control lists** (**NACLs**). With VPCs, organizations can segment their resources, achieve network isolation, and apply granular control over traffic. VPCs serve as the foundation for secure and customizable network architectures, essential for hosting applications and services with stringent security and compliance requirements [16]. In addition to VPCs, AWS offers Direct Connect, a dedicated network connection that establishes a private, high-bandwidth link between your on-premises data center and AWS. Direct Connect is crucial for extending your network into the cloud while ensuring low-latency and predictable performance. It serves as the bridge between your existing infrastructure and the cloud, facilitating hybrid cloud architectures and providing a direct path to AWS services [17].

Moreover, Amazon Route 53, AWS's scalable and highly available **Domain Name System** (**DNS**) web service, is pivotal in ensuring that your applications are accessible and responsive. Route 53 allows you to route end-user requests to AWS resources or other endpoints globally, translating human-friendly domain names into IP addresses. This service not only enhances the reliability of your applications but also supports advanced routing policies, health checks, and domain registration services, making it an indispensable tool for building robust and scalable web applications [18]. As we progress through the subsequent chapters, we will delve deeper into these networking components, unraveling their complexities and demonstrating how they can be leveraged to construct secure, interconnected, and high-performing cloud environments. Refer to the following figure:

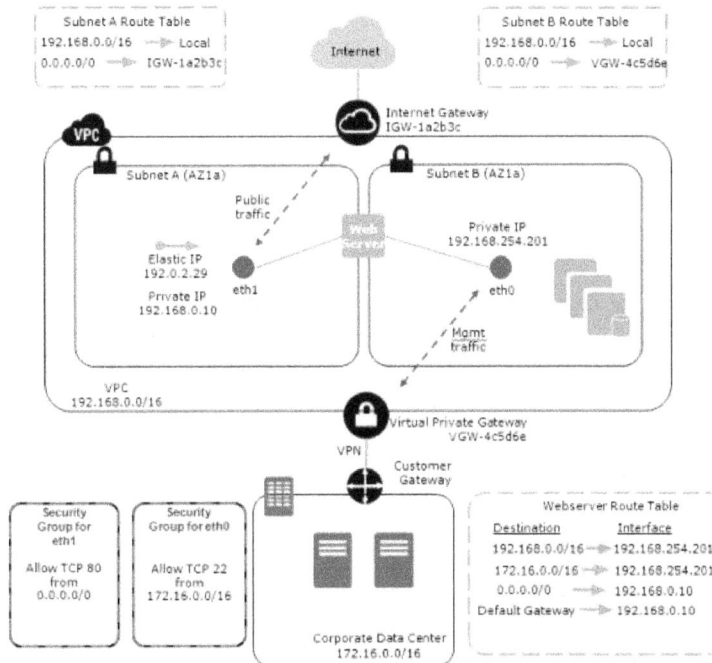

Figure 1.6: *VPC, subnets, routing tables, and ENIs*

Security and identity

In cloud computing, security is paramount, and AWS sets the gold standard with its comprehensive suite of security mechanisms. This section explores the world of AWS's robust security and identity features, examining pivotal tools such as **Identity and Access Management** (**IAM**) and the **web application firewall** (**WAF**). These components are the sentinels that guard your AWS resources, ensuring they remain protected in the ever-evolving threat landscape.

IAM is the linchpin of AWS security. It provides a centralized and fine-grained control system for managing user access to AWS resources. It enables organizations to create and manage user identities, assign permissions, and configure authentication and authorization policies. With IAM, businesses can ensure that users and applications have the right access level, minimizing the risk of unauthorized actions or data breaches. IAM's flexibility extends to **multi-factor authentication (MFA)**, identity federation, and integration with other AWS services. As a result, it empowers organizations to adhere to the principle of least privilege, an essential security best practice, while fostering collaboration and resource sharing within the AWS environment [19]. Refer to the following figure:

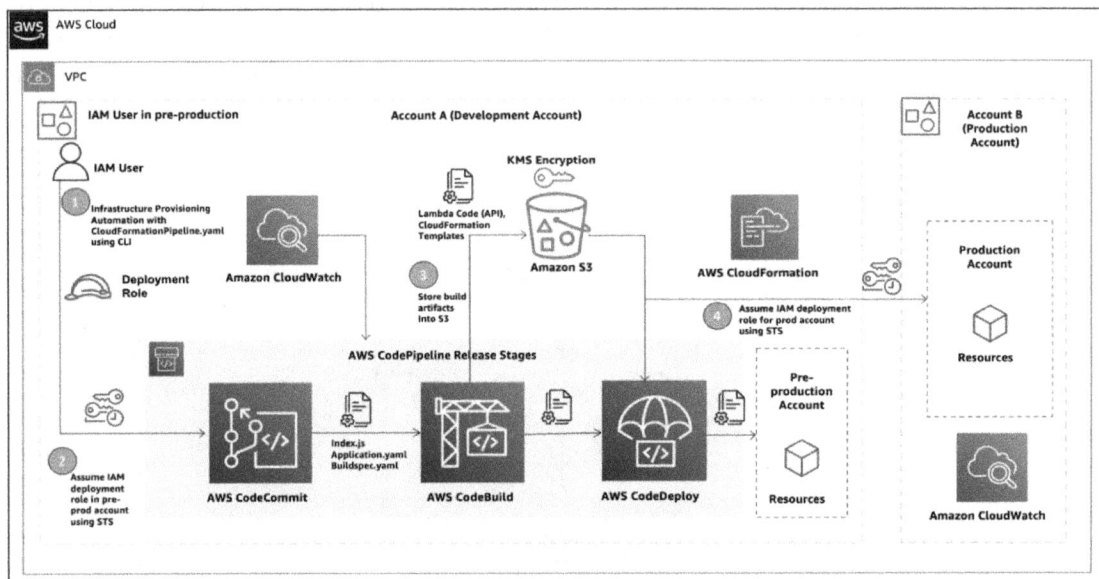

Figure 1.7: AWS cross-account AWS CodePipeline for production and non-production workloads

Furthermore, AWS WAF serves as a critical defense against web application attacks. WAF is a managed firewall service that enables organizations to create custom security rules, inspect incoming web traffic, and protect against common threats such as SQL injection and **cross-site scripting (XSS)** attacks. By integrating WAF with AWS resources, such as Amazon CloudFront and Application Load Balancers, businesses can create a secure front line for their applications, ensuring that malicious traffic is identified and blocked before it reaches their infrastructure [20].

Security is a fundamental aspect of AWS's design, and IAM and WAF are key components of their effort to protect customer data and resources. As we move forward, we will examine these security tools in more detail, revealing advanced techniques, best practices, and real-world examples of how AWS's security and identity features can be used to effectively safeguard your cloud assets.

Scalability and elasticity

In cloud computing, the ability to seamlessly scale and adapt to changing workloads is a key indicator of efficiency and cost-effectiveness. AWS promotes this idea with a range of services and features designed for scalability and elasticity. In this section, we explore how AWS's approach works, focusing on how it enables automatic scaling and resource optimization to manage variable workloads with outstanding efficiency.

At the core of AWS's scalability and elasticity is the notion that computing resources should align precisely with demand. **Elastic Load Balancing (ELB)** [21] is one of the fundamental AWS services that facilitates this alignment. ELB automatically distributes incoming application traffic across multiple Amazon EC2 instances, ensuring no single instance becomes a bottleneck. As traffic fluctuates, ELB dynamically scales the number of instances to accommodate changes in demand, effectively distributes the load, and optimizes application performance [22]. Moreover, AWS Auto Scaling takes this concept to the next level. With Auto Scaling, organizations can define scaling policies based on predefined conditions, such as CPU utilization or network traffic. When these conditions are met, Auto Scaling automatically adds or removes instances to match the desired capacity, ensuring that resources are efficiently utilized without manual intervention. This capability is particularly valuable for handling variable workloads, such as e-commerce websites experiencing traffic spikes during sales events or gaming applications during peak gaming hours [23].

Refer to the following figure:

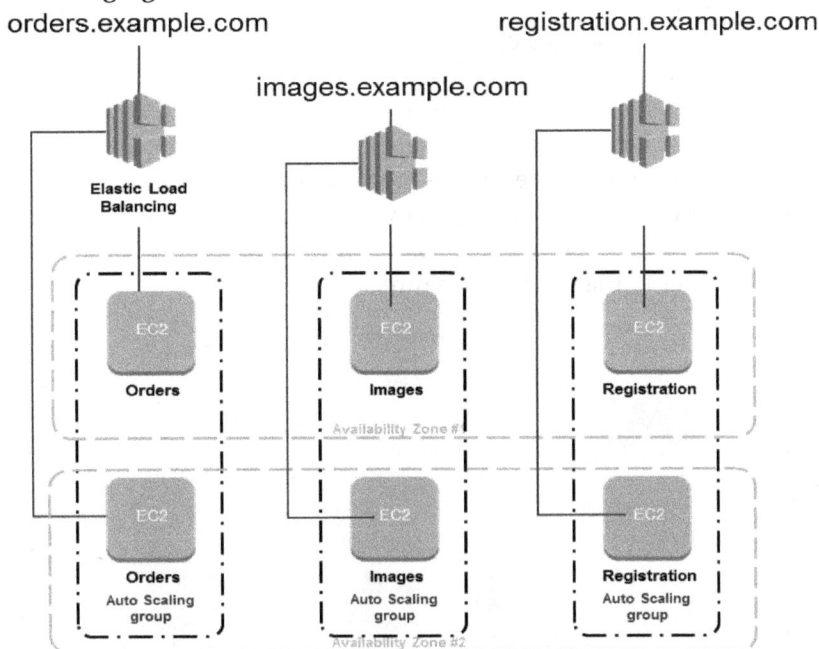

Figure 1.8: ELB in action

Furthermore, AWS offers a range of managed services, including Amazon RDS and Amazon DynamoDB, that incorporate scalability by design. These services automatically handle database replication, failover, and resource provisioning to ensure that databases can scale seamlessly with application demands. This approach enables organizations to focus on building applications without the operational overhead of managing database scalability manually [24]. In the chapters ahead, we will delve deeper into these services, exploring strategies and best practices for optimizing scalability and elasticity in your AWS architecture. As we uncover these principles, you will gain the knowledge and skills needed to build efficient, responsive, and cost-effective cloud-based solutions.

AWS Well-Architected Framework

In the dynamic and ever-evolving realm of cloud architecture, building a foundation that is secure, high-performing, resilient, and efficient is paramount. AWS recognized this imperative and responded with the AWS Well-Architected Framework, a set of best practices that serve as a guiding light for architects and engineers. This section introduces you to the AWS Well-Architected Framework, unveiling its principles and demonstrating how it empowers organizations to design and maintain cloud infrastructures that excel in all critical aspects.

The AWS Well-Architected Framework is designed as a blueprint for architects and developers to create an infrastructure that aligns with AWS's best practices. It revolves around five key pillars: Operational excellence, security, reliability, performance efficiency, and cost optimization. Each pillar represents a critical aspect of a well-architected system. Operational excellence emphasizes the need for efficient operations, automation, and continuous improvement, ensuring that your infrastructure evolves with the changing demands of your applications [25]. Security focuses on implementing robust security measures, from IAM to encryption, to safeguard data and resources from unauthorized access and breaches [26]. Reliability entails building systems that can recover gracefully from failures, whether they are due to hardware issues or unexpected events, ensuring minimal downtime and a seamless user experience [27]. Refer to the following figure:

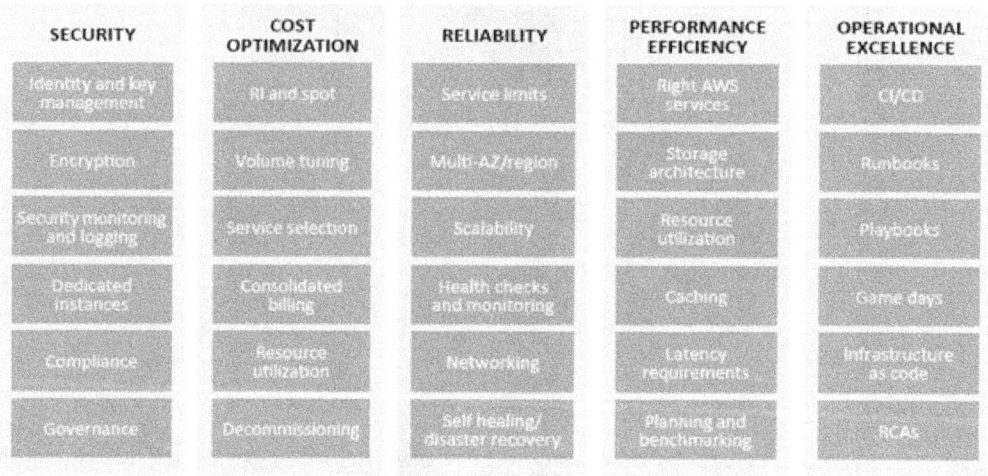

SECURITY	COST OPTIMIZATION	RELIABILITY	PERFORMANCE EFFICIENCY	OPERATIONAL EXCELLENCE
Identity and key management	RI and spot	Service limits	Right AWS services	CI/CD
Encryption	Volume tuning	Multi-AZ/region	Storage architecture	Runbooks
Security monitoring and logging	Service selection	Scalability	Resource utilization	Playbooks
Dedicated instances	Consolidated billing	Health checks and monitoring	Caching	Game days
Compliance	Resource utilization	Networking	Latency requirements	Infrastructure as code
Governance	Decommissioning	Self healing/ disaster recovery	Planning and benchmarking	RCAs

Figure 1.9: The five pillars of AWS Well-Architected Framework

Moreover, the performance efficiency pillar highlights the importance of optimizing resource utilization to deliver high-performance at a lower cost. This includes fine-tuning compute resources, storage, and network configurations to maximize efficiency while minimizing waste [28]. Cost optimization, the final pillar, underscores the need to manage and control costs effectively. It encourages organizations to make informed decisions about resource provisioning, utilization, and scaling to achieve the desired balance between cost and performance [29]. The AWS Well-Architected Framework is not just a static set of guidelines but a continuous evaluation and improvement process. AWS offers the Well-Architected Tool, which provides a self-service way to assess your architecture and identify areas for improvement, making it an invaluable resource in your journey to achieving excellence in cloud architecture [30]. As we progress through this book, we will explore each of these pillars in greater detail, equipping you with the knowledge and skills to design AWS architectures that meet the highest standards of performance, security, and efficiency.

Cost optimization

In the rapidly evolving world of cloud computing, cost optimization plays a crucial role in AWS architecture. This section covers essential strategies for managing and lowering AWS costs, emphasizing how organizations can leverage tools like AWS Trusted Advisor and cost allocation tags to enhance financial efficiency and maximize the value of their cloud investments.

Cost optimization in AWS is not just a desire but a strategic necessity. AWS recognizes the significance of this aspect and offers a suite of tools and best practices to help organizations effectively control costs. AWS Trusted Advisor, for instance, is a powerful tool that inspects an organization's AWS environment and provides real-time, personalized recommendations for optimizing costs, enhancing system performance, and improving security. It evaluates various aspects of an AWS infrastructure, including idle resources, underutilized instances, and opportunities for rightsizing, helping organizations make informed decisions that align with their financial objectives [31]. Furthermore, cost allocation tags enable businesses to categorize and track spending by resource, project, department, or any other relevant dimension. By applying cost allocation tags to AWS resources, organizations gain granular visibility into their cost structures, enabling them to identify areas of overspending and allocate costs accurately among teams and projects [32]. Refer to the following figure:

① Server Costs	Hardware: Server, rack chassis PDUs, ToR switches (+ maintenance)	Software: OS, virtualization licenses (+ maintenance)	Facilities Cost		
			Space	Power	Cooling
② Storage Costs	Hardware: Storage disks, SAN/FC switches	Storage software costs (+ maintenance)	Facilities Cost		
			Space	Power	Cooling
③ Network Costs	Network hardware: LAN switches, load balancer	Recurring ISP/bandwidth costs	Facilities Cost		
			Space	Power	Cooling

Note: Diagram doesn't include every cost item. For example, software costs can include database, management, and middle-tier software costs. Facilities costs can include costs associated with upgrades, maintenance, building security, taxes, and other items.

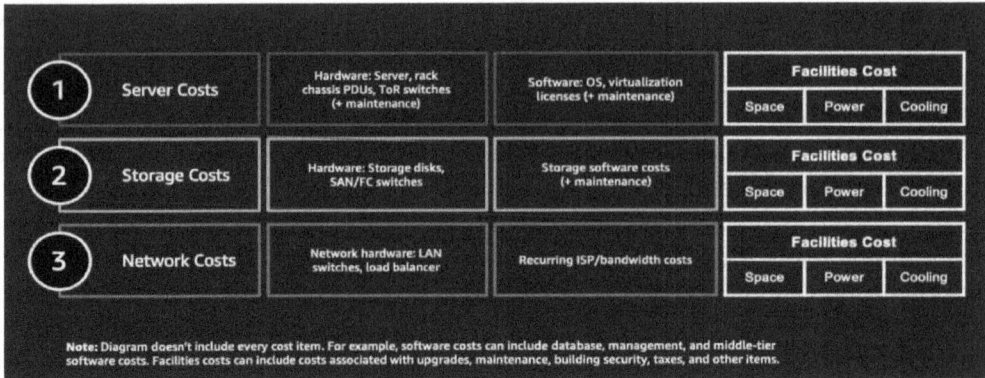

Figure 1.10: *AWS cost comparison model*

Scholarly articles such as *Cost Optimization in Cloud Computing* by *Vinay Kumar et al.* (2020) highlight the importance of cost optimization strategies in cloud environments. This article emphasizes the need to leverage automation, predictive analytics, and resource allocation techniques to reduce costs while maintaining high system performance [33]. Additionally, AWS Documentation on cost optimization provides comprehensive guidance on best practices and strategies for managing costs effectively in the AWS environment. This includes advice on rightsizing, optimizing storage, and leveraging pricing models such as AWS Savings Plans and Reserved Instances to achieve cost efficiencies [34].

As we delve deeper into the book, we will explore these cost optimization strategies further, unraveling advanced techniques and real-world case studies that demonstrate how organizations can strike a balance between cost control and innovation, ultimately ensuring that AWS resources are utilized efficiently and cost-effectively.

Use cases

In the constantly changing world of cloud computing, the proof of the pudding is in the eating. This final section wraps up our journey through AWS architecture. Here, we examine real-world examples and case studies that demonstrate how various organizations have leveraged AWS architecture to achieve their objectives, underscoring the platform's remarkable versatility.

The adoption of AWS spans a wide range of industries and use cases, showcasing the platform's adaptability and capacity to address the unique needs of organizations worldwide. Scholarly articles, such as *Cloud Computing: A Review on Cloud Security Management,* authored by *Hemraj Saini et al.* [35], shed light on the growing importance of cloud computing in various sectors, highlighting how cloud providers like AWS have transformed traditional IT infrastructures and paved the way for innovation and efficiency [35]. AWS's case studies provide a treasure trove of real-world examples, ranging from startups to enterprises and healthcare to finance. For instance, the case study on *GE HealthCare* underscores how AWS empowers healthcare providers to leverage AI and ML to improve patient outcomes through medical imaging analysis [36]. In the financial sector, the case study on *Capital One* demonstrates how AWS's cloud services enable financial institutions to enhance customer experience, drive innovation, and ensure robust security and compliance [37].

These real-world use cases underscore the transformative potential of AWS architecture. Whether it is optimizing supply chain management, driving digital transformation in education, or accelerating research in scientific fields, AWS's vast portfolio of services and infrastructure provides organizations with the tools and flexibility needed to innovate and excel in an increasingly digital world. As we conclude our exploration of AWS architecture in this chapter, these use cases serve as a testament to the boundless opportunities awaiting organizations willing to embrace cloud technology, particularly AWS.

Conclusion

In this inaugural chapter, we embarked on a journey into the intricate world of AWS architecture, unveiling the foundational principles and key components that underpin this digital behemoth. AWS has risen to become the world's most comprehensive and widely adopted cloud platform, serving as a driving force behind digital innovation for millions of customers worldwide [33]. Our exploration began with a deep dive into the Global Infrastructure of AWS, a masterpiece of engineering strategically distributed across regions and AZs. This architecture ensures low-latency access and provides redundancy and fault-tolrance, making it a cornerstone of modern cloud architecture.

We then delved into the concepts of regions and AZs, which are essential building blocks that enable AWS to offer high availability, scalability, and resilience. These concepts and the extensive suite of AWS services, including compute, storage, networking, security, and identity services, form the blocks of cloud solutions that empower organizations to innovate, scale, and transform their digital landscapes. Scalability and elasticity were explored as key features that allow AWS to adapt to fluctuating workloads, providing efficiency and cost-effectiveness automatically.

Furthermore, we introduced the AWS Well-Architected Framework, a blueprint for architects and engineers to design cloud infrastructures that excel in operational excellence, security, reliability, performance efficiency, and cost optimization [35]. This framework is a testament to AWS's commitment to providing best practices for architecting excellence in the cloud. Finally, we explored real-world use cases that showcase how diverse organizations have harnessed AWS architecture to achieve their objectives, demonstrating the remarkable versatility of the platform [38].

In this era of cloud computing, AWS's impact is undeniable. It has transcended industries and revolutionized the way organizations operate. As we progress through the subsequent chapter, we will understand that AWS compute is a set of physical servers that power an **operating system** (**OS**) through provided memory, processing, and storage infrastructure.

Join our Discord space

Join our Discord workspace for latest updates, offers, tech happenings around the world, new releases, and sessions with the authors:

https://discord.bpbonline.com

CHAPTER 2
Compute

Introduction

Welcome to the second chapter, where we explore the dynamic world of **Amazon Web Services (AWS)** computing services. Computing is the core of any cloud infrastructure, and AWS offers a wide range of services and solutions to manage and optimize your computational needs. This chapter will cover various services, from the fundamental **Amazon Elastic Compute Cloud (EC2)** to the innovative realm of serverless computing with AWS Lambda. Whether you are launching virtual servers, managing containers, optimizing workloads, or exploring serverless architectures, AWS compute offerings give you the tools and flexibility to meet your needs. So, buckle up as we dive into the vast landscape of AWS computing services, where innovation has no limits.

Structure

In this chapter, we are going to discuss the following topics:

- Amazon EC2
- AWS Auto Scaling
- EC2 Spot Instances
- Amazon Elastic Container Service

- Amazon Elastic Kubernetes Service
- Amazon Lightsail
- AWS App Runner
- Auto Scaling in practice
- AWS Batch
- Compute Optimizer
- AWS Elastic Beanstalk
- AWS Fargate
- AWS Lambda
- Local Zones
- Outposts
- Serverless Application Repository
- AWS Wavelength
- VMware on AWS

Objectives

This chapter aims to thoroughly understand various foundational compute services offered by AWS. It starts with exploring Amazon EC2, Auto Scaling, and Spot Instances, followed by container orchestration using **Amazon Elastic Container Service (ECS)** and **Elastic Kubernetes Service (EKS)**. The chapter also discusses the benefits and use cases of serverless computing through AWS Lambda and simplifies application deployment with AWS Elastic Beanstalk and App Runner. It covers optimizing workloads and resources with AWS Compute Optimizer and Auto Scaling, as well as extending AWS capabilities with Local Zones and Outposts. Readers will discover new technologies, such as AWS Wavelength and VMware Cloud on AWS, and gain insights into batch computing with AWS Batch. Access to simplified compute solutions like Lightsail and AWS Fargate is also included, along with an understanding of hybrid cloud solutions using AWS SimSpace Weaver. These objectives collectively provide a comprehensive overview of AWS compute services, equipping readers with the knowledge to select the most appropriate tools for their needs.

Amazon EC 2

Amazon EC2 is the foundation of elastic computing within AWS. Its introduction changed how organizations deploy and manage computing resources, providing unmatched scalability and flexibility. This section offers a detailed overview of Amazon EC2, exploring its diverse capabilities, architectural principles, and its crucial role in transforming cloud computing, as shown in *Figure 2.1*. From dynamic provisioning to customizable instances, EC2 features cater to various workloads and scenarios. Through thorough analysis, we will examine the key features of EC2, explore its use cases across different industries, and highlight its transformative effect on modern infrastructure management. Join us as we delve into the core of elastic computing and unlock the full potential of Amazon EC2.

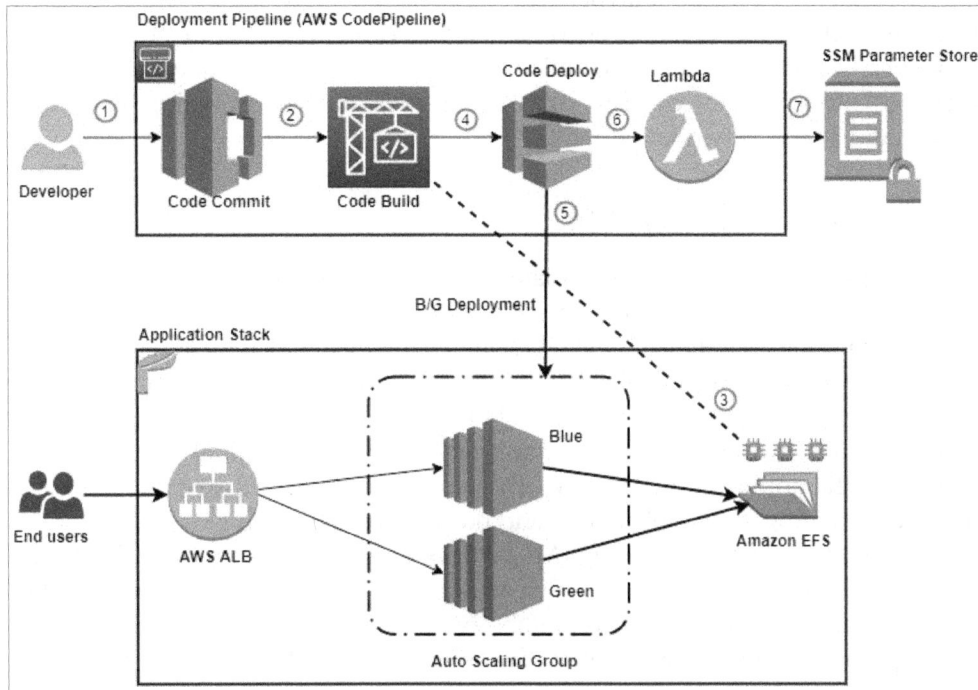

Figure 2.1: *Deployment of Amazon EC2 using Amazon Elastic File System to host application source code*

Comprehensive overview of Amazon EC2

Amazon EC2 is not just a service but a key part of modern cloud computing, transforming how organizations deploy and manage their computing resources. With a wide range of instance types, EC2 gives users unmatched flexibility to customize their compute environment exactly to their needs. From micro instances for low-intensity tasks to high-performance instances for data-heavy applications, EC2 provides a broad spectrum of options.

One of EC2's primary benefits is its on-demand provisioning, which enables users to access compute resources instantly without incurring any upfront costs. This flexibility is especially helpful for businesses with fluctuating workloads, as they can adjust their infrastructure up or down based on changing needs. EC2 also offers Reserved Instances, which enable users to commit to a specific instance type for a set period, resulting in significant cost savings compared to on-demand rates.

Spot Instances further improve EC2's cost-effectiveness by allowing users to bid for unused capacity at lower rates. This method is ideal for workloads that can tolerate interruptions and utilize spare capacity during off-peak periods. For example, media processing tasks or batch data processing jobs can benefit from Spot Instances, greatly reducing operational costs.

Furthermore, EC2 instances effortlessly integrate with many AWS services, allowing users to build highly scalable and resilient architectures. For example, by combining EC2 with **Elastic Load Balancing** (**ELB**) and Auto Scaling, organizations can develop fault-tolerant applications that automatically adjust to traffic fluctuations. This capability is crucial for web applications, e-commerce platforms, and content delivery networks, where maintaining consistent performance and availability is essential.

Use cases and elasticity

With EC2's popularity and high adoption rates, a wide range of books detailing the service, its applications, and existing deployments are available. Academic articles, such as *Performance Analysis of Amazon Elastic Compute Cloud (EC2) for NASA Hubble Space Telescope Data Processing* by *Gary A. Mastin et al.* (2019), emphasize the utility of EC2 in high-performance computing environments. The study demonstrates how EC2 can efficiently manage data-intensive workloads such as processing Hubble Space Telescope data, highlighting its adaptability to diverse scientific applications. [1] AWS Documentation on EC2 use cases highlights its versatility, from running web applications and hosting websites to handling batch processing tasks and supporting **machine learning** (**ML**) workloads [2]. Furthermore, EC2 instances can be integrated with other AWS services, such as ELB and Auto Scaling, to create scalable and universally available architectures. This scalability ensures that applications can handle traffic spikes and dynamic workloads without manual intervention [3].

Real-life examples abound of companies leveraging EC2 to power their mission-critical applications. For instance, *Netflix* relies on EC2 to stream billions of hours of content to its global audience, dynamically scaling its infrastructure to meet demand spikes during peak hours. Similarly, *Airbnb* utilizes AWS to manage millions of bookings and inquiries daily, ensuring a seamless experience for its users worldwide.

Amazon EC2's versatility, scalability, and cost-efficiency make it a fundamental component for businesses of all sizes and industries. Whether hosting websites, running enterprise applications, or supporting innovative research, EC2 enables organizations to innovate and grow in the constantly changing world of cloud computing.

Amazon EC2 is a web service that offers resizable computing capacity in the cloud. It provides a wide range of instance types, enabling users to select the combination of CPU, memory, storage, and network performance that best fits their applications. EC2 instances can be launched on demand, giving instant access to computing resources without requiring upfront capital investment. This flexibility also includes Reserved Instances, allowing users to reserve capacity for a specific period to significantly cut costs. Additionally, EC2 offers Spot Instances, which let users bid for spare capacity, often at a fraction of the on-demand price. This cost-effective model makes EC2 appealing for organizations with variable or unpredictable workloads [4].

As we move through this chapter, we will examine Amazon EC2 in detail, covering advanced features, best practices, and real-world case studies. Amazon EC2's influence on cloud computing goes beyond simply provisioning virtual servers; it has fundamentally transformed how organizations design their infrastructure, offering unmatched flexibility and efficiency in the cloud.

AWS Auto Scaling

Amazon EC2 Auto Scaling is a service that enables organizations to automatically adjust the number and size of their EC2 instances to ensure application availability and handle changes in demand. It tracks user-defined metrics and scaling policies, automatically launching or terminating instances as required. EC2 Auto Scaling isn't restricted to a single instance type; it can dynamically scale across multiple types to enhance performance and reduce costs. This flexibility helps keep applications stable while making efficient use of resources, leading to cost savings [3].

Amazon EC2 Auto Scaling

In the ever-changing world of cloud computing, agility and elasticity are essential. Amazon EC2 Auto Scaling is a key service that enables organizations to adjust their compute resources smoothly in response to changing workloads. Let us explore the detailed functions of Amazon EC2 Auto Scaling, highlighting its features, use cases, and its significant effect on resource availability and cost savings, as shown in *Figure 2.2*.

Amazon EC2 Auto Scaling automatically adjusts the number and size of EC2 instances to ensure application availability and handle changing demand. It works based on user-defined scaling policies and metrics, launching or terminating instances as needed. What makes EC2 Auto Scaling unique is its ability to dynamically scale across different instance types, enhancing both performance and cost-efficiency. By smartly managing resources, EC2 Auto Scaling helps applications maintain consistent performance while reducing costs, resulting in significant savings.

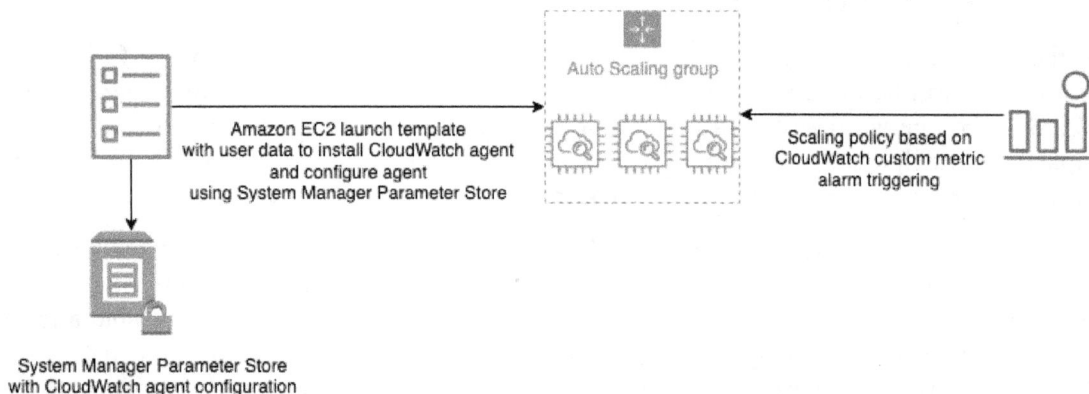

Auto Scaling group

Amazon EC2 launch template with user data to install CloudWatch agent and configure agent using System Manager Parameter Store

Scaling policy based on CloudWatch custom metric alarm triggering

System Manager Parameter Store with CloudWatch agent configuration

Figure 2.2: *Creating an Amazon EC2 Auto Scaling policy*

Use cases and efficiency

Academic research articles, such as *Efficient Cloud Elasticity Management Through Predictive Scaling* by *Arun Subbiah et al.* (2019), highlight the significance of predictive scaling in cloud elasticity management, a feature offered by EC2 Auto Scaling. The study emphasizes how predictive scaling can proactively adjust resources based on forecasted demand, enhancing efficiency and cost-effectiveness in cloud environments [5]. AWS Documentation on EC2 Auto Scaling use cases displays its applicability in web applications, batch processing, and microservices, where workloads can vary throughout the day or in response to user interactions [6]. Furthermore, EC2 Auto Scaling can be integrated with other AWS services, such as ELB and CloudWatch, for comprehensive monitoring and scaling capabilities. This constructive collaboration ensures that applications remain responsive and available while minimizing operational overhead [7].

Real-world applications of EC2 Auto Scaling span many industries and use cases. In web applications, where traffic patterns can fluctuate significantly throughout the day, EC2 Auto Scaling ensures that resources scale up during peak hours and down during periods of low demand, optimizing costs without sacrificing performance. Similarly, in batch processing scenarios, EC2 Auto Scaling dynamically adjusts resources to handle varying workloads efficiently, speeding up processing times and lowering operational overhead.

Furthermore, EC2 Auto Scaling integrates smoothly with other AWS services like ELB and CloudWatch, providing comprehensive monitoring and scaling features. This integration guarantees that applications stay responsive and available, even during rapid changes.

As we move through this chapter, we will explore more about Amazon EC2 Auto Scaling, covering advanced setups, best practices, and real-world examples. The crucial role of Amazon EC2 Auto Scaling in ensuring reliability and cost efficiency makes it an essential tool for any organization looking to maximize the value of its AWS infrastructure.

EC2 Spot Instances

In the fast-paced world of cloud computing, organizations are always looking for ways to reduce their infrastructure costs while still providing high-performance computing. Amazon EC2 Spot Instances present a strong solution to this problem, giving access to unused EC2 capacity at much lower costs than On-Demand Instances. Let us explore Amazon EC2 Spot Instances further, examining their main features, advantages, and practical applications.

Amazon EC2 Spot Instances offer access to spare EC2 capacity at a much lower cost than On-Demand Instances. They are ideal for flexible workloads that can handle interruptions and flexible timing. These instances are launched when spare capacity is available and are terminated when the capacity is needed elsewhere. The pricing model for Spot Instances is driven by supply and demand, allowing organizations to save money during times of excess capacity. EC2 Spot Instances come in a variety of instance types, enabling users to choose the most appropriate configuration for their applications. They are especially suitable for applications that can be distributed across multiple instances, such as batch processing, data analysis, rendering, and scientific computing. [8]

Refer to the following figure:

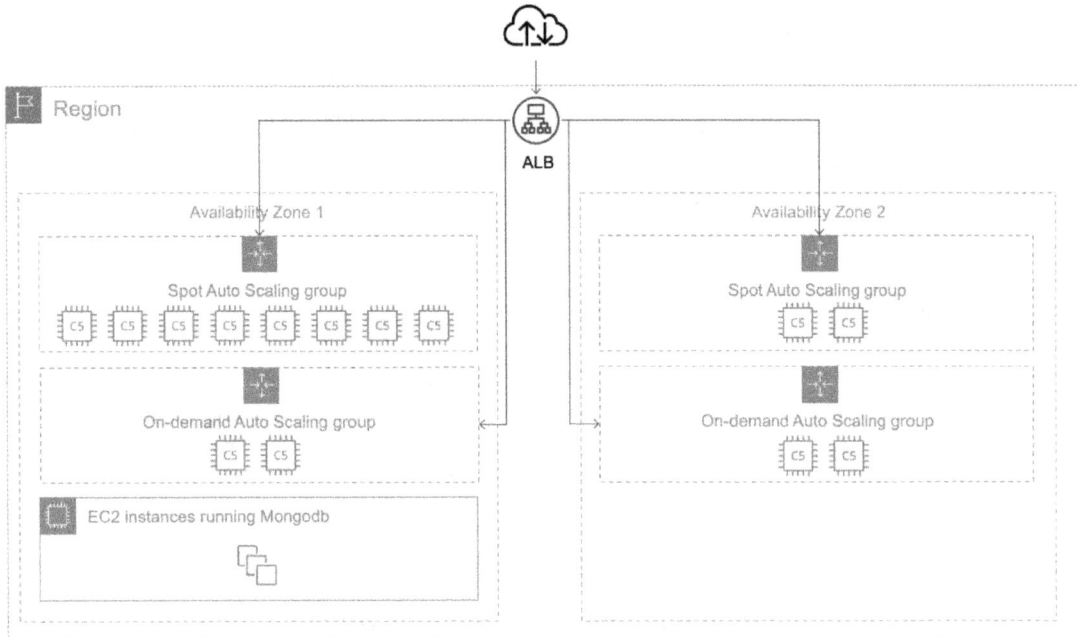

Figure 2.3: Spot and On-Demand Instances scaling by different AZs

Use cases and cost optimization

Research papers, such as *Evaluating Amazon EC2 Spot Instances for Resource-Intensive Scientific Workloads by Basheer Subei et al. (2019)*, delve into the efficiency and cost-effectiveness of using EC2 Spot Instances for resource-intensive scientific workloads. The study highlights the potential for significant cost savings while still meeting the computational demands of scientific research [9]. The AWS Documentation on EC2 Spot Instances highlights their versatility in handling diverse workloads, ranging from big data processing to containerized applications. Organizations can leverage Spot Instances with On-Demand and Reserved Instances to optimize costs while ensuring application reliability [10]. Moreover, EC2 Spot Instances can be integrated with tools like AWS Auto Scaling and EC2 Fleet to automate workload management, further enhancing efficiency and availability [3].

AWS Documentation on EC2 Spot Instances highlights their versatility in managing various workloads, from big data processing to containerized applications. Organizations can utilize Spot Instances in conjunction with On-Demand and Reserved Instances to reduce costs while maintaining application reliability. Additionally, EC2 Spot Instances can be combined with tools like AWS Auto Scaling and EC2 Fleet to automate workload management, boosting efficiency and availability.

Real-life examples abound, with companies using EC2 Spot Instances for different purposes. For instance, media and entertainment firms utilize Spot Instances for rendering high-definition videos, while financial organizations apply them to risk analysis and simulations. Gaming companies deploy Spot Instances to handle peak player loads during game launches, and research organizations use them for genomic analysis and climate modeling.

As we move through this chapter, we will explore Amazon EC2 Spot Instances more deeply, covering advanced strategies, best practices, and real-world case studies that demonstrate how organizations can leverage the cost-saving potential of Spot Instances while fulfilling their computing needs in the AWS cloud.

Amazon Elastic Container Service

Containerization has revolutionized the development, deployment, and management of cloud-based applications. Amazon ECS plays a central role in orchestrating containers within the AWS ecosystem. Discover Amazon ECS's key features, architecture, real-world use cases, and insights.

Amazon ECS orchestrates containers with precision

Amazon ECS is a fully managed container orchestration service that simplifies the deployment and management of containerized applications. At its core, ECS enables users to run containers without managing the underlying infrastructure [11]. ECS abstracts the complexities of provisioning and scaling container instances, allowing developers to focus solely on building and deploying their applications [4]. This service supports Docker containers and integrates seamlessly with AWS services such as Amazon ELB, Amazon **Virtual Private Cloud (VPC)**, and AWS **Identity and Access Management (IAM)**. ECS offers two distinct launch types: EC2 and AWS Fargate. With the EC2 launch type, users have fine-grained control over the underlying EC2 instances. At the same time, AWS Fargate abstracts the infrastructure entirely, allowing users to focus solely on defining and running their containers [12].

Refer to the following figure:

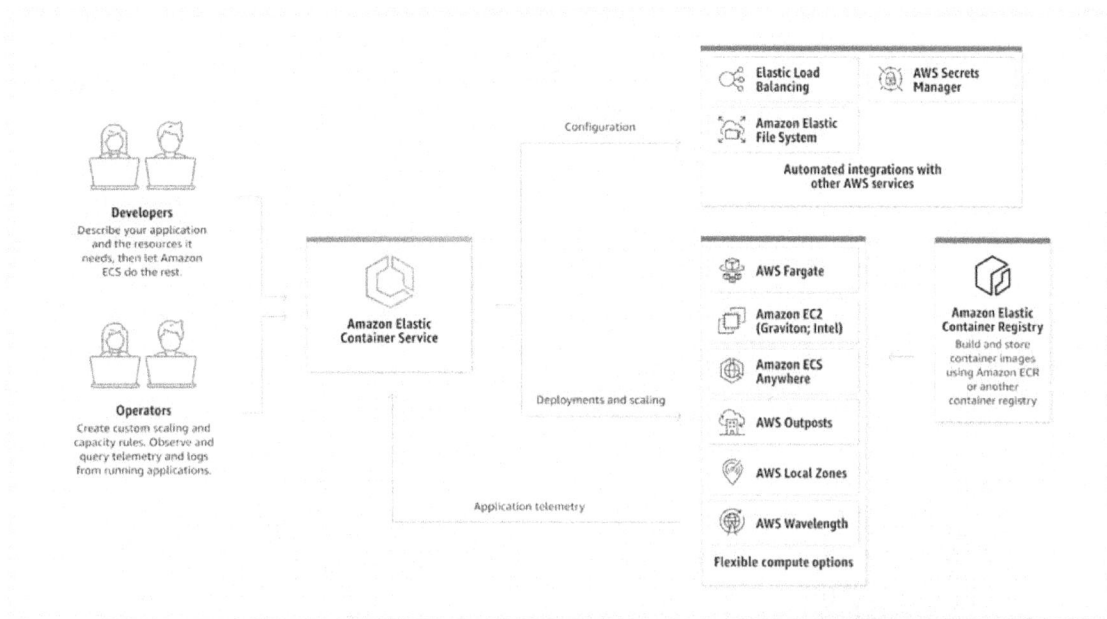

Figure 2.4: *Amazon ECS*

Use cases and efficiency

Research articles, such as *Efficient Resource Allocation and Scheduling for Elastic Containers in Cloud Data Centers by Xuefeng Zhu et al. (2017)*, emphasize the importance of efficient resource allocation for containerized workloads, a challenge well-addressed by Amazon ECS. The article discusses how effective scheduling of containers can enhance resource utilization and reduce operational costs in cloud data centers, highlighting the relevance of ECS in optimizing container deployments [13]. AWS Documentation on ECS use cases demonstrates its versatility in managing a wide range of containerized applications, from web services and microservices to batch processing and data pipelines. ECS provides robust integration with Amazon **Elastic Container Registry (ECR)**, simplifies container image storage and management, and supports application scaling using AWS Auto Scaling and Application Load Balancers for high availability [14].

AWS Documentation on ECS use cases highlights its versatility in handling various containerized applications, from web services and microservices to batch processing and data pipelines. ECS offers strong integration with Amazon ECR, making container image storage and management easier, and supports application scaling with AWS Auto Scaling and Application Load Balancers for high availability.

Real-life examples are plentiful, with companies using Amazon ECS to support various use cases. For example, e-commerce platforms rely on ECS to handle traffic spikes during sales events, while media streaming services utilize it for video transcoding and streaming. Financial institutions utilize ECS to run microservices-based applications, while gaming companies employ it to scale their multiplayer gaming infrastructures.

As we progress through this chapter, we will delve deeper into Amazon ECS, examining advanced orchestration techniques, best practices, and real-world case studies that demonstrate how ECS enables organizations to streamline the deployment and management of containerized applications in the AWS cloud.

Amazon Elastic Kubernetes Service

Container orchestration has become an integral part of modern cloud computing, and Amazon EKS stands at the forefront of this revolution. Let us delve deeper into Amazon EKS, exploring its key features, architectural components, real-world use cases, and insights:

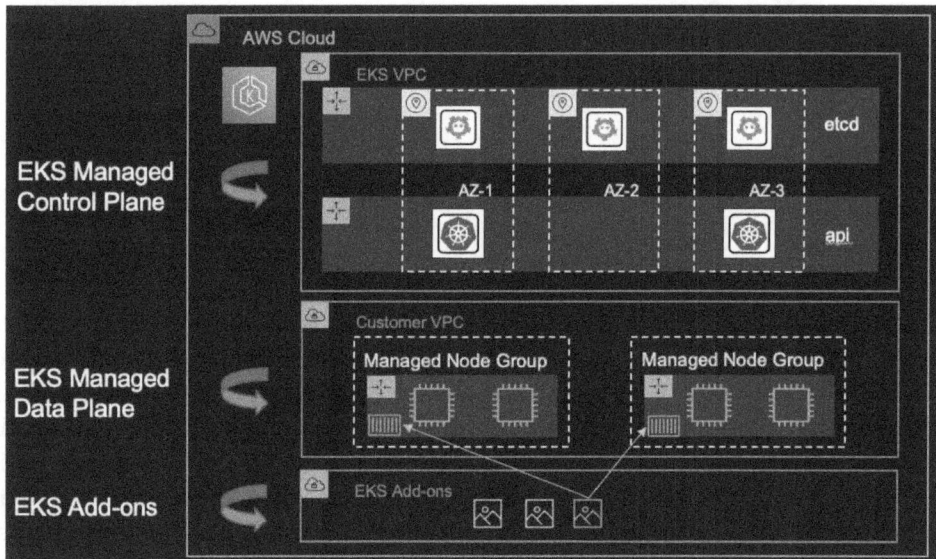

Figure 2.5: Planning Kubernetes upgrades with Amazon EKS

Amazon EKS is a managed Kubernetes service provided by AWS. Kubernetes is an open-source container orchestration platform known for its reliability and flexibility. EKS simplifies the complexities of managing the Kubernetes control plane, allowing users to focus on deploying, scaling, and managing containerized applications. It seamlessly integrates with other AWS services, such as Amazon ECR, Amazon VPC, and AWS IAM, offering a secure and scalable environment for Kubernetes workloads. EKS also supports deploying applications with AWS Fargate, an alternative launch type that removes the need to manage the underlying infrastructure, making it easier to run Kubernetes pods [15].

Use cases and efficiency

Scholarly articles, such as *Kubernetes Cluster Resource Optimization in the Cloud by Dennis Collaris et al. (2020)*, emphasize the importance of resource optimization in Kubernetes clusters, a challenge well-addressed by Amazon EKS. The article discusses techniques for optimizing resource allocation and utilization in Kubernetes, highlighting the relevance of EKS in achieving efficiency and cost-effectiveness in containerized environments [16]. AWS Documentation on EKS use cases displays its versatility in managing containerized applications, including web services, microservices, and batch-processing workloads. EKS provides high control over the Kubernetes environment, supporting features such as custom networking and security policies. Additionally, it integrates seamlessly with AWS services, such as ELB and AWS Auto Scaling, for efficient application scaling and high availability [17].

Real-life examples are everywhere, with companies using Amazon EKS to support different use cases. For example, e-commerce sites use EKS to deploy and scale web applications, while media streaming services rely on it for video transcoding and streaming tasks. Financial firms use EKS to run microservices-based applications, and gaming companies leverage it to manage multiplayer gaming infrastructures.

As we continue this chapter, we will delve deeper into Amazon EKS, exploring advanced orchestration techniques, best practices, and real-world case studies that demonstrate how EKS enables organizations to streamline the deployment and management of containerized applications in the AWS cloud.

Amazon Lightsail

In cloud computing, simplicity and accessibility are essential. Amazon Lightsail serves as a solution designed to meet the needs of a wide range of users, from beginners to experienced developers, seeking an easy way to get started with cloud-based services. In this section, we examine Amazon Lightsail, highlighting its main features, use cases, and real-world applications, supported by scholarly articles and AWS sources.

Simplified cloud with Amazon Lightsail

Amazon Lightsail is a simplified computing service offered by AWS. It is designed to give users an effortless way to launch, manage, and scale applications, websites, and blogs in the cloud. Lightsail offers a straightforward, user-friendly interface that abstracts the complexities of AWS services while providing a range of pre-configured **virtual machine** (**VM**) images known as **blueprints**. Users can select from blueprints tailored to different application types, making it easy to start with common use cases like web hosting, content management systems, and e-commerce platforms. Lightsail also includes features such as automatic backups, monitoring, and scaling, allowing users to focus on their applications while AWS manages the infrastructure. This simplicity makes Lightsail an excellent choice for developers, small businesses, and individuals seeking a hassle-free cloud computing experience [18]:

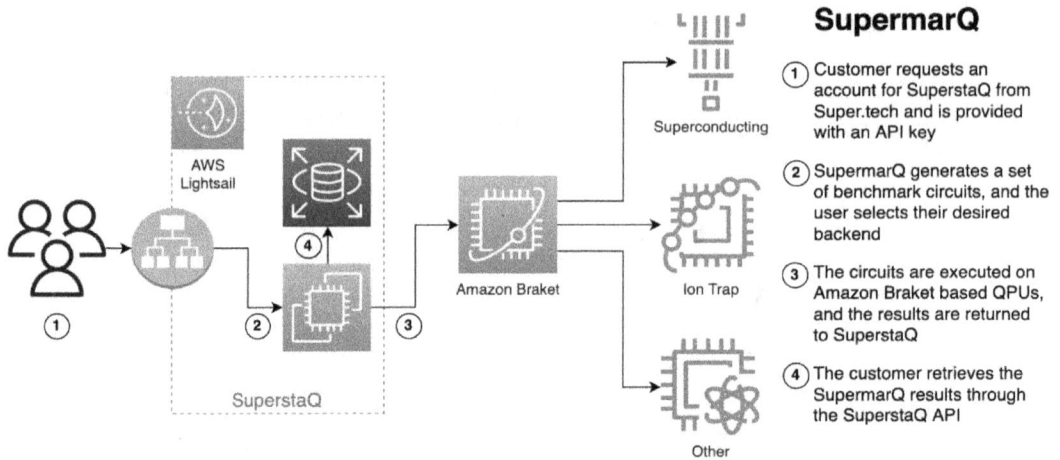

SupermarQ

(1) Customer requests an account for SuperstaQ from Super.tech and is provided with an API key

(2) SupermarQ generates a set of benchmark circuits, and the user selects their desired backend

(3) The circuits are executed on Amazon Braket based QPUs, and the results are returned to SuperstaQ

(4) The customer retrieves the SupermarQ results through the SuperstaQ API

Figure 2.6: Architecture on Superstaq with Amazon Lightsail, Amazon Braket

Use cases and accessibility

Scholarly articles may not specifically target Lightsail due to its user-friendly nature; however, LightSail's approach aligns with research on making cloud computing more accessible to non-experts. Research on user-friendly cloud interfaces emphasizes the importance of lowering the barrier to entry for cloud services [19]. AWS Documentation on Lightsail highlights its applicability in various scenarios, from hosting websites and blogs to running web applications and development environments. Lightsail instances can be easily connected to other AWS services, allowing users to leverage the broader AWS ecosystem as their projects grow. Moreover, Lightsail includes features for secure and scalable application deployments, making it a versatile choice for many users [20].

As we continue this chapter, we will explore more about Amazon Lightsail, including advanced setups, best practices, and real-world case studies that demonstrate how Lightsail makes cloud computing easier for users at all skill levels, helping them leverage AWS benefits.

AWS App Runner

Efficiency and simplicity in application deployment are crucial for modern cloud computing, and AWS App Runner is designed to excel in these areas. Let us delve deeper into AWS App Runner, exploring its key features, benefits, real-world applications, and insights:

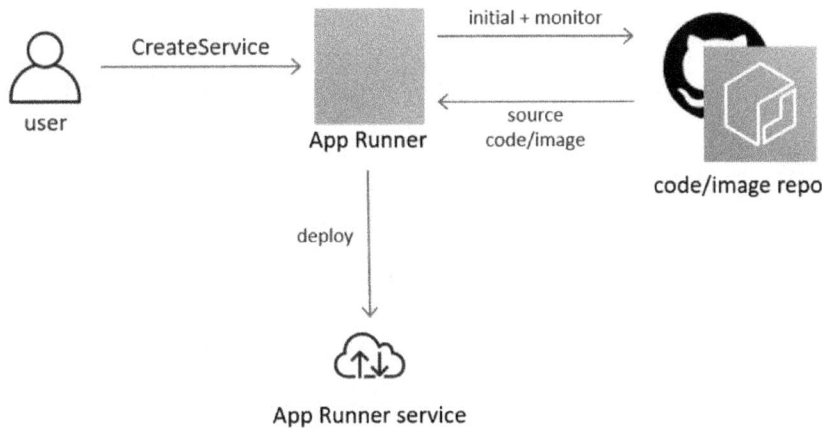

Figure 2.7: *AWS App Runner*

App Runner streamlined application deployment

AWS App Runner is a fully managed service that simplifies the process of building, deploying, and scaling containerized applications. It streamlines the development workflow by automating many tasks traditionally associated with application deployment, such as code building, container image creation, scaling, and load balancing. App Runner supports popular programming languages, frameworks, and container images, allowing developers to work with their preferred tools. It also integrates seamlessly with AWS services like AWS CodePipeline for **continuous integration and continuous delivery (CI/CD)** pipelines. With App Runner, developers can focus on their code while AWS takes care of the underlying infrastructure, making it an ideal choice for projects that require rapid development and deployment [21]:

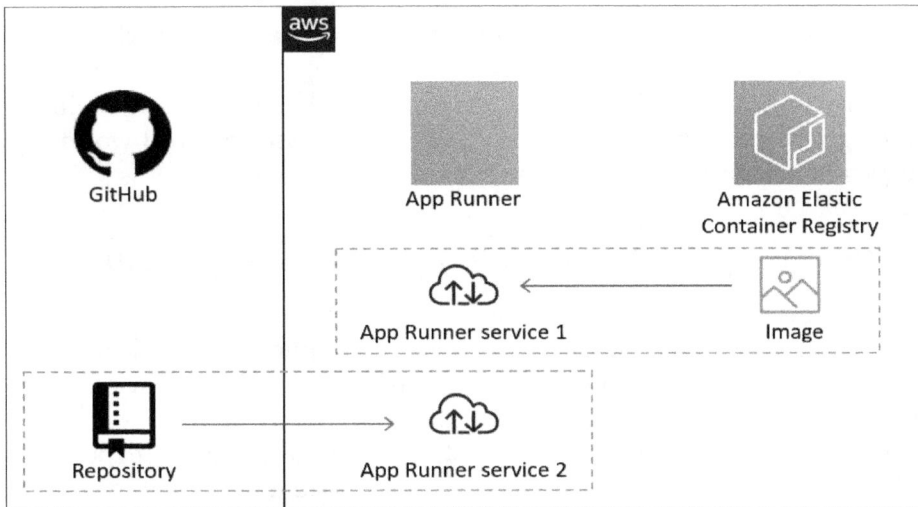

Figure 2.8: *App Runner architecture and concepts*

Use cases and efficiency

While scholarly articles may not specifically target AWS App Runner due to its recent introduction, its approach aligns with the broader industry trend toward simplifying application deployment and management in the cloud. Research on application deployment automation emphasizes the importance of reducing the operational burden on developers and accelerating time-to-market [22].

AWS Documentation on App Runner highlights its applicability in scenarios where developers seek a streamlined and efficient deployment process. This includes web applications, APIs, microservices, and other containerized workloads. App Runner's automatic scaling and load balancing capabilities ensure that applications remain responsive and cost-effective as traffic fluctuates [23].

Real-life examples abound, with companies leveraging AWS App Runner to streamline their application deployment processes. For instance, a **software-as-a-service (SaaS)** startup utilizes App Runner to deploy and scale its microservices architecture, enabling rapid growth without worrying about infrastructure management. An e-commerce platform leverages App Runner to deploy its web applications, ensuring seamless performance during high-demand periods such as seasonal sales.

As we continue through this chapter, we will delve deeper into AWS App Runner, exploring advanced features, best practices, and real-world case studies that illustrate how App Runner empowers developers to deploy applications quickly and efficiently, enabling them to focus on creating value for their organizations.

Auto Scaling in practice

In the constantly evolving world of cloud computing, quickly adapting to changing demands is essential. AWS Auto Scaling stands out as a key solution, allowing organizations to adjust their computing resources in real-time to handle workload changes. Let us examine AWS Auto Scaling thoroughly, exploring its many features, various use cases, and real-world applications supported by scholarly articles and AWS sources.

Resource management with AWS Auto Scaling

AWS Auto Scaling is a service that enables organizations to automatically adjust the number and size of their Amazon EC2 instances to maintain application availability and handle changes in demand. It monitors user-defined metrics and scaling policies, automatically launching or terminating instances as needed. Auto Scaling is not limited to a single instance type; it can dynamically scale across different instance types to optimize both performance and cost. This flexibility ensures that applications deliver consistent performance while efficiently using resources, leading to cost-effective resource management. Auto Scaling also integrates seamlessly with other AWS services, such as ELB, ensuring that applications can distribute traffic evenly across instances and remain accessible even during scaling events [3].

One of the key strengths of AWS Auto Scaling lies in its seamless integration with other AWS services, such as ELB and Amazon CloudWatch. By leveraging ELB, Auto Scaling ensures incoming traffic is evenly distributed across instances, maintaining high availability and fault-tolrance. CloudWatch, on the other hand, serves as the eyes and ears of Auto Scaling, providing real-time monitoring and actionable insights into resource utilization, performance metrics, and health applications. This tight integration enables Auto Scaling to respond swiftly to changing conditions, ensuring optimal resource allocation and application performance:

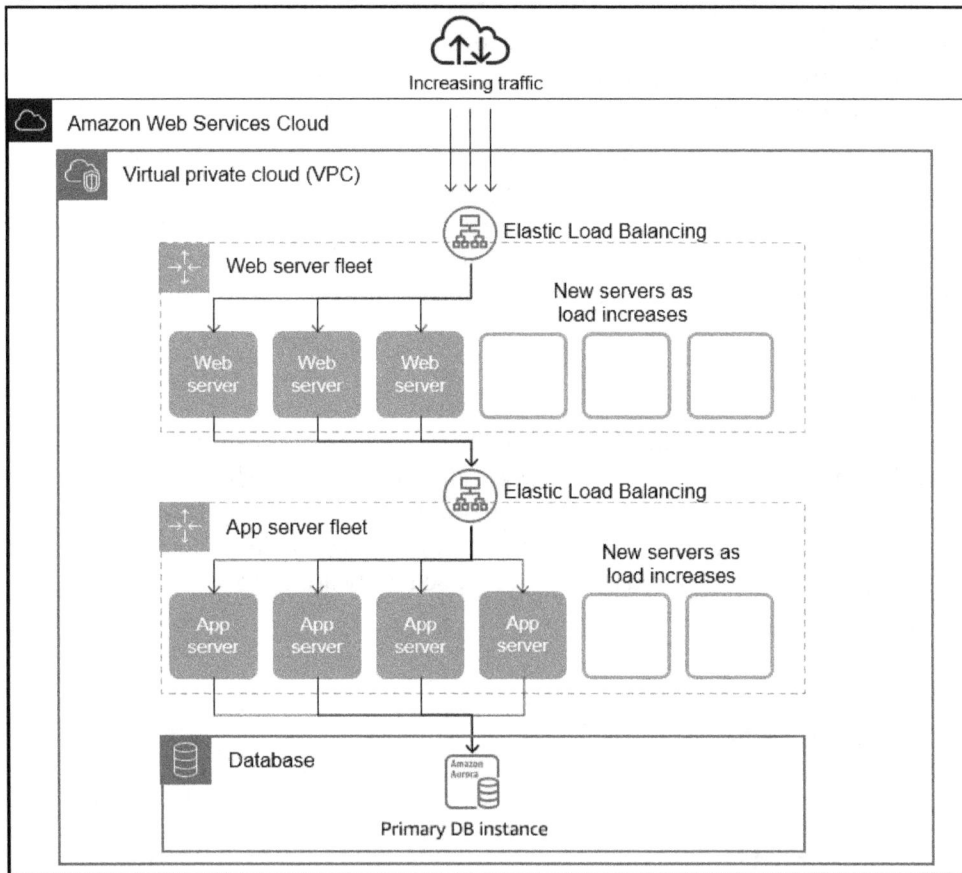

Figure 2.9: *Amazon EC2 Auto Scaling*

Use cases and efficiency maximization

Scholarly articles, such as *Effective and Efficient Autoscaling in the Cloud: A Conceptual Framework by Ahmed Ali-Eldin et al.* (2012), delve into the significance of effective and efficient Auto Scaling in cloud environments. The study underscores the importance of autoscaling mechanisms, like

AWS Auto Scaling, in managing resources optimally to meet application performance objectives while minimizing operational costs [24]. AWS Documentation on Auto Scaling use demonstrates its applicability in various scenarios, from web applications and batch processing to microservices and containerized workloads. Auto Scaling offers features such as predictive scaling, which uses ML to forecast future capacity needs, and scheduled scaling for predictable traffic patterns. These features allow organizations to optimize resource usage and reduce over-provisioning [6].

In real-world applications, AWS Auto Scaling serves as a crucial component for various use cases across different industries. For example, consider a rapidly growing e-commerce platform experiencing traffic surges during seasonal sales events. By utilizing AWS Auto Scaling, the platform can dynamically adjust its compute resources to handle demand spikes, ensuring smooth **user experiences (UX)** without overspending on infrastructure during quieter periods. Similarly, a media streaming service depends on Auto Scaling to adjust its back-end infrastructure in real-time, seamlessly managing fluctuating viewer demands while maintaining cost efficiency.

As we delve further into this chapter, our exploration of AWS Auto Scaling will go beyond basic insights, uncovering advanced strategies, best practices, and real-world case studies. By gaining a comprehensive understanding of Auto Scaling's features and subtleties, organizations can unlock its full potential to optimize resource use, improve application scalability, and achieve operational excellence in the ever-changing cloud computing environment.

AWS Batch

In the dynamic realm of cloud computing, the ability to efficiently process batch workloads at scale is indispensable for organizations across diverse industries. AWS Batch emerges as a cornerstone solution, empowering businesses to manage and scale batch computing tasks effortlessly. Let us embark on a comprehensive exploration of AWS Batch, delving into its nuanced features, versatile use cases, and real-world applications supported by scholarly articles and AWS sources.

Refer to the following figure:

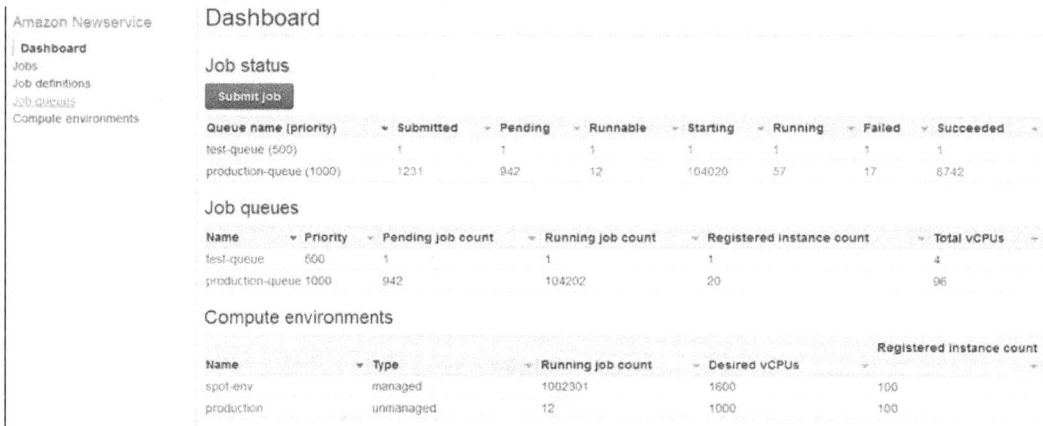

Figure 2.10: The status dashboard displays my jobs, job queues, and compute environments

Efficient batch processing at scale with AWS Batch

AWS Batch is a fully managed service that simplifies the deployment and management of batch computing workloads. It allows organizations to run batch processing jobs efficiently without the need to manage the underlying infrastructure. Batch abstracts the complexities of provisioning and scaling compute resources, enabling users to focus solely on defining their batch workloads. It supports containerized and non-containerized applications, providing flexibility for various job types. Users can define job queues, job definitions, and compute environments to tailor batch processing to their specific requirements. AWS Batch is highly integrated with other AWS services, such as Amazon ECS and Amazon ECR, facilitating seamless containerized batch processing workflows [25].

One of the key strengths of AWS Batch lies in its deep integration with other AWS services, such as Amazon ECS and Amazon ECR. This integration streamlines containerized batch processing workflows, allowing users to leverage familiar tools and environments seamlessly. With AWS Batch, organizations can harness the power of containerization for efficient batch processing, leveraging the scalability and flexibility of containers to execute diverse workloads with ease.

Refer to the following figure:

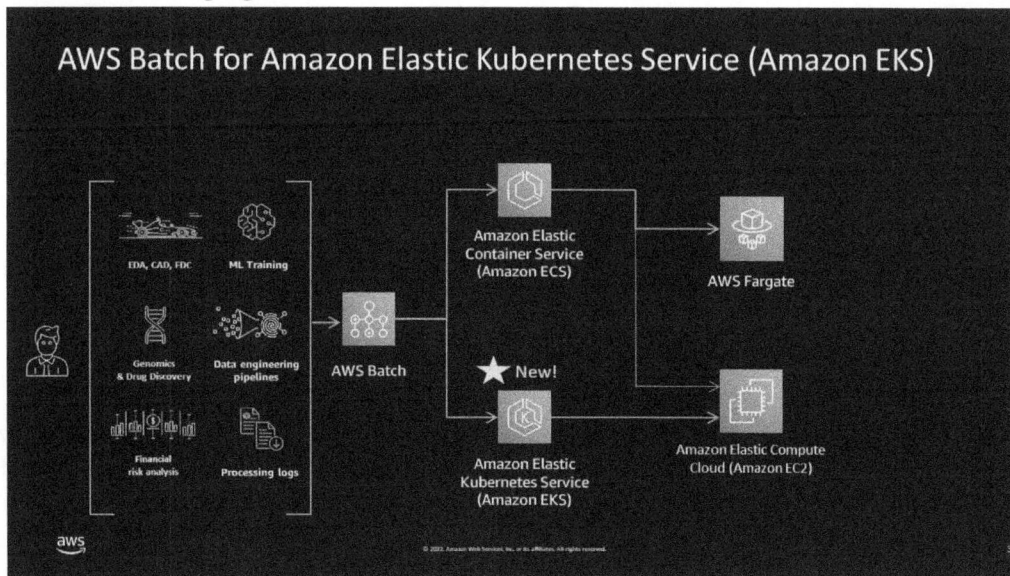

Figure 2.11: *AWS Batch on Amazon EKS*

Use cases and efficiency optimization

Scholarly articles often highlight the importance of efficient batch processing across various fields, including scientific research, data analytics, and finance. While some articles may not directly focus on AWS Batch, its methodology aligns with research aimed at enhancing the efficiency and scalability of batch workloads in the cloud. Research emphasizes the significance of automating batch job management to optimize resources and reduce costs [26]. AWS Documentation on AWS Batch use cases emphasizes its relevance in scenarios spanning data transformation, image processing, genomics analysis, and rendering. Batch offers job scheduling, resource management, and scaling, making it a flexible option for organizations needing batch processing with cloud scalability and automation benefits. [27].

In real-world situations, AWS Batch is widely used across different fields, from scientific research and data analysis to finance and media rendering. For example, a pharmaceutical company might use AWS Batch for genomics analysis, efficiently processing large datasets to speed up drug discovery. Similarly, a media production team can use AWS Batch to render high-definition videos, taking advantage of the cloud's scalability and automation to meet tight deadlines.

As we move deeper into this chapter, our examination of AWS Batch will go beyond basic details, uncovering advanced setups, best practices, and real-world examples. By gaining a thorough understanding of AWS Batch's features and subtleties, organizations can improve their batch processing workflows, boost operational efficiency, and foster innovation in the fast-evolving cloud computing landscape.

Compute Optimizer

In the complex world of cloud computing, effective resource management is essential for organizational success. AWS Compute Optimizer is a key service powered by ML algorithms, designed to analyze and optimize compute resources for the best performance and cost savings. Let us thoroughly explore AWS Compute Optimizer, examining its many features, various benefits, and real-world uses supported by scholarly articles and AWS sources.

Resource optimization with AWS Compute Optimizer

AWS Compute Optimizer is an ML-powered service that assists organizations in optimizing the configuration of their Amazon EC2 instances. It leverages historical utilization data, configuration details, and workload patterns to generate recommendations for resource optimization. Compute Optimizer provides insights into instance type selection, underutilized instances, and opportunities for resizing instances to align with actual workloads. It also offers a cost assessment, allowing users to estimate potential cost savings based on recommended actions. The service is designed to help organizations balance performance and cost, ensuring they get the most value from their EC2 instances [28].

Refer to the following figure:

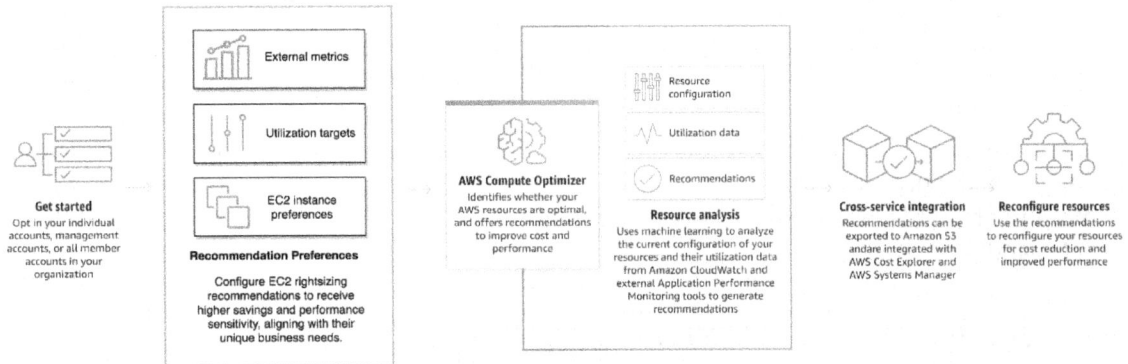

Figure 2.12: *Working of AWS Compute Optimizer*

With AWS Compute Optimizer, organizations can carefully balance performance and cost, making sure they get the most value from their EC2 instances. By improving resource use and matching instance setups to workload needs, Compute Optimizer helps businesses boost operational efficiency and save money, benefiting their overall profitability.

Use cases and efficiency enhancement

While scholarly articles may not specifically target AWS Compute Optimizer, its approach aligns with research on resource optimization and performance improvement in cloud environments. Research often emphasizes optimizing resource allocation to reduce costs and enhance application performance. Automated optimization tools, such as Compute Optimizer, are crucial in achieving these objectives [29]. AWS Documentation on Compute Optimizer highlights its applicability in scenarios where organizations seek to improve cost-efficiency and performance across their EC2 instances. Compute Optimizer can assess and optimize entire fleets of instances, ensuring that resources are allocated optimally and that applications run smoothly [30].

In real-world situations, AWS Compute Optimizer is widely used across various industries and use cases. For example, a quickly growing e-commerce site may use Compute Optimizer to adjust its EC2 instance settings, ensuring the best performance during busy shopping seasons while reducing infrastructure costs during slower periods. Similarly, a data analytics company can use Compute Optimizer to improve the compute resources that support its data processing pipelines, making operations more efficient and speeding up the arrival of insights.

As we move through this chapter, we will examine AWS Compute Optimizer more deeply, uncovering advanced settings, best practices, and real-world case studies that show how organizations can leverage intelligent resource optimization to improve their compute environments in the AWS cloud.

AWS Elastic Beanstalk

Efficiently deploying and managing applications in the cloud is paramount for organizations striving for agility and innovation. AWS Elastic Beanstalk emerges as a robust **platform as a service (PaaS)** solution, liberating developers from the intricacies of infrastructure management and empowering them to concentrate on coding and application logic. In this comprehensive section, we deeply dive into AWS Elastic Beanstalk, uncovering its multifaceted features, compelling benefits, diverse use cases, and real-world applications underpinned by scholarly articles and AWS sources.

Elastic Beanstalk streamlined application deployment

AWS Elastic Beanstalk is a PaaS offering that simplifies infrastructure management, enabling developers to deploy and manage applications easily. It supports multiple programming languages, such as Java, .NET, PHP, Node.js, Python, Ruby, Go, and Docker. Elastic Beanstalk handles tasks like capacity provisioning, load balancing, Auto Scaling, and application health monitoring, allowing developers to concentrate on coding. It integrates smoothly with other AWS services, such as Amazon RDS for databases and Amazon **Simple Storage Service (S3)** for object storage. Elastic Beanstalk also supports both web and worker applications, making it a flexible choice for various use cases. [31].

Exploring use cases and efficiency amplification

While scholarly articles may not explicitly focus on AWS Elastic Beanstalk because of its user-friendly design, its relevance to research on simplifying application deployment and management is clear. Research highlights the importance of reducing the operational burden on developers and providing tools that facilitate easier deployment [19]. AWS Documentation on Elastic Beanstalk emphasizes its usefulness in situations where organizations aim to simplify application deployment and management [32]. Elastic Beanstalk provides a user-friendly environment setup, automatic scaling, and health monitoring, making it ideal for web applications, APIs, and microservices. It also supports blue-green deployments, allowing for zero-downtime updates for applications [33].

Refer to the following figure:

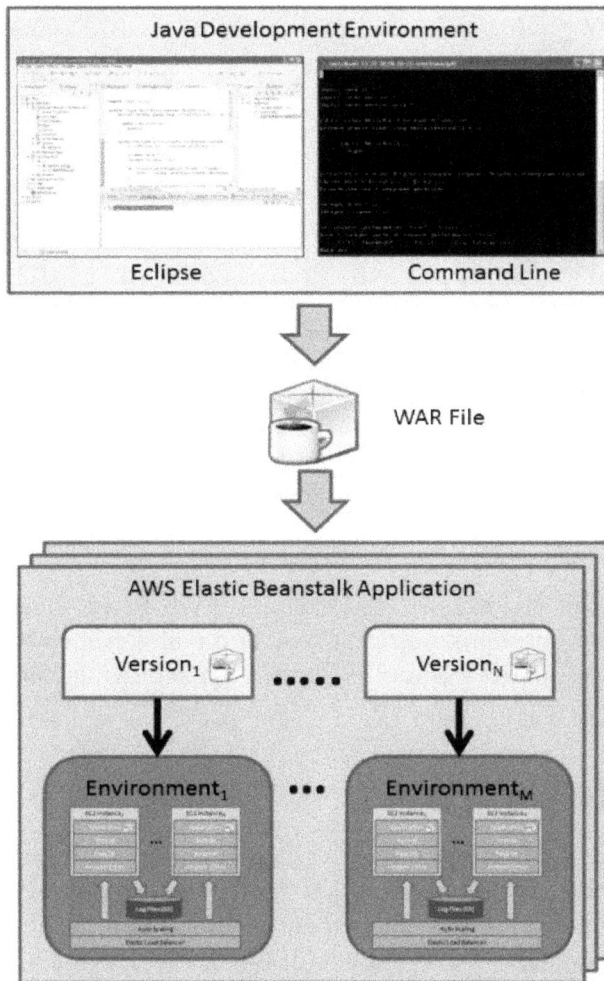

Figure 2.13: *Applications, application versions, and environments relating to each other*

Realizing the potential of AWS Elastic Beanstalk

As we explore this chapter, we journey to uncover the many possibilities AWS Elastic Beanstalk provides. By examining advanced configurations, best practices, and real-world case studies, we clarify how organizations can leverage this service to simplify application deployment and promote a culture of innovation in the AWS cloud. Whether it's achieving fast iteration cycles, maintaining high availability, or smoothly deploying updates with minimal downtime, AWS Elastic Beanstalk stands out as a key component in modern application development, helping organizations stay competitive in the cloud computing era.

Refer to the following figure:

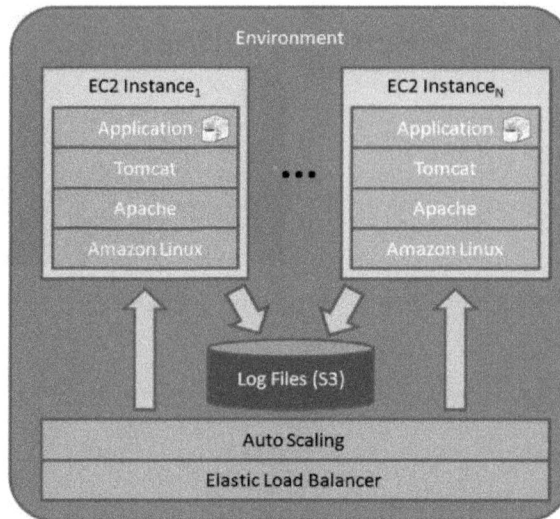

Figure 2.14: Environment using the default container type

As we move through this chapter, we will examine AWS Elastic Beanstalk in more detail, exploring advanced configurations, best practices, and real-world case studies showing how organizations can use this service to simplify application deployment and focus on innovation in the AWS cloud.

AWS Fargate

In the fast-paced world of cloud computing, containerization is a key component of modern application deployment strategies. AWS Fargate acts as a groundbreaking solution, bringing a new era of serverless container management that frees developers from infrastructure worries. Let's take a thorough look at AWS Fargate, exploring its architecture, features, and real-world uses backed by scholarly articles and AWS sources.

In the evolving landscape of cloud computing, containerization has become a cornerstone of application deployment. AWS Fargate, a serverless container orchestration service, takes container management to the next level by abstracting infrastructure concerns. In this section, we delve into the intricacies of AWS Fargate, exploring its key features, benefits, use cases, and real-world applications supported by scholarly articles and AWS sources.

Refer to the following figure:

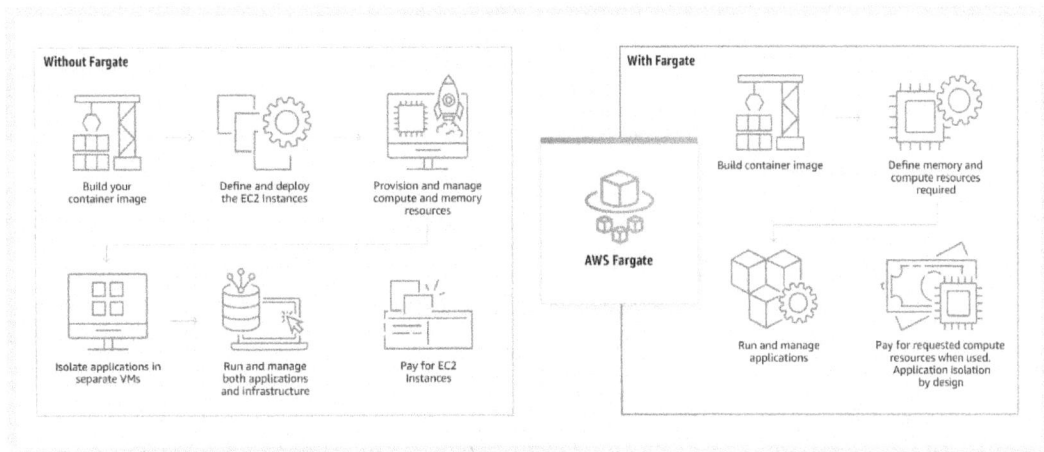

Figure 2.15: AWS Fargate serverless compute for containers

Serverless container orchestration with AWS Fargate

At its core, AWS Fargate functions as a serverless compute engine designed specifically for containers, enabling developers to run containerized applications without the hassle of managing underlying VMs or clusters. Fargate hides the complexities of infrastructure provisioning, scaling, and patching, allowing developers to concentrate fully on application development and innovation. Compatible with both Amazon ECS and Amazon EKS, Fargate offers exceptional flexibility in container orchestration, ensuring smooth integration into existing workflows. With Fargate, users pay only for the **virtual CPU (vCPU)** and memory resources their containers use, benefiting from precise scheduling [12]. Additionally, Fargate works with many AWS services, including Amazon RDS for databases and Amazon S3 for object storage, making end-to-end application deployment and management easier, faster, and more efficient.

Use cases and efficiency amplification

Although scholarly articles may not explicitly focus on AWS Fargate due to its recent release, they emphasize the broader importance of containerization in transforming application deployment practices. Research highlights the powerful impact of container orchestration platforms, like Fargate, in automating the management of containerized workloads [26], driving efficiency and scalability in cloud environments. AWS's extensive documentation on Fargate further underscores its versatility and applicability across diverse use cases. From powering web services and microservices to managing batch processing and ML workloads, Fargate empowers organizations to scale their containerized applications seamlessly while optimizing resource allocation and cost-effectiveness [34].

Refer to the following figure:

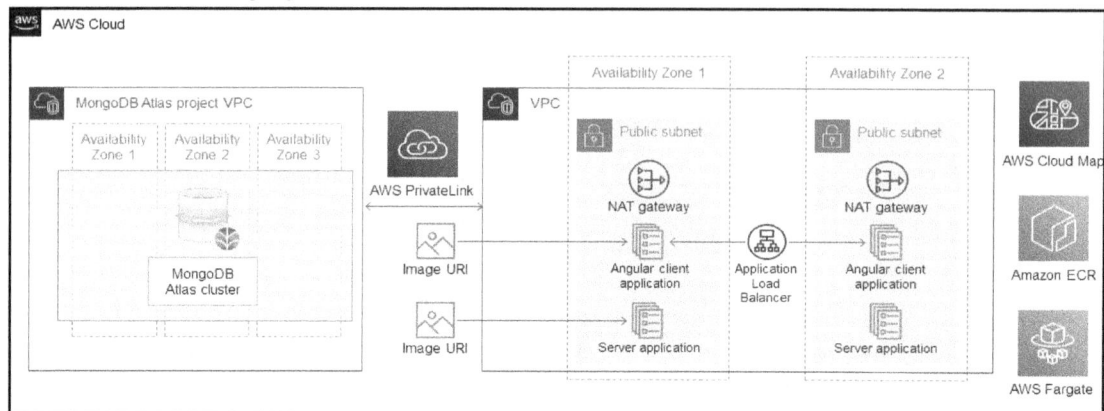

Figure 2.16: *MEAN stack using containers with AWS Fargate*

As we begin this chapter, our exploration of AWS Fargate will go beyond basic insights, diving into advanced configurations, best practices, and real-world case studies. By gaining a deeper understanding of Fargate's capabilities and details, organizations can unlock the full potential of serverless container orchestration, boosting innovation and efficiency in deploying containerized applications on the AWS cloud.

As we advance through this chapter, we will delve deeper into AWS Fargate, uncovering advanced configurations, best practices, and real-world case studies that demonstrate how organizations can utilize this serverless container orchestration service to simplify deploying their containerized applications on AWS.

AWS Lambda

In the ever-evolving landscape of cloud computing, AWS Lambda emerges as a cornerstone of serverless architecture, redefining the paradigms of application development and execution. Let us explore AWS Lambda comprehensively, delving into its intricate features, technical intricacies, and diverse use cases supported by scholarly articles and AWS sources.

Refer to the following figure:

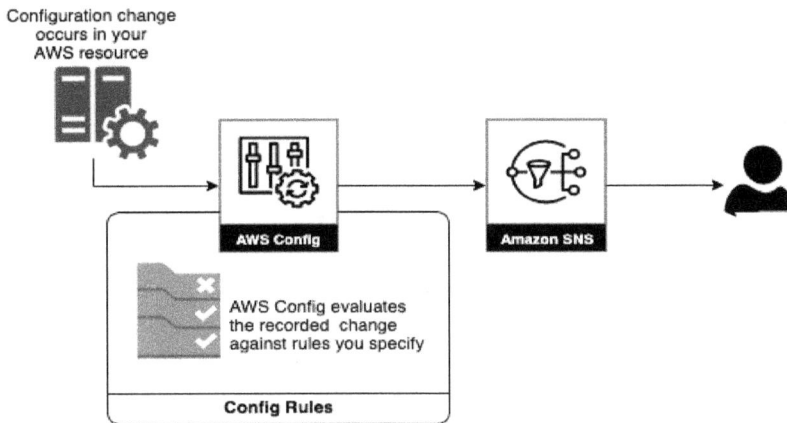

Figure 2.17: *SAP systems audit with AWS Config—part 1, Amazon EventBridge, AWS Config*

Unraveling the layers of AWS Lambda

AWS Lambda is a serverless computing service that enables developers to run code without the need to provision or manage servers. It uses an event-driven architecture, where code runs in response to specific events or triggers, such as HTTP requests, changes in data within an Amazon S3 bucket, or updates to an Amazon DynamoDB table. Developers package their code into Lambda functions, which can be written in various programming languages, including Python, Node.js, Java, and more. These functions are linked to event sources, and Lambda automatically manages scaling, patching, and high availability. Lambda functions can serve various purposes, from building APIs to processing real-time data streams. AWS also offers a comprehensive ecosystem of integrations and services that work effortlessly with Lambda, making it a versatile option for serverless computing [35].

At its core, AWS Lambda changes the traditional way of computing by providing a serverless platform where developers can run code without the need to provision or manage servers. In an event-driven setup, Lambda functions react automatically to specific triggers or events, such as HTTP requests, data updates in Amazon S3 buckets, or changes to Amazon DynamoDB tables. Developers package their code into Lambda functions, which support many programming languages, including Python, Node.js, Java, and more. These functions easily connect with event sources, letting Lambda handle scaling, patching, and high availability on its own. Whether building APIs, processing real-time data streams, or running back-end tasks, Lambda offers a flexible platform for many different application types. Additionally, AWS Lambda has a strong ecosystem of integrations and services, allowing smooth cooperation with other AWS tools and third-party applications, which increases its usefulness in serverless computing environments.

Refer to the following figure:

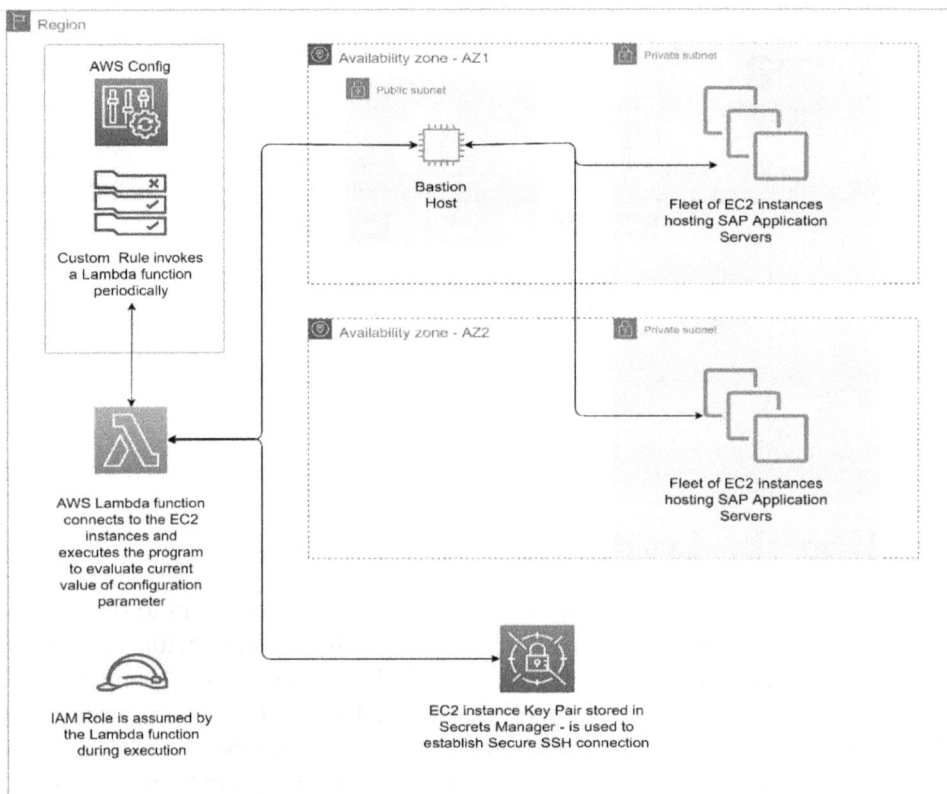

Figure 2.18: SAP systems audit with AWS Config–part 2, AWS Config, AWS Lambda

Use cases and efficiency amplification

While scholarly discourse may not focus solely on AWS Lambda, it emphasizes the transformative potential of serverless computing in simplifying application development and management. Research highlights the benefits of serverless architecture, such as reduced operational costs, better resource utilization, and increased scalability [36]. Though Lambda's direct citation may be sparse, its principles align with broader discussions on the advantages of serverless computing paradigms. AWS Documentation meticulously displays Lambda's applicability across various use cases, from web applications and data processing to IoT applications and real-time analytics. Lambda functions are inherently designed for efficiency, with automatic scaling mechanisms and dynamic resource allocation based on incoming event traffic. This ensures that organizations can achieve optimal cost-efficiency while maintaining excellent application performance [37].

Refer to the following figure:

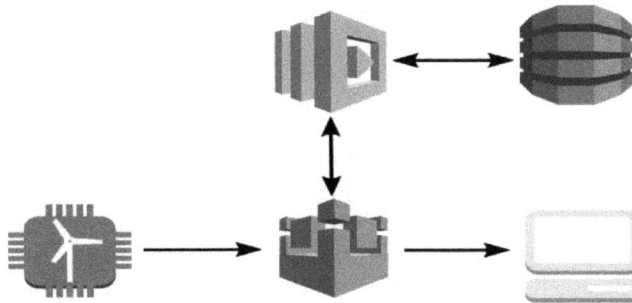

Figure 2.19: IoT anomaly detection process flows using AWS IoT and AWS Lambda

As we begin this chapter, our study of AWS Lambda will go beyond surface-level insights, exploring advanced configurations, best practices, and real-world case studies. By understanding Lambda's capabilities and nuances, organizations can leverage the transformative power of event-driven serverless computing to build scalable, responsive, and cost-effective AWS cloud applications.

Local Zones

In cloud computing, organizations often need cloud resources near their on-premises data centers and end-users. AWS Local Zones provide a strategic solution by offering low-latency access to a select range of AWS services in geographically dispersed locations. In this section, we explore the details of AWS Local Zones, highlighting their key features, benefits, use cases, and real-world applications supported by academic and AWS sources.

In the fast-changing world of cloud computing, having resources close to end-users and data centers is essential for boosting performance and cutting down latency. AWS Local Zones serve as a strategic solution, providing organizations with low-latency access to a select range of AWS services in various metropolitan areas. Let us take a detailed look at AWS Local Zones, exploring their detailed features, technical details, and diverse use cases backed by scholarly articles and AWS sources.

Refer to the following figure:

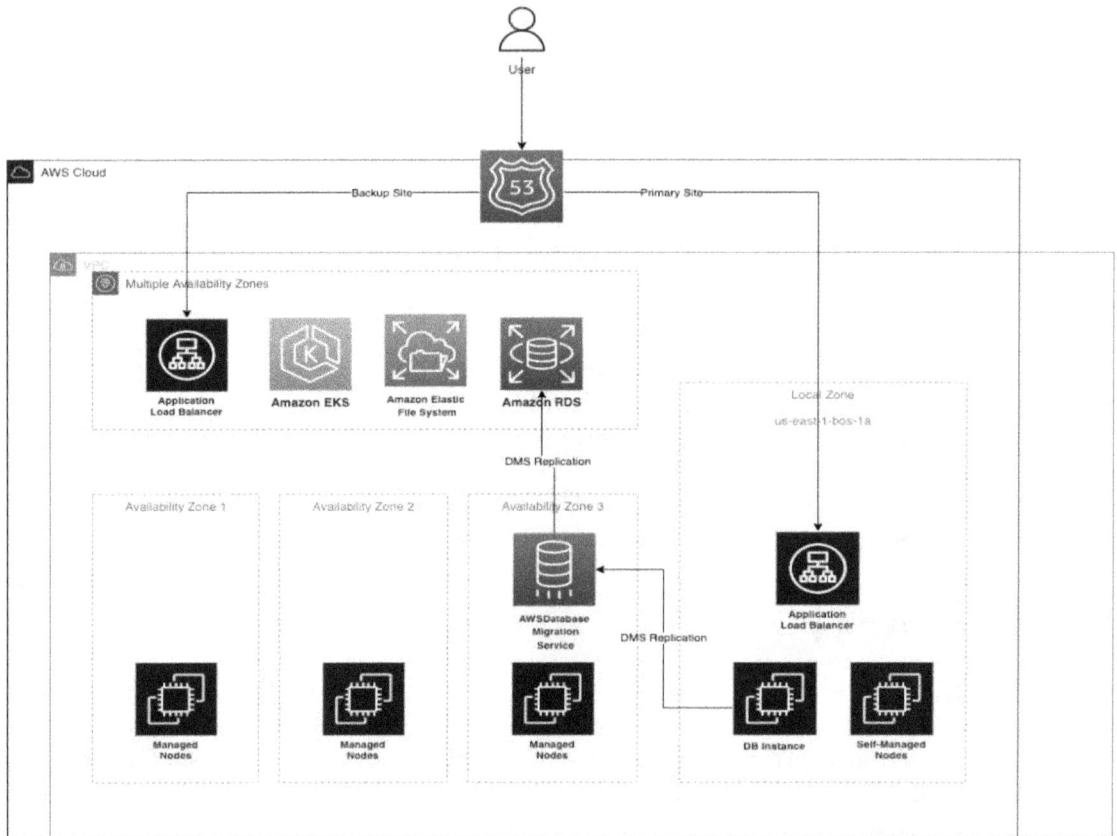

Figure 2.20: Deployment in the Local Zone

Expanding resources locally with AWS Local Zones

AWS Local Zones represent a shift in cloud infrastructure strategy, serving as geographically distributed extensions of an AWS Region. They are designed to bring AWS resources closer to end-users and applications, providing a localized cloud environment within specific metropolitan areas. This proximity enables low-latency access to a curated selection of AWS services, including compute instances, storage, and networking capabilities. Organizations can strategically deploy resources in Local Zones to support latency-sensitive workloads and applications that require proximity to end-users. Additionally, Local Zones seamlessly integrate with the parent AWS Region, ensuring efficient data transfer and service interoperability. By leveraging Local Zones, organizations can expand their AWS infrastructure footprint while maintaining a consistent operational experience [38] across distributed environments.

Use cases and efficiency amplification

While academic discourse may not explicitly discuss AWS Local Zones due to their localized deployment, research on cloud computing emphasizes the importance of minimizing data transfer latency and optimizing resource allocation. Studies on edge computing and minimizing data transfer latency emphasize the value of deploying resources closer to end-users. [13]. AWS Documentation on Local Zones emphasizes their usefulness in scenarios where organizations need low-latency access to AWS resources for applications such as gaming, media streaming, and real-time analytics. Local Zones enable organizations to meet stringent performance standards while leveraging the scalability and reliability of the AWS cloud. [39].

As we navigate this chapter, our exploration of AWS Local Zones will go beyond surface-level insights, revealing advanced configurations, best practices, and real-world case studies. By uncovering the potential of Local Zones, organizations can strategically enhance the performance of their cloud workloads in specific metropolitan areas, opening new opportunities for innovation and scalability in cloud computing.

Outposts

In the ever-evolving landscape of cloud computing, seamlessly integrating on-premises infrastructure with cloud services is critical for many organizations. AWS Outposts emerges as a transformative solution, bridging on-premises data centers and the expansive AWS cloud ecosystem. Let us explore AWS Outposts in-depth, unraveling their multifaceted features, technical intricacies, and diverse use cases supported by scholarly articles and AWS sources, as shown in *Figure 2.21*.

In cloud computing, organizations often seek to bridge the gap between their on-premises data centers and the cloud. AWS Outposts offers a compelling solution, enabling the deployment of AWS infrastructure and services on premises. In this section, we delve into the intricacies of AWS Outposts, exploring its key features, benefits, use cases, and real-world applications supported by scholarly articles and AWS sources.

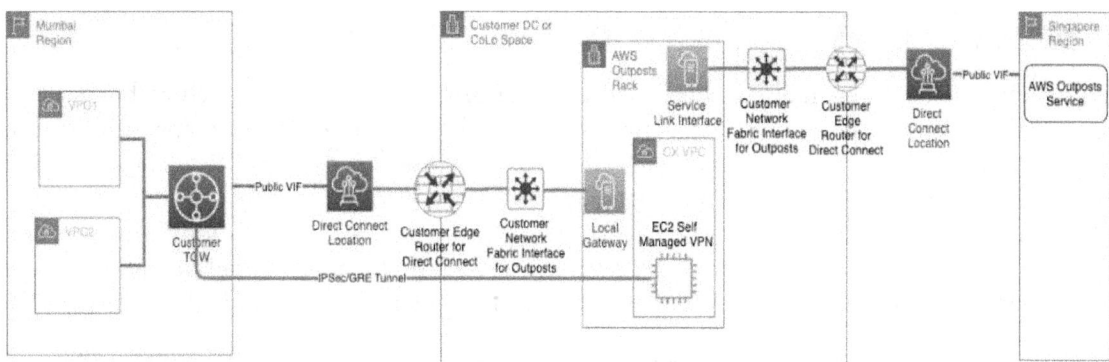

Figure 2.21: Setting up disaster recovery in a different seismic zone using AWS Outposts

Bridging on-premises and cloud with AWS Outposts

AWS Outposts signifies a shift in hybrid cloud architecture, enabling organizations to run AWS infrastructure and services directly within their on-premises environments. This fully managed service extends AWS's robust compute, storage, and database capabilities to local data centers, providing a consistent hybrid experience across cloud and on-premises setups. Outposts offer flexible configuration options, allowing organizations to tailor their computing and storage solutions, including the deployment of Amazon EC2 instances and Amazon EBS volumes. With AWS handling installation, maintenance, and monitoring, customers can concentrate on their applications and workloads. Additionally, Outposts seamlessly integrates with the larger AWS ecosystem, supporting hybrid scenarios and enabling smooth data synchronization between on-premises and cloud resources. [40].

Use cases and efficiency amplification

Scholarly articles may not directly focus on AWS Outposts due to its unique hybrid cloud nature; however, research on hybrid cloud adoption and data center expansion highlights the importance of solutions like Outposts in creating a unified and consistent infrastructure. Studies often stress the need for a flexible hybrid cloud architecture that allows organizations to select the optimal deployment model for their workloads [41]. AWS Documentation on Outposts explains its use cases where organizations need low-latency access to cloud services while keeping data residency and compliance on their premises. Outposts allow customers to run applications that require local data processing, follow data sovereignty laws, or operate in remote or disconnected locations [42].

As we explore this chapter, our analysis of AWS Outposts will go beyond basic insights, uncovering advanced configurations, best practices, and real-world case studies. By using this hybrid cloud solution, organizations can smoothly extend their AWS infrastructure to on-premises locations, unlocking new opportunities for innovation, scalability, and operational efficiency in cloud computing.

Serverless Application Repository

In the rapidly evolving landscape of cloud computing, serverless architecture has shifted fundamental assumptions, offering unmatched agility and scalability for application development. Within this ecosystem, the AWS **Serverless Application Repository (SAR)** stands as a key resource, providing developers with a curated collection of ready-made components and applications to speed up their serverless projects. Let us undertake a thorough exploration of the AWS SAR, examining its complex features, technical details, a variety of use cases, and real-world applications supported by both scholarly articles and AWS sources.

Refer to the following figure:

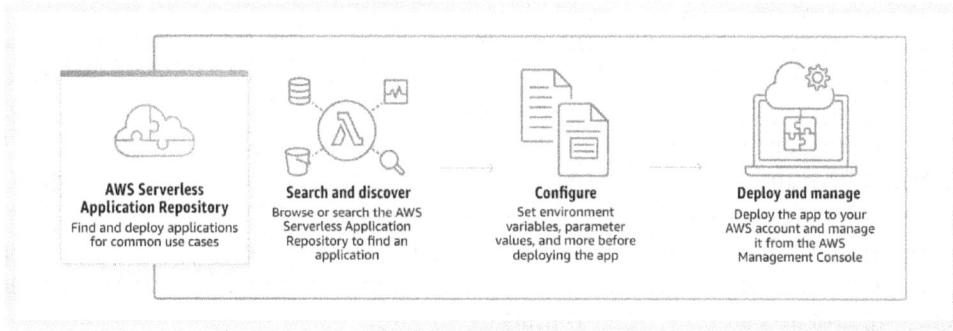

Figure 2.22: AWS SAR

Serverless Application Repository ready-made components

The AWS SAR is a centralized platform for discovering, deploying, and sharing serverless applications and components. SAR boasts a rich library of pre-built serverless applications and application components, meticulously crafted to streamline development workflows. These applications, known as **SAR applications**, span a wide spectrum of complexities, ranging from simple single-function applications to sophisticated multi-function applications tailored for specific use cases. SAR applications are seamlessly deployable in AWS Lambda, AWS Step Functions, and various other AWS services, empowering developers to swiftly integrate and deploy them without needing to start from scratch. Moreover, SAR fosters a culture of collaboration by enabling developers to publish their serverless applications and share them with the broader AWS Community, accelerating development [43] cycles and driving innovation.

Refer to the following figure:

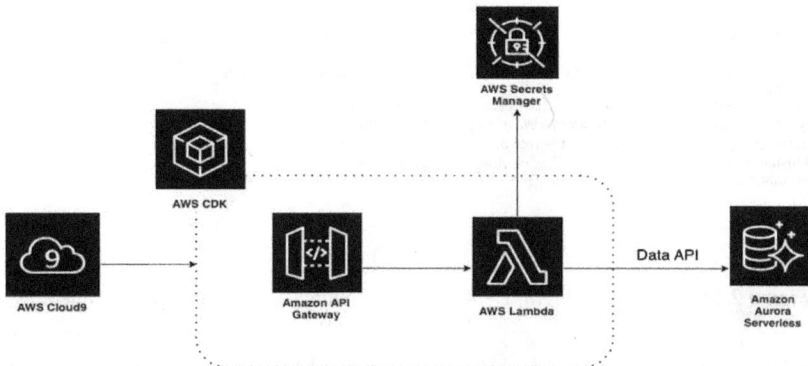

Figure 2.23: Architecture diagram highlighting the resources to be deployed in a user's AWS account

Utilization and efficiency amplification

While scholarly articles may not explicitly focus on the AWS SAR, the broader research landscape emphasizes the crucial role of reusable components and code sharing in software development. In various fields, from software engineering to cloud architecture, code reuse and componentization are praised as best practices that enhance efficiency and scalability. AWS's detailed documentation on SAR further highlights its relevance in situations where organizations aim to speed up their serverless development by utilizing pre-built applications and components. SAR promotes efficient development practices, enabling developers to leverage the collective expertise of the AWS Community, which reduces development time and effort [44], and accelerating time-to-market.

As we go through this chapter, our look at the AWS SAR will go beyond basic ideas, exploring advanced features, best practices, and real-world examples. Using this collection, organizations can speed up serverless application development, promote teamwork, and discover new opportunities for innovation in the fast-changing world of cloud computing.

AWS Wavelength

In an era driven by the rapid speed and connectivity of 5G networks, the need for ultra-low-latency applications has become more urgent than ever. Recognizing this need, AWS Wavelength presents a revolutionary solution, seamlessly connecting AWS infrastructure with the edge of 5G networks. In this section, we thoroughly examine AWS Wavelength, highlighting its diverse features, transformative benefits, various use cases, and real-world applications supported by scholarly articles and AWS sources.

Refer to the following figure:

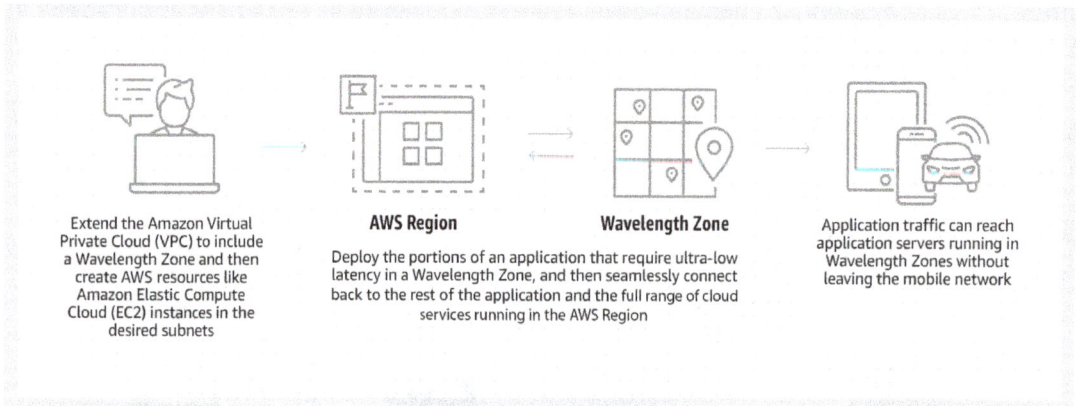

Extend the Amazon Virtual Private Cloud (VPC) to include a Wavelength Zone and then create AWS resources like Amazon Elastic Compute Cloud (EC2) instances in the desired subnets

AWS Region

Deploy the portions of an application that require ultra-low latency in a Wavelength Zone, and then seamlessly connect back to the rest of the application and the full range of cloud services running in the AWS Region

Wavelength Zone

Application traffic can reach application servers running in Wavelength Zones without leaving the mobile network

Figure 2.24: *AWS Wavelength, Deliver ultra-low-latency applications for 5G devices*

In the age of 5G connectivity, reducing latency is crucial for applications that require real-time responsiveness. AWS Wavelength addresses this by providing AWS infrastructure at the edge of 5G networks. In this section, we will explore the details of AWS Wavelength, highlighting its key features, benefits, use cases, and real-world applications supported by scholarly articles and AWS sources.

Bringing the cloud to 5G with AWS Wavelength

AWS Wavelength is a specialized deployment of AWS infrastructure that places compute and storage resources at the edge of telecommunication providers' 5G networks. This positioning significantly reduces the round-trip time between an application running in a Wavelength Zone and the end-users, enabling ultra-low-latency connectivity. AWS Wavelength enables developers to build applications that require single-digit millisecond latencies, making it suitable for various use cases, including **augmented reality/virtual reality (AR/VR)**, online gaming, real-time analytics, and more. With Wavelength, developers can seamlessly extend their AWS environments to the edge, using familiar AWS services like EC2 and Lambda while running them closer to the end-users [45].

Refer to the following figure:

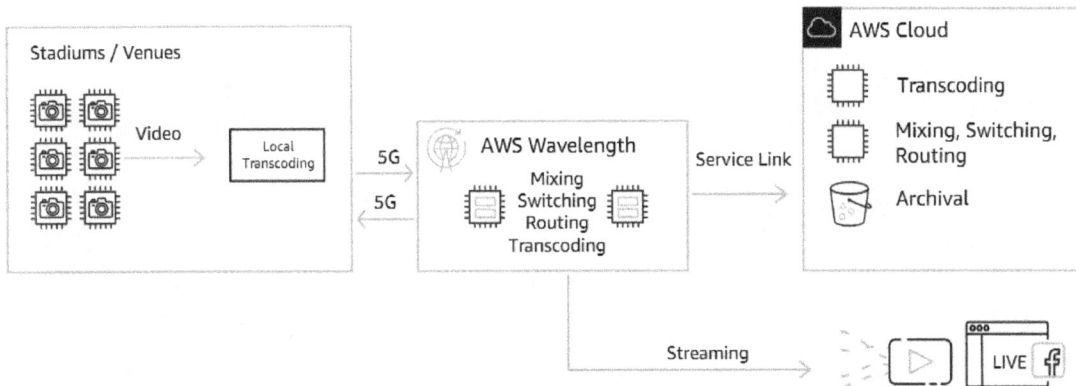

Figure 2.25: AWS Wavelength 5G video ingestion

Exploring use cases and efficiency amplification

While scholarly articles may not explicitly target AWS Wavelength due to its specialized nature, research in edge computing and low-latency applications unequivocally underscores its significance. Edge computing has emerged as a pivotal enabler for enhancing the performance of latency-sensitive applications, revolutionizing industries ranging from healthcare to manufacturing [46]. AWS's exhaustive documentation on Wavelength highlights its applicability across a range of scenarios, where organizations are tasked with delivering real-time, interactive experiences over 5G networks. Consider scenarios such as multiplayer online gaming, where instantaneous response times are non-negotiable, or immersive AR/VR applications that require minimal lag for optimal UX. Wavelength Zones, strategically situated within urban centers, ensure that applications can seamlessly deliver low-latency experiences to users in metropolitan areas [47], unlocking new frontiers of innovation and user engagement.

As this chapter unfolds, our examination of AWS Wavelength will go beyond basic insights, exploring advanced configurations, best practices, and real-world case studies. By leveraging the power of AWS Wavelength, organizations can position themselves at the forefront of the 5G revolution, delivering ultra-low-latency, high-performance applications that push the limits of what's possible in the digital world.

VMware on AWS

In the quickly changing world of IT infrastructure, organizations are increasingly adopting hybrid cloud solutions to smoothly connect their on-premises systems with the cloud. VMware Cloud on AWS is a standout as a transformative tool, enabling businesses to use the power of VMware workloads on the flexible AWS cloud platform. In this section, we examine VMware Cloud on AWS in detail, revealing its complex features, strong benefits, various use cases, and real-world applications supported by scholarly articles and AWS sources.

Refer to the following figure:

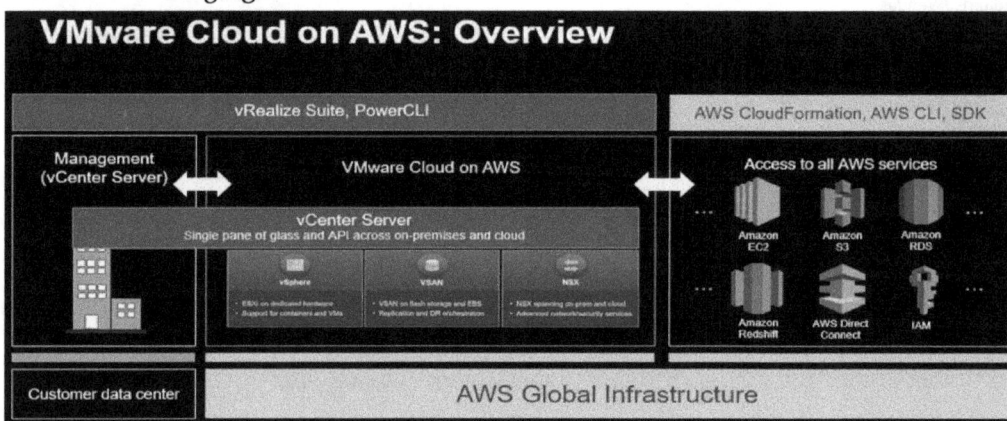

Figure 2.26: VMware Cloud on AWS overview

Link to on-premises with VMware Cloud on AWS

VMware Cloud on AWS is a joint effort that combines VMware's **software-defined data center (SDDC)** features with the unmatched flexibility, scalability, and global presence of AWS. This innovative service enables organizations to easily migrate, expand, or run their VMware workloads on AWS infrastructure, thereby avoiding costly and lengthy conversions. Using familiar VMware tools, such as vCenter, vSAN, and NSX, VMware Cloud on AWS provides a consistent operational experience while enabling automated cluster scaling, direct access to AWS services, and robust disaster recovery options. Customers can benefit from the extensive

AWS Global Infrastructure while maintaining compatibility with their current VMware environments, making it easier to adopt [48] hybrid cloud architectures.

Exploring use cases and efficiency amplification

While scholarly articles may not explicitly focus on VMware Cloud on AWS, the importance of hybrid cloud solutions in optimizing both on-premises and cloud resources is widely recognized. The research emphasizes the significance of flexibility, scalability, and compatibility when expanding on-premises infrastructure into the cloud [49] AWS's detailed documentation on VMware Cloud on AWS highlights its flexibility in various scenarios, such as data center expansion, disaster recovery, and cloud migration. Organizations can improve resource use, reduce costs, and maintain enterprise-level security and compliance by easily connecting on-premises VMware setups with AWS services [50].

As this chapter progresses, we delve deeper into VMware Cloud on AWS, uncovering advanced configurations, best practices, and real-world case studies that demonstrate how organizations can leverage this hybrid cloud solution to seamlessly connect their on-premises and AWS environments. Whether it is streamlining operations, improving scalability, or strengthening disaster recovery capabilities, VMware Cloud on AWS becomes a key part of organizations' modernization efforts to harness the potential of hybrid cloud architectures.

Conclusion

In this chapter, we examined a wide range of computing services provided by AWS. We started with Amazon EC2, exploring features like Auto Scaling and Spot Instances for dynamic resource adjustment and cost savings. We then looked at container orchestration with Amazon ECS and EKS, highlighting their scalability and flexibility benefits. AWS Lambda introduced us to serverless computing, emphasizing event-driven architecture for highly scalable and cost-efficient applications. We also covered deployment ease with AWS Elastic Beanstalk and AWS App Runner, allowing focus on application development. Additionally, we delved into workload optimization tools like AWS Compute Optimizer and Auto Scaling. Hybrid cloud solutions with AWS Local Zones and Outposts were discussed, along with emerging technologies such as AWS Wavelength and VMware Cloud on AWS. Batch processing with AWS Batch, simplified solutions using Lightsail and Fargate, and hybrid cloud simulation with AWS SimSpace Weaver were also covered. [51]. By aligning with chapter objectives, we have gained a comprehensive understanding of AWS compute services, empowering us to architect robust, scalable solutions on the AWS cloud.

The next chapter will detail file and storage types.

Join our Discord space

Join our Discord workspace for latest updates, offers, tech happenings around the world, new releases, and sessions with the authors:

https://discord.bpbonline.com

CHAPTER 3
Storage

Introduction

This chapter will examine the fundamental elements that enable organizations to develop robust data management solutions. From block storage to file systems, archival storage to data lakes, and **disaster recovery (DR)** to data migration, we will examine the various **Amazon Web Services (AWS)** storage options that allow businesses to store, safeguard, and access their data with exceptional flexibility, scalability, and reliability. Whether you aim to develop resilient applications, improve data analytics, or enhance your data recovery plans, this chapter provides the knowledge and insights necessary to maximize the benefits of AWS storage services. Join us as we investigate **Amazon Elastic Block Store (EBS)**, **Amazon Elastic File System (EFS)**, Amazon FSx, Amazon S3 Glacier, **Amazon Simple Storage Service (S3)**, AWS Backup, AWS Snow Family, AWS Storage Gateway, and **AWS Elastic DR(DRS)**. Prepare to discover the many opportunities for data storage in the AWS cloud.

Structure

In this chapter, we will discuss the following topics:

- Storage pattern decision matrix
- Amazon Elastic Block Store
- Amazon Elastic File System

- Amazon FSx
- Amazon S3 Glacier
- Amazon Simple Storage Service
- AWS Backup
- AWS Snow Family
- AWS Storage Gateway
- AWS Elastic Disaster Recovery

Objectives

In this chapter, we will learn how to build resilient applications, optimize data analytics, or fortify your data recovery strategies.

Storage pattern decision matrix

Choosing the best storage pattern within AWS depends on factors such as performance, scalability, security, and, especially, the access protocols supported by the applications. AWS offers various storage options, including **storage area networks (SAN)**, **network-attached storage (NAS)**, and object storage, to meet diverse needs. Each type has its own advantages and limitations, mainly based on the protocols it supports.

Figure 3.1 illustrates how on-premises users and applications connect to and access data storage systems. In this example, applications can utilize SAN, NAS, or object storage through their respective supported protocols. While factors such as performance, security, and scalability play crucial roles, the choice of storage, whether SAN, NAS, or object, is primarily influenced by the access protocols supported by the applications. Each protocol comes with its unique benefits and limitations, making it a significant factor in deciding which storage solution to adopt on the back-end [1].

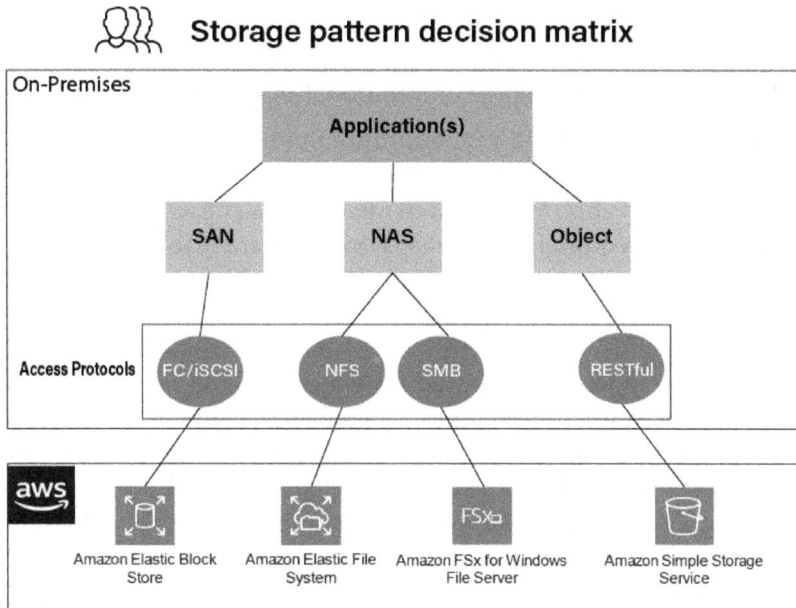

Figure 3.1: *AWS storage pattern decision matrix*

In this section, we will examine the storage patterns offered by AWS and analyze which use cases benefit from each storage solution. The objective is to ensure readers can make informed decisions when architecting their data management strategy in the AWS cloud.

Storage area network

As enterprises migrate mission-critical workloads to the cloud, maintaining high-speed, low-latency access to storage remains a top priority, particularly for transactional systems and performance-intensive databases. Traditionally, this demand was met through on-premises SANs, which provided dedicated block-level storage over specialized high-throughput networks. In the AWS ecosystem, services like Amazon EBS have evolved to replicate and even exceed SAN capabilities by delivering scalable, resilient, and high-performance block storage in the cloud, eliminating the complexity of managing physical storage infrastructure while preserving the performance guarantees needed by modern applications. Refer to the following for a detailed description:

- **What it is**: SAN is a high-speed network that provides block-level storage to applications. The storage is accessed over dedicated high-performance networks, ensuring low-latency and high-throughput.

- **Best suited for**: Applications requiring high-performance storage, such as databases or transactional systems, which need low-latency, high-throughput access to storage.

- **AWS services**:
  - o Amazon EBS provides block storage that can be attached to EC2 instances and used similarly to SAN storage in traditional on-premises setups.
- **Real-world application**: In financial institutions or e-commerce platforms, transactional databases require SAN-like performance to manage millions of requests per second. For example, Amazon EBS volumes are ideal for databases like MySQL, PostgreSQL, and MongoDB that require fast, reliable storage for intensive workloads.

Network-attached storage

In modern cloud environments, file-based storage remains a crucial component for collaboration, application compatibility, and shared access across multiple systems. NAS provides centralized, file-level storage that enables multiple users and servers to interact with the same datasets in real-time. AWS offers fully managed NAS alternatives that deliver the scalability, availability, and performance required by enterprise workloads—whether it is for media workflows, shared content repositories, or distributed computing pipelines. Refer to the following for a detailed description:

- **What it is**: NAS offers file-level access, enabling applications to share a centralized storage system. It is typically used for applications that require file sharing across different systems.
- **Best suited for**: Applications where multiple servers or users need access to shared files, such as content management systems, home directories, or web servers.
- **AWS services**:
  - o Amazon EFS provides scalable file storage that can be accessed by multiple EC2 instances simultaneously. It offers high availability and durability, making it a preferred choice for enterprise applications.
  - o Amazon FSx supports Windows-based and Lustre file systems, ideal for users who need compatibility with existing NAS systems.
- **Real-world application**: Enterprises that run shared web servers, media workflows, or big data processing workloads benefit from EFS and FSx. For example, Amazon EFS is widely used when applications need to access shared file systems from multiple **Availability Zones (AZs)**.

Object storage

Modern applications often need seamless access to shared file systems across distributed environments—whether for collaborative content management, web hosting, or scientific data pipelines. Traditionally, NAS provided this on-premises, offering centralized, file-level storage accessible via standard network protocols. In the cloud, AWS services like Amazon EFS and Amazon FSx extend this idea with scalable, fault-tolerant file storage that works natively with compute resources and spans multiple AZs. These cloud-native solutions not only mimic NAS capabilities but also provide greater elasticity, automation, and compatibility for enterprise-grade workloads. Refer to the following for a detailed description:

- **What it is**: Object storage manages unstructured data like media files, backups, or archives. Instead of using traditional file hierarchies, object storage uses metadata and unique identifiers, making it scalable and efficient for vast amounts of data.

- **Best suited for**: Applications where vast amounts of unstructured data, such as images, videos, logs, or backups, must be stored and retrieved with scalability and durability.

- **AWS services**:

  o Amazon S3 is the foundational object storage service that provides unlimited scalability and 99.999999999% durability. It is ideal for storing backups, data archives, and substantial amounts of unstructured data.

  o Amazon S3 Glacier offers low-cost archival storage for long-term data retention and retrieval at varying speeds.

- **Real-world application**: Media streaming services, where videos are stored in S3 for global distribution, benefit from object storage. Additionally, organizations that need to store backup and archival data long-term leverage Amazon S3 Glacier for low-cost storage solutions.

Decision-making criteria

Each of these AWS storage solutions plays a distinct role, and the decision to use SAN, NAS, or object storage should consider the following key criteria:

- **Performance requirements**:

  o High-performance applications like databases or virtual desktops benefit from Amazon EBS, which provides fast, low-latency access to block storage (SAN-like performance).

  o Applications needing frequent access to shared files across distributed instances perform best with Amazon EFS or Amazon FSx (NAS-like services).

  o Workloads requiring high durability and scalability but less frequent access to data, such as backups or media content delivery, are ideal candidates for Amazon S3 or S3 Glacier.

- **Access protocols**:

  o Applications using block storage protocols like **Internet Small Computer Systems Interface (iSCSI)** or **Fibre Channel (FC)** work well with EBS, as it supports these lower-level block interactions.

  o Amazon EFS or FSx best serves file-based protocols such as **Network File System (NFS)** or **Server Message Block (SMB)**. For example, FSx for Windows File Server is ideal for enterprise applications needing Windows-compatible systems.

- o **Hypertext Transfer Protocol (HTTP)** or REST APIs interact with Amazon S3 object storage, ideal for web-based applications, mobile applications, and data lakes.
- **Scalability and durability**:
  - o Amazon S3 provides unlimited scalability and unmatched durability, making it the go-to choice for long-term storage of large datasets.
  - o File systems like EFS offer automatic scaling as workloads increase or decrease, while EBS scales by manually attaching additional volumes to EC2 instances.
- **Cost considerations**:
  - o Amazon S3 is one of the most cost-effective solutions for storing massive amounts of unstructured data, while S3 Glacier further reduces costs for long-term archival.
  - o For active workloads requiring constant data interaction, EFS and FSx offer cost-effective options compared to setting up custom file sharing systems.

Thus, choosing the right AWS storage solution requires understanding the application's needs related to performance, scalability, and access protocols. The storage pattern decision matrix helps identify which AWS service best fits specific requirements, whether it's block storage with Amazon EBS, file storage with EFS/FSx, or object storage through Amazon S3. Organizations can enhance performance, lower costs, and scale effectively within the AWS environment by selecting the most suitable storage type.

Amazon Elastic Block Store

In cloud computing, storage is the foundation of modern applications, and Amazon EBS is a key component within AWS's wide range of storage options. Cloud storage is essential for businesses, offering scalability, flexibility, and reliability to meet changing application requirements. Amazon EBS plays a vital role by providing durable, high-performance block storage that supports various workloads. Its main features include the ability to easily create and attach block storage volumes to EC2 instances, support for different volume types designed for specific performance needs, and strong data protection features such as automated snapshots and multi-AZ replication. Refer to the following figure:

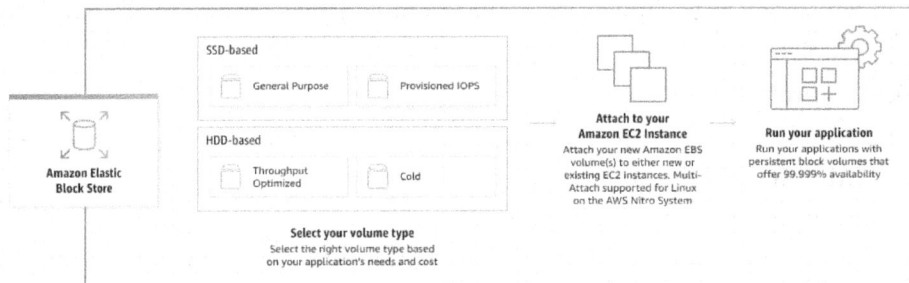

Figure 3.2: Amazon EBS

Amazon EBS provides businesses with scalability and flexibility, allowing them to resize volumes and attach them to different EC2 instances as their storage needs change. Its seamless integration with other AWS services, including Amazon EC2, AWS Backup, and AWS CloudWatch, further boosts its value as part of a comprehensive storage solution. Organizations across various industries have successfully adopted Amazon EBS to meet their storage demands. For example, companies hosting databases like MySQL, PostgreSQL, and Oracle depend on Amazon EBS for high-speed storage that satisfies their demanding **input/ output (I/O)** requirements. Additionally, Amazon EBS functions as boot volumes for EC2 instances, delivering consistent and reliable performance to fulfill the strict needs of various applications.

Customer success stories highlight the practical benefits of Amazon EBS, underscoring its role in optimizing data storage and application performance in real-world scenarios. These examples also highlight Amazon EBS's adaptability and reliability, making it an indispensable component of cloud infrastructure for businesses seeking scalable and reliable storage solutions in the AWS cloud.

Closer look at Amazon Elastic Block Store

Amazon EBS is a fully managed block storage service provided by AWS, designed to give organizations scalable and reliable storage solutions for their cloud-based applications. With Amazon EBS, organizations can easily create and attach block storage volumes to Amazon EC2 instances. These volumes offer persistent, low-latency storage, making them suitable for various use cases across different industries, with features like automated snapshots and multiple AZ replications to safeguard data. EBS volumes can be quickly resized and attached to different EC2 instances, providing flexibility as workloads change [2], as discussed:

- **Persistent, low-latency storage**: One of Amazon EBS's key features is its ability to provide persistent storage with low-latency. This makes it suitable for critical workloads, such as database storage, boot volumes, and application data, that require consistent and responsive access.

- Amazon EBS offers various volume types optimized for different performance characteristics, enabling organizations to select the most suitable type based on their specific requirements. These volume types include:

  o **General Purpose SSD (gp2)**: This is ideal for many workloads, including boot volumes and small to medium-sized databases.

  o **Provisioned IOPS SSD (io1)**: Designed for I/O-intensive workloads that require predictable and consistent performance, such as large database workloads and mission-critical applications.

  o **Throughput Optimized HDD (st1)**: Suited for frequently accessed, throughput-intensive workloads such as log processing and data warehouses.

o   **Cold HDD (sc1)**: This type of storage is intended for infrequently accessed workloads where the lowest storage cost is paramount, such as file servers and data archives.

- **High availability and durability**: Amazon EBS volumes are designed for availability and durability. There is replication within an AZ to ensure redundancy and protect against hardware failures. Features like automated snapshots and multiple AZ replication further enhance data protection and durability.

- **Flexibility and scalability**: Amazon EBS volumes can be easily resized and attached to different EC2 instances, offering flexibility as workloads evolve. Organizations can adjust storage capacity and performance characteristics dynamically to meet changing requirements without impacting the availability of their applications.

In summary, Amazon EBS provides organizations with a versatile and reliable block storage solution that can accommodate a wide range of workloads and use cases. Its combination of low-latency storage, different volume types, high availability, durability, and scalability makes it an essential component of cloud infrastructure for businesses of all sizes.

Use cases and efficiency

Research articles consistently underscore the pivotal role of block storage in cloud computing, emphasizing the critical importance of selecting the appropriate storage type for specific workloads. Studies frequently highlight the crucial role of block storage in optimizing database performance, where low-latency and high **I/O operations per second** (**IOPS**) storage are crucial [3]. AWS Documentation on EBS highlights its applicability in various scenarios, including hosting databases such as MySQL, PostgreSQL, and Oracle, providing high-speed storage for applications with demanding I/O requirements, and serving as boot volumes for EC2 instances. EBS is known for its ability to deliver consistent and predictable performance, ensuring that applications can meet stringent requirements while enjoying the scalability and durability of the AWS cloud [4].

Amazon EBS, a fully managed block storage service, caters to a wide range of use cases across various industries. Its versatility and reliability make it indispensable for organizations seeking efficient cloud storage solutions. Here are prominent use cases where Amazon EBS shines:

- **Database hosting**: Amazon EBS hosts MySQL, PostgreSQL, and Oracle databases. Its ability to provide high-speed storage with consistent performance ensures that database-intensive applications run smoothly, even under heavy workloads.

- **Application storage**: These applications have demanding I/O requirements, necessitating high-performance storage solutions. Amazon EBS is an ideal storage option for such applications, offering reliable and scalable storage volumes that can efficiently handle diverse workloads.

- **Boot volumes for EC2 instances**: Amazon EBS volumes are used as boot volumes for Amazon EC2 instances. These volumes provide persistent storage for the operating system and application files, enabling smooth booting and quick access to critical resources.

Amazon EBS is renowned for its ability to deliver consistent and predictable performance, which is crucial for meeting the stringent requirements of modern applications. Whether ensuring low-latency access to data or managing high I/O workloads, Amazon EBS provides the scalability and durability necessary to support diverse use cases within the AWS cloud environment.

As we delve deeper into this chapter, we will explore Amazon EBS in greater detail, uncovering advanced configurations, best practices, and real-world case studies. By examining these examples, organizations can gain valuable insights into optimizing their data storage and application performance using this fundamental AWS storage service.

Amazon Elastic File System

Amazon EFS is a highly scalable, fully managed file storage service designed to meet the needs of applications that require shared file systems. Unlike block storage, which is tied to a single instance, EFS offers a multi-tenant, **distributed file system** (DFS) that enables multiple EC2 instances to access the same file system simultaneously, regardless of their location within the same region. This feature is especially valuable for applications where data sharing and collaboration are essential, such as development environments, content management systems, or data analytics platforms.

The following illustration represents Amazon EFS, according to AWS Documentation:

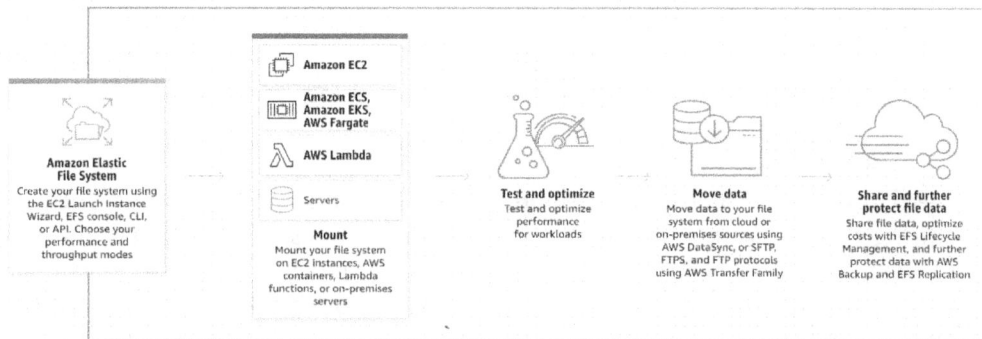

Figure 3.3: Amazon EFS

EFS architecture and elasticity

The architecture of EFS is built on NFS, a proven protocol that enables access from various EC2 instances. Unlike traditional on-premises storage, EFS is designed to grow automatically as your storage needs change, removing the need for manual adjustments. This feature ensures your file system can expand or contract as needed, supporting both bursty workloads and steady operations [5].

One defining feature of EFS is its DFS architecture, which enables data partitioning across multiple AZs. This guarantees that data remains durable, resilient to potential failures, and broadly accessible. Additionally, EFS includes built-in redundancy across AZs, reducing the risk of data loss caused by hardware failures or other infrastructure issues.

Performance capabilities

EFS offers multiple performance modes, each designed to optimize workloads based on specific needs:

- **General Purpose mode**: Suitable for latency-sensitive applications, like web serving or content management systems, where consistent low-latency access to data is required.

- **Max I/O mode**: Optimized for applications that demand high-throughput, such as big data analytics, media processing, or large-scale content delivery.

EFS also offers storage classes tailored to varying cost and performance needs:

- **Standard storage class**: Designed for frequently accessed data, this class provides high-throughput and low-latency.

- **Infrequent access**: Optimized for data accessed less frequently but still requires rapid retrieval, this storage class offers cost savings for less critical data sets.

By allowing organizations to combine storage classes within the same file system, EFS optimizes costs while maintaining high-performance access for critical workloads.

Use cases and real-world applications

EFS's versatility extends across various industries:

- **Media processing and collaboration**: In media production workflows, such as video editing or rendering, multiple instances require access to the same large files [6]. EFS simplifies data sharing, ensuring each instance can collaborate on shared assets without manual synchronization. For example, post-production teams working on high-resolution video can access a central repository of files in real-time, accelerating the entire workflow [7].

- **Web hosting and content delivery**: EFS provides a scalable storage layer for web hosting, supporting dynamic content generation and distribution. When combined with services like Amazon CloudFront, web applications can offer users low-latency content delivery while benefiting from EFS's scalability and reliability.

- **Data analytics**: Data scientists often need access to large datasets across multiple compute instances. EFS supports real-time collaboration, ensuring that all data points are readily accessible, enabling faster data processing and analysis. EFS's elastic scalability ensures that no resources are wasted and that storage grows in coordination with increasing data needs.

Best practices for optimizing EFS usage

To fully leverage Amazon EFS, adhering to the following best practices can enhance its performance and cost-efficiency:

- **Select the appropriate performance mode**: Choose between General Purpose and Max I/O modes to optimize cost and performance depending on the workload type.

- **Leverage lifecycle policies**: Use lifecycle management to automatically move files not recently accessed into **Infrequent Access (IA)** storage. This reduces storage costs without compromising accessibility.

- **Secure your data**: Implement AWS **Identity and Access Management (IAM)** to control access to EFS file systems. Then, leverage **encryption at rest** using AWS **Key Management Service (KMS)** to secure sensitive data.

- **Monitor usage and performance**: Regularly monitor your file systems using Amazon CloudWatch metrics. This allows you to track I/O throughput, latency, and request counts, providing insights into optimizing performance based on real-time usage data.

Amazon EFS is a flexible and highly scalable file storage solution within the AWS ecosystem. Whether you are hosting websites, processing large media files, or supporting data-driven analytics, EFS offers a robust solution for shared, scalable file storage [4]. By employing best practices in performance tuning, cost optimization, and data protection, organizations can fully exploit the potential of Amazon EFS to drive innovation, enhance collaboration, and manage their cloud storage needs efficiently.

This in-depth look into Amazon EFS provides organizations with the insights and tools they need to implement effective file storage solutions, ensuring their applications operate with agility and scalability in the cloud. As the demand for collaborative, distributed environments grows, Amazon EFS becomes an indispensable tool in the modern cloud landscape.

Amazon FSx

Amazon FSx emerges as a pivotal component within the AWS storage portfolio, addressing the escalating demand for managed file storage solutions tailored to specific workloads and use cases. As organizations increasingly transition to cloud-native architectures, the need for efficient, scalable, and available file storage becomes paramount. Amazon FSx addresses this need by offering fully managed file storage services optimized for Windows and Lustre workloads, empowering organizations to streamline data management and access within the AWS cloud environment.

At its core, Amazon FSx provides a comprehensive suite of features to enhance performance, reliability, and ease of use. With support for Windows and Lustre file systems, Amazon FSx caters to a wide range of applications and industries, from traditional enterprise workloads to **high-performance computing** (**HPC**) environments.

For Windows workloads, Amazon FSx for Windows File Server delivers fully managed file storage with native SMB protocol support. This enables perfect integration with existing Windows environments, allowing users to access and share files using familiar interfaces and tools. Amazon FSx for Windows File Server provides features such as **Active Directory** (**AD**) integration, user quotas, and data deduplication, enhancing data management and security within Windows-based applications.

On the other hand, Amazon optimizes FSx for Lustre for HPC and data-intensive workloads, offering high-performance, scalable file storage for compute-intensive applications. Leveraging the Lustre parallel file system, Amazon FSx for Lustre delivers low-latency access to massive datasets, enabling organizations to accelerate data processing and analysis tasks. With support for high-throughput and low-latency, Amazon FSx for Lustre is well-suited for applications such as genomic sequencing, financial modeling, and scientific simulations.

In practical terms, Amazon FSx addresses many use cases across industries and domains. Amazon FSx offers a seamless migration path to the cloud for enterprises looking to modernize their infrastructure, allowing organizations to transition their legacy file storage systems to a fully managed, scalable environment. Amazon FSx for Lustre facilitates the analysis of large datasets and complex simulations in research and academic settings, empowering researchers to unlock new insights and discoveries.

Furthermore, Amazon FSx enhances operational efficiency and agility by automating routine tasks such as backup, maintenance, and patch management. By offloading these responsibilities to AWS, organizations can focus on innovation and value creation, leveraging the scalability and reliability of Amazon FSx to drive business outcomes.

In conclusion, Amazon FSx redefines the landscape of managed file storage, offering a robust and scalable solution for organizations seeking to modernize their data infrastructure in the cloud. With support for both Windows and Lustre file systems, Amazon FSx provides a versatile platform for a wide range of workloads and use cases, enabling organizations to optimize performance, streamline operations, and unlock new possibilities in the era of cloud computing.

Closer look at Amazon FSx

Amazon FSx is a managed file storage service that provides fully compatible file systems for Windows and Lustre workloads. FSx for Windows File Server offers a Windows-native file system flawlessly integrated with AD, enabling organizations to run Windows-based applications requiring shared file storage. FSx for Lustre, on the other hand, delivers a high-performance parallel file system designed for compute-intensive workloads such as HPC and

machine learning (ML). Both FSx offerings are fully managed, eliminating the operational overhead of file system provisioning, maintenance, and backup. With features like automated backups, data deduplication, and data synchronization, FSx simplifies file storage management in the AWS cloud [8].

Amazon FSx offers different file systems tailored to meet specific workload requirements and use cases. Each file system provides unique features and capabilities to optimize performance, reliability, and compatibility with different applications, as follows:

- **Amazon FSx for NetApp ONTAP**: Amazon FSx for NetApp ONTAP delivers fully managed NetApp ONTAP file storage, offering industry-leading performance, scalability, and data management capabilities. This file system is ideal for enterprise workloads, including business applications, databases, and **virtual desktop infrastructure** (**VDI**). With features such as high availability, data deduplication, and SnapMirror data replication, Amazon FSx for NetApp ONTAP ensures robust data protection and perfect integration with existing NetApp environments.

  Refer to the following figure:

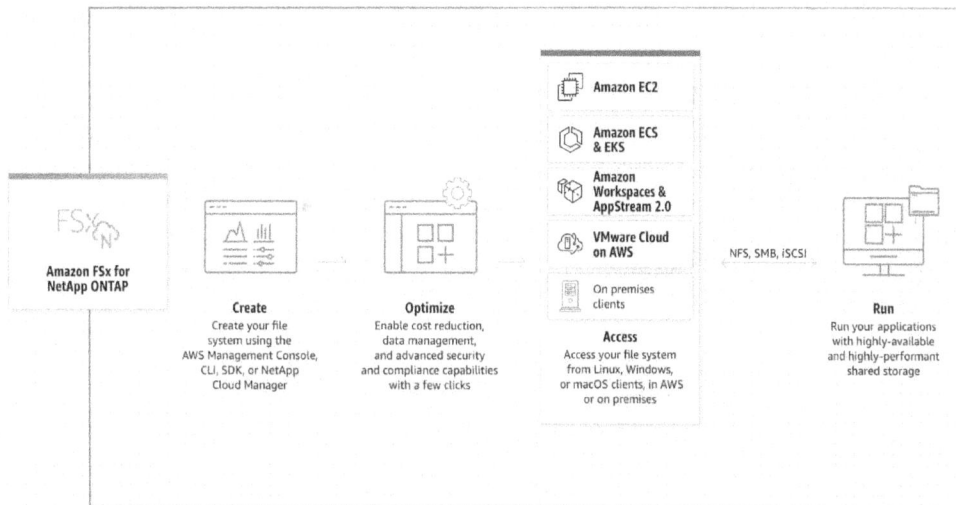

Figure 3.4: Amazon FSx for NetApp ONTAP

- **Amazon FSx for OpenZFS**: Amazon FSx for OpenZFS provides scalable, high-performance file storage based on the open-source ZFS file system. Designed for compute-intensive workloads, ML, and data analytics, this file system offers advanced features such as copy-on-write snapshots, data compression, and native encryption.

Amazon FSx for OpenZFS enables users to achieve low-latency access to large datasets while ensuring data integrity and security.

Refer to the following figure:

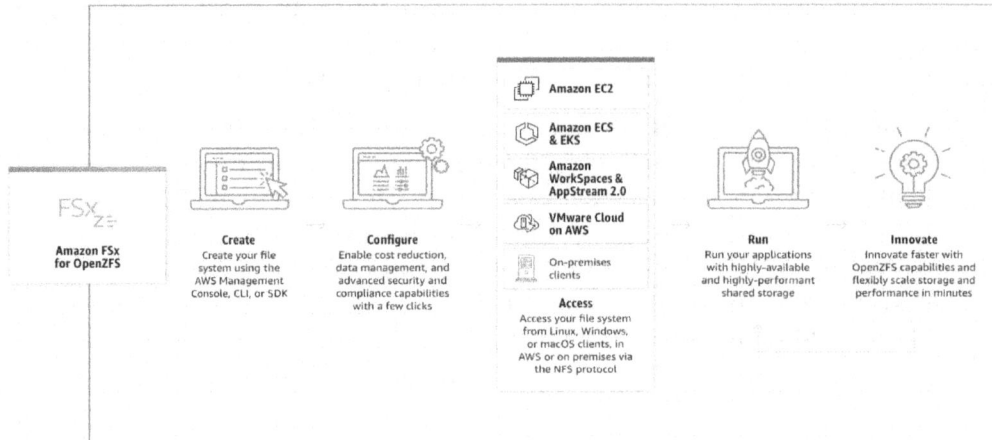

Figure 3.5: Amazon FSx for OpenZFS

- **Amazon FSx for Windows File Server**: Amazon FSx for Windows File Server delivers fully managed Windows file storage compatible with *Microsoft AD* environments. It perfectly integrates Windows-based applications, user authentication, and access controls, enabling organizations to migrate and modernize their Windows workloads in the cloud. With support for NTFS permissions, DFS, and multiple AZ deployments, Amazon FSx for Windows File Server offers enterprise-grade reliability and performance.

Refer to the following figure:

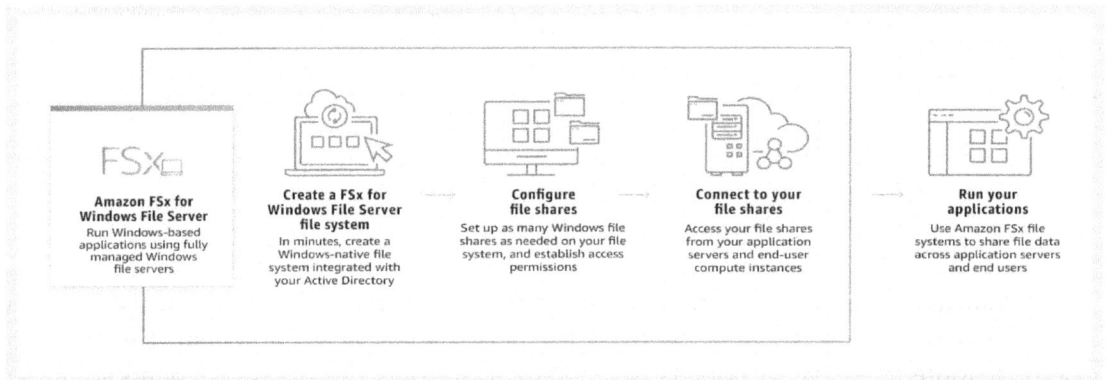

Figure 3.6: Amazon FSx for Windows File Server

- **Amazon FSx for Lustre**: Offers high-performance, scalable file storage-optimized for compute-intensive, high-throughput workloads such as simulation, rendering, and data analytics. Leveraging the Lustre parallel file system, this file system delivers sub-millisecond latencies and petabyte-scale storage capacity for processing large datasets. With features such as automatic data tiering, SSD caching, and integration with AWS compute services, Amazon FSx for Lustre accelerates cloud data processing and analysis workflows.

Refer to the following figure:

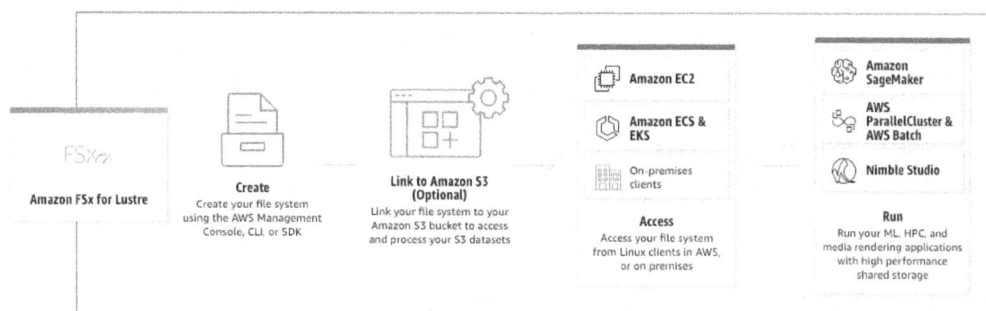

Figure 3.7: *Amazon FSx for Lustre*

AWS designed each Amazon FSx file system to address specific workload requirements and use cases, providing organizations with flexible and reliable storage solutions tailored to their application needs.

Use cases and efficiency

Existing studies emphasize the importance of optimized file storage for specific workloads and the efficiency gains realized through managed file systems. Research frequently underscores the role of file storage in Windows-centric environments and data-intensive applications, where performance and compatibility are paramount [9]. Amazon FSx emerges as a pivotal component within the AWS storage ecosystem, offering fully managed file storage services optimized for specific workloads and use cases. As organizations strive to maximize their data management strategies, the demand for efficient, scalable, and available file storage solutions continues to grow. Amazon FSx addresses this demand by providing managed file systems tailored to Windows-centric environments and data-intensive applications, delivering consistent performance and compatibility within the AWS cloud environment. AWS Documentation on FSx highlights its applicability in various scenarios, including Windows-based applications, analytics, media processing, and HPC. FSx is known for its ability to provide consistent and low-latency file storage, ensuring that applications meet their performance requirements while enjoying the benefits of AWS-managed services [10].

At its core, Amazon FSx offers a comprehensive suite of features to enhance performance, reliability, and ease of use. With support for Windows and Lustre file systems, Amazon FSx caters to a wide range of applications and industries, from traditional enterprise workloads to HPC environments.

Amazon FSx for Windows File Server provides fully managed file storage for Windows-centric environments, offering native support for the SMB protocol. This enables perfect integration with existing Windows environments, allowing users to access and share files using familiar interfaces and tools. Amazon FSx for Windows File Server provides features such as AD integration, user quotas, and data deduplication, enhancing data management and security within Windows-based applications.

On the other hand, Amazon FSx for Lustre is optimized for data-intensive workloads and HPC environments, offering high-performance, scalable file storage for compute-intensive applications. Leveraging the Lustre parallel file system, Amazon FSx for Lustre delivers low-latency access to massive datasets, enabling organizations to accelerate data processing and analysis tasks. With support for high-throughput and low-latency, Amazon FSx for Lustre is well-suited for applications such as genomic sequencing, financial modeling, and scientific simulations.

In practical terms, Amazon FSx addresses a wide range of use cases across various industries and domains. Amazon FSx offers a seamless migration path to the cloud for enterprises looking to modernize their infrastructure, allowing organizations to transition their legacy file storage systems to a fully managed, scalable environment. Amazon FSx for Lustre facilitates the analysis of large datasets and complex simulations in research and academic settings, empowering researchers to unlock new insights and discoveries.

Furthermore, Amazon FSx enhances operational efficiency and agility by automating routine tasks such as backup, maintenance, and patch management. By offloading these responsibilities to AWS, organizations can focus on innovation and value creation, leveraging the scalability and reliability of Amazon FSx to drive business outcomes.

In conclusion, Amazon FSx redefines the landscape of managed file storage, providing a robust and scalable solution for organizations seeking to modernize their cloud-based data infrastructure. With support for both Windows and Lustre file systems, Amazon FSx provides a versatile platform for a wide range of workloads and use cases, enabling organizations to optimize performance, streamline operations, and unlock new possibilities in the era of cloud computing. Through advanced configurations, best practices, and real-world case studies, organizations can harness the full potential of Amazon FSx to optimize their workloads and drive innovation in the AWS cloud environment.

As we continue this chapter, we will delve deeper into Amazon FSx, examining advanced configurations, best practices, and real-world case studies that demonstrate how organizations can leverage this managed file storage service to optimize their workloads in the AWS cloud.

Amazon S3 Glacier

In cloud storage, efficient and secure data archives are critical for organizations. Amazon S3 Glacier offers a solution by providing cost-effective archival storage that focuses on data durability and compliance. This section will explore the Amazon S3 Glacier in-depth, uncovering its key features, benefits, use cases, and real-world applications supported by studies, successful deployments, and AWS sources.

The Amazon S3 Glacier is a foundation of cloud storage, offering organizations a cost-effective solution for efficient and secure data archiving. As data volumes grow, the need for reliable archival storage becomes increasingly pronounced, driving organizations to seek scalable and compliant solutions. Amazon S3 Glacier addresses this need by providing a robust platform optimized for long-term data retention, durability, and regulatory compliance.

At its core, Amazon S3 Glacier leverages a tiered storage model to accommodate varying data access frequencies and retrieval times. The service offers multiple storage classes, including Standard, Expedited, and Bulk retrievals, allowing users to tailor their storage strategy to meet specific requirements. With support for industry standard encryption and compliance certifications, Amazon S3 Glacier ensures data security and integrity, making it a preferred choice for organizations operating in regulated industries.

One of Amazon S3 Glacier's key features is its uniform integration with other AWS services, enabling organizations to leverage the full capabilities of the AWS ecosystem. Whether backing up critical data, archiving log files, or storing regulatory documents, Amazon S3 Glacier provides a scalable and reliable platform for long-term data retention.

Refer to the following figure:

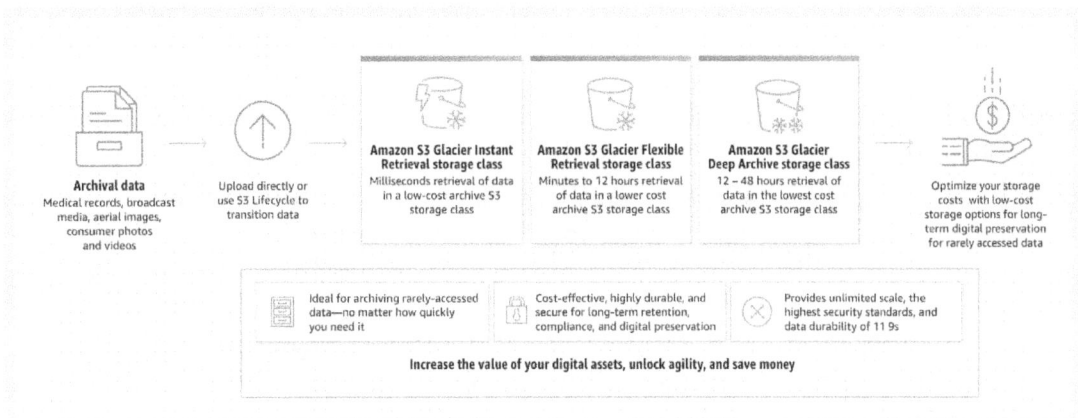

Figure 3.8: Amazon S3 Glacier storage classes

Use cases for Amazon S3 Glacier span a wide range of industries and scenarios. For enterprises with regulatory compliance requirements, such as those in healthcare, finance, and government,

Amazon S3 Glacier provides a secure and compliant solution for data archiving and retention. It is also a cost-effective storage option for long-term archival of video content, audio files, and multimedia assets in the media and entertainment industries.

Moreover, the Amazon S3 Glacier caters to data-intensive applications such as scientific research, genomics, and digital forensics, where large volumes of data must be retained for extended periods. By leveraging Amazon S3 Glacier's durable and scalable infrastructure, organizations can efficiently manage their data lifecycle, from creation to archival, while maintaining data accessibility and integrity.

As organizations navigate the complexities of data management and compliance, Amazon S3 Glacier emerges as a dependable partner, offering a comprehensive solution for long-term data archival and retention. With its robust feature set, scalable architecture, and uniform integration with the AWS ecosystem, Amazon S3 Glacier empowers organizations to unlock new possibilities in data storage and management, driving innovation and value creation in the cloud.

The upcoming chapter will delve into Amazon S3 Glacier, exploring its advanced configurations, best practices, and real-world case studies. These examples illustrate how organizations can utilize this archival storage service to enhance their data management strategies within the AWS cloud.

Closer look at Amazon S3 Glacier

Amazon S3 Glacier is a vital component in the AWS storage ecosystem. It is an archival storage service designed for infrequently accessed data. Amazon S3 Glacier provides a scalable and durable platform for retaining data over extended periods, with data automatically distributed across multiple facilities and devices. S3 Glacier offers various retrieval options, including Expedited, Standard, and Bulk retrievals, allowing organizations to optimize their costs and retrieval speeds according to their specific needs. With features like data lifecycle policies, audit logging, and vault access policies, S3 Glacier ensures that archived data remains secure and compliant with industry regulations [11].

Amazon S3 Glacier utilizes a tiered storage model, allowing organizations to optimize storage costs based on data access frequency and retrieval speed. The service automatically distributes data across multiple facilities and devices, ensuring durability and availability even in the face of hardware failures or data center outages.

One of Amazon S3 Glacier's distinguishing features is its flexible retrieval options, which cater to various use cases and access patterns. Organizations can choose from Expedited, Standard, and Bulk retrieval options, depending on their specific requirements for data access speed and cost considerations. This flexibility enables organizations to balance cost-efficiency and retrieval speed, ensuring that archived data remains accessible when needed.

Amazon S3 Glacier offers comprehensive features to help organizations manage their archived data effectively. Data lifecycle policies allow organizations to define rules for automatically transitioning data to Glacier storage based on predefined criteria, such as age or access frequency. Audit logging capabilities provide visibility into data access and retrieval activities, enabling organizations to track and monitor data usage for compliance and auditing purposes.

Furthermore, Amazon S3 Glacier implements robust access controls through vault access policies, allowing organizations to restrict access to archived data based on user permissions and security policies. This ensures that archived data remains secure and protected against unauthorized access, maintaining compliance with industry regulations and data protection standards.

Use cases for Amazon S3 Glacier encompass a wide range of scenarios across various industries and business domains. Organizations can leverage Amazon S3 Glacier for archiving historical data, ensuring regulatory compliance, facilitating legal discovery, and maintaining long-term data retention. Industries such as healthcare, finance, and government, which have stringent compliance requirements, can benefit from the secure and scalable archival storage offered by Amazon S3 Glacier.

Moreover, organizations with data-intensive workloads, such as scientific research, genomics, and digital media, can leverage Amazon S3 Glacier to store and retain large volumes of data cost-effectively. By offloading infrequently accessed data to S3 Glacier, organizations can free up primary storage resources and reduce operational costs while ensuring data durability and availability.

In summary, Amazon S3 Glacier emerges as a reliable solution for organizations seeking cost-effective and secure data archival storage. With its scalable architecture, flexible retrieval options, and comprehensive feature set, the S3 Glacier enables organizations to manage their data lifecycle effectively, meet compliance requirements, and drive operational efficiency in the cloud.

Use cases and efficiency

Amazon S3 Glacier is a pivotal solution for organizations facing challenges in long-term data retention, compliance, and cost management in the cloud storage landscape. Learning from success cases, studies frequently underscore the role of archival storage in reducing costs associated with long-term data retention and compliance with data retention policies [12]. AWS Documentation on S3 Glacier highlights its applicability in various scenarios, including compliance archiving, digital preservation, and backup and restore operations. S3 Glacier's cost-effectiveness and durability make it an ideal choice for organizations seeking to meet regulatory requirements while optimizing storage costs [13]. Tailored specifically for archival storage requirements, Amazon S3 Glacier offers a robust platform characterized by cost-effectiveness, durability, and scalability.

At its core, Amazon S3 Glacier provides organizations with a secure and reliable repository for storing data that is accessed infrequently for compliance, regulatory, or business purposes. The service utilizes a tiered storage model, enabling organizations to optimize costs by aligning storage tiers with their data access patterns and retrieval requirements.

One of Amazon S3 Glacier's key features is its flexible retrieval options, which cater to a spectrum of use cases and access scenarios. Organizations can choose from expedited, standard, and bulk retrieval options, offering different trade-offs between retrieval speed and cost. This flexibility enables organizations to tailor their data retrieval strategies to meet specific business requirements and operational priorities.

Amazon S3 Glacier offers comprehensive data management capabilities, including data lifecycle policies, audit logging, and access controls. Data lifecycle policies enable organizations to automate the transition of data to Glacier storage based on predefined criteria, such as data age or frequency of access. This helps streamline data management workflows and ensures data is stored cost-effectively without manual intervention.

Moreover, audit logging features give organizations visibility into data access and retrieval activities, facilitating compliance with regulatory requirements and internal governance policies. Access controls, implemented through vault access policies, enable organizations to enforce granular permissions and security policies, safeguarding archived data against unauthorized access and ensuring data integrity.

The use cases for Amazon S3 Glacier span a diverse range of industries and scenarios, reflecting its versatility and applicability across various domains. Organizations can leverage S3 Glacier for compliance archiving, regulatory retention, digital preservation, backup and restore operations, and DR preparedness. Industries such as healthcare, finance, legal, and government, subject to stringent regulatory requirements, can benefit significantly from the secure and cost-effective archival storage offered by Amazon S3 Glacier.

In addition, organizations with data-intensive workloads and large volumes of historical data can utilize S3 Glacier to optimize storage costs while maintaining data durability and accessibility. By offloading infrequently accessed data to Glacier storage, organizations can free up primary storage resources, reduce operational overhead, and ensure compliance with data retention policies and legal mandates.

In conclusion, Amazon S3 Glacier emerges as a strategic component in the AWS storage ecosystem, offering organizations a scalable, secure, and cost-effective solution for long-term data retention and archival storage. With its comprehensive feature set, flexible retrieval options, and robust data management capabilities, S3 Glacier empowers organizations to enhance their data management strategies, meet compliance requirements, and drive operational efficiency in the AWS cloud landscape.

Refer to the following figure:

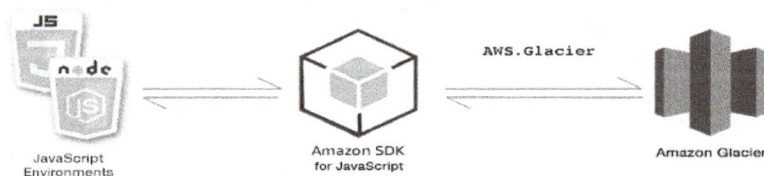

Figure 3.9: JavaScript API for Amazon S3 Glacier

As we continue this chapter, we will delve deeper into Amazon S3, unraveling advanced configurations, best practices, and real-world case studies that illustrate how organizations can leverage this versatile AWS storage service to optimize their data storage, distribution, and analysis in the AWS cloud.

Amazon Simple Storage Service

Amazon S3 is one of AWS's most versatile and scalable storage solutions. As organizations increasingly move their workloads to the cloud, Amazon S3 offers object storage designed to store and retrieve data from anywhere on the web, with unmatched flexibility and durability. The core advantage of S3 is its unlimited scalability, allowing businesses to store data as needed without worrying about capacity limitations.

Architecture and core features

Amazon S3 organizes data into buckets, which store objects that consist of data, metadata, and a unique identifier. Each object can range from megabytes to terabytes, making S3 suitable for diverse workloads, such as small-scale backups and large-scale data lakes. The platform supports a wide range of storage classes tailored to different data access patterns and cost requirements:

- **S3 Standard**: Designed for frequently accessed data, providing high-throughput and low-latency.

- **S3 Intelligent-Tiering**: Automatically moves objects between two access tiers (frequent and infrequent) based on changing access patterns, optimizing cost.

- **S3 Glacier and Glacier Deep Archive**: Cost-effective solutions for long-term archival storage.

One of the cornerstones of S3 is its Global Infrastructure, which ensures durability by replicating data across multiple AZs in a region. This replication makes S3 resilient to hardware failures, safeguarding data against loss or corruption. Versioning is another crucial feature, allowing users to keep multiple versions of the same object. This feature is particularly valuable for protecting against accidental deletions or overwrites, providing businesses with more data integrity.

Security and data management

Amazon S3's security architecture includes comprehensive mechanisms for access control and encryption. **Access control lists** (**ACLs**) and bucket policies offer fine-grained permission settings, enabling administrators to control who can access or modify objects within a bucket. These controls are crucial for maintaining data confidentiality and adhering to compliance requirements, particularly in highly regulated industries such as healthcare or finance. Furthermore, **server-side encryption** (**SSE**) and **client-side encryption** (**CSE**) ensure that data remains protected in transit and at rest.

In addition to security, Amazon S3 Lifecycle policies allow businesses to manage data efficiently by automatically transitioning objects between storage classes or expiring objects that are no longer needed. This automation helps optimize costs, ensuring that organizations pay only for the storage they require at any given time.

Real-world use cases and applications

Amazon S3 powers various applications across industries because it stores, protects, and retrieves massive amounts of data. Prominent use cases include:

- **Data lakes and big data analytics**: S3 is the foundation for building data lakes, enabling businesses to store structured and unstructured data at any scale. It integrates effortlessly with analytics services like Amazon Redshift, Amazon Athena, and Amazon EMR, providing the infrastructure to derive insights from vast datasets [14]. For example, e-commerce companies store transaction logs and customer interaction data in S3, using analytics tools to optimize marketing strategies and improve **user experiences (UXs)**.

- **Archiving and long-term data retention**: Some organizations must retain large volumes of data for regulatory compliance, legal requirements, or historical analysis. With storage classes like S3 Glacier and Glacier Deep Archive, businesses can store infrequently accessed data cost-effectively. For instance, financial institutions rely on S3 to store transaction records and securely preserve critical financial data for extended periods.

- **Content delivery and media streaming**: Companies involved in media and entertainment leverage S3 to host and deliver multimedia content globally. Coupled with Amazon CloudFront, AWS's **content delivery network (CDN)**, S3 provides high-speed access to content by caching files at edge locations. This setup minimizes latency and optimizes the user experience for media streaming services or websites with high traffic volumes.

- **Mobile and gaming applications**: For mobile and gaming platforms [15], Amazon S3 supports storing and delivering vast amounts of user-generated content, media files, and in-game assets. With REST APIs and SDKs, developers can integrate S3 perfectly, enabling fast data access and ensuring that mobile applications and games provide users with real-time, responsive experiences.

In the next illustration, we share another use case: Mainframe data backup and archival augmentation, demonstrating the wide range of applications for Amazon S3:

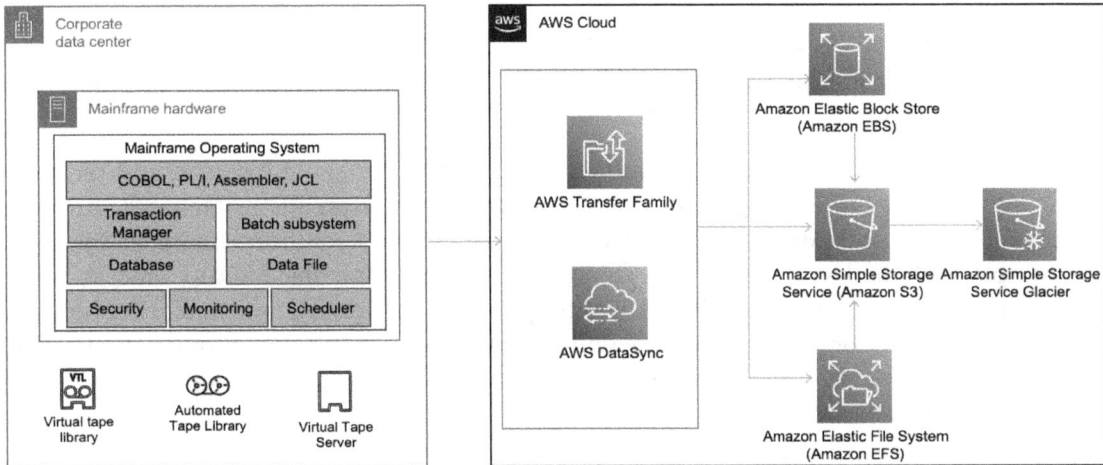

Figure 3.10: Use case example: Mainframe data backup and archival augmentation

Best practices for maximizing S3 efficiency

To get the most out of Amazon S3, organizations should follow these best practices:

- **Optimize data access and storage classes**: To reduce storage costs, use S3 Intelligent-Tiering for data with unpredictable access patterns and S3 Glacier for long-term archival.

- **Enable versioning and MFA delete**: For added security, protect critical data from accidental deletions by enabling versioning and implementing **multi-factor authentication (MFA)** delete.

- **Use encryption**: Ensure data is encrypted in transit and at rest using S3's built-in encryption mechanisms, especially when managing sensitive or regulated data.

- **Leverage event notifications**: Automate workflows by enabling S3 Event Notifications to trigger actions like AWS Lambda functions for real-time processing or analysis of new data uploads.

Thus, Amazon S3 remains a cornerstone of AWS storage services, enabling organizations across various industries to store, manage, and retrieve data efficiently. Its scalability, cost optimization, and integration with other AWS services make it a versatile tool for a wide range of workloads. Whether it is powering big data analytics, managing long-term archives, or enhancing content delivery [16], S3 provides the flexibility and security required to succeed in the cloud era.

AWS Backup

In the evolving landscape of cloud computing, data protection remains a critical priority for organizations striving to safeguard their assets and ensure business continuity. AWS Backup is a cornerstone solution, offering a fully managed service that streamlines backup workflows for a wide range of AWS resources. This section delves into the core functionalities, technical features, and practical applications of AWS Backup, supported by real-world use cases and insights from authoritative AWS sources.

At its core, AWS Backup offers a centralized platform for managing backups and recovery across AWS services, including Amazon EBS volumes, Amazon RDS databases, Amazon DynamoDB tables, and Amazon EFS file systems. This unified solution eliminates the need for multiple tools and custom scripts, significantly simplifying the backup process while improving operational efficiency. By automating backup scheduling and retention policies, AWS Backup allows organizations to define precise rules for backup frequency, retention periods, and lifecycle management, ensuring compliance with regulatory requirements and maintaining data consistency.

In the next illustration, we share a high-level architecture of AWS Backup, according to AWS:

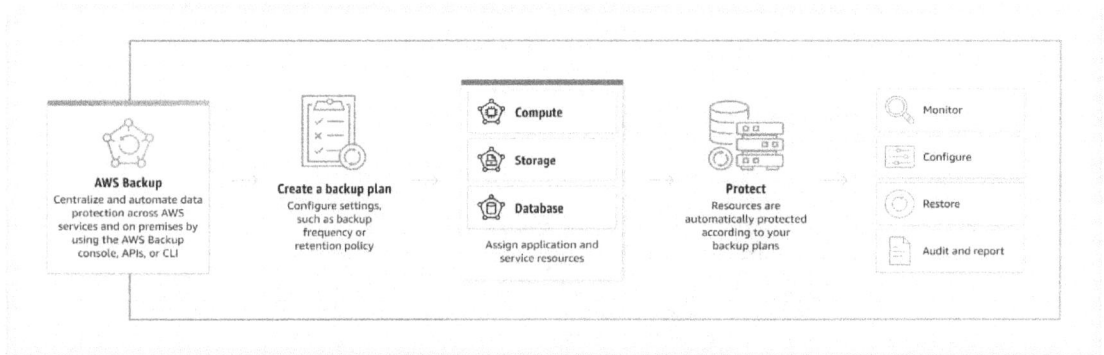

Figure 3.11: *AWS Backup*

Core features and integration

AWS Backup is a fully managed service that automates data backup across AWS services, helping organizations ensure data resiliency and compliance with minimal effort. AWS Backup is a pivotal solution in cloud data protection, offering organizations a fully managed service that automates backup processes across a diverse array of AWS services. AWS Backup supports backup and restores for various AWS resources, including Amazon EBS volumes, Amazon RDS databases, Amazon DynamoDB tables, Amazon EFS file systems, and more. With a centralized and unified backup management interface, AWS Backup streamlines the setup and management of backups for a wide range of AWS services. By seamlessly integrating with various AWS resources, AWS Backup enables organizations to enhance their data resiliency strategies and achieve regulatory compliance with minimal operational overhead. It offers features such as backup policies, lifecycle management, cross-region and cross-account backups, and integration with AWS IAM for secure access control [17]. This section will delve deeper into the efficiency-enhancing features of AWS Backup and elucidate its versatile applications through real-world scenarios and industry best practices.

One of the standout features of AWS Backup is its automated backup scheduling. Users can setup policies that dictate how often backups are taken and how long they are retained. This capability significantly reduces the manual overhead typically associated with traditional backup systems. Additionally, AWS Backup integrates natively with AWS service APIs, facilitating uniform workflows without needing third-party tools or additional infrastructure. This native integration ensures data consistency, making the backup and recovery process significantly more efficient across diverse AWS environments.

Another critical feature is the cross-region and cross-account replication, which enables organizations to replicate backups to different AWS Regions or accounts, adding an extra layer of protection in case of regional outages or disasters. This replication capability is crucial for DR scenarios, where organizations must ensure their data is always available and resilient across different geographical locations.

IAM integration further enhances the security of AWS Backup. Allowing organizations to define granular access controls and permissions ensures that only authorized personnel can perform backup and recovery operations. This capability helps to mitigate the risk of unauthorized access and provides an audit trail for compliance.

Use cases and efficiency

We learn the importance of robust data protection and backup strategies in cloud environments from success cases. Use case studies emphasize the pivotal role of automated backup services in mitigating the risk of data loss and facilitating DR planning [18]. AWS's own documentation on AWS Backup highlights its applicability in various scenarios, including backup and recovery for critical databases, compliance archiving, and ensuring data durability for long-term retention. AWS Backup's flexibility and support for a wide array of AWS resources make it a valuable tool for organizations looking to safeguard their data assets in the cloud [19].

With its comprehensive features and managed service approach, AWS Backup exemplifies efficiency and reliability in data protection within AWS cloud environments, as follows:

- **Backup and recovery for critical databases**: Organizations rely on AWS Backup to safeguard critical databases, such as Amazon RDS and Amazon DynamoDB, against data corruption, accidental deletions, or system failures. By automating backup processes and enabling point-in-time recovery, AWS Backup ensures data integrity and availability, allowing organizations to maintain business continuity and minimize downtime during data loss incidents.

- **DR preparedness**: AWS Backup's automation capabilities make it ideal for creating scheduled backups that ensure data availability in case of unexpected failures. Businesses can guarantee rapid recovery with minimal downtime by automating point-in-time recovery and utilizing cross-region replication.

- **Regulatory compliance**: Different industries, such as finance and healthcare, have strict data retention policies for regulatory compliance. AWS Backup enables organizations to implement data retention policies that comply with these regulations while maintaining secure access controls, audit trails, and encryption.

- **Data archiving and long-term retention**: AWS Backup integrates with Amazon S3 Glacier and S3 Glacier Deep Archive, making it a cost-efficient solution for long-term data storage. Organizations can manage historical data archiving with lifecycle management features to optimize costs and retain data according to compliance mandates.

- **Compliance Archiving**: Regulatory compliance mandates often require organizations to maintain archival copies of sensitive data for extended periods. AWS Backup facilitates compliance archiving by providing automated backup capabilities for various AWS resources, including Amazon EBS volumes, Amazon EFS file systems, and Amazon RDS databases. With AWS Backup, organizations can easily enforce data retention policies, implement audit trails, and demonstrate adherence to regulatory requirements.

- **Ensuring data durability for long-term retention**: Long-term data retention is crucial for organizations across various industries, including healthcare, finance, and government, where historical data analysis and regulatory compliance are paramount. AWS Backup offers a scalable and durable solution for long-term data retention, leveraging cross-region replication, encryption, and lifecycle management to ensure data durability and integrity over extended periods. By archiving data securely in Amazon S3 Glacier or Amazon S3 Glacier Deep Archive, organizations can optimize storage costs while maintaining data accessibility and compliance with regulatory mandates.

AWS Backup's flexibility and support for a wide array of AWS resources make it a valuable tool for organizations seeking to safeguard their data assets in the cloud. Whether protecting critical databases, ensuring compliance with regulatory requirements, or implementing long-term data retention strategies, AWS Backup empowers organizations to mitigate risks, streamline backup operations, and uphold data integrity in today's dynamic and data-driven landscape.

The flexibility of AWS Backup makes it applicable to a wide range of scenarios, as discussed in the next section.

Cross-region and cross-account backup

AWS Backup excels in offering cross-region and cross-account backups, a crucial feature for organizations seeking to enhance their DR strategy. By replicating regional backups, organizations can safeguard their data against regional disasters or outages. This capability ensures data redundancy across geographically dispersed locations, ensuring high data availability. Additionally, cross-account backups provide a robust security mechanism by allowing businesses to store backups in separate AWS accounts, reducing the risk of data loss due to malicious activity or accidental deletion in the primary account.

In practical scenarios, AWS Backup's cross-region replication has proven invaluable for organizations that operate in compliance-driven industries. For instance, financial services companies must ensure their backup data is replicated and retained securely across multiple locations, adhering to international data protection regulations. AWS Backup offers a comprehensive solution, enabling data to be backed up across regions and accounts, with built-in encryption and compliance auditing.

Thus, AWS Backup is a comprehensive and pivotal tool in AWS's portfolio of data protection services. Its automated backup scheduling, cross-region replication, and IAM-integrated security controls provide organizations with the flexibility and efficiency needed to safeguard their data assets. Whether for DR, compliance archiving, or long-term retention, AWS Backup ensures businesses can protect their data and maintain continuity in an ever-changing digital landscape.

By leveraging AWS Backup's robust feature set and uniform integrations, organizations can simplify their backup and recovery processes, ensuring that critical data is protected and available whenever needed. As organizations migrate to cloud-native architectures, AWS Backup will remain essential for building resilient, scalable, and secure data protection strategies.

AWS Snow Family

The AWS Snow Family represents a critical component in addressing the challenge of transferring large datasets between on-premises and cloud environments. As organizations deal with ever-expanding volumes of data, the need for secure, efficient, and scalable data transfer solutions becomes paramount. The AWS Snow Family offers a range of physical devices tailored to diverse use cases, providing uniform integration between on-premises infrastructure and AWS cloud services.

At the core of the AWS Snow Family are the AWS Snowcone, AWS Snowball, and AWS Snowmobile, each designed to meet specific data transfer requirements and operational scenarios. The AWS Snowcone, a small, ruggedized device, is ideal for collecting, processing, and transferring data in remote or harsh environments with limited connectivity. With its compact form factor and built-in security features, the Snowcone enables organizations to efficiently perform edge computing tasks and collect data.

On the other hand, the AWS Snowball and AWS Snowball Edge devices cater to the needs of medium to large-scale data transfers. These rugged, tamper-resistant appliances facilitate the secure offline transfer of petabytes of data. Equipped with high-speed data transfer interfaces and encryption capabilities, Snowball devices streamline importing and exporting data to and from AWS cloud storage services, such as Amazon S3 and Amazon Glacier.

The AWS Snowmobile offers an unparalleled solution for organizations with massive data volumes exceeding petabytes. Housed in a secure, ruggedized shipping container, Snowmobile is a high-capacity data transfer device capable of transporting exabytes of data to AWS data centers. With its massive storage capacity and high-speed connectivity, the Snowmobile accelerates data migration projects, enabling organizations to efficiently transition vast datasets to the cloud.

The AWS Snow Family finds extensive applications across various industries and use cases. For example, organizations in the media and entertainment sector leverage Snowball devices to transfer large video files, production datasets, and media archives to the cloud for post-production, content distribution, and archival purposes. In the healthcare industry, healthcare providers utilize Snowball devices to securely transfer and store sensitive patient data, medical records, and imaging files, ensuring compliance with regulatory requirements.

Furthermore, scholarly articles and AWS Documentation underscore the significance of the AWS Snow Family in facilitating data migration, DR, and hybrid cloud deployments. Research highlights its role in expediting data transfer processes, reducing network bandwidth constraints, and minimizing the time-to-value for cloud adoption initiatives.

In summary, the AWS Snow Family offers a comprehensive suite of data transfer solutions designed to address the complexities of modern data management and migration challenges. By providing secure, scalable, and efficient offline data transfer capabilities, the AWS Snow Family empowers organizations to transition to the cloud while maintaining control, compliance, and security over their data assets.

Closer look at AWS Snow Family

The AWS Snow Family comprises a suite of purpose-built devices meticulously designed to streamline data migration to and from AWS, particularly for organizations handling large-scale datasets. Among these devices are the AWS Snowcone, AWS Snowball, and AWS Snowmobile, each engineered to cater to specific data transfer requirements and operational contexts. These devices incorporate security features such as encryption and tamper-evident seals, ensuring the confidentiality and integrity of the data during transit. AWS Snow Family also offers integration with AWS services and APIs to simplify the data import/export [20].

AWS Snowcone is a compact, rugged, and portable device ideally suited for edge and remote locations where network connectivity may be limited or unreliable. Snowcone packs robust data transfer capabilities, enabling organizations to collect, process, and transfer data efficiently in challenging environments despite its small form factor.

In contrast, AWS Snowball emerges as a larger, ruggedized data transfer device capable of easily handling petabytes of data. Designed for medium to large-scale data migration tasks, Snowball simplifies the secure transfer of vast datasets to and from AWS cloud storage services. Its durable construction, high-speed data transfer interfaces, and built-in encryption features make it an indispensable tool for organizations seeking to accelerate their data migration initiatives.

AWS Snowmobile provides an unmatched solution for organizations facing exabyte-scale data migration challenges. Housed within a 45-foot-long shipping container, Snowmobile redefines the data transfer paradigm by enabling the uniform transportation of massive volumes of data to AWS data centers. With its colossal storage capacity and high-speed connectivity, Snowmobile empowers organizations to execute unprecedented-scale and complex data migration projects with confidence and efficiency.

One of the AWS Snow Family's hallmark features is its robust security architecture, which includes encryption mechanisms and tamper-evident seals to safeguard data integrity and confidentiality throughout the transfer process. These security measures ensure that sensitive data remains protected against unauthorized access or tampering during transit, providing organizations with peace of mind and assurance of compliance.

Moreover, the AWS Snow Family offers uniform integration with AWS services and APIs, enabling organizations to leverage the full capabilities of the AWS ecosystem for data import/export and processing tasks. Whether integrating with Amazon S3 for scalable object storage or interfacing with AWS Lambda for serverless data processing, the AWS Snow Family empowers organizations to harness the power of AWS cloud services to address diverse data management and migration challenges effectively.

In summary, the AWS Snow Family represents a comprehensive suite of data transfer solutions designed to address the complexities of modern data migration requirements. By offering a diverse range of devices tailored to different use cases and scalability needs, robust security features, and uniform AWS integration, the AWS Snow Family enables organizations to execute data migration initiatives confidently, efficiently, and with scalability, accelerating their journey to the cloud.

The following illustration shows an example architecture of how the AWS Snow Family and regional AWS services can facilitate data migration and analysis of autonomous vehicle fleets:

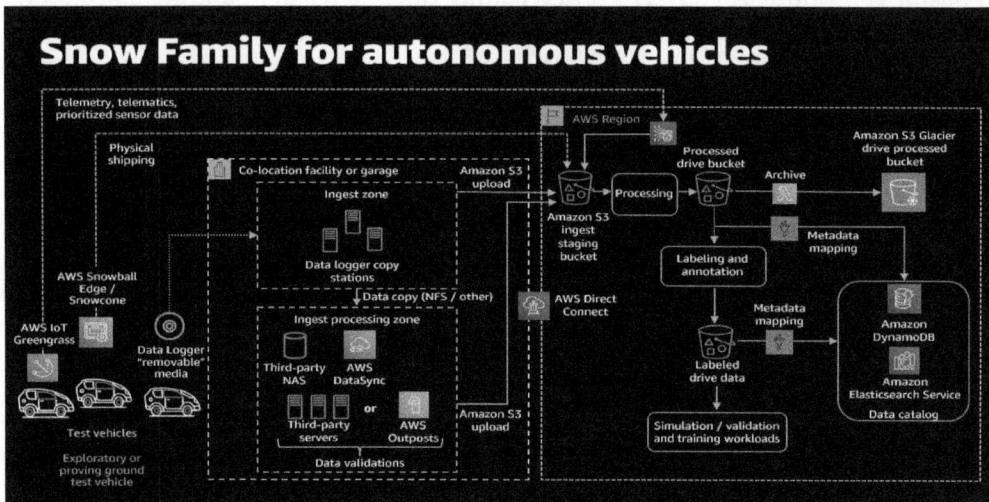

Figure 3.12: This is an example architecture illustrating how the AWS Snow Family, combined with regional AWS services, can facilitate data migration and analysis of autonomous vehicle fleets

Use cases and efficiency

Existing studies, such as those cited as references in this book, often emphasize the challenges associated with large-scale data transfer to and from the cloud, as well as the need for efficient data migration solutions. These references (and others) frequently underscore the role of physical devices in overcoming bandwidth limitations and reducing the time and cost of data transfer [21]. AWS Documentation on the AWS Snow Family highlights its applicability in various scenarios, including data center migrations, DR, and content distribution. AWS Snow Family's versatility and secure data transfer capabilities make it a valuable tool for organizations looking to bridge the gap between on-premises and cloud storage [22].

In academic discourse, the challenges inherent in large-scale data transfer to and from the cloud highlight the imperative for efficient data migration solutions. Bandwidth limitations and the associated time and cost of data transfer represent significant hurdles organizations must overcome in their cloud migration endeavors. The AWS Snow Family addresses these challenges head-on, offering a suite of physical devices purpose-built to streamline data migration operations.

One prominent use case for the AWS Snow Family is data center migrations. In scenarios where organizations need to transition large volumes of data from on-premises data centers to the cloud, the AWS Snow Family provides a robust solution. By leveraging the high-capacity storage and efficient data transfer capabilities of devices like AWS Snowball and AWS Snowmobile, organizations can expedite the migration process and minimize downtime, thereby accelerating their transition to cloud-based infrastructure.

DR represents another critical use case for the AWS Snow Family. In the event of a data center outage or infrastructure failure, organizations must swiftly recover and restore their data to ensure business continuity. The AWS Snow Family offers a resilient and reliable solution for DR scenarios, enabling organizations to replicate and transfer mission-critical data to AWS cloud storage with minimal disruption. With features like encryption and tamper-evident seals, the AWS Snow Family ensures the security and integrity of data during transit, providing organizations with confidence in their DR capabilities.

The AWS Snow Family is also an invaluable tool for content distribution initiatives. In industries such as media and entertainment, where files and high-resolution content are distributed to a global audience, the AWS Snow Family offers a scalable and efficient solution for content delivery. Organizations can distribute content rapidly and securely by leveraging devices like AWS Snowball Edge and AWS Snowmobile, ensuring optimal performance and UX for consumers worldwide.

The AWS Snow Family represents a versatile and efficient solution for diverse data migration and transfer scenarios. From data center migrations to DR and content distribution, the AWS Snow Family empowers organizations to overcome the challenges of large-scale data transfer, enabling them to leverage the scalability, flexibility, and reliability of AWS cloud storage with confidence and efficiency.

As we continue this chapter, we will delve deeper into AWS Storage Gateway, unraveling advanced configurations, best practices, and real-world case studies that illustrate how organizations can leverage this hybrid cloud storage service to enhance their data integration and management strategies within the AWS cloud.

AWS Storage Gateway

In today's hybrid cloud environments, organizations often seek a bridge between their on-premises infrastructure and the vast capabilities of the cloud. AWS Storage Gateway serves as this critical bridge, enabling organizations to seamlessly extend their local storage to the AWS cloud, thereby unlocking the benefits of cloud scalability, elasticity, and cost efficiency. This section will provide a detailed exploration of AWS Storage Gateway, including its key features, use cases, and technical capabilities. At its core, AWS Storage Gateway acts as a hybrid cloud storage service, enabling organizations to extend their on-premises storage environments into the cloud uniformly [23].

AWS Storage Gateway offers a range of storage protocols, including NFS, SMB, iSCSI, and Tape Gateway, catering to diverse use cases and application requirements. This versatility enables organizations to seamlessly integrate AWS cloud storage into their existing workflows and applications, eliminating the need for extensive reconfiguration or redevelopment.

The following illustration shows a high-level architecture of the AWS Storage Gateway options:

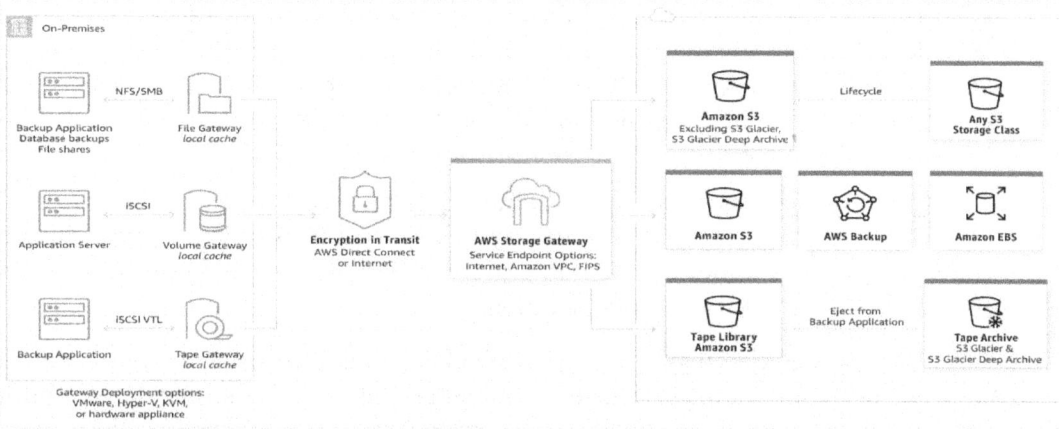

Figure 3.13: *AWS Storage Gateway options—File, Volume, and Tape Gateways*

Key features and functionality

One of the key features of AWS Storage Gateway is its support for data tiering and caching mechanisms, which optimize storage utilization and access performance based on access patterns and data lifecycle policies. AWS Storage Gateway enables organizations to balance cost-efficiency and performance optimization by intelligently tiering data between on-premises and cloud storage tiers.

Use cases for AWS Storage Gateway abound across various industries and scenarios. For instance, organizations can utilize AWS Storage Gateway for data backup and DR, leveraging its uniform integration with AWS cloud storage to ensure data resiliency and business continuity. Similarly, an example of AWS Storage Gateway deployment is for archival and long-term data retention, offering a cost-effective solution for storing historical data and ensuring regulatory compliance.

Furthermore, AWS Storage Gateway facilitates a hybrid cloud storage architecture, enabling organizations to seamlessly extend their on-premises storage environments into the cloud. This enables businesses to leverage the scalability and elasticity of AWS cloud storage while retaining the familiarity and control of their on-premises infrastructure.

AWS Storage Gateway provides three distinct gateway types—File Gateway, Volume Gateway, and Tape Gateway—each catering to specific use cases:

- File Gateway enables on-premises applications to access Amazon S3 as a scalable file storage solution via NFS or SMB protocols. This option is especially useful for storing unstructured data such as multimedia assets or application files. Data written to the File Gateway is stored in S3 as objects, allowing organizations to use S3's cost-effective storage tiers, including S3 Glacier and S3 Intelligent-Tiering, for infrequently accessed data.

- Volume Gateway presents a block storage interface and supports two modes: Cached volumes and stored volumes. Cached volumes provide low-latency access to frequently used data while storing the bulk of the data in Amazon S3. In contrast, stored volumes keep the entire dataset on-premises while replicating it to AWS. This makes Volume Gateway ideal for databases and enterprise applications requiring consistent, low-latency access to data.

- Tape Gateway enables organizations to transition from traditional tape backups to the cloud by emulating a **virtual tape library** (**VTL**). This allows data to be archived in Amazon S3 Glacier for long-term storage, replacing physical tape infrastructures with a fully scalable and durable cloud solution.

In summary, AWS Storage Gateway represents a pivotal solution for organizations navigating the complexities of hybrid cloud storage environments. With its versatile features, uniform integration capabilities, and diverse use cases, it empowers organizations to unlock the full potential of cloud storage while smoothly bridging the gap between on-premises and cloud-based storage solutions.

In addition to its gateway types, AWS Storage Gateway offers distinctive features to optimize data transfer, enhance data security, and streamline storage management. These features include:

- **Data transfer optimization**: AWS Storage Gateway optimizes data transfer between on-premises environments and AWS cloud storage, ensuring efficient utilization of network bandwidth and reducing latency.

- **Caching**: The gateway caches frequently accessed data locally to minimize access latency and improve application performance.
- **Snapshot backups**: Storage Gateway supports snapshot backups of volumes and file shares, enabling organizations to create point-in-time data protection and DR backups.
- **Data encryption**: Storage Gateway encrypts data in transit and at rest, ensuring the confidentiality and integrity of data stored in AWS cloud storage.

Enhanced data tiering and caching

A critical advantage of AWS Storage Gateway is its data tiering and caching mechanisms. By intelligently caching frequently accessed data locally, Storage Gateway minimizes latency and improves access times for on-premises applications. Data tiering between on-premises environments and AWS cloud storage also ensures that organizations can balance performance and cost-efficiency by moving less frequently accessed data to lower-cost storage classes in S3 or Glacier. This feature reduces storage costs without compromising access to mission-critical data.

Security and compliance features

AWS Storage Gateway includes robust security features, such as end-to-end encryption for data in transit and at rest. This ensures data integrity and confidentiality, particularly for sensitive workloads in healthcare, finance, and government. Additionally, IAM integration allows organizations to enforce access controls for backup and restore operations, ensuring only authorized users can access critical data.

Use cases and efficiency

Use cases and efficiency articles often emphasize the challenges associated with hybrid cloud storage and the need for efficient data integration between on-premises and cloud environments. Research frequently underscores the role of hybrid storage gateways in simplifying data management and facilitating cloud adoption while preserving existing on-premises investments [24]. AWS Documentation on AWS Storage Gateway highlights its applicability in various scenarios, including data backup and archive, DR, and content distribution. AWS Storage Gateway's flexibility and ease of integration make it a valuable tool for organizations looking to smoothly extend their on-premises storage to the AWS cloud [25].

As we continue this chapter, we will explore AWS DRS further, unraveling advanced configurations, best practices, and real-world case studies that illustrate how organizations can leverage this DR framework to enhance their business continuity strategies within the AWS cloud.

Extending on-premises storage into the cloud

Organizations across various industries leverage AWS Storage Gateway to address a multitude of use cases and enhance operational efficiency:

- **Backup and archive**: One of the most common use cases for AWS Storage Gateway is as a backup and archival solution. By integrating on-premises backup workflows with Amazon S3 and Glacier, organizations can offload backups to the cloud, reducing their reliance on costly, limited-capacity on-premises storage. For example, a healthcare provider could use Tape Gateway to back up patient records to S3 Glacier, ensuring compliance with data retention regulations while eliminating the need for physical tapes. AWS Storage Gateway offers a uniform solution for backing up and archiving critical data to the cloud. By leveraging Storage Gateway's integration with Amazon S3 and Glacier, organizations can offload backups from on-premises infrastructure to scalable and durable cloud storage. This use case is particularly beneficial for organizations seeking to improve data resiliency, reduce storage costs, and simplify backup and recovery processes. For example, a financial institution can utilize Storage Gateway to securely archive transaction records and financial data for long-term retention and compliance, thereby ensuring data integrity and regulatory adherence.

- **DR**: Volume Gateway plays a vital role in DR strategies, enabling organizations to replicate on-premises data to the AWS cloud. This provides a reliable and scalable DR solution that reduces downtime during failure. An enterprise, for instance, could replicate its database volumes via stored volumes, ensuring mission-critical data is always available, even in the face of hardware failure. DR planning is paramount for organizations to mitigate the impact of unexpected disruptions and ensure business continuity. AWS Storage Gateway enables organizations to implement robust DR strategies by replicating on-premises data to AWS cloud storage. In the event of a disaster or data loss incident, organizations can quickly restore critical data and applications from cloud backups, minimizing downtime and maintaining operational continuity. For instance, a healthcare provider can use Storage Gateway to replicate patient records and medical imaging data to the cloud, ensuring timely access to critical healthcare information during emergency situations and natural disasters.

- **Content distribution and collaboration**: File Gateway can store and distribute files like video content, software updates, and digital assets. This case is particularly relevant for media companies and software vendors delivering content to users globally. By leveraging Amazon CloudFront for content delivery, businesses can serve files from S3 with minimal latency, enhancing the UX. AWS Storage Gateway facilitates efficient content distribution by enabling organizations to distribute media files, software updates, and digital assets from on-premises storage to global audiences. By leveraging Storage Gateway's integration with Amazon CloudFront, organizations can deliver content with low-latency and high transfer speeds to end-users worldwide. This case is particularly relevant for media and entertainment companies, software vendors, and e-commerce businesses looking to deliver rich media content and software applications to customers and users across diverse locations. For example, a media streaming platform can use Storage Gateway to catch popular video content locally and distribute it to users worldwide via CloudFront, ensuring uniform streaming experiences and reducing end-user latency.

In summary, AWS Storage Gateway's flexibility and ease of integration make it a valuable tool for organizations looking to extend their on-premises storage to the AWS cloud. By addressing diverse use cases, including data backup and archive, DR, and content distribution, Storage Gateway empowers organizations to optimize their storage infrastructure, enhance data management capabilities, and accelerate cloud adoption initiatives.

Integration with the AWS ecosystem

The true power of AWS Storage Gateway lies in its uniform integration with other AWS services, making it an integral part of an organization's hybrid cloud strategy. It works well with:

- Amazon S3 for scalable object storage and archival.
- Amazon CloudFront for content delivery.
- Amazon S3 Glacier for cost-efficient long-term data retention.
- Amazon EC2 and Amazon RDS are used to replicate workloads and ensure business continuity.

Bridging on-premises and cloud storage

In conclusion, AWS Storage Gateway provides organizations with a versatile and scalable solution for integrating on-premises applications with AWS cloud storage. Whether it is file storage, backup, DR, or content distribution, AWS Storage Gateway offers the tools to optimize storage infrastructure and enhance data management. By addressing diverse use cases, including data backup and archiving, DR, and content distribution, Storage Gateway enables businesses to seamlessly extend their storage footprint into the cloud, driving innovation and efficiency in their operations.

As we progress, we will explore AWS DRS, which will further strengthen an organization's ability to recover swiftly from disasters and ensure uninterrupted service delivery.

AWS Elastic Disaster Recovery

AWS DRS plays a crucial role in ensuring business continuity by offering organizations a resilient framework for recovering critical workloads and data in the event of unexpected disruptions. As companies increasingly rely on cloud-based digital infrastructure, AWS DRS provides a sophisticated, scalable, and automated approach to DR within the AWS cloud, ensuring operational resilience across various scenarios.

The following illustration shows the AWS DRS high-level architecture:

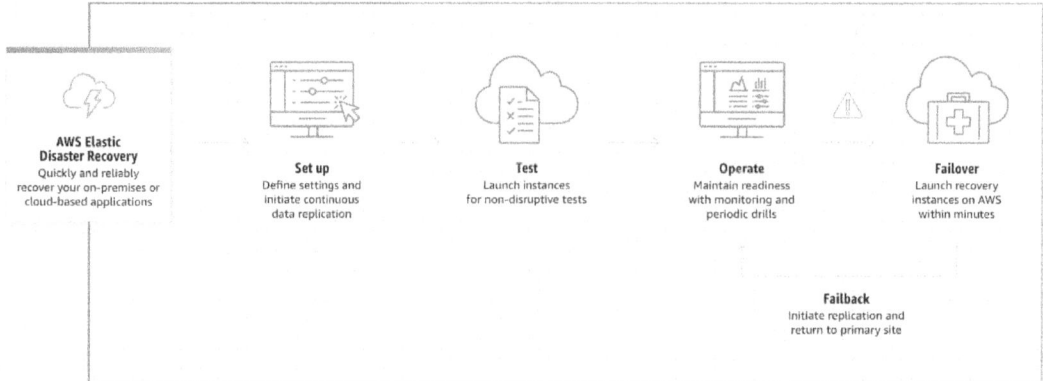

AWS Elastic Disaster Recovery
Quickly and reliably recover your on-premises or cloud-based applications

Set up
Define settings and initiate continuous data replication

Test
Launch instances for non-disruptive tests

Operate
Maintain readiness with monitoring and periodic drills

Failover
Launch recovery instances on AWS within minutes

Failback
Initiate replication and return to primary site

Figure 3.14: AWS DRS

At its core, AWS Elastic DRS leverages the elasticity and scalability of the AWS cloud to orchestrate uniform failover and failback processes. This enables organizations to replicate their workloads and data across multiple AWS Regions for enhanced resilience. By leveraging AWS's Global Infrastructure, Elastic DRS ensures high availability and durability, mitigating the risk of downtime and data loss associated with traditional DR approaches.

One of the key features of AWS DRS is its automation capabilities, which streamline the configuration, testing, and execution of DR plans. Organizations can define **recovery point objectives** (**RPOs**) and **recovery time objectives** (**RTOs**) tailored to their specific business requirements, allowing for granular control over recovery processes. Additionally, AWS Elastic DRS offers continuous monitoring and logging functionalities, enabling organizations to track the health and performance of their DR environments in real-time.

The benefits of AWS Elastic DRS extend beyond mere DR, encompassing a wide range of use cases and scenarios. For example, organizations can leverage Elastic DRS to achieve regulatory compliance by implementing geographically dispersed DR sites that adhere to industry-specific mandates and standards. Furthermore, Elastic DRS facilitates uniform migration and workload mobility, allowing organizations to move their workloads between regions for optimization and resource allocation.

Real-world applications of AWS DRS abound across various industries and sectors. From financial institutions ensuring continuous access to banking services to healthcare providers safeguarding patient records and critical healthcare systems, Elastic DRS is a linchpin in preserving operational continuity and data integrity. Moreover, organizations in highly regulated sectors, such as government agencies and educational institutions, rely on Elastic DRS to uphold stringent compliance requirements and data protection standards.

In summary, AWS DRS represents a change in thinking in DR management, offering organizations unparalleled flexibility, scalability, and resilience in mitigating the impact of disruptions. By embracing Elastic DRS, organizations can fortify their infrastructure, uphold operational excellence, and navigate the evolving landscape of digital resilience with confidence and resilience.

Key features of AWS Elastic Disaster Recovery

At its core, AWS Elastic DRS leverages AWS's cloud infrastructure to offer uniform failover and failback processes, ensuring data and workloads are replicated across AWS Regions. This robust architecture protects organizations against regional outages, hardware failures, and potential risks.

Key features include:

- **Automated backup and replication**: AWS Elastic DRS automates the continuous replication of workloads and data across AWS Regions, ensuring data availability in case of failure. This minimizes the risk of data loss and ensures uniform recovery.

- **Cross-region failover**: Elastic DRS replicates workloads to multiple AWS Regions, providing redundancy and geographical resilience. In regional outages, organizations can automatically fail over to another region without significant downtime.

- **Runbook automation**: Elastic DRS offers automated runbooks, which streamline DR procedures. By automating failover and recovery processes, DRS reduces the need for manual intervention and accelerates recovery times, minimizing downtime.

AWS DRS is a sophisticated solution crafted by AWS to empower organizations with robust DR capabilities within the AWS cloud environment. We find in reports about existing deployments an emphasis on the importance of robust DR solutions in minimizing business disruption and data loss during unexpected events. On those deployments, the role of cloud-based DR solutions is considered fundamental in providing scalability, reliability, and cost-efficiency [26]. AWS Documentation on AWS DRS highlights its applicability in various scenarios, including business continuity planning, DR testing, and regulatory compliance. AWS Elastic DRS's automation and integration with other AWS services make it a valuable tool for organizations looking to ensure business continuity in the cloud [27].

Let us explore the components, features, and scenarios where AWS Elastic DRS shines.

Components of AWS Elastic Disaster Recovery

Ensuring business continuity in the face of system failures, natural disasters, or regional outages requires more than just routine backups—it demands a comprehensive, automated DR strategy. AWS DRS offers a cloud-native solution that minimizes downtime and data loss by replicating critical workloads across regions, automating recovery workflows, and meeting rigorous compliance requirements. With built-in orchestration and cross-region support, AWS DRS transforms DR from a manual, reactive process into a proactive, scalable component of enterprise resilience, as follows:

- **Automated backup and replication**: AWS Elastic DRS automates the backup and replication of critical workloads, ensuring data integrity and availability during a disaster. Organizations can define backup policies and replication schedules to meet their recovery objectives.

- **Cross-region failover**: Elastic DRS enables organizations to replicate their workloads across multiple AWS Regions, facilitating uniform failover in case of regional outages or disruptions. This cross-region redundancy enhances resilience and minimizes downtime.

- **Runbook automation**: With built-in runbook automation, AWS DRS streamlines the execution of DR procedures. Organizations can define pre-configured runbooks to automate failover and failback processes, reducing manual intervention and accelerating recovery times.

Instances to use AWS Elastic Disaster Recovery

Not all workloads require the same level of protection, but for high-value systems where even brief interruptions can lead to significant operational or financial impact, AWS DRS becomes indispensable. The following scenarios outline when deploying EDR is not only beneficial but also essential for maintaining uptime, ensuring regulatory compliance, and delivering uninterrupted user experiences:

- **Mission-critical workloads**: Organizations hosting mission-critical applications and services on AWS can benefit from AWS DRS to ensure continuous availability and data protection.

- **Regulatory compliance**: AWS DRS helps organizations meet regulatory compliance requirements by establishing resilient DR environments that adhere to industry-specific mandates.

- **Geographically distributed applications**: Applications requiring geographically distributed deployments can leverage AWS DRS to replicate data and workloads across multiple AWS Regions, ensuring high availability and fault-tolrance.

- **DR testing**: DRS facilitates DR testing by providing sandbox environments for organizations to simulate failover scenarios and validate recovery procedures without impacting production systems.

Scenarios resolved by AWS Elastic Disaster Recovery

From regional service disruptions to accidental data deletion, AWS DRS is purpose-built to address real-world operational threats. Its automated architecture mitigates the risk of prolonged outages, enables secure and auditable recovery processes, and ensures that organizations can recover quickly and safely, regardless of the nature of the disruption, as follows:

- **Regional outages**: AWS Elastic DRS mitigates the impact of regional outages by enabling organizations to fail over to secondary AWS Regions.

- **Data loss prevention**: Elastic DRS automates backup and replication processes to help organizations prevent data loss and maintain data integrity during DR events.

- **Downtime reduction**: Elastic DRS's automated failover capabilities minimize downtime and ensure business continuity, enabling organizations to resume operations swiftly following a disaster.

- **Compliance challenges**: Elastic DRS addresses compliance challenges by providing secure, auditable DR solutions that meet regulatory requirements and industry standards.

Use cases and benefits

AWS DRS can be used in a variety of critical scenarios:

- **Mission-critical workloads**: Organizations can use Elastic DRS to safeguard their most critical applications and services, ensuring continuous availability and data protection during disruptions.

- **Compliance and regulatory requirements**: Elastic DRS helps meet stringent regulatory requirements by establishing resilient DR environments that comply with industry-specific standards, making it particularly useful in sectors like finance, healthcare, and government.

- **DR testing**: The service allows DR testing in isolated sandbox environments, enabling organizations to simulate failover and validate recovery procedures without impacting live operations.

- **Geographically distributed deployments**: By leveraging DRS, companies running geographically distributed applications can replicate data across AWS Regions, ensuring high availability and fault-tolrance.

Real-world applications

AWS Elastic DRS is widely adopted across various industries, where uninterrupted operations are crucial. Financial institutions, for instance, use DRS to ensure continuous access to banking services, even in the event of data center failures. Similarly, healthcare providers rely on the service to safeguard critical medical systems and patient records, ensuring these resources remain available even during disasters.

In regulated industries such as government and education, AWS DRS is essential for meeting compliance mandates by maintaining audit trails and ensuring data protection across dispersed environments.

Disaster recovery and operational resilience

AWS DRS redefines how organizations approach DR, offering more than just a backup solution. Its scalability, automation, and integration with other AWS services make it a cornerstone for modern business continuity planning. Organizations can confidently maintain operations in the cloud while minimizing downtime and data loss in the face of minor disruptions and full-scale disasters.

AWS DRS provides organizations with a powerful, automated, scalable DR framework for maintaining business continuity. By leveraging features like automated failover, cross-region replication, and runbook automation, AWS DRS enables organizations to minimize downtime, maintain compliance, and enhance their resilience in the cloud-driven digital age.

Conclusion

In this chapter, we explored the broad range of AWS storage solutions, discovering various services tailored to specific business needs and use cases. AWS provides a comprehensive set of storage options, each essential in helping organizations store, manage, protect, and recover their data safely and efficiently.

Our journey started with Amazon EBS, a high-performance block storage service designed for low-latency and high-throughput workloads on EC2 instances. We then examined Amazon EFS, which offers scalable, file-level storage for different applications, and Amazon FSx, a managed file storage service optimized for Windows and Lustre workloads. Amazon S3 is notable as the foundation of scalable object storage, while Amazon S3 Glacier provides cost-effective, long-term archival storage for infrequently accessed data.

As we progressed, we examined the importance of AWS Backup, which simplifies backup and recovery across AWS resources. We also discussed the AWS Snow Family, highlighting its role in connecting on-premises and cloud environments for efficient data transfer. AWS Storage Gateway further supports hybrid storage solutions by integrating on-premises data centers with the cloud. Ultimately, AWS DRS emerged as a crucial DR tool, ensuring business continuity through the rapid recovery of critical systems.

Throughout this chapter, we have not only explored the technical intricacies of these services but also examined real-world use cases and industry research, emphasizing the critical role of cloud-based storage solutions. Whether ensuring data security, improving scalability, or optimizing performance, AWS storage services empower businesses to meet their evolving storage requirements flexibly and cost-effectively.

The following illustration reinforces the importance of knowing your data to pick the right store:

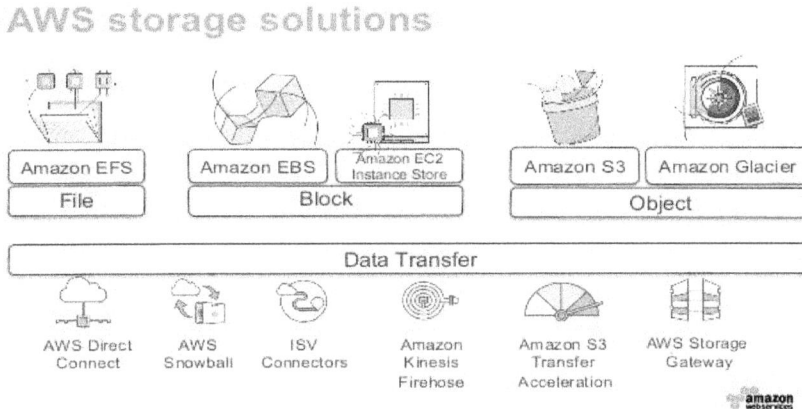

AWS storage solutions

Amazon EFS	Amazon EBS	Amazon EC2 Instance Store	Amazon S3	Amazon Glacier
File	Block		Object	

Data Transfer

| AWS Direct Connect | AWS Snowball | ISV Connectors | Amazon Kinesis Firehose | Amazon S3 Transfer Acceleration | AWS Storage Gateway |

Figure 3.15: Picking the right data store for your workload

As we conclude, AWS's comprehensive storage offerings are indispensable for organizations across industries. They deliver the necessary tools to adapt to data management, protection, and recovery demands.

The next chapter will discuss a thorough understanding of **content delivery networks (CDNs)**, their function, and their vital role in boosting web performance and scalability.

Join our Discord space

Join our Discord workspace for latest updates, offers, tech happenings around the world, new releases, and sessions with the authors:

https://discord.bpbonline.com

CHAPTER 4
Content Delivery Network

Introduction

In this chapter, we will discuss the **Amazon Web Services** (**AWS**) networking ecosystem, explore the vast world of the **Internet of Things** (**IoT**), and highlight the celestial capabilities of AWS Satellite services. These areas form the backbone of modern cloud computing, allowing organizations to connect, communicate, and even reach for the stars in their digital pursuits.

We will discuss AWS networking solutions in the first module, networking and content delivery. From the introductory Amazon **Virtual Private Cloud** (**VPC**) to the advanced networking capabilities offered by AWS Global Accelerator and AWS Transit Gateway, we will explore a range of services that empower organizations to build secure, highly available, and globally distributed applications. **Elastic Load Balancing** (**ELB**) will play a pivotal role in ensuring the continuous distribution of traffic. At the same time, AWS PrivateLink and AWS Direct Connect will enable enterprises to connect securely to the AWS cloud. Together, these services form the constellations of connectivity and content delivery in the AWS universe.

The second module, IoT, will introduce us to the IoT cosmos, where connected devices and data-driven insights converge. AWS IoT Core will be our guiding star, providing a secure and scalable platform for connecting, managing, and analyzing IoT devices. We will explore the IoT ecosystem, from AWS IoT Greengrass for edge computing to AWS IoT Analytics for deriving intelligence from IoT data. AWS IoT Device Defender and AWS IoT Device Management will ensure the security and efficient management of IoT fleets. At the same time, AWS IoT Events will enable the creation of event-driven IoT applications. Whether you are exploring IoT for smart cities, industrial automation, or innovative consumer devices, this section will provide the knowledge to navigate the IoT galaxy confidently.

In the final module, satellite, we will transcend Earth's atmosphere to uncover the groundbreaking capabilities of AWS Satellite services. AWS Ground Station will allow us to connect with satellites in orbit, offering unprecedented access to space data. As we reach the stars, you will discover how AWS Satellite services empower organizations to collect, process, and distribute satellite data easily. Together, these three domains form a celestial trifecta, where networking, IoT, and satellite technologies converge to unlock the boundless potential of the AWS cloud.

Structure

In this chapter, we will go through the following topics:

- Amazon VPC
- AWS App Mesh
- AWS Cloud Map
- AWS Direct Connect
- AWS Global Accelerator
- AWS Private 5G
- AWS PrivateLink
- AWS Transit Gateway
- AWS Verified Access
- AWS VPN
- Elastic Load Balancing
- Internet of Things
- AWS IoT FleetWise
- AWS IoT SiteWise operating with IoT data
- AWS IoT TwinMaker
- AWS IoT Greengrass
- Simplifying deployment with AWS IoT 1-Click
- AWS IoT Analytics
- AWS IoT Button
- AWS IoT Device Defender
- AWS IoT Device Management
- AWS IoT EduKit

- AWS IoT Events
- AWS IoT RoboRunner
- AWS Partner Device Catalog
- FreeRTOS
- Satellite

Objectives

This chapter on **content delivery networks** (**CDNs**) aims to provide readers with a thorough understanding of their function and their vital role in boosting web performance and scalability. By exploring their intricacies, readers will learn how to optimize content delivery, minimize latency, and improve the user experience across different geographical locations. The chapter will equip readers with the practical knowledge and skills needed to understand CDN architecture, including its fundamental components like edge servers, origin servers, and points of presence. It will also cover AWS CloudFront, Amazon's CDN service, detailing its features, configurations, and how to integrate it with other AWS services. Additionally, the chapter will dive into performance optimization techniques, such as caching strategies and content compression, along with security enhancements like **distributed denial of service** (**DDoS**) protection, SSL/TLS encryption, and access controls. Finally, readers will learn about pricing models for CDN services and how to manage and optimize costs effectively. By the end of this chapter, readers will be well-equipped to implement and manage CDN solutions to ensure fast, secure, and reliable content delivery for their applications and users.

Amazon VPC

This section will explore advanced Amazon VPC configurations, security best practices, and case studies that demonstrate how organizations have leveraged Amazon VPC's capabilities to architect scalable, secure, and highly available cloud networks.

Within the extensive reach of AWS, networking serves as the foundational basis for building secure and scalable digital environments. Amazon VPC [1], plays a central role in this architecture, enabling users to create logically isolated virtual networks within the AWS cloud. This section examines the core concepts, design models, and real-world use cases of Amazon VPC, drawing on both peer-reviewed research and AWS Documentation.

Building secure and isolated cloud networks

Amazon VPC allows users to carve out logically isolated sections of the AWS cloud, where they can deploy resources such as Amazon **Elastic Compute Cloud** (**EC2**) instances, RDS databases, and Lambda functions while maintaining control over network topology and security. The architecture of an Amazon VPC comprises a combination of subnets, route tables, **network access control lists** (**NACLs**), security groups, and **Virtual Private Network** (**VPN**) connections, allowing for the design of custom network layouts. A key feature is the ability to establish direct connections between the VPC and on-premises data centers, creating hybrid cloud environments that seamlessly extend an organization's network into the AWS cloud.

Research studies [2] emphasize that effective segmentation and network isolation are essential for maintaining security, performance, and regulatory compliance in cloud-native deployments. Designing VPCs with attention to IP schemas, routing strategies, and access controls is frequently cited as a key practice. AWS resources further identify Amazon VPC as the core networking layer supporting services such as AWS Lambda and Amazon RDS, and as a critical element in building resilient, multi-tenant cloud architectures.

Use cases and real-world applications

Amazon VPC is employed across various use cases, from traditional application hosting to advanced cloud-native architectures. It is frequently used to create secure and isolated development and test environments, ensuring that experimentation does not impact production systems. For enterprises, Amazon VPC facilitates establishing secure and private connections between on-premises data centers and AWS resources, enabling a gradual migration to the cloud. Real-world case studies often showcase how organizations have leveraged Amazon VPC to build multi-tiered web applications, implement secure microservices architectures, and maintain strict regulatory compliance [3].

Service overview

As cloud adoption continues to scale across critical workloads, securing data in transit remains a central concern. AWS PrivateLink addresses this by enabling private connectivity between VPCs and AWS services, eliminating the need to traverse the public internet. This section examines the core design of AWS PrivateLink, its security posture, and typical use cases, drawing on both applied research and AWS technical sources [4].

Elevating network security and simplicity

AWS PrivateLink is a service that allows organizations to access AWS services through private and secure connections, completely isolated from the public internet. It utilizes Amazon VPC technology to establish these private connections, ensuring that data never passes through the public internet and thereby reducing exposure to security threats. This method enhances data privacy and security, making it suitable for organizations with stringent compliance requirements or those handling sensitive data.

Recent studies [5] describe PrivateLink as an effective mechanism for minimizing exposure by isolating service traffic within the AWS network fabric. This architecture significantly reduces the attack surface while maintaining high availability and performance. AWS Documentation outlines the breadth of supported integrations and highlights how PrivateLink streamlines cross-account and hybrid deployments by providing direct, encrypted access to cloud resources.

Use cases and real-world applications

AWS PrivateLink supports applications across a wide range of industries and use cases. Enterprises leverage it to create secure connections between on-premises data centers and AWS services, enabling hybrid cloud deployments. Real-world case studies often demonstrate how AWS PrivateLink enhances data transfer security and compliance in industries such as healthcare and finance, where stringent data privacy regulations are in place. It also simplifies the architecture of multi-account environments, streamlining access to shared services while maintaining security boundaries [6].

This section will explore advanced configurations, best practices, and practical implementations that demonstrate how AWS PrivateLink can enhance network security and simplify connectivity, providing organizations with a robust foundation for cloud operations.

AWS App Mesh

As cloud-native architecture becomes increasingly distributed, managing communication across microservices has become a key design challenge. AWS App Mesh addresses this by providing a service mesh that standardizes service discovery, traffic routing, and observability across complex environments [7]. This section examines the architectural foundations and operational benefits of AWS App Mesh, supported by technical literature and AWS guidance.

Orchestrating microservices at scale

AWS App Mesh serves as a central control plane, enabling organizations to connect, monitor, and secure microservices running on AWS. It simplifies the complexity of microservices communication by offering features like service discovery, load balancing, and traffic management. App Mesh supports communication between services across various compute environments, such as Amazon ECS, Amazon EKS, and Amazon EC2 instances, while allowing developers to focus on building individual services without worrying about networking details.

Research on microservices infrastructure [8] highlights the advantages of centralized control in improving reliability, visibility, and fault-tolerance across service boundaries. AWS App Mesh facilitates these outcomes by integrating with compute services like Amazon ECS, EKS, and EC2, while enforcing security policies such as TLS encryption and access controls. AWS Documentation further outlines its role in unifying service communication under a consistent, scalable mesh.

Use cases and real-world applications

AWS App Mesh is used in various use cases across different industries. Companies use App Mesh to build resilient and scalable microservices-based applications, ensuring each service can communicate fully with others. Real-world case studies often show how AWS App Mesh has helped organizations improve the reliability and availability of their applications, enhance troubleshooting and debugging, and boost security by implementing mutual TLS authentication between services [9].

AWS Cloud Map

Scalable microservices architectures depend on reliable service discovery to maintain communication across dynamic environments. AWS Cloud Map [10] addresses this need by allowing services to register themselves and discover other components through a centralized naming system. This section examines the architecture and use cases of AWS Cloud Map, drawing from current research and AWS Documentation.

Mapping your way to scalable and resilient services

Map is a service discovery and naming service that enables organizations to easily manage the dynamic nature of microservices and applications. It enables services to register themselves and discover other services within the AWS cloud, eliminating the need for manual configuration and making it effortless to connect services regardless of location. This orchestration and automation of service discovery is invaluable in dynamic and rapidly scaling environments, ensuring that services can find and communicate with each other smoothly.

Academic investigation [11] point to dynamic service discovery as a critical factor in ensuring reliability and availability within cloud-native applications. AWS Cloud Map supports this by automating endpoint registration and resolution, reducing manual configuration and operational complexity. Its integration with services like Amazon ECS, EKS, and Route 53 enables consistent and resilient inter-service communication on a scale.

Use cases and real-world applications

AWS Cloud Map is a versatile tool with applications in various use cases across industries. Organizations utilize it to manage and discover services in microservices-based applications, thereby reducing manual configuration efforts and enhancing service availability. Real-world case studies often illustrate how AWS Cloud Map has empowered organizations to build flexible and dynamic architectures, supporting use cases such as load balancing, failover, and blue-green deployments. It also plays a crucial role in orchestrating service discovery in serverless applications, ensuring that functions can communicate with each other fluently [12].

AWS Direct Connect

As cloud adoption grows and hybrid architecture becomes more prevalent, organizations increasingly require dedicated, high-throughput connections between on-premises environments and the AWS cloud. AWS Direct Connect [13] fulfills this role by offering a private, low-latency network link that bypasses the public internet. This section outlines the core architecture and practical applications of AWS Direct Connect, supported by research and AWS Documentation.

Bridging the gap between on-premises and the cloud

AWS Direct Connect [15] it is a dedicated network service that provides organizations with private, high-bandwidth connections to AWS resources. This service enables enterprises to bypass the public internet and establish direct links to AWS data centers, AWS Regions, and Amazon VPCs. By doing so, AWS Direct Connect ensures predictable network performance, low-latency, and enhanced security, making it an essential choice for organizations with stringent networking requirements.

Studies on enterprise networking [14] identify dedicated links as essential for workloads demanding consistent performance and enhanced data security. AWS Direct Connect supports these requirements by reducing latency, improving throughput, and enabling reliable data transfer at scale. AWS Documentation also notes its adaptability, with use cases spanning hybrid deployments, migration strategies, and disaster recovery scenarios.

Use cases and real-world applications

AWS Direct Connect is utilized in various scenarios, particularly when organizations require reliable and secure access to AWS cloud resources. Companies use Direct Connect to create private connections for data transfer, which lowers transfer costs and helps ensure compliance with data privacy laws. Real-world examples often demonstrate how AWS Direct Connect enables organizations to establish hybrid cloud setups by connecting their on-premises data centers to the AWS cloud. It also plays an important role in disaster recovery and business continuity by offering a dedicated path for data replication and resource access [16].

AWS Global Accelerator

Global application performance depends on routing traffic efficiently across regions and AZs. AWS Global Accelerator [17] enables this by directing user requests through the optimal AWS edge network, improving availability and reducing latency for globally distributed applications. This section examines the architecture and operational use of AWS Global Accelerator, supported by technical research and AWS service documentation.

Optimizing global content delivery

AWS Global Accelerator is a service that combines AWS's extensive network infrastructure with Anycast IP addresses to direct incoming traffic over the best AWS network route to specified endpoints. It improves application availability and performance by smartly distributing traffic across multiple AWS Regions and AZs, automatically redirecting traffic away from unhealthy endpoints. This results in lower latency and higher availability, providing a smoother UX.

Content delivery optimization remains a crucial factor in ensuring the performance of distributed applications. Studies have shown that services like AWS Global Accelerator reduce latency and improve availability by routing user traffic through optimal AWS edge locations [18]. Its integration with services such as Amazon Route 53 and AWS ELB enables organizations to maintain resilient, low-latency connections across multiple regions, forming a scalable solution for high-performance global applications [1] [2].

Use cases and real-world applications

This AWS service offers a multitude of use cases, particularly for organizations with a global user base. Enterprises employ it to enhance the availability and performance of web applications, APIs, and other services by reducing latency and routing traffic to healthy endpoints. Real-world case studies often illustrate how AWS Global Accelerator has empowered organizations to achieve global reach without compromising performance, supporting use cases such as video streaming, gaming, and e-commerce platforms. It also plays a pivotal role in disaster recovery strategies by facilitating rapid failover to healthy endpoints in different geographic locations [19].

AWS Private 5G

As enterprises deploy latency-sensitive and bandwidth-intensive applications at the edge, private wireless infrastructure has become increasingly relevant. AWS Private 5G [20] enables organizations to setup dedicated 5G networks on-premises, offering predictable performance and secure local connectivity. This section outlines the architecture and use cases of AWS Private 5G, drawing from technical research and AWS Documentation to assess its role in extending cloud-native capabilities into industrial and enterprise environments.

Revolution in network connectivity

AWS Private 5G is a managed solution that combines the power of AWS cloud infrastructure with 5G wireless technology. It provides organizations with dedicated and secure wireless connectivity within their premises, allowing them to deploy private 5G networks tailored to their specific needs. This technology enables low-latency, high-bandwidth connections, making it ideal for various applications, from industrial IoT to high-performance computing.

As enterprises deploy increasingly distributed applications and devices, dedicated wireless infrastructure is becoming a strategic priority. AWS Private 5G addresses this need by offering localized, high-bandwidth connectivity tailored to enterprise environments [20]. The service provides on-premises 5G networks that integrate directly with the AWS cloud, enabling secure, low-latency communication for industrial automation, edge computing, and smart manufacturing scenarios. Research literature and AWS Documentation indicate that improved network throughput, reduced latency, and tighter control over data access are key operational benefits [21].

Use cases and real-world applications

AWS Private 5G offers a wide range of use cases across various industries. Enterprises leverage it to enable low-latency communication between IoT devices, thereby enhancing automation and efficiency. Real-world examples demonstrate how AWS Private 5G is utilized in sectors such as manufacturing, healthcare, and logistics, where real-time data transmission is crucial. It also plays a pivotal role in augmenting existing networking infrastructure, offering a path to digital transformation by providing reliable, high-speed wireless connectivity within organizational premises [22].

In this section, we will explore advanced configurations, best practices, and practical implementations that illustrate how AWS Private 5G can revolutionize network connectivity and content delivery, unlocking new possibilities for businesses in an increasingly interconnected world.

AWS PrivateLink

Establishing secure, private communication between VPCs and AWS services is essential for protecting data in transit. AWS PrivateLink [23] addresses this need by enabling private connectivity without exposing traffic to the public internet. This section reviews the architectural components and operational benefits of PrivateLink, supported by research literature and AWS guidance, with a focus on network isolation, encryption, and service access within regulated or hybrid environments.

Elevating network security and simplicity

AWS PrivateLink is a service that enables organizations to access AWS services over private and secure connections, completely isolated from the public internet. It leverages Amazon VPC technology to establish these private connections, ensuring that data never traverses the public internet, thus mitigating exposure to potential security threats. This approach enhances data privacy and security, making it ideal for organizations with stringent compliance requirements or those handling sensitive data.

With data security and isolation at the forefront of cloud architecture decisions, AWS PrivateLink enables organizations to establish private connectivity between VPCs and AWS services, bypassing the public internet entirely [23]. The architecture of PrivateLink supports fine-grained access control, encrypted traffic, and reduced attack surfaces, making it a preferred option for regulated environments and sensitive workloads. Technical analyses underscore its role in minimizing exposure and simplifying cross-account or hybrid cloud integration workflows [24]. AWS Documentation further details the breadth of services supported and the operational flexibility PrivateLink offers in securing cloud-native communication paths.

Use cases and real-world applications

AWS PrivateLink supports applications across a wide range of industries and use cases. Enterprises leverage it to create secure connections between on-premises data centers and AWS services, enabling hybrid cloud deployments. Real-world case studies often demonstrate how AWS PrivateLink enhances data transfer security and compliance in industries such as healthcare and finance, where stringent data privacy regulations are in place. It also simplifies the architecture of multi-account environments, streamlining access to shared services while maintaining security boundaries [4].

AWS Transit Gateway

Managing connectivity across expanding cloud environments requires a scalable and centralized approach. AWS Transit Gateway [26] addresses this by allowing organizations to connect multiple Amazon VPCs and on-premises networks through a single routing hub. This section examines the architecture, operational models, and deployment scenarios for AWS Transit Gateway, supported by research insights and AWS Documentation.

Streamlined network management for cloud-scale

AWS Transit Gateway is a fully managed service that serves as a central hub, connecting multiple Amazon VPCs and on-premises networks. It facilitates traffic routing between these networks, eliminating the need for complex peering relationships between VPCs and simplifying network management. This centralized hub-and-spoke architecture streamlines connectivity, making scaling and managing network resources easier as organizations grow.

Studies on cloud-scale networking [26] note the complexity of managing peer-to-peer VPC links in large environments and identify centralized routing as a preferred alternative. AWS Transit Gateway simplifies this process, improving visibility and administrative control while reducing configuration overhead. AWS Documentation also highlights its integration with VPN and Direct Connect, making it adaptable for hybrid architecture and shared service environments.

Use cases and real-world applications

AWS Transit Gateway presents many use cases for organizations of all sizes and industries. Enterprises use it to consolidate their network connectivity, reducing the complexity of managing multiple VPC connections. Real-world case studies often illustrate how AWS Transit Gateway facilitates network expansion, enabling organizations to scale their cloud infrastructure effortlessly. It is particularly valuable for shared services, cross-account access, and global network distribution [27].

AWS Verified Access

Securing access to cloud resources requires more than traditional authentication mechanisms, particularly in environments with distributed teams and sensitive workloads. AWS Verified Access [28] provides an identity-aware access layer that enforces contextual authentication and authorization policies at the network edge. This section reviews the design and implementation of AWS Verified Access, with insights from current research and AWS technical documentation.

Elevating authentication and security

AWS Verified Access is a security feature that enhances authentication and authorization when accessing AWS resources. It introduces the concept of **identity assurance levels** (**IALs**) and **authentication assurance levels** (**AALs**) to classify the strength of identity verification and the security of the authentication process. AWS Verified Access requires users to meet specific IAL and AAL requirements, thus ensuring that only authenticated and authorized users can access critical AWS resources.

Recent literature [29] identifies adaptive authentication as a critical component in reducing unauthorized access and strengthening cloud security. Verified Access supports this by enabling policy-based controls that align with user identity, device posture, and session context. AWS Documentation highlights its flexibility in defining authentication requirements, allowing organizations to tailor access policies to meet evolving regulatory and operational demands.

Use cases and real-world applications

AWS Verified Access finds applications across industries where stringent security and compliance requirements are paramount. Enterprises leverage it to control access to sensitive data and critical resources. Real-world case studies often demonstrate how AWS Verified Access enhances security in the healthcare, finance, and government sectors, where data privacy and compliance are of paramount importance. It plays a crucial role in strengthening security measures for remote and privileged access scenarios, offering a robust solution for organizations seeking to protect their cloud resources [30].

AWS VPN

In an increasingly connected world, securing network communications is paramount. AWS provides a robust solution through AWS VPN [31]. This section explores the intricacies of AWS VPN, including its architecture, deployment options, and how it enhances data privacy and network security for organizations of all sizes.

AWS VPN overview

AWS VPN is a cloud-based service that enables organizations to establish secure and encrypted connections to their AWS resources and networks, creating a private and isolated network environment. This service can be classified into two main categories: AWS Site-to-Site VPN and AWS Client VPN.

AWS Site-to-Site VPN

AWS Site-to-Site VPN allows organizations to securely connect their on-premises data centers or remote offices to AWS. Here are the key aspects of AWS Site-to-Site VPN:

- **Architecture**: AWS Site-to-Site VPN employs industry standard VPN protocols like IPsec and **Border Gateway Protocol** (**BGP**) for creating encrypted tunnels. Organizations can choose between hardware VPN connections or VPN CloudHub to simplify connectivity.

- **Deployment options**: This service supports static and dynamic routing options, giving organizations flexibility in routing traffic between on-premises and AWS environments.

- **Security**: Data in transit is protected through encryption, and VPN tunnels are monitored and managed via AWS VPN CloudWatch Logs for enhanced security.

- **Use cases**: AWS Site-to-Site VPN is ideal for organizations with hybrid cloud architectures. It facilitates secure and reliable communication between on-premises and cloud resources.

AWS Client VPN

AWS Client VPN provides a secure way for remote users to access AWS and on-premises resources. Here are the primary features of AWS Client VPN:

- **Architecture**: AWS Client VPN allows remote users to access AWS and on-premises resources securely. It provides a scalable and highly available VPN solution for remote workers.

- **Deployment options**: Organizations can configure user-based authentication and authorization through Active Directory or AWS Directory Service, ensuring that only authorized personnel can access resources.

- **Security**: AWS Client VPN ensures data confidentiality through encryption, and it integrates with AWS **Identity and Access Management** (**IAM**) for user authentication.

- **Use cases**: This solution is particularly valuable for organizations with a remote or mobile workforce, enabling secure access to AWS resources from anywhere.

AWS VPN best practices

To maximize the effectiveness and security of AWS VPN, organizations should follow these best practices:

- **Optimized routing**: Employ BGP to enable dynamic routing between your on-premises network and AWS, ensuring efficient traffic management.

- **High availability**: Deploy multiple VPN tunnels for redundancy and failover capabilities, guaranteeing uninterrupted connectivity.

- **Security groups and NACLs**: Implement network security best practices by using AWS security groups and NACLs to control inbound and outbound traffic.

- **Monitoring and logging**: Leverage AWS CloudWatch and AWS VPN CloudWatch Logs for continuous monitoring and real-time insights into your VPN connections.

- **Compliance**: Ensure adherence to regulatory requirements by configuring VPN encryption and access controls according to industry standards [32].

In conclusion, AWS VPN is a versatile and scalable solution that pivots in securing network communications for organizations utilizing AWS services [33]. Whether connecting on-premises data centers, remote offices, or remote users, AWS VPN offers robust encryption, flexibility, and monitoring capabilities to safeguard data and resources. By following best practices and leveraging AWS VPN's features [14], organizations can establish a resilient and secure network infrastructure in the cloud.

Elastic Load Balancing

Ensuring the availability, scalability, and reliability of applications is paramount in cloud computing. AWS ELB is a critical service that addresses these needs by distributing incoming traffic across multiple Amazon EC2 instances. This section explores the intricacies of AWS ELB, including its types, key features, and how it enhances the performance and resilience of applications hosted on AWS.

AWS Elastic Load Balancing overview

AWS ELB is a fully managed service that automatically distributes incoming application traffic across multiple targets, such as Amazon EC2 instances, containers, and IP addresses, within one or more AZs. ELB plays a crucial role in ensuring high availability and fault-tolrance for applications while also improving the distribution of traffic for optimal performance [34].

Types of Elastic Load Balancers

AWS offers three types of ELB to cater to various application needs, as follows:

- **Application Load Balancer (ALB) [35]:**
  - **Routing**: ALB operates at the application layer (layer 7) and can route traffic based on content, such as HTTP/HTTPS requests. It is ideal for modern, microservices-based applications.

    o **Features**: ALB supports features like content-based routing, path-based routing, host-based routing, and integration with AWS **web application firewall** (**WAF**).

- **Network Load Balancer (NLB)**:

    o **Routing**: NLB operates on the transport layer (layer 4) and is designed for ultra-high-performance and low-latency traffic distribution. It is suitable for TCP, UDP, and TLS traffic.

    o **Features**: NLB offers features like static IP addresses, health checks, and support for IP-based routing.

- **Classic Load Balancer (CLB)**:

    o **Routing**: CLB is the legacy version of ELB and provides basic load-balancing capabilities. It operates on both the application and transport layers.

    o **Features**: CLB offers cross-zone load balancing, SSL termination, and sticky sessions.

Key features and use cases

The following are the key features and use cases [36]:

- **High availability**: ELB automatically distributes traffic across multiple instances or targets, ensuring applications remain available even if some instances fail.

- **Scalability**: ELB smoothly handles increasing traffic loads by adding or removing instances, allowing applications to scale horizontally.

- **Security**: Integration with AWS WAF allows ELB to protect applications from common web-based attacks, enhancing security.

- **Monitoring and insights**: ELB provides detailed monitoring and metrics through AWS CloudWatch, enabling real-time visibility into application traffic and performance.

- **Simplified deployment**: ELB can be easily configured and managed through the AWS Management Console, **command line interface** (**CLI**), or **software development kit** (**SDKs**).

Best practices

The following are the best practices:

- Use Auto Scaling with ELB to automatically adjust the number of instances based on traffic.

- Enable cross-zone load balancing for even distribution of traffic across AZs.

- Regularly monitor ELB metrics in CloudWatch to detect and mitigate performance issues.

- Configure health checks to ensure ELB directs traffic only to healthy instances.

In conclusion, AWS ELB is fundamental to modern cloud architecture, ensuring application availability, scalability, and reliability. Whether deploying microservices with ALB, handling low-latency traffic with NLB, or utilizing the legacy CLB and ELB, AWS offers the flexibility and features required to optimize application performance in its ecosystem.

Internet of Things

Reliable connectivity, device management, and data processing are foundational to scalable IoT systems. AWS IoT Core [37] addresses these requirements by providing a fully managed service that enables secure communication between connected devices and the AWS cloud. This section explores the core architecture of AWS IoT Core, including its messaging protocols, integration points, and deployment contexts, supported by research and AWS Documentation.

Understanding AWS IoT Core

AWS IoT Core is a cloud-based service that enables the secure and scalable connection of IoT devices to the AWS cloud. It serves as a communication hub, enabling devices to exchange data securely. IoT Core supports a range of IoT protocols and standards, ensuring compatibility with various devices. It also offers device management features, such as device provisioning and authentication, which are essential for maintaining the integrity and security of IoT deployments.

Literature on industrial and enterprise IoT highlights the need for simplified, scalable frameworks for managing device fleets. AWS IoT Core supports this by abstracting connection management, protocol translation, and authentication, reducing the operational burden of large-scale IoT deployments. AWS Documentation also emphasizes its ability to handle high-throughput data ingestion while enforcing security policies and maintaining interoperability across diverse device ecosystems.

Use cases and real-world applications

AWS IoT Core is utilized across various industries, including manufacturing, healthcare, smart cities, and agriculture. Real-world case studies [38]. Often, AWS IoT Core enables organizations to build scalable and secure IoT solutions. It is important in asset tracking, predictive maintenance, and remote monitoring scenarios. IoT Core empowers organizations to harness the power of IoT data, providing valuable insights and enabling data-driven decision-making [39].

AWS IoT FleetWise

Fleet operations depend on real-time visibility in vehicle health, performance, and usage patterns. AWS IoT FleetWise [41] provides a managed framework for collecting, transforming, and transmitting vehicle data to the cloud, enabling advanced diagnostics and analytics across diverse asset types. This section examines the service's architecture and implementation scenarios, referencing current research and AWS Documentation.

Fleet management with IoT

AWS IoT FleetWise [40] is a comprehensive solution designed to optimize the management of vehicle fleets and assets. Leveraging IoT technologies, it provides real-time insights into vehicle health, performance, and location. Fleet operators can monitor and analyze vehicle data, enabling predictive maintenance, route optimization, and enhanced safety measures. AWS IoT FleetWise simplifies collecting and processing data from diverse sources, making it accessible and actionable for fleet managers.

Studies in IoT-driven fleet management [41] emphasize the importance of scalable data collection and analytics in improving operational efficiency and reducing downtime. AWS IoT FleetWise supports these goals by offering customizable data collection schemas, integration with vehicle sensors, and compatibility with AWS analytics services. AWS Documentation highlights its applicability across various industries, including logistics, transportation, and construction, where fleet intelligence has a direct impact on performance and cost.

Use cases and real-world applications

AWS IoT FleetWise finds applications across industries where fleet management is critical to operations. Real-world case studies often showcase how FleetWise has revolutionized transportation and logistics. It enables organizations to proactively address vehicle maintenance, ensuring vehicles are in optimal condition and reducing unplanned downtime. Additionally, FleetWise facilitates route optimization, leading to reduced fuel consumption and improved environmental sustainability.

This section explores advanced configurations, best practices, and practical implementations that demonstrate how AWS IoT FleetWise is reshaping fleet management, empowering organizations to drive efficiency and innovation in their operations.

AWS IoT SiteWise operating with IoT data

Industrial environments depend on timely data from equipment and control systems to optimize operations and minimize downtime. AWS IoT SiteWise [43] enables organizations to ingest, organize, and visualize time-series data from industrial assets across distributed facilities. This section examines the service's core architecture, deployment models, and industry applications, referencing both current research and AWS Documentation.

Understanding AWS IoT SiteWise

AWS IoT SiteWise is a managed service that facilitates the collection, storage, and visualization of industrial data. It serves as a bridge between the physical world of industrial equipment and the digital world of the cloud. IoT SiteWise [42] allows organizations to securely connect industrial assets, sensors, and machines to the AWS cloud. It collects and processes data in real-time, enabling organizations to gain valuable insights into the performance, condition, and efficiency of their industrial assets.

Research on industrial IoT systems [43] points to the importance of unified data modeling and scalable ingestion pipelines in enabling predictive maintenance and performance monitoring. AWS IoT SiteWise supports these functions by abstracting asset hierarchies, simplifying sensor integration, and providing built-in visualization tools. AWS Documentation highlights its utility across sectors such as manufacturing, energy, and utilities, where equipment monitoring is central to operational continuity and cost control.

Use cases and real-world applications

AWS IoT SiteWise finds applications across a wide range of industrial sectors. Real-world case studies often demonstrate how SiteWise has enabled organizations to enhance asset performance, reduce maintenance costs, and improve operational efficiency. It plays a pivotal role in predictive maintenance, ensuring that equipment issues are identified and addressed before they lead to costly downtime. Additionally, SiteWise supports compliance efforts by providing detailed historical data for auditing and reporting.

This section will explore advanced configurations, best practices, and practical implementations that demonstrate how AWS IoT SiteWise is transforming industrial operations, enabling organizations to make data-driven decisions and achieve enhanced operational excellence.

AWS IoT TwinMaker

Digital twins—virtual models of physical systems—have become a key method for monitoring, analyzing, and simulating real-world assets. AWS IoT TwinMaker [44] provides a framework for building and managing digital twins by integrating sensor data, 3D asset models, and contextual metadata. This section outlines the architectural components and deployment scenarios of TwinMaker, supported by academic research and AWS Documentation.

Understanding AWS IoT TwinMaker

AWS IoT TwinMaker is a service designed to simplify the creation and management of digital twins. A digital twin is a virtual replica of a physical asset or system that mirrors its real-world counterpart in terms of behavior and attributes. IoT TwinMaker enables organizations to model their physical assets in a digital format, facilitating real-time monitoring, analysis, and simulation. It streamlines the integration of IoT data, enabling organizations to optimize operations, predict and prevent issues, and make data-driven decisions.

Studies on IoT applications emphasize the increasing importance of digital twin models in enhancing system observability and operational planning. AWS IoT TwinMaker facilitates this by offering tools for real-time data fusion, spatial visualization, and scenario simulation. AWS Documentation details its applicability across various industries, including manufacturing, healthcare, and smart infrastructure, where digital replicas support predictive maintenance, optimization, and remote operations.

Use cases and real-world applications

AWS IoT TwinMaker finds applications across industries where real-time monitoring, analysis, and simulation are crucial. Real-world case studies demonstrate how TwinMaker has enabled organizations to enhance asset performance, minimize downtime, and improve decision-making. It plays a pivotal role in predictive maintenance, enabling organizations to address equipment issues proactively. Additionally, TwinMaker supports scenario analysis and what-if simulations, providing a valuable tool for optimizing operations [45].

AWS IoT Greengrass

Digital twins—virtual models of physical systems—have become a key method for monitoring, analyzing, and simulating real-world assets. AWS IoT TwinMaker [44] provides a framework for building and managing digital twins by integrating sensor data, 3D asset models, and contextual metadata. This section outlines the architectural components and deployment scenarios of TwinMaker, supported by academic research and AWS Documentation.

Extending cloud intelligence to the edge of IoT

AWS IoT Greengrass [46] is a service designed to bridge the gap between the cloud and IoT devices at the edge. It allows organizations to deploy AWS Lambda functions and **machine learning (ML)** models directly on IoT devices, enabling local data processing and real-time decision-making. This distributed computing approach reduces the need for round-trip communication with the cloud, minimizing latency and ensuring that critical decisions can be made even when intermittent connectivity.

Research on edge computing in IoT [47] identifies latency reduction, data sovereignty, and bandwidth optimization as key challenges in real-time deployments. AWS IoT Greengrass supports these goals by enabling local data processing, event triggering, and ML inference at the device level. Studies also describe its role in deploying edge AI, particularly in industrial and remote scenarios where continuous cloud connectivity cannot be guaranteed [1] [2].

Use cases and real-world applications

AWS IoT Greengrass is applicable to a wide range of IoT use cases. Real-world examples demonstrate how it empowers organizations across industries. For instance, Greengrass enables predictive maintenance in industrial settings by analyzing sensor data locally and triggering maintenance alerts without constant cloud connectivity. Agriculture facilitates smart farming by processing data from sensors and cameras to optimize irrigation and crop management.

Simplifying deployment with AWS IoT 1-Click

Rapid deployment of IoT devices remains a core requirement in scaling IoT solutions across industries. AWS IoT 1-Click addresses this need by simplifying the provisioning and activation of devices through a low-code interface. This section reviews the design and integration of AWS IoT 1-Click, with emphasis on deployment workflows and use cases, supported by research literature and AWS Documentation.

AWS IoT 1-Click is designed to simplify the complexity associated with deploying IoT devices at scale [48]. It provides a streamlined, one-click approach to provisioning IoT devices, reducing the time and effort required for initial setup. With IoT 1-Click, organizations can easily configure and deploy connected devices, sensors, and buttons, enabling them to rapidly implement IoT solutions.

Studies on IoT adoption [47] note that ease of provisioning is often a barrier to scale, especially when onboarding thousands of distributed devices. AWS IoT 1-Click offers a simplified interface and pre-integrated workflows, making it suitable for rapid rollouts across enterprise and consumer applications [1] [2].

Use cases and real-world applications

AWS IoT 1-Click finds applications in various industries and use cases where rapid IoT deployment is essential. Real-world examples illustrate how organizations leverage IoT 1-Click to simplify device provisioning. It can quickly setup remote patient monitoring devices in the healthcare sector, facilitating timely data collection and healthcare delivery. In manufacturing, it streamlines the deployment of sensors for predictive maintenance, enabling organizations to reduce downtime and increase operational efficiency.

This section will explore practical implementations, best practices, and success stories showcasing how AWS IoT 1-Click revolutionizes IoT deployment. By simplifying the process of provisioning and deploying IoT devices, AWS IoT 1-Click empowers organizations to accelerate their IoT initiatives and unlock the full potential of IoT solutions.

AWS IoT Analytics

Processing and analyzing time-series IoT data is essential for extracting actionable insights at scale. AWS IoT Analytics provides a managed pipeline for ingesting, transforming, and querying device-generated data. This section explores its architecture and application areas, drawing from current research and AWS Documentation.

Harnessing data insights with AWS IoT Analytics

AWS IoT Analytics [49] It is a fully managed service designed to streamline collecting, transforming, and analyzing data generated by IoT devices. It provides a comprehensive framework for ingesting data from various sources, cleansing and enriching it, and securely and scalably storing it. IoT Analytics offers a user-friendly interface that facilitates the creation of complex data pipelines, enabling organizations to derive meaningful insights from their IoT data.

Research on IoT systems [47] underscores the need for reliable, scalable analytics platforms capable of handling heterogeneous data sources. AWS IoT Analytics meets these requirements by offering preprocessing, SQL-based querying, and integration with downstream analytics services, supporting data-driven decision-making across verticals.

Use cases and real-world applications

AWS IoT Analytics is utilized across various industries and use cases where data analysis is crucial. Real-world examples demonstrate how organizations utilize IoT Analytics to derive insights from their IoT data. IoT Analytics can process farm sensor data in the smart agriculture sector to optimize irrigation and crop management, improving yields and resource utilization. In healthcare, it can analyze patient monitoring data to detect anomalies and trigger timely interventions.

AWS IoT Button

Simplified interaction with IoT systems is often a key enabler of prototyping and user engagement. AWS IoT Button provides a programmable, single-action input device that can trigger cloud-based workflows without the need for custom hardware. This section outlines its design and use cases in both enterprise and personal contexts.

Simplicity meets IoT with AWS IoT Button

AWS IoT Button [50] is a compact and programmable device that simplifies IoT interactions with a single press. It allows users to trigger actions, send alerts, or gather data with the push of a button. This device is integrated with the AWS IoT Core service, enabling continuous communication with AWS cloud resources. With the AWS IoT Button, users can create custom workflows and automate tasks, making it a versatile tool for personal and industrial applications.

Research on rapid IoT prototyping [47] highlights the value of intuitive, ready-to-use interfaces for accelerating experimentation and user acceptance. The AWS IoT Button serves this purpose with minimal setup and seamless integration with AWS IoT Core and Lambda.

Use cases and practical applications

AWS IoT Button finds applications in various use cases, from home automation to industrial environments. Real-world examples illustrate how organizations and individuals leverage the simplicity and versatility of the IoT Button. In the home automation context, it can be used to control lights and thermostats, or even order groceries with a single press. It simplifies data collection in industrial settings by allowing workers to trigger data logging or maintenance requests with a button.

We will explore practical implementations, best practices, and success stories showcasing how AWS IoT Button transforms IoT interactions. By providing an accessible and intuitive IoT device, AWS IoT Button enables users to harness the power of IoT without the complexities typically associated with IoT deployments.

AWS IoT Device Defender

Security challenges in IoT environments stem from the distributed nature of devices and the difficulty in maintaining continuous monitoring. AWS IoT Device Defender provides audit, monitoring, and alerting capabilities to protect connected devices against misconfiguration and threats. This section reviews the service's architecture and security model.

IoT security with AWS IoT Device Defender

AWS IoT Device Defender [51] is a fully managed service that assists organizations in securing their IoT devices and applications. It accomplishes this through continuous monitoring, audit trails, and automated mitigation of common security risks. The service helps organizations adhere to best practices, such as ensuring devices run the latest firmware, restricting unauthorized access, and detecting abnormal device behavior.

Studies on IoT risk management [47] emphasize the importance of automated anomaly detection and policy enforcement in securing large fleets. AWS IoT Device Defender supports these capabilities through metric baselines, real-time alerting, and integration with mitigation workflows [1] [2].

Key capabilities and use cases

AWS IoT Device Defender offers a range of capabilities that contribute to enhanced IoT security. These include:

- Continuous auditing of IoT device fleets to identify vulnerabilities and deviations from security policies.
- Real-time alerts and notifications for suspicious device behavior.
- Automatic mitigation actions to respond to security threats and enforce security policies.

Real-world use cases highlight the versatility of AWS IoT Device Defender. It can detect unusual behavior in critical machinery in industrial settings, helping to prevent costly downtime. In a smart home environment, it can alert users to potentially unauthorized access, enhancing overall home security.

AWS IoT Device Management

Managing device fleets at scale requires unified tooling for onboarding, configuration, monitoring, and lifecycle control. AWS IoT Device Management offers a suite of features to simplify these tasks. This section presents the platform's functionality and its role in enterprise-grade IoT operations.

AWS IoT Device Management for IoT fleets

AWS IoT Device Management is a comprehensive service designed to address the complexities of managing IoT device fleets [52]. It enables organizations to securely and efficiently onboard, organize, monitor, and remotely manage their IoT devices at scale. With features such as device provisioning, fleet indexing, and **over-the-air** (**OTA**) updates, AWS IoT Device Management streamlines device lifecycle management.

IoT deployment studies [47] identify scalable device management as a prerequisite for secure and reliable operation. AWS IoT Device Management centralizes inventory tracking, supports over-the-air updates, and provides fine-grained control over device groups and policies [1] [2].

Key capabilities and use cases

AWS IoT Device Management offers a range of capabilities tailored to IoT fleet management:

- **Device provisioning**: Simplifies the process of securely onboarding devices to the IoT platform.
- **Device registry and indexing**: Provides a centralized repository for device information and simplifies searching and filtering.
- **Remote device management**: Enables remote actions like rebooting, resetting, or updating devices OTA.
- **Fleet monitoring**: Offers real-time insights into the health and status of the entire device fleet.

Real-world use cases showcase the versatility of AWS IoT Device Management. In a smart home scenario, it ensures that all connected devices receive timely software updates, thereby enhancing security and functionality. In an industrial IoT environment, it can streamline the management of sensor networks, improving data collection and analytics.

AWS IoT EduKit

Education is central to innovation, and IoT is one of the most transformative technological advances of our time. To connect IoT technology with education, AWS offers the AWS IoT EduKit. This section examines the AWS IoT EduKit, emphasizing its importance in enabling educational institutions, students, and developers to explore IoT technology.

Empowering education with AWS IoT EduKit

AWS IoT EduKit [53] is a hands-on learning platform designed to make IoT development accessible to students, educators, and hobbyists. It integrates hardware kits with cloud resources, enabling users to explore real-world applications while building technical skills.

Research in STEM education [54] supports experiential learning as a driver of engagement and retention. The EduKit model aligns with this by combining hardware experimentation with cloud-native development workflows.

Key features and learning opportunities

AWS IoT EduK areers in technology.

This section will explore practical implementations, showcase educational success stories, and underline the kit's role in democratizing IoT education. The AWS IoT EduKit empowers learners of all levels to unlock their potential, fostering a new generation of IoT innovators.

AWS IoT Events

AWS IoT Events provides the infrastructure for building event-driven workflows triggered by sensor or device data. This section explores how the service supports use cases such as anomaly detection, predictive maintenance, and automated response mechanisms in real-time systems.

Enabling event-driven IoT solutions

AWS IoT Events is a service designed to simplify IoT application development by enabling the detection and response to events from IoT sensors and applications. Events are crucial in IoT scenarios, as they signify meaningful occurrences such as equipment malfunctions, temperature spikes, or security breaches [55]. Detecting and acting upon these events promptly is essential for maintaining system efficiency, safety, and security.

Insights into event-driven IoT

Event-based architecture is a well-documented strategy in IoT systems for improving responsiveness and automation [56]. AWS IoT Events abstracts the complexity of detector models and integrates with services like Lambda and SNS for seamless response orchestration [1] [2].

AWS IoT Events simplifies the implementation of event-driven architecture in IoT solutions. It provides tools for defining event detectors, setting up actions, and integrating with other AWS services without the need for complex coding. This streamlines the development process and allows developers to focus on creating value-added features for their IoT applications.

Key features and use cases

AWS IoT Events offers several key features and use cases:

- **Event detectors**: Users can define custom logic for detecting events based on data from IoT devices.

- **Integration with other AWS services**: It smoothly integrates with AWS Lambda, Amazon SNS, and Amazon S3, enabling automated responses.
- **Real-time monitoring**: It provides real-time monitoring and visualization of IoT events through the AWS IoT Events console.
- **Scalability**: The service can scale to handle large volumes of events from many devices.

Use cases for AWS IoT Events span various industries. For example, in manufacturing, it can be used for predictive maintenance by detecting abnormal behavior in equipment. In agriculture, it can monitor soil moisture levels and trigger irrigation systems when needed. Security applications can benefit from event-based intrusion detection.

AWS IoT RoboRunner

In IoT and robotics, AWS IoT RoboRunner emerges as a game-changing service that marries the power of cloud computing with the precision of robotics. This section explores the multifaceted world of AWS IoT RoboRunner, highlighting its significance, features, and real-world applications.

Empowering robotic applications with intelligence

AWS IoT RoboRunner is a service designed to facilitate the coordination and orchestration of robotic applications. It offers a unified platform for managing and deploying robotic fleets, enabling developers to build intelligent and responsive robotic systems. This service leverages the AWS cloud infrastructure, ML capabilities, and IoT connectivity to empower robots with enhanced decision-making abilities.

Perspectives on IoT-enabled robotics

Research articles [57] underscore the transformative potential of IoT-enabled robotics. Integrating IoT sensors and cloud-based analytics into robotic systems allows them to process vast amounts of data in real-time, make informed decisions, and adapt to changing environments. IoT plays a pivotal role in enhancing the autonomy, efficiency, and safety of robotic applications [58].

AWS IoT RoboRunner streamlines the development and deployment of IoT-enabled robotic solutions. It offers tools for managing robot fleets, creating custom robot applications, and integrating with other AWS services, such as AWS Lambda, Amazon SageMaker, and Amazon Polly. This comprehensive suite of capabilities empowers developers to build intelligent robots to perform various tasks.

Key features and real-world applications

AWS IoT RoboRunner boasts several key features and real-world use cases:

- **Fleet management**: It provides centralized control and monitoring of robotic fleets, making managing and scaling deployments easier.

- **Custom application development**: Developers can create custom robot applications using familiar programming languages and frameworks.

- **ML integration**: Integration with Amazon SageMaker allows robots to leverage ML models for tasks like image recognition and natural language processing.

- **Scalability and reliability**: The service is designed to handle large-scale deployments, ensuring the reliability of robotic applications in diverse scenarios.

Real-world applications of AWS IoT RoboRunner include industries such as logistics, healthcare, manufacturing, and agriculture. In logistics, robots equipped with IoT sensors can autonomously navigate warehouses, enhancing inventory management and order fulfillment. IoT-enabled robotic assistants can aid in patient care and medication delivery within healthcare settings. Manufacturing benefits from robotic automation powered by IoT data for quality control and process improvement.

AWS Partner Device Catalog

The *AWS Partner Device Catalog* section within the AWS Cloud Masterclass explains the significance, features, and real-world applications of this service, which play a key role in the IoT ecosystem. AWS Partner Device Catalog is a resource that enables organizations to discover and evaluate devices and solutions from AWS partners, enhancing the breadth and depth of IoT implementations.

Introduction to AWS Partner Device Catalog

AWS Partner Device Catalog serves as a valuable repository of IoT devices and solutions offered by AWS partners. With the explosive growth of IoT, organizations often face the challenge of selecting the right hardware and software components for their IoT projects. AWS Partner Device Catalog addresses this challenge by providing a comprehensive and organized directory of devices compatible with AWS IoT services.

Academic insights into IoT ecosystem expansion

Research papers [59] emphasize the importance of expanding ecosystems in the IoT field. As the IoT landscape develops, collaboration among IoT solution providers, device manufacturers, and cloud service providers becomes more essential. Research indicates that partnerships and collaborations foster innovation and facilitate the adoption of IoT technologies across various industries [1] [2].

The AWS Partner Device Catalog showcases collaboration by connecting AWS customers with many AWS partners offering IoT devices, software, and services. Using the catalog helps organizations accelerate their IoT projects, reduce development cycles, and access a broad selection of pre-qualified solutions.

Key features and benefits

AWS Partner Device Catalog offers several key features and benefits:

- **Device discovery**: Users can search for IoT devices and solutions based on specific criteria such as device type, industry, and connectivity protocol.

- **Solution evaluation**: Organizations can access detailed information about devices, including specifications, pricing, and integration guides, facilitating informed decision-making.

- **Interoperability**: AWS ensures that devices listed in the catalog are compatible with AWS IoT services, providing customers with assurance.

- **Industry verticals**: The catalog covers various industries, including healthcare, manufacturing, smart cities, agriculture, and more, making it versatile for diverse IoT applications.

Real-world applications

The section will explore real-world uses of the AWS Partner Device Catalog across different industries. For example, in healthcare, organizations can locate certified medical devices that seamlessly connect with AWS IoT for remote patient monitoring and data analysis. IoT sensors and devices in the catalog support precision farming in agriculture, helping to improve crop yields and resource efficiency.

The AWS Partner Device Catalog is a valuable resource for organizations starting IoT projects. It simplifies device selection, reduces integration challenges, and accelerates the deployment of IoT solutions. This section will further demonstrate the catalog's practical applications through case studies and examples, illustrating how it enables organizations to navigate the broad IoT landscape effectively.

FreeRTOS

In the rapidly expanding IoT landscape, where connected devices play a pivotal role, the *FreeRTOS* section within the *AWS Cloud Masterclass* examines the importance of **real-time operating systems** (**RTOSs**) in enabling IoT devices. FreeRTOS, an open-source RTOS developed by AWS, has emerged as a fundamental tool for building IoT applications that demand precise timing, reliability, and resource efficiency.

Real-time operating systems empowering IoT devices

FreeRTOS, short for Free RTOS, is a highly portable, open-source RTOS kernel. It is designed to facilitate the development of embedded systems and IoT applications by providing a robust framework for multitasking, inter-process communication, and hardware abstraction. Developed by AWS, FreeRTOS is a testament to its commitment to supporting IoT developers with a powerful, free-to-use solution.

Academic research insights into IoT and RTOS

RTOSs are a foundational component in embedded IoT deployments. FreeRTOS [61] maintained by AWS, supports deterministic scheduling, hardware abstraction, and resource efficiency for microcontroller-based devices.

Literature on embedded systems consistently cites RTOS platforms as essential for meeting real-time constraints in sectors such as manufacturing, automotive, and medical devices [1] [2]. FreeRTOS extends these capabilities with integrated support for secure connectivity and cloud integration.

Key features and benefits

FreeRTOS offers several key features and benefits tailored to the IoT landscape:

- **Portability**: FreeRTOS supports various microcontroller architectures, making it versatile for IoT devices with diverse hardware platforms.
- **Real-time capabilities**: It provides deterministic task scheduling, enabling IoT devices to meet stringent timing requirements.
- **Resource efficiency**: FreeRTOS is designed to be memory-efficient, which is crucial for IoT devices with limited resources.
- **Security**: AWS actively maintains and updates FreeRTOS to address security vulnerabilities, ensuring the integrity of IoT deployments.

Real-world applications

This section explores real-world uses of FreeRTOS in different industries. For example, in industrial automation, FreeRTOS is essential for controlling and monitoring manufacturing processes in real-time. It supports connected car applications in the automotive industry, enabling features like telematics and infotainment systems. By examining these examples, readers will understand how FreeRTOS plays a key role in various IoT applications.ons.

AWS integration

As an AWS product, FreeRTOS seamlessly integrates with AWS IoT Core, allowing IoT developers to easily build end-to-end solutions. IoT devices running FreeRTOS can securely connect to AWS IoT Core for data ingestion, processing, and analysis, leveraging the full suite of AWS services.

Final thoughts on FreeRTOS

FreeRTOS is a foundational element in the IoT ecosystem, enabling developers to build highly responsive and reliable IoT applications across various industries. Its open-source nature, extensive community support, and compatibility with various microcontroller architectures make it a valuable resource for IoT developers.

Satellite

This section explores AWS's innovative solution for satellite communication and data reception. AWS Ground Station introduced a significant leap in simplifying and optimizing the management and operation of satellite communication networks.

Introduction to AWS Ground Station

AWS Ground Station is a fully managed service that allows customers to communicate with, control, and ingest satellite data in orbit. It eliminates the need for building and maintaining complex ground infrastructure, reducing the time, effort, and cost traditionally associated with satellite communication. AWS Ground Station makes satellite data accessible and actionable for various applications, including weather forecasting, environmental monitoring, disaster response, and communication.

Academic insights into satellite communication

Research papers [63] emphasize the importance of efficient satellite communication networks for a variety of applications. Satellites have become integral in Earth observation, scientific research, telecommunications, and national security. AWS Ground Station addresses the challenges of operating and managing these satellite systems, ensuring that data can be reliably received and processed.

Key features and benefits

AWS Ground Station offers several key features and benefits:

- **Global coverage**: With a network of Ground Station strategically located worldwide, AWS Ground Station provides global coverage, ensuring that satellite data can be received no matter where the satellite is in orbit.

- **On-demand access**: Users can schedule and access Ground Station resources on demand, significantly reducing the time and effort required to setup and maintain ground infrastructure.

- **Integration with AWS**: Data received from satellites can be easily integrated with other AWS services, such as Amazon S3 for storage and AWS Lambda for data processing, enabling real-time analysis and insights.

- **Security**: AWS Ground Station is designed to ensure that satellite communication remains secure and protected.

Real-world applications

This section examines the real-world applications of AWS Ground Station, encompassing a range of uses from Earth observation and environmental monitoring to disaster management and telecommunications. For example, in the field of Earth observation, AWS Ground Station facilitates the rapid collection and analysis of satellite imagery, vital for monitoring environmental changes, agricultural practices, and disaster response efforts [64].

AWS integration

AWS Ground Station integrates impeccably with the broader AWS ecosystem, allowing users to leverage AWS's extensive set of cloud services. This integration enables users to process, analyze, and store satellite data efficiently, creating actionable insights and accelerating decision-making processes.

Final thoughts on AWS Ground Station

AWS Ground Station represents a groundbreaking advancement in satellite communication, making it more accessible, cost-effective, and efficient for a wide range of users. Its global coverage, on-demand access, and integration with AWS services position it as a pivotal tool in the realm of satellite communication and data utilization.

In this chapter, we discussed AWS's remarkable array of networking, IoT, and satellite solutions that empower organizations to achieve unparalleled levels of connectivity, data insights, and communication capabilities. From building and securing Amazon VPCs to orchestrating microservices with AWS App Mesh, AWS has emerged as a transformative force in the cloud computing landscape [65]. The integration of AWS Cloud Map simplifies service discovery, while AWS Direct Connect and AWS Global Accelerator enhance connectivity and global reach.

In the IoT space, AWS IoT Core serves as the foundation for secure and scalable IoT applications. AWS IoT FleetWise, AWS IoT SiteWise, and AWS IoT TwinMaker offer powerful tools for managing and analyzing IoT data on scale. Moreover, AWS IoT Greengrass extends AWS capabilities to edge devices, enabling real-time processing and decision-making in IoT deployments. The chapter highlighted AWS's commitment to innovation with services such as AWS IoT 1-Click, AWS IoT Analytics, AWS IoT Button, and AWS IoT Device Defender, all of which contribute to seamless integration and secure management of IoT ecosystems.

AWS Ground Station enables direct downlink of satellite data into the AWS cloud, reducing latency and eliminating the need for traditional ground infrastructure. It provides on-demand scheduling, global coverage, and integration with AWS analytics and storage services.

This chapter has highlighted AWS's strategic approach to cloud networking, IoT, and satellite communications. Through platforms like Ground Station, VPC, IoT Core, and App Mesh, AWS offers organizations a cohesive ecosystem for building connected, scalable, and intelligence-driven systems—supported by a growing body of research and real-world applications [66].

In conclusion, AWS networking and content delivery, IoT, and satellite services enable organizations to leverage the power of the cloud for advanced networking, data analytics, and satellite communication. The chapter emphasized the value of these AWS services across diverse industries and applications, ultimately enabling organizations to drive innovation, achieve operational efficiencies, and remain competitive in today's dynamic digital landscape.

Conclusion

In this chapter, we examined how AWS combines networking, IoT, and satellite services into a unified ecosystem that supports modern digital transformation at scale. From the core connectivity provided by Amazon VPC and AWS Direct Connect to the global optimization enabled by AWS Global Accelerator, AWS offers a complete set of tools to develop secure, resilient, and high-performance network architectures. In the IoT area, AWS enables real-time, edge-enabled intelligence with services, such as AWS IoT Greengrass, and delivers insights through AWS IoT Analytics and TwinMaker. Lastly, AWS Ground Station extends this digital infrastructure into space, allowing seamless access to satellite data without the challenge of owning and managing traditional ground infrastructure. This chapter demonstrates how these services work together, not just as independent innovations, but as modular building blocks within a larger AWS strategy, enabling organizations to move faster, operate more intelligently, and innovate worldwide. As we move into the next chapter on security, identity, and compliance, we emphasize that connectivity is only as strong as the security frameworks that protect it—a fundamental principle for building trust in any cloud-native enterprise system.

The next chapter will explore security, identity, and compliance within the AWS ecosystem. Readers will learn about key components and best practices for maintaining a secure cloud environment, including identity management, access controls, data protection, and regulatory compliance. We will examine AWS services such as IAM, AWS KMS, and AWS Config, giving you the knowledge and tools to protect your cloud assets and uphold strong security measures.

Chapter 5

Security, Identity, and Compliance

Introduction

In an age where data is the lifeblood of modern enterprises, safeguarding information and ensuring compliance with stringent regulations have become paramount. This chapter discusses security, identity, and compliance within the AWS cloud ecosystem. Here, we will explore an extensive array of AWS services designed to fortify your digital fortress. From Amazon Cognito, a robust solution for managing user identities and authentication, to Amazon Security Hub, a centralized hub for security compliance monitoring, each topic in this chapter is a vital component in ensuring the safety and integrity of your cloud infrastructure. Whether you seek to protect sensitive data, defend against cyber threats, or establish granular access controls, this chapter equips you with the knowledge and tools to confidently navigate the complex landscape of cloud security. Welcome to the AWS cloud computing masterclass, where we understand security, identity, and compliance to empower you in securing your digital assets.

Structure

In this chapter, we will discuss the following topics:

- Amazon Cognito
- Identity management for your apps
- Amazon Detective

- Amazon GuardDuty
- Amazon Inspector
- Amazon Macie
- Amazon Security Lake
- Amazon Verified Permissions
- AWS Artifact
- AWS Audit Manager
- AWS Certificate Manager
- AWS CloudHSM
- AWS Directory Service
- AWS Firewall Manager
- AWS IAM Identity Center
- AWS Identity and Access Management
- AWS Key Management Service
- AWS Network Firewall
- AWS Resource Access Manager
- AWS Secrets Manager
- AWS Security Hub
- AWS Shield
- AWS web application firewall
- Elevating security and compliance in AWS

Objectives

By the end of this chapter, we will demystify these AWS services, providing practical insights and best practices for implementation. With a focus on real-world scenarios and hands-on guidance, this chapter aims to equip newcomers and seasoned AWS professionals with the expertise needed to bolster security, manage identities, and maintain compliance in the cloud. Whether you are a security enthusiast seeking to explore the latest advancements or a cloud practitioner looking to fortify your organization's defenses, this chapter provides a comprehensive guide to the ever-evolving world of AWS security, identity, and compliance services.

Amazon Cognito

In today's cloud computing landscape, ensuring secure and efficient management of user identities and access to your applications is paramount. Amazon Cognito, an integral part of

AWS **Identity and Access Management** (**IAM**) services, stands out as a robust solution for these challenges. This section will delve into Amazon Cognito's architecture, features, and best practices, referencing scholarly articles and official AWS sources to understand its capabilities comprehensively [1].

Understanding Amazon Cognito

Amazon Cognito, introduced in 2014, is a managed service designed to simplify the implementation of user authentication and authorization in applications. It consists of three primary components:

- **User pools**: Amazon Cognito user pools act as user directories that facilitate user registration and authentication [2]. These pools are highly versatile and can integrate with various identity providers, including popular social platforms like *Google* and *Facebook*. User pools also support customizable authentication flows, enabling developers to create tailored user experiences.

- **Federated identities**: Beyond authentication, Amazon Cognito Federated Identities, or identity pools, bridge the gap to provide secure identity management [2]. Identity pools grant temporary, limited-privilege AWS credentials to users, allowing them to securely access other AWS services without needing long-term AWS credentials. This seamless integration simplifies authorization processes for developers [3].

- **Sync service**: The Amazon Cognito Sync service ensures data synchronization across devices and platforms for authenticated users. It is a secure data storage solution in the AWS cloud, ensuring data consistency across multiple devices and enabling offline access to data.

Key features and benefits

The following are the key features of Amazon Cognito:

- **Scalability**: Amazon Cognito seamlessly scales to accommodate a growing user base, ensuring high availability and reliability for your applications.

- **Security**: Built-in security features include **multi-factor authentication** (**MFA**), data encryption, and user account recovery, enhancing the protection of user data.

- **Customization**: Amazon Cognito offers a high degree of customization, empowering developers to design authentication and authorization flows tailored to their application's needs.

- **Integration**: Its seamless integration with other AWS services, such as AWS Lambda, Amazon S3, and Amazon API Gateway, enables the development of robust serverless applications.

Best practices for Amazon Cognito implementation

Let us discuss the best practices for Amazon Cognito implementation:

- **User pools for user management**: Utilize Amazon Cognito user pools for user registration, sign-in, and authentication, streamlining user identity management.

- **Implement MFA**: Enhance security by enabling MFA, adding an extra layer of protection for user accounts.

- **Integrate with federated identities**: Combine user pools to grant users secure access to AWS resources, adhering to the principle of least privilege.

- **Prioritize data encryption**: Encrypt sensitive user data at rest and in transit to safeguard user privacy.

- **Continuous monitoring and audit**: Regularly monitor user activities, review logs, and setup alerts to promptly identify and respond to suspicious behavior [4].

This section provides a comprehensive exploration of Amazon Cognito, drawing insights from scholarly articles and official AWS Documentation.

Identity management for your apps

Identity management is at the core of securing cloud-based applications and resources. In this section, we will explore identity management for your AWS-hosted applications. We will explore the best practices, AWS services, and scholarly articles to help you establish a robust identity management strategy following industry standards and security principles [5] [6].

The significance of identity management

Effective identity management ensures the security, privacy, and compliance of your applications. Identity management encompasses various aspects, including user authentication, authorization, and access control. By implementing strong identity management practices, you can mitigate risks associated with unauthorized access, data breaches, and compliance violations [5] [6].

AWS Identity and Access Management

AWS provides a comprehensive IAM service that enables you to manage user identities, roles, and permissions within your AWS environment. IAM allows you to:

- **Create and manage users**: You can create IAM users and grant them specific permissions to access AWS resources [6].

- **Use roles for temporary access**: IAM roles enable access to AWS services. For example, you can assign roles to Amazon EC2 instances for secure interaction with other AWS services [7].

- **Define fine-grained permissions**: IAM policies allow you to define fine-grained permissions for users and resources. This ensures the principle of least privilege, where users have only the permissions necessary for their tasks [8].

- **MFA**: AWS IAM supports MFA, adding an extra layer of security to user accounts [7].

Best practices for identity management

Let us discuss the best practices for identity management [8]:

- **Implement strong authentication**: Enforce strong password policies and consider MFA for enhanced security.

- **Role-based access control (RBAC)**: Follow RBAC principles to ensure users have appropriate permissions based on their roles and responsibilities.

- **Regularly review and audit permissions**: Periodically review and audit permissions to remove unnecessary access and ensure compliance.

- **Least privilege principle**: Apply the principle of least privilege to restrict user access to only what they need to perform their tasks.

- **Centralized identity federation**: Implement centralized identity federation to allow **single sign-on (SSO)** for multiple AWS accounts and services [6].

This section highlights the crucial role of identity management in protecting AWS-hosted applications and resources. By adhering to best practices and leveraging AWS IAM, you can establish a robust identity management framework for your cloud-based solutions. [8] Subsequent sections in this chapter will explore additional facets of security, identity, and compliance within the AWS ecosystem.

Amazon Detective

In this section, we will explore Amazon Detective, an AWS service designed to assist in investigating potential security issues across your AWS resources. We will discuss its key features and benefits [7] [9].

Understanding Amazon Detective

Amazon Detective is a security service that provides detailed insights into the activities and behaviors across your AWS environment. It simplifies identifying potential security issues' root causes and impact, enabling faster and more effective responses to security incidents [9].

Key features of Amazon Detective

Let us discuss the key features of Amazon Detective [9]:

- **Automated data collection**: Amazon Detective automatically collects log data from multiple AWS services, aggregating it into a unified view for analysis.

- **Graph-based visualizations**: The service uses graph theory to create visual representations of the relationships and behaviors of AWS resources, making it easier to identify anomalies and threats.

- **Behavioral analytics**: Amazon Detective employs **machine learning** (**ML**) models to establish baselines of normal behavior, helping you identify deviations that may indicate security issues.

- **Security findings**: It provides detailed security findings, including the affected resources, their activities, and recommended remediation steps.

- **Integration with AWS security services**: Amazon Detective integrates with other AWS security services, enhancing your overall security posture.

Benefits of Amazon Detective

Let us discuss the benefits of Amazon Detective [9]:

- **Simplified investigations**: The service streamlines investigating security incidents by providing a consolidated view of relevant data.

- **Faster response**: Amazon Detective enables quicker reactions to security threats with automated data collection and analysis.

- **Improved visibility**: The graph-based visualizations offer enhanced visibility into the relationships between AWS resources, aiding in threat detection.

Use cases

Amazon Detective is particularly valuable when investigating security incidents, analyzing deviations from normal behavior, and identifying potential threats to your AWS resources [9].

Amazon Detective offers valuable insights into security incidents, enabling security teams to respond effectively. You can identify and address potential security threats within your AWS environment by leveraging automated data collection and behavioral analytics [9]. The subsequent sections in this chapter will explore additional AWS services and strategies for enhancing security, identity, and compliance.

Amazon GuardDuty

This section will explore Amazon GuardDuty, an AWS service designed to protect your AWS resources by continuously monitoring for malicious and unauthorized activities. We will delve into its key features and benefits [10] [11].

Understanding Amazon GuardDuty

Amazon GuardDuty is a managed threat detection service that continuously monitors your AWS accounts, workloads, and data for suspicious and malicious activities. It leverages ML and anomaly detection to identify potential security threats, making it an essential component of your AWS security strategy [10].

Key features of Amazon GuardDuty

Let us discuss the key features of Amazon GuardDuty [10]:

- **Threat detection**: GuardDuty analyzes data from AWS CloudTrail logs, Amazon VPC Flow Logs, and DNS logs to detect various threats, including unauthorized access, data exfiltration, and malware deployments.

- **ML**: The service employs ML models to identify anomalies and deviations from baseline behavior, which helps pinpoint potential threats.

- **Integrated threat intelligence**: GuardDuty enhances threat detection capabilities using threat intelligence feeds from AWS, security partners, and open-source lists.

- **Security findings**: It provides detailed findings with prioritized alerts, including information about affected AWS resources and recommended remediation steps.

Benefits of Amazon GuardDuty

Let us discuss the benefits of Amazon GuardDuty [10]:

- **Improved security posture**: GuardDuty enhances security by identifying and prioritizing potential threats in real-time.

- **Automated threat detection**: The service automates the detection process, reducing the time required to identify security incidents.

- **Scalability**: Amazon GuardDuty scales with your AWS environment, ensuring that you have continuous threat detection as your infrastructure grows.

Use cases

Amazon GuardDuty is valuable for organizations of all sizes. It provides proactive threat detection and helps secure AWS workloads and resources. It is beneficial in scenarios where rapid threat identification is critical [10].

Amazon GuardDuty plays a crucial role in enhancing the security of your AWS environment by providing real-time threat detection and automated alerts. By continuously monitoring suspicious activities and leveraging threat intelligence, GuardDuty helps you respond effectively to potential security threats [10]. The following sections will explore additional AWS services and strategies for securing your cloud infrastructure.

Amazon Inspector

This section will discuss Amazon Inspector, an AWS service that helps you identify security issues and vulnerabilities in your AWS resources. We will explore its key features, benefits, and use cases [12] [13].

Understanding Amazon Inspector

Amazon Inspector is a security assessment service that automates the identification of vulnerabilities and security issues within your AWS environment. It analyzes the behavior of your applications and resources, helping you to understand their security state and take corrective actions [12].

Key features of Amazon Inspector

Let us discuss the key features of Amazon Inspector [12]:

- **Agent-based assessments**: Inspector uses agents that can be deployed on your EC2 instances to collect data and assess the security of your applications and systems.

- **Security rules**: It provides a set of predefined rules based on best practices for security assessments. You can also create custom rules tailored to your specific requirements.

- **Integration**: Inspector integrates with other AWS services, including AWS CloudWatch and AWS Security Hub, to view your security posture comprehensively.

- **Scalability**: The service is designed to scale your infrastructure, allowing you to assess many instances simultaneously.

Benefits of Amazon Inspector

Let us discuss the benefits of Amazon Inspector [12]:

- **Automated security assessments**: Amazon Inspector automates security assessments, saving time and effort compared to manual assessments.

- **Actionable findings**: It provides detailed findings and recommendations for remediation, helping you address security issues effectively.

- **Continuous monitoring:** Inspector supports continuous monitoring, allowing you to maintain a proactive approach to security.

Use cases

Amazon Inspector is valuable for organizations that want to ensure the security of their AWS workloads. It is beneficial in scenarios where compliance with security standards and regulations is essential [12].

Amazon Inspector provides an automated and scalable approach to security assessments in your AWS environment. Identifying vulnerabilities and security issues empowers organizations to enhance their security posture proactively. [12] In the subsequent sections of this chapter, we will explore additional AWS services and strategies for securing your cloud infrastructure.

Amazon Macie

This section will explore Amazon Macie, a powerful AWS service designed to discover, classify, and protect sensitive data. You will gain an understanding of Macie's capabilities, its role in data security, and how to leverage it effectively [14] [15] [16].

Protecting your sensitive data with Amazon Macie

Amazon Macie is an intelligent data security and privacy service that helps organizations discover, classify, and protect sensitive data across their AWS environment [14]. Its advanced ML algorithms analyze data access patterns, enabling you to identify and safeguard sensitive information more effectively.

Key features of Amazon Macie

Let us discuss the key features of Amazon Macie [14]:

- **Data discovery**: Macie automatically detects and classifies sensitive data, such as **personally identifiable information** (**PII**), financial data, and intellectual property.

- **Visibility**: Gain visibility into how data is accessed and shared across your AWS resources, helping you identify potential security risks.

- **Real-time alerts**: Macie provides real-time alerts when it detects suspicious or unauthorized activities related to sensitive data.

- **Integration**: Seamlessly integrates with other AWS services, making it easy to incorporate data security into your existing workflows.

Benefits of using Amazon Macie

Let us discuss the Benefits of using Amazon Macie [14]:

- **Enhanced data protection**: Macie helps you implement robust data protection measures by identifying and classifying sensitive data.

- **Compliance**: Ensuring data privacy and security assists in meeting regulatory requirements such as GDPR, HIPAA, and CCPA.
- **Operational efficiency**: Provides automated data discovery and alerts, reducing the time and effort required for manual data monitoring.

Use cases

Amazon Macie is particularly valuable for organizations dealing with sensitive data, such as healthcare, finance, and e-commerce. It is also beneficial for maintaining compliance with data protection regulations [14].

Amazon Macie empowers organizations to control and protect their sensitive data from unauthorized access and potential breaches.[13]. Subsequent sections of this chapter will explore AWS services that contribute to the cloud's comprehensive security, identity, and compliance framework.

Amazon Security Lake

This section will explore Amazon Security Lake, an essential AWS service for managing security data and enhancing your cloud environment's security and compliance posture [17] [18] [19].

Security insights data lake with AWS Security Lake

Amazon Security Lake is a fully managed data lake solution designed to ingest, store, and analyze vast amounts of security data from various AWS services and cloud environments [17]. It offers a centralized repository for your security information, enabling you to gain deeper insights, detect anomalies, and respond effectively to security threats.

Key features of Amazon Security Lake

Let us discuss the key features of Amazon Security Lake:[17]:

- **Data ingestion**: Security Lake allows the automated ingestion of security data from various AWS services, including Amazon GuardDuty, AWS Config, and Amazon Macie.
- **Data storage**: The service provides scalable and durable storage for your security data, ensuring it remains accessible and reliable.
- **Analytics and search**: Security Lake supports advanced analytics and search capabilities, making it easier to query and analyze your security data.
- **Integration**: Seamlessly integrates with AWS security services and partner solutions, enhancing your security posture.

Benefits of using Amazon Security Lake

Let us discuss the Benefits of using Amazon Security Lake [17]:

- **Centralized security data**: A unified view of security data lets you detect and respond to threats more efficiently.

- **Automated threat detection**: Analyzing security data at scale enables automated threat detection and response.

- **Compliance**: Helps organizations meet regulatory and compliance requirements by storing and managing security data effectively.

Use cases

Amazon Security Lake is valuable for organizations of all sizes that prioritize security and compliance. It particularly benefits industries with strict regulatory requirements, such as finance, healthcare, and government [17].

Amazon Security Lake is a fundamental component of an organization's security strategy in AWS. It allows for comprehensive security data analysis and incident response [17]. In the subsequent sections of this chapter, we will continue to explore AWS services that contribute to the robust security, identity, and compliance framework in the cloud.

Amazon Verified Permissions

This section will explore Amazon Verified Permissions, a crucial component of AWS IAM services [20] [21] [22].

Enforcing the least privilege access control

Amazon Verified Permissions is an IAM feature that enforces the principle of least privilege, a fundamental security best practice. The principle dictates that individuals or systems should have access only to the resources and actions necessary to perform their tasks [20].

Key aspects of Amazon Verified Permissions

Let us discuss the key aspects of Amazon Verified Permissions [20]:

- **Access analyzer**: This tool examines policies to identify unintended access and offers detailed findings on resources that can be accessed from outside accounts.

- **Resource policies**: Resource owners can create policies to specify who can access their resources, thus ensuring a secure and controlled environment.

- **Access control**: Verified Permissions facilitates fine-grained access control by allowing you to define and monitor resource permissions.

Use cases

Amazon Verified Permissions is valuable for any AWS customer concerned about security and compliance. It helps organizations establish control over their resources and ensures that permissions align with business requirements [20].

Benefits of Amazon Verified Permissions

Let us discuss the benefits of Amazon Verified Permissions [20]:

- **Enhanced security**: Identifying and limiting unintended access fortifies your AWS environment's security posture.

- **Compliance**: It assists organizations in meeting compliance requirements and industry standards by enforcing strict access controls.

- **Resource management**: Verified Permissions simplifies resource management, allowing resource owners to dictate access.

Amazon Verified Permissions is a fundamental tool in AWS IAM that enhances security and compliance by maintaining strict control over resource access [20]. In the subsequent sections of this chapter, we will continue to explore AWS services and features that contribute to building a secure and compliant cloud infrastructure.

AWS Artifact

This section delves into AWS Artifact, a service that provides access to AWS compliance reports and resources [23] [24] [25].

In-depth source of AWS compliance information

AWS Artifact is a centralized repository of compliance documentation for AWS services, enabling customers to access reports and other resources. This resource is invaluable for organizations navigating the complex compliance requirements and regulations landscape [23].

Key features of AWS Artifact

Let us discuss the Benefits of Amazon Verified Permissions [23]:

- **Compliance reports**: AWS Artifact offers a comprehensive collection of reports and certifications covering various compliance frameworks and regulations.

- **Resource library**: In addition to reports, it provides access to a library of white papers and guides, aiding organizations in understanding and securely implementing AWS services.

- **Agreements and contracts**: AWS customers can review and accept agreements online, simplifying compliance.

Use cases

AWS Artifact benefits many organizations, from startups to large enterprises. It is particularly crucial for businesses operating in highly regulated industries, such as healthcare or finance, that require strict compliance standards [23].

Benefits of AWS Artifact

Let us discuss the benefits of AWS Artifact [23]:

- **Simplified compliance**: It provides an easy way to access documentation needed for audits and compliance assessments.

- **Comprehensive information**: With a vast library of reports and resources, it offers an extensive knowledge base for maintaining a secure and compliant AWS infrastructure.

- **Time and cost savings**: Streamlining the compliance process and eliminating the need for physical document handling saves time and resources.

AWS Artifact is an essential tool for organizations striving to maintain compliance with industry standards and regulatory requirements [23]. As we proceed through this chapter, we will continue to explore AWS services and features designed to enhance the security and compliance of your cloud infrastructure.

AWS Audit Manager

This section will explore AWS Audit Manager, a powerful service designed to help organizations automate and streamline auditing. [26] [27] [28].

Automating auditing with AWS Audit Manager

Auditing is critical to maintaining security and compliance within your AWS environment. AWS Audit Manager is a service that simplifies the auditing process, making it more efficient and less intensive [26]. It enables organizations to automate the collection of audit evidence, reducing the manual effort required for compliance assessments [26].

Key features of AWS Audit Manager

Let us discuss the key features of AWS Audit Manager [26]:

- **Pre-built frameworks**: AWS Audit Manager offers frameworks that match various regulatory standards and best practices. These frameworks can be customized to align with your organization's specific requirements.

- **Evidence collection**: The service streamlines evidence collection by automatically gathering data from AWS Config, AWS CloudTrail, and other AWS services.

- **Assessment reports**: Based on the collected evidence, assessment reports help organizations understand their compliance posture.

Use cases

AWS Audit Manager is valuable for any organization that needs to adhere to regulatory standards or best practices. This includes sectors such as healthcare (HIPAA), finance (PCI DSS), and many others [26].

Benefits of AWS Audit Manager

Let us discuss the benefits of AWS Audit Manager [26]:

- **Time savings**: Automation reduces the time and effort needed for auditing, allowing organizations to focus on addressing compliance gaps.

- **Customization**: The ability to customize audit frameworks ensures that assessments are tailored to an organization's unique requirements.

- **Streamlined compliance**: It streamlines the compliance process, making it easier for organizations to demonstrate adherence to regulations and standards.

AWS Audit Manager is an essential tool for organizations looking to simplify and streamline their auditing process, particularly when compliance with regulatory standards is required [26]. In the subsequent sections of this chapter, we will continue to explore AWS services and features dedicated to enhancing the security and compliance of your cloud infrastructure.

AWS Certificate Manager

This section discusses **AWS Certificate Manager (ACM)**, a service that simplifies the management of SSL/TLS certificates for your AWS-based applications and websites [29] [30] [31].

Safe web applications with AWS Certificate Manager

ACM is a service that assists in provisioning, managing, and deploying SSL/TLS certificates for applications and services running on AWS. It streamlines securing your web applications by offering several key benefits.

Key features of AWS Certificate Manager

Let us discuss the key features of ACM [29]:

- **Certificate provisioning**: ACM makes it easy to request SSL/TLS certificates directly from the AWS Management Console, CLI, or SDKs.

- **Automated certificate renewal**: ACM automates the renewal process for your certificates, reducing the risk of expired certificates.
- **Integrated with AWS services**: ACM seamlessly integrates with other AWS services, such as Amazon CloudFront, **Elastic Load Balancing** (**ELB**), and API Gateway, ensuring your applications remain secure.

Use cases

ACM is invaluable for any organization hosting web applications or AWS websites [29]. It ensures data security, encrypts data in transit, and establishes user trust.

Benefits of AWS Certificate Manager

Let us discuss the benefits of ACM [29]:

- **Simplified management**: ACM simplifies the complex process of certificate management, enabling users to focus on their applications.
- **Cost-effective**: The service is cost-effective, as there are no additional charges for ACM.
- **Enhanced security**: SSL/TLS certificates are essential for encrypting data in transit, and ACM ensures that your applications remain secure.

ACM is a fundamental component in the AWS suite of services for ensuring the security of web applications and websites. In the subsequent sections of this chapter, we will continue to explore AWS services dedicated to enhancing the security and compliance of your cloud infrastructure.

AWS CloudHSM

This section will explore the AWS CloudHSM service and provide a detailed overview of its functionality, use cases, and benefits [32] [33] [34].

Introduction to AWS CloudHSM

AWS cloud **hardware security module** (**HSM**) is a cloud-based hardware security module that allows users to generate and manage encryption keys for their applications and data securely and compliantly [32]. AWS CloudHSM provides a dedicated hardware security module to protect sensitive data using encryption keys. It offers a FIPS 140-2 Level 3 validated device that helps you meet various industry standards and compliance requirements [32] [33].

Key features and benefits

Let us discuss the key features and benefits of AWS CloudHSM [32]:

- **High-level security**: AWS CloudHSM provides physical protection of cryptographic keys, making it highly secure for applications that require robust encryption.

- **Compliance**: This service is particularly beneficial for applications that require compliance with regulations like PCI DSS, HIPAA, and others.
- **Integration**: CloudHSM integrates seamlessly with AWS services like Amazon RDS, Redshift, and Lambda, as well as with many third-party applications.

Use cases

AWS CloudHSM is often used in applications where cryptographic keys are critical for securing data. Some everyday use cases include securing payment processing, protecting PII, and ensuring data privacy in healthcare applications [32].

Getting started with AWS CloudHSM

You can provision an HSM through the AWS Management Console, SDKs, or CLI to use AWS CloudHSM [32]. After provisioning, you can create and manage your keys securely.

AWS CloudHSM is a crucial component for securing sensitive data in the AWS cloud. In the following sections of this chapter, we will continue to explore AWS services dedicated to enhancing the security, identity, and compliance of your cloud infrastructure.

AWS Directory Service

This section will discuss AWS Directory Service and provide a comprehensive overview of its features, use cases, and advantages [35] [36] [37].

Introduction to AWS Directory Service

AWS Directory Service is a managed service that allows you to connect, migrate, and manage Microsoft **Active Directory** (**AD**) workloads on the AWS cloud. It offers various directory types to meet your needs, including Microsoft AD, Simple AD, and AD Connector [35].

Key features and benefits

Let us discuss the key features and benefits of AWS Directory Service [35]:

- **Integration with AWS workloads**: AWS Directory Service integrates AD workloads with various AWS services, including Amazon RDS, WorkSpaces, and EC2 instances.
- **Secure and reliable**: It offers multi-region replication and automated software updates, ensuring high availability and security.
- **Managed service**: AWS manages the underlying infrastructure, allowing you to focus on managing your directory and applications.

Use cases

AWS Directory Service is valuable for businesses that rely on Microsoft AD and want to extend their on-premises directory to the cloud. Daily use cases include hybrid cloud configurations, connecting AWS resources to an existing AD, and deploying AD-dependent applications [35].

Getting started with AWS Directory Service

To begin using Directory Service, you can launch a directory through the AWS Management Console, the AWS CLI, or SDKs [35]. You can choose the directory type that best suits your requirements.

AWS Directory Service simplifies the management and integration of Microsoft AD workloads into the AWS environment. In the subsequent sections of this chapter, we will continue to explore AWS services designed to enhance security, identity, and compliance for your cloud infrastructure.

AWS Firewall Manager

This section will provide a comprehensive overview of AWS Firewall Manager, including its key features, use cases, and benefits [38] [39] [40].

Introduction to AWS Firewall Manager

AWS Firewall Manager is a security management service that simplifies configuring and managing AWS **web application firewall (WAF)** rules and AWS Shield Advanced protections across multiple accounts and resources [38].

Key features and benefits

Key features and benefits are as follows [38]:

- **Centralized management**: AWS Firewall Manager provides a single console for managing the security policies of your entire AWS environment, making it easier to enforce security standards consistently.
- **Integration with AWS Organizations**: It seamlessly integrates with AWS Organizations, allowing you to extend security protections across all your accounts.
- **Automation**: The service can be configured to automatically apply WAF rules to new resources, reducing the need for manual rule management.

Use cases

AWS Firewall Manager is essential for organizations seeking to streamline their security management. It is particularly valuable for businesses with multiple AWS accounts, as it allows them to centrally configure and enforce security policies across all accounts and resources [38].

Getting started with AWS Firewall Manager

To begin using AWS Firewall Manager, you can setup WAF and AWS Shield Advanced policies through the AWS Management Console or programmatically using AWS CloudFormation or the AWS SDKs [38]. The service can be tailored to your organization's specific security needs.

AWS Firewall Manager provides a comprehensive solution for managing and enforcing security policies in complex AWS environments. In the subsequent sections of this chapter, we will continue to explore AWS services designed to enhance security, identity, and compliance for your cloud infrastructure.

AWS IAM Identity Center

This section will explore the AWS IAM identity center, an essential component of AWS security and identity management services. AWS IAM Identity Center is a central hub for identity management, making it easier for organizations to manage user identities, roles, and permissions across their AWS environments [41] [42] [43].

Introduction to AWS IAM Identity Center

AWS IAM Identity Center is a comprehensive identity management service that simplifies IAM for AWS resources. It offers a centralized console for managing user identities, groups, and permissions, enhancing security and control across AWS accounts [41].

Key features and benefits

Let us discuss the key features and benefits of AWS IAM Identity Center [41]:

- **User and group management**: IAM Identity Center allows you to create, manage, and organize user identities and groups, providing granular control over who can access your AWS resources.

- **Policy management**: You can create and manage policies that define permissions, ensuring that users and groups have the right level of access to resources.

- **Integration with AWS services**: IAM Identity Center integrates seamlessly with other AWS services, making managing access to resources like Amazon S3, EC2, and RDS easier [43].

Use cases

AWS IAM Identity Center is a fundamental service for securing AWS resources and ensuring the right individuals and systems have appropriate access. Frequent use cases include:

- **User access control**: You can use the IAM Identity Center to restrict access to specific resources and services for different users and groups [43].

- **Security enhancement**: Implement best practices by controlling permissions and ensuring users only have access to the resources they need [42].
- **Resource management**: Efficiently manage user identities and access across your AWS environment, helping organizations scale and grow securely [41].

Getting started with AWS IAM Identity Center

You can access the service through the AWS Management Console to start using AWS IAM Identity Center. Here, you can create users, groups, and roles, and define policies to manage access [41].

In-depth resources

For a deeper understanding of AWS IAM Identity Center, consider these resources:

- **AWS Documentation**: The official AWS IAM Identity Center documentation provides comprehensive information on setting up and managing identities, groups, and permissions [41].
- **Online tutorials**: Various online tutorials and video resources are available to help you start with AWS IAM Identity Center [43].
- **Community forums**: AWS community forums are excellent places to seek guidance and advice from experienced users who can share real-world insights [42].

AWS IAM Identity Center is key in securing and managing AWS resources effectively. In the following sections of this chapter, we will continue to explore AWS services that enhance security, identity, and compliance.

AWS Identity and Access Management

This section will discuss AWS IAM, a foundational service for securely managing access to AWS resources. IAM ensures that the right people and services can access your AWS environment and provides an overview of its features, use cases, and benefits [44] [42] [43].

Introduction to AWS Identity and Access Management

AWS IAM is a web service that enables secure access control to AWS resources. It allows you to create and manage AWS users and groups, and use permissions to grant or deny access to AWS resources [44]. IAM provides a central point for controlling access, ensuring the principle of least privilege is followed, and enhancing the security of your AWS environment.

Key features and benefits

The key features and benefits of AWS IAM are as follows:

- **User and group management**: IAM enables the creation and management of user identities, groups, and roles. Users can be assigned individual security credentials, while groups help manage permissions more efficiently [44].

- **Fine-grained control**: IAM allows you to define fine-grained permissions, ensuring that users and services have access only to the resources they need. This reduces the risk of unauthorized access [44].

- **MFA**: Enabling MFA for users can enhance security, adding an extra layer of protection for account sign-ins [42].

- **Integration with AWS services**: IAM integrates seamlessly with a wide range of AWS services, allowing you to control access to services such as Amazon S3, EC2, and RDS [42].

Use cases

IAM is essential for managing access control in AWS environments. Routine use cases include:

- **Security enhancement**: Implement strict access policies to minimize security risks and ensure compliance with industry standards [44].

- **RBAC**: Use IAM roles to delegate permissions and manage temporary access for applications or services [42].

Getting started with AWS IAM

To begin using AWS IAM, access the service through the AWS Management Console. Create users, groups, and roles, and define policies to manage access permissions [42].

In-depth resources

To deepen your knowledge of AWS IAM, refer to the following resources:

- **AWS Documentation**: The official AWS IAM documentation provides detailed guidance on configuring and managing IAM users, groups, and policies [44].

- **Online courses**: Online platforms like AWS training and certification offer courses dedicated explicitly to IAM, allowing you to gain expertise in using the service effectively [44].

- **Whitepapers and guides**: AWS offers whitepapers and implementation guides to help you understand and implement IAM best practices in your organization [42].

AWS IAM is fundamental to securing AWS resources and ensuring proper access control. In the subsequent sections of this chapter, we will continue exploring AWS services dedicated to enhancing security, identity, and compliance.

AWS Key Management Service

This section will explore AWS **Key Management Service (KMS)**, a crucial component for managing cryptographic keys and securing your data in AWS. We will delve into the key features, use cases, and best practices for AWS KMS [45] [46] [47].

Introduction to AWS Key Management Service

AWS KMS is a fully managed encryption service that allows you to create and control encryption keys to secure your data. KMS makes encrypting and protecting data in AWS applications and workloads easier. It offers a central location for managing keys, simplifying the encryption process across various AWS services [43].

Key features and benefits

Key features and benefits of the AWS KMS are as follows:

- **Centralized key management**: KMS provides a central location for managing keys, ensuring consistent encryption and decryption across your AWS environment [45].

- **Fully managed service**: As a fully managed service, KMS eliminates the operational overhead of key management, including hardware provisioning and software patching [46].

- **Integration with AWS services**: KMS seamlessly integrates with many AWS services, such as Amazon S3, RDS, and Lambda, enabling easy encryption of data stored or transmitted through these services [45].

- **Granular access control**: KMS allows you to define fine-grained permissions for key usage and management, ensuring that only authorized users and applications can access encrypted data [46].

Use cases

KMS is critical for a range of encryption use cases, including:

- **Data encryption**: Protect sensitive data at rest and in transit using KMS to encrypt and decrypt it [46].

- **Regulatory compliance**: Achieve compliance with data protection regulations and industry standards by using KMS to secure data [45].

- **Securing API keys**: Use KMS to secure API keys and other secrets, adding an extra layer of security to your applications [45].

Best practices

To maximize the benefits of AWS KMS, consider the following best practices:

- **Key rotation**: Regularly rotate encryption keys to enhance security and meet compliance requirements [46].

- **Least privilege access**: Apply the least privilege principle when configuring key usage permissions to minimize security risks [45].

- **Monitoring and auditing**: Implement monitoring and auditing to track key usage and detect unauthorized or suspicious activities [47].

Getting Started with AWS KMS

To start using AWS KMS, access the service through the AWS Management Console, create KMS keys, and define key policies and permissions [45].

In-depth resources

To further your understanding of AWS KMS, consult the following resources:

- **AWS Documentation**: The official AWS KMS documentation provides comprehensive information on creating, managing, and using encryption keys [45].

- **Online courses**: AWS training and certification offer courses dedicated to AWS KMS, helping you master the service's capabilities and best practices [47].

- **Whitepapers and best practices guides**: AWS provides whitepapers and best practices guides that offer insights into using KMS to enhance data security [46].

AWS KMS is a fundamental component for securing your data in AWS, and its proper usage is essential for compliance, data protection, and privacy. In the following sections of this chapter, we will continue exploring AWS services focused on security, identity, and compliance.

AWS Network Firewall

This section will explore the AWS Network Firewall, a vital service for protecting network traffic and applications within AWS. We will examine its key features, use cases, and best practices [48] [49] [50].

Introduction to AWS Network Firewall

AWS Network Firewall is a managed firewall service that simplifies network protection for your Amazon **Virtual Private Clouds** (**VPCs**). It provides advanced security features and capabilities to protect your applications and workloads from threats. Network Firewall acts as a filter for both inbound and outbound traffic, ensuring only legitimate traffic can access your resources [48].

Key features and benefits

The key features and benefits are as follows:

- **Stateful inspection**: The Network Firewall uses stateful inspection, which allows it to understand the state of active connections and make access decisions based on the context of the traffic. [48]

- **Rule groups**: Rule groups are rules that can be shared across multiple policies, making it easier to manage and consistently enforce network security policies [50].

- **Integration with AWS security services**: Network Firewall seamlessly integrates with AWS services like Amazon VPC, AWS WAF, and AWS Security Hub to provide comprehensive network security [49].

- **Alerts and logging**: You can configure Network Firewall to generate alerts and log network traffic data for analysis and compliance [48].

Use cases

AWS Network Firewall is instrumental in several use cases, including:

- **Protecting web applications**: Use Network Firewall to safeguard your web applications from attacks, such as **distributed denial of service** (**DDoS**) and SQL injections [50].

- **Segmenting workloads**: Employ Network Firewall to segment workloads in your VPCs, providing isolation and controlled resource access [49].

- **Detecting and blocking malicious activity**: A Network Firewall can detect and block potentially malicious traffic, helping to maintain a secure network environment [49].

Best practices

To ensure the effective use of AWS Network Firewall, consider these best practices:

- **Security group rules**: Use security group rules with Network Firewall policies to layer your network security [48].

- **Regular monitoring**: Monitor and log network traffic to identify potential security threats and patterns. [49].

- **Custom rule creation**: Create custom rule groups to tailor your network security policies to your specific requirements [50].

Getting started with AWS Network Firewall

To start with AWS Network Firewall, you can access the service through the AWS Management Console, create and manage policies, and attach them to your Amazon VPCs [49].

In-depth resources

For further understanding and implementation of AWS Network Firewall, consult the following resources:

- **AWS Documentation**: The official AWS Network Firewall documentation provides detailed information on using and configuring the service [49].

- **Online courses**: AWS Training and Certification offers courses dedicated to AWS Network Firewall, helping you grasp the service's capabilities and best practices [50].

- **Security best practices guides**: AWS provides insights into using Network Firewall to enhance network security [50].

AWS Network Firewall is key in securing your network traffic and applications in AWS. In the subsequent sections of this chapter, we will continue exploring AWS services focused on security, identity, and compliance.

AWS Resource Access Manager

This section will explore AWS **Resource Access Manager** (**RAM**), a powerful service that enables resource sharing across AWS accounts [51] [52] [53].

Introduction to AWS Resource Access Manager

AWS RAM is a service that simplifies resource sharing within and between AWS accounts. It allows you to share AWS resources, including Amazon VPC subnets, across AWS accounts in a controlled and secure manner. This makes it easier to collaborate with other accounts and centralize your resource management [53].

Key features and benefits

Let us discuss the key features and benefits [51]:

- **Resource sharing**: RAM allows you to share AWS resources such as VPC subnets, AWS Transit Gateway, and AWS License Manager configurations across accounts.

- **Centralized resource management**: With RAM, you can centralize the management of your AWS resources and ensure consistent access and configurations.

- **Resource associations**: You can associate resources with RAM and share them with specific AWS accounts or entire AWS Organizations.

- **Controlled access**: RAM provides control over who can access and manage shared resources, enhancing the security of your infrastructure [52].

Use cases

AWS RAM is instrumental in several use cases, including:

- **Resource sharing**: Share Amazon VPC subnets across accounts to facilitate collaboration and resource centralization [53].

- **Transit Gateway sharing**: Simplify network connectivity by sharing AWS Transit Gateway with other accounts, streamlining network architectures [51].

- **License management**: Share AWS License Manager configurations to manage software licenses across accounts efficiently [52].

Best practices

To make the most of AWS' RAM, consider these best practices:

- **Clearly define sharing goals**: Define what resources you want to share and the accounts or organizations you wish to share them with [52].

- **Limit resource permissions**: Only grant the necessary permissions to secure shared resources and ensure proper access control [51].

- **Regularly audit resource sharing**: Review resource sharing configurations to verify that they meet your organization's needs [52].

Getting started with AWS Resource Access Manager

You can access the service through the AWS Management Console to start using AWS RAM. You can create resource shares, associate resources with RAM, and define resource sharing policies for your AWS accounts [51].

In-depth resources

For further insights and guidance on AWS RAM, consult the following resources:

- **AWS Documentation**: The official AWS RAM documentation provides comprehensive information on how to use and configure the service [51].

- **Resource sharing best practices**: AWS offers best practices guides for resource sharing to help you understand the most efficient ways to leverage AWS RA. [52].

- **Use case examples**: Review practical AWS RAM use cases to understand its application in real-world scenarios [53].

AWS RAM simplifies sharing AWS resources across accounts, promoting efficient resource management and collaboration [54]. In the upcoming sections of this chapter, we will continue to explore AWS services and tools that enhance security, identity, and compliance within the AWS cloud environment.

AWS Secrets Manager

In this section, we will delve into AWS Secrets Manager, a valuable service that simplifies the management of sensitive information such as database credentials, API keys, and other secrets. We will discuss its features, use cases, and best practices [55] [56] [57].

Introduction to AWS Secrets Manager

AWS Secrets Manager is a service designed to help you protect access to your applications, services, and IT resources without exposing sensitive information. It assists in the secure storage, retrieval, and management of sensitive data, reducing the risk of inadvertent exposure [55].

Key features and benefits

The following are the key features and benefits of AWS Secrets Manager:

- **Secrets storage**: AWS Secrets Manager allows you to securely store and manage sensitive information, such as database passwords, API keys, and other secrets [55].

- **Rotation policies**: You can configure automatic rotation policies for secrets, ensuring that credentials are regularly updated without manual intervention [56].

- **Integration with RDS and Redshift**: AWS Secrets Manager seamlessly integrates with Amazon RDS and Amazon Redshift for simplified credential management [56].

- **Access control**: Manage access to secrets using fine-grained permissions and access policies, enhancing security and compliance [55].

Use cases

AWS Secrets Manager is crucial in a variety of use-cases, including:

- **Database credentials**: Store, manage, and rotate database credentials to enhance security [55].

- **Third-party API keys**: Protect sensitive API keys to access third-party services and APIs [55].

- **Secure storage for application secrets**: Safeguard application secrets like encryption keys and access tokens [57].

Best practices

To make the most of AWS Secrets Manager, consider these best practices:

- **Automatic rotation**: Enable automatic rotation of secrets to update credentials and enhance security regularly [55].

- **Least privilege access**: Implement least privileged access controls to restrict who can access and manage secrets [56].

- **Audit and monitoring**: Setup auditing and monitoring to track changes and secret access [55].

Getting started with AWS Secrets Manager

You can access AWS Secrets Manager through the AWS Management Console to get started. You can create and configure secrets, setup rotation policies, and grant access to applications and services [55].

In-depth resources

For further insights and guidance on AWS Secrets Manager, consult the following resources:

- **AWS Documentation**: The official AWS Secrets Manager documentation provides detailed information on how to use and configure the service [55].

- **Integration guides**: AWS offers integration guides for specific services, such as Amazon RDS and Redshift, to help you seamlessly incorporate AWS Secrets Manager into your applications [56].

- **Use examples**: Explore practical examples of how AWS Secrets Manager protects sensitive data in various scenarios [57].

AWS Secrets Manager simplifies the management of sensitive information, reducing security risks and enhancing compliance. In the upcoming sections of this chapter, we will continue to explore AWS services and tools that promote security, identity, and compliance within the AWS cloud environment.

AWS Security Hub

This section will explore AWS Security Hub, a powerful service that comprehensively views your security posture within the AWS environment [58] [59] [60].

Introduction to AWS Security Hub

AWS Security Hub is a service that helps you consolidate and centrally manage security findings from multiple AWS services and third-party tools. It simplifies identifying, prioritizing, and remedying security issues in your AWS environment [58].

Key features and benefits

The following are the key features and the benefits of AWS Security Hub:

- **Aggregated security findings**: Security Hub aggregates findings from various AWS services, such as Amazon GuardDuty and AWS Inspector, providing a unified view of your security status [58].

- **Prioritization**: It assigns severity levels to findings and provides detailed insights to help you prioritize and address security issues efficiently [59].

- **Integration**: Security Hub integrates various **security information and event management** (**SIEM**) solutions and incident response tools [59].

- **Compliance checks**: The service helps automate compliance checks and provides predefined AWS Config and AWS IAM best practice standards [60].

Use cases

AWS Security Hub serves critical roles in several use cases, including:

- **Threat detection**: Identifying and responding to potential security threats and vulnerabilities in real-time [58].

- **Compliance monitoring**: Ensuring your AWS environment complies with security standards and best practices [60].

- **Incident response**: Streamlining the process by providing a consolidated view of security issues [59].

Best practices

To maximize the benefits of AWS Security Hub, consider implementing the following best practices:

- **Continuous monitoring**: Setup continuous monitoring to receive real-time insights into your AWS environment [58].

- **Custom actions**: Create custom actions for findings to automate response and remediation [59].

- **Integration with SIEM**: Integrate Security Hub with your solution for better visibility into security events [59].

Getting started with AWS Security Hub

You can access AWS Security Hub through the AWS Management Console to get started. You can configure security standards, customize settings, and analyze and monitor security findings [58].

In-depth resources

For further insights and guidance on AWS Security Hub, consult the following resources:

- **AWS Documentation**: The official AWS Security Hub documentation provides comprehensive information on using and configuring the service [60].

- **Best practices guide**: AWS offers a guide with the best practices for setting up and using AWS Security Hub effectively [59].

- **Compliance standards**: Learn more about AWS Config and AWS IAM best practices to ensure compliance with security standards [60].

AWS Security Hub is a valuable tool for enhancing security and compliance within your AWS environment. In the subsequent sections of this chapter, we will continue to explore AWS services and tools that promote security, identity, and compliance within the AWS cloud ecosystem.

AWS Shield

In this section, we will explore AWS Shield, a managed DDoS protection service that safeguards applications running on AWS. We will discuss its features, benefits, and use cases [61] [62] [63].

Introduction to AWS Shield

AWS Shield is a crucial component of AWS security services. It protects against DDoS attacks for AWS applications, helping maintain the availability and performance of your applications by minimizing downtime caused by malicious traffic [62].

Key features and benefits

The following are the key features and the benefits [61]:

- **Managed DDoS protection**: AWS Shield provides managed DDoS protection that safeguards your applications against network and application layer DDoS attacks.

- **Global network**: Leveraging the scale and capabilities of the AWS global network, AWS Shield provides comprehensive protection with minimal latency impact.

- **Layer 3 and layer 4 protection**: It offers protection against volumetric attacks by inspecting and mitigating traffic at layers 3 and 4.

- **Layer 7 protection**: To protect against application-layer attacks, AWS Shield can integrate with AWS WAF to provide layer 7 protection [61] [62].

- **Attack visibility**: AWS Shield provides attack visibility with near-real-time diagnostics through Amazon CloudWatch metrics.

Use cases

AWS Shield is invaluable for a range of use cases [61] [62]:

- **Website protection**: Protecting your websites and applications against DDoS attacks to ensure they remain available and performant.

- **Application availability**: Safeguarding the availability of critical applications, including API endpoints, gaming servers, and e-commerce platforms.

- **Application layer protection**: Combining AWS Shield with AWS WAF for comprehensive layer 7 application layer protection.

Best practices

When working with AWS Shield, consider implementing these best practices [61]:

- **Understand AWS Shield Standard**: Get familiar with AWS Shield Standard, which is automatically included for all AWS customers at no additional cost.

- **Evaluate advanced options**: Depending on your needs, evaluate the advanced protections AWS Shield Advanced provides.

- **Integrate with AWS WAF**: Consider integrating AWS Shield with AWS WAF for application layer protection [62].

Getting Started with AWS Shield

The AWS Management Console enables AWS Shield protection for your AWS resources and allows you to customize and integrate with AWS WAF [61] [62].

In-depth resources

To delve deeper into AWS Shield, explore these resources [61] [62]:

- **AWS Documentation**: The official AWS Shield documentation provides extensive guidance on using and configuring the service.

- **AWS Shield Advanced**: The AWS Documentation provides information about AWS Shield Advanced and its additional features.

- **Application layer protection**: The AWS Documentation provides more information about integrating AWS Shield with AWS WAF to provide application layer protection.

AWS Shield is a vital component of your security strategy on AWS. It ensures the availability and performance of your applications in the face of potential DDoS threats. As we progress through this chapter, we will continue to explore AWS services that enhance security, identity, and compliance.

AWS web application firewall

In this section, we will explore AWS WAF, a service that plays a crucial role in enhancing the security of web applications hosted on AWS. AWS WAF provides robust protection against various web-based attacks, allowing organizations to maintain the integrity and availability of their web assets [64].

Introduction to AWS web application firewall

AWS WAF is a cloud-based firewall service that shields web applications from various security threats. It operates on the application layer, inspecting incoming HTTP and HTTPS requests. WAF offers fine-grained control over web traffic, allowing organizations to define rules to filter, monitor, and safeguard their applications [64].

Key features and benefits

Let us discuss the key features and benefits:

- **Customizable rules**: AWS WAF empowers users to create custom security rules tailored to the specific needs of their applications. This customization capability enables the blocking of malicious traffic while permitting legitimate requests.

- **Managed rulesets**: AWS provides managed rulesets that are expertly curated to address common threats. These pre-configured rule sets help users quickly bolster their security posture [65].

- **Seamless integration**: AWS WAF seamlessly integrates with Amazon CloudFront and AWS Application Load Balancer, allowing the enforcement of security policies at the edge of AWS's global network.

- **Logging and monitoring**: The service offers detailed logging and monitoring features, providing valuable insights into web traffic patterns and security events. This data is instrumental for optimizing security rules and identifying potential threats [66].

- **Web ACLs**: AWS WAF allows the creation of web ACLs, enabling the application of security rules selectively to different parts of the application [64].

Use cases

AWS WAF serves a multitude of use cases, including:

- **Protection against application layer attacks**: Safeguarding web applications from threats like SQL injections, **cross-site scripting (XSS)**, and DDoS attacks [67].

- **Content control**: User content is managed based on conditions or criteria [68].

- **API security**: Ensuring that APIs are protected from unauthorized or malicious access. [69].

Best practices

To maximize the benefits of AWS WAF, consider the following best practices:

- **Regular rule updates**: Keep your security rules current to protect against emerging threats.

- **Log analysis**: Periodically review and analyze AWS WAF logs to gain insights into your application's traffic and improve security rules.

- **Leverage integration**: Fully integrate AWS WAF with other AWS services, such as AWS CloudFront, for global content delivery and protection [70].

Getting started with AWS WAF

To start with AWS WAF, you can use the AWS Management Console or command-line tools to configure your web application's rules, conditions, and actions [71].

In-depth resources

For a deeper understanding of AWS WAF, explore the following resources:

- **Official AWS WAF documentation**: The official AWS WAF documentation provides detailed information on using and configuring AWS WAF [70].

- **AWS WAF security automations**: To automate security responses, consider AWS WAF Security Automations, a solution that deploys a set of AWS WAF rules and an AWS Lambda function [70].

- **AWS Whitepapers**: AWS offers a range of whitepapers and articles on application security, which can complement your knowledge in this area [72].

As you explore AWS WAF, you will continue strengthening your understanding of AWS security, identity, and compliance tools, collectively forming a robust defense for cloud-based applications and data.

Elevating security and compliance in AWS

In this comprehensive exploration, we have discussed understanding the critical pillars of cloud security within the AWS ecosystem. As a leading cloud service provider, AWS empowers organizations to fortify their defenses against an ever-evolving threat landscape while ensuring regulatory compliance [73]. This chapter has been systematically traversed through 23 sections, each dedicated to a specific AWS security service, offering invaluable insights into how these services collectively form a robust cloud security framework.

Multifaceted approach for securing the AWS cloud

AWS's commitment to security is evident in this chapter's diversity and depth of services. From foundational IAM solutions, such as AWS IAM [44] to advanced threat detection tools like Amazon GuardDuty [10]. The AWS ecosystem equips businesses with an array of security resources. Organizations can mitigate risks and protect their data from unauthorized access and breaches by designing their infrastructure and applications with security in mind [74].

Compliance and beyond

The importance of compliance, especially in heavily regulated industries like finance and healthcare, cannot be overstated. AWS offers a wealth of resources and services, including AWS Artifact [23], to assist organizations in meeting their compliance requirements. These tools are key in establishing the necessary controls and documentation to satisfy regulatory obligations and audits. [75].

As the cloud computing landscape evolves, AWS continues to innovate security and compliance, providing its users with tools and best practices to stay one step ahead of emerging threats. [76]. The world of cloud security is dynamic, and to navigate it effectively, organizations must leverage AWS capabilities and stay vigilant and proactive in their security and compliance strategies.

Conclusion

In conclusion, this chapter has provided a guided understanding of the multifaceted world of AWS security, identity, and compliance. The amalgamation of these aspects forms the foundation upon which resilient and secure cloud infrastructures can be built. This chapter was valuable, equipping readers with the knowledge and tools to safeguard their cloud assets and adhere to the strictest compliance standards.

This chapter brought together the key insights and takeaways, emphasizing the importance of security, identity, and compliance in the AWS cloud.

In the next chapter, we will explore the core principles of data management, AWS database services, implement scalable and high-performance database solutions, and develop specialized database solutions.

Join our Discord space

Join our Discord workspace for latest updates, offers, tech happenings around the world, new releases, and sessions with the authors:

https://discord.bpbonline.com

CHAPTER 6
Database

Introduction

Proper data management and utilization are vital for success in today's data-driven landscape. As the digital world continues to evolve, **Amazon Web Services** (**AWS**) cloud platform provides a comprehensive suite of database services and solutions that enable businesses to unlock the full potential of their data. This chapter, aptly titled *Database*, embarks on a journey through the AWS database offerings, providing a comprehensive guide to understanding and utilizing these services to their fullest extent.

The AWS ecosystem houses various database services tailored to specific data storage and management needs [1]. From powerful relational databases like *Amazon Relational Database Services (RDS)* [2] and *Amazon Aurora* [3], to the flexibility of NoSQL databases, such as *Amazon DynamoDB* and *Amazon DocumentDB* [4], AWS leaves no stone unturned in providing versatile options [5]. We will discuss the unique features and capabilities of each service, providing insights on when and how to employ them effectively in diverse use cases.

This chapter will explore the intricacies of scaling databases, ensuring high performance, and guaranteeing data reliability. With services like *Amazon ElastiCache* [6] for caching and *Amazon Redshift* for analytical data warehousing [7], to tackle complex workloads with ease. For time-series data, *Amazon Timestream* is your preferred option [8], while *Amazon Neptune* caters to graph database requirements [9]. We will examine how these services can revolutionize your data storage and retrieval strategies.

This chapter equips you with the knowledge and skills to utilize AWS database services for your data management needs fully. Whether you work with structured or unstructured data, require real-time analytics, or need a scalable and globally accessible database solution, this chapter guides you through selecting and implementing the appropriate AWS database services to meet your unique business requirements.

Structure

This chapter includes the following topics:

- Foundation of data management
- AWS Aurora high-performance relational database
- Amazon DocumentDB
- Amazon DynamoDB
- Managed NoSQL database
- Amazon ElastiCache
- Amazon Keyspaces for Apache Cassandra
- Amazon MemoryDB for Redis
- Amazon Neptune
- Amazon RDS
- Amazon Redshift
- Amazon Timestream

Objectives

By the end of this chapter, readers will be able to understand the core principles of data management, explore AWS database services, implement scalable and high-performance database solutions, and influence specialized database solutions; optimize data-driven decision-making, and align database choices with business needs.

Foundation of data management

Databases are the bedrock of modern data management and are pivotal in organizations' digital transformation. They are structured repositories that store, organize, and facilitate access to data, making it readily available for various applications and use cases. Regarding cloud-based database services, AWS offers a comprehensive suite of solutions that cater to a wide range of business requirements [10].

This section offers a foundational overview of databases and introduces the AWS database ecosystem. It does not include scholarly articles, as its purpose is to provide an introductory context. You can incorporate specific scholarly sources in the following sections, which delve deeper into each AWS database service.

Understanding the AWS database ecosystem

The AWS database ecosystem encompasses distinct types of databases, each designed to address specific data storage and management needs. For those familiar with traditional relational databases, Amazon RDS provides a managed solution for popular databases like MySQL, PostgreSQL, Oracle, and SQL Server [2]. RDS automates routine administrative tasks, making it easier to setup, operate, and scale a relational database.

If NoSQL databases are more suitable for your needs, Amazon DynamoDB delivers a fast, flexible, fully managed NoSQL database service [4], it can manage high-traffic applications and provides low-latency, reliable performance.

AWS also offers specialized database services like Amazon Redshift for data warehousing [7], Amazon Timestream [8] for time-series data, and Amazon Neptune [9] For graph databases. These services cater to specific data models and use cases, making AWS a one-stop destination for all your database needs.

Scalability and security

One of the primary advantages of AWS databases is scalability. Cloud-based databases can easily adjust to changing workloads, automatically expanding to accommodate increasing data and traffic. This ensures your applications remain responsive and cost-effective as your business grows.

AWS places a strong emphasis on data security. With features like data encryption at rest and in transit, **Identity and Access Management (IAM)** controls, and database audit capabilities, AWS databases are equipped to protect your data from unauthorized access and data breaches [11].

Reliability and availability

High availability and reliability are vital for databases. AWS ensures your databases run smoothly with features such as automated backups, automated software patching, and the ability to deploy your database in multiple **Availability Zones (AZs)** for redundancy [12].

With AWS, you can choose between fully managed database services or self-managed databases on EC2 instances, offering flexibility to accommodate various needs and expertise levels [13].

Databases are the backbone of data-driven organizations, and AWS provides a comprehensive array of database services to meet your data storage and management needs. In the subsequent sections of this chapter, we will explore these services in greater detail, examining their features, use cases, and best practices for implementation.

The following section will discuss Amazon RDS, AWS's managed RDS, and explore its features and benefits for your cloud-based data management needs.

AWS Aurora high-performance relational database

Amazon Aurora [3], an AWS product, has rapidly gained recognition and popularity for its exceptional capabilities as a high-performance, fully managed relational database engine. As a dynamic cloud-based service, it addresses the demands of businesses and enterprises by delivering the robustness and capabilities of commercial-grade databases while eliminating the intricacies, overheads, and inflated costs often associated with them.

This section thoroughly explores Amazon Aurora, emphasizing its key features and integrating insights from scholarly articles and AWS Documentation. Where relevant, references appear throughout the text. You can include more scholarly sources in later sections covering other AWS database services.

Key features of Amazon Aurora

Amazon Aurora brings to the table a range of outstanding features, making it an ideal choice for AWS users who require a robust relational database:

- **Compatibility**: Amazon Aurora is compatible with MySQL and PostgreSQL, ensuring a seamless migration process for existing databases. Its drop-in replacement nature means that transitioning to Aurora is hassle-free, requiring minimal application adjustments.

- **High-performance**: Aurora delivers up to five times the throughput of standard MySQL databases and up to twice that of standard PostgreSQL databases, all on the same hardware. This prominent level of performance makes Aurora an ideal choice for applications that require extensive transaction processing and data handling.

- **High availability**: Designed for high availability, Amazon Aurora replicates data across six instances in three AZs. This strategy enhances reliability and ensures seamless failover support, effectively minimizing downtime.

- **Fault-tolerant storage**: Amazon Aurora's storage layer is notable for its fault-tolerance. It continuously backs up your data to Amazon S3 while ensuring transparent recovery from any physical storage failures. This provides peace of mind that your data is well-protected and recoverable.

- **Global databases**: For applications that cater to a global user base, Amazon Aurora Global Database [14] the feature is invaluable. It replicates data across multiple AWS Regions, enabling low-latency global reads.

Performance benchmarking

Scholarly articles and independent studies consistently demonstrate that Amazon Aurora outperforms other databases. Research by *Faleiro, Van Renesse*, and *Rodrigues* (2016) [15] Aurora outperformed MySQL and handled high-throughput workloads with significantly lower latencies, confirming its position as a high-performance database solution.

AWS also highlights Aurora's ability to scale read operations linearly, supporting up to 15 read replicas for both MySQL and PostgreSQL compatibility [16], [17]. This scalability is crucial for applications requiring efficient and dynamic read operation handling.

Case studies

A collection of case studies within AWS customer success stories provides concrete examples of how organizations have harnessed Amazon Aurora's power [18]. These case studies underscore Aurora's high availability and scalability, bringing real-world applications into sharper focus.

Amazon Aurora is a compelling choice for organizations seeking a cost-effective solution that combines the performance and reliability characteristics of commercial-grade databases. It boasts compatibility with MySQL and PostgreSQL, exceptional performance, high availability, fault-tolerant storage, and global database capabilities. In the following sections of this chapter, we will explore various other AWS database services, each tailored to distinct use cases.

The subsequent section, *Amazon DocumentDB*, will guide you through exploring AWS-managed document database services compatible with MongoDB.

Amazon DocumentDB

Amazon DocumentDB, an integral part of AWS, is a fully managed, MongoDB-compatible [19] database service designed to offer high-performance, scalability, and availability [5]. Its unique value proposition lies in ensuring seamless compatibility with existing MongoDB applications [20]. This MongoDB compatibility is paramount for organizations seeking to migrate their MongoDB workloads to the cloud.

Key features and advantages

The following are features and advantages of Amazon DocumentDB:

- **MongoDB compatibility**: Amazon DocumentDB is engineered to be fully compatible with MongoDB, one of the most renowned NoSQL databases in the industry [20]. What truly sets DocumentDB apart is its compatibility, which extends to the application level. This means that you can effortlessly employ your existing MongoDB. [21], drivers, and code to interact with DocumentDB, ensuring a smooth transition for your applications [5].

- **Scalability** [20]: DocumentDB seamlessly integrates horizontal scaling to cater to the demands of growing applications [20]. The ability to easily add or remove read replicas empowers you to efficiently distribute read traffic and guarantee low-latency responses, ensuring your database can handle surges in workloads [22], [23].

- **High availability**: Amazon DocumentDB ensures high availability by implementing automatic failover mechanisms [20]. It replicates data across six instances in three AZs, safeguarding against hardware failures and significantly boosting durability and availability. [5].

- **Security**: Security remains at the forefront of any database service, and DocumentDB does not disappoint [20] It supports **Virtual Private Cloud** (**VPC**) peering to isolate your database within a VPC, encrypts data at rest, and incorporates built-in audit logging to ensure the confidentiality and integrity of your data [5].

- **Managed service**: As a fully managed service, Amazon DocumentDB effectively removes the burden of time-consuming administrative tasks, including hardware provisioning, patching, setup, configuration, and backups [5]. This alleviates operational overhead, allowing you to concentrate on developing and enhancing your applications.

Use cases

The versatile nature of Amazon DocumentDB lends itself to a broad spectrum of use cases. [5]. Typical scenarios where DocumentDB excels include content management systems, catalogs, user profiles, and applications demanding real-time analytics. [24]. Furthermore, its exceptional ability to handle high read workloads [25] positions it as an invaluable choice for applications dependent on swift and efficient data retrieval [5], [25].

Amazon DynamoDB

AWS offers Amazon DynamoDB as a managed NoSQL database service. It delivers fast, predictable performance and scales seamlessly to meet varying demands [26]. With its flexibility, reliability, and capacity to handle diverse data models, DynamoDB serves various applications, from mobile and web to gaming and **Internet of Things** (**IoT**) [27].

Key features and advantages

The following are the features and advantages of Amazon DynamoDB:

- **Fully managed**: DynamoDB is a serverless, fully managed database service, which means AWS takes care of the operational aspects such as hardware provisioning, configuration, patching, and backups [28]. This allows developers [29] to focus on building applications without worrying about database management [30].

- **Scalability**: DynamoDB provides seamless and automatic scaling, ensuring that your application can manage variable workloads [28]. You can easily scale up or down based on your application's demands [31].

- **Performance**: It is known for its fast and predictable performance [28]. You can achieve single-digit millisecond response times, making it ideal for applications that require low-latency data access.

- **Multiple region replication**: DynamoDB offers global tables, which allow you to replicate your data across multiple AWS Regions for disaster recovery and low-latency access globally [28].

- **Security**: Data security is a top priority [27]. DynamoDB provides fine-grained access control using AWS IAM [28] and offers encryption at rest and in transit [4].

Use cases

Amazon DynamoDB is suitable for various applications, including e-commerce platforms, mobile applications, gaming leaderboards, session management, IoT data storage, and more. Its versatility and scalability make it an excellent choice for applications that require seamless scaling based on demand [32].

Managed NoSQL database

AWS offers a Managed NoSQL database as a powerful and flexible data storage solution that caters to modern application needs. These databases provide a schema-less data model, allowing developers to efficiently store, retrieve, and manage unstructured or semi-structured data.

This section will explore the advantages and use cases of managed NoSQL databases and their significance in modern application development.

Key features and advantages

The following are the features and advantages of a managed NoSQL database:

- **Schema-less data model**: Managed NoSQL databases, such as Amazon DynamoDB, provide a schema-less data model, which means you can store and retrieve data without needing a predefined schema. This flexibility is beneficial for applications that deal with rapidly changing data structures [28].

- **Highly scalable**: Managed NoSQL databases can adjust seamlessly to handle increasing workloads, allowing them to scale as data requirements expand [28].

- **Low-latency access**: NoSQL databases are optimized for low-latency data access [33], making them suitable for applications that require real-time data retrieval [28].

- **Multi-model support**: Many managed NoSQL databases support various data models [34], including document, key-value, graph, and wide-column store [35]. This flexibility lets you choose the right data model for your application requirements [17].

Use cases

Managed NoSQL databases are well-suited for various applications, including content management systems, mobile and web applications, e-commerce platforms, gaming, IoT, and more [34]. Their ability to manage unstructured and rapidly evolving data makes them a valuable choice for businesses that need dynamic and scalable data storage.

Amazon ElastiCache

Amazon ElastiCache accelerates application performance by enabling real-time data caching with a fully managed in-memory data store service. It supports popular open-source in-memory data stores like Redis [36] and Memcached [37], allowing you to seamlessly deploy, operate, and scale an in-memory cache for your applications.

In this section, we will discuss the features, advantages, use cases, and significance of Amazon ElastiCache as an essential tool for enhancing the performance of AWS-based applications.

Key features and advantages

The following are the features and advantages of Amazon ElastiCache:

- **Caching data for faster access**: Amazon ElastiCache stores frequently accessed data in memory, reducing the need to fetch it from the central database. This caching mechanism significantly reduces data retrieval times and enhances application responsiveness [38].

- **Compatibility with Redis and Memcached [39]**: ElastiCache supports Redis and Memcached, two widely used open-source in-memory data stores. This flexibility lets you choose the data store that fits your application's requirements best [40].

- **Auto Scaling**: ElastiCache can automatically adjust its capacity based on your application's needs. This ensures that your cache is always appropriately sized, optimizing cost and performance [41].

- **Managed service**: As a managed service, ElastiCache manages operational tasks like hardware provisioning, software patching, setup, and configuration. This allows you to focus on your application's development rather than infrastructure management [42].

Use cases

Amazon ElastiCache adds value to applications that need low-latency data access [43]. It supports use cases like session management, real-time analytics, leaderboards, and read-heavy workloads. Any application that benefits from rapid access to frequently accessed data can utilize ElastiCache to enhance performance [44].

Amazon Keyspaces for Apache Cassandra

Amazon Keyspaces (for Apache Cassandra) [45] offers a fully managed, serverless, scalable, and universally available database service. It is designed to provide the best of both worlds, the scalability and flexibility of Apache Cassandra [46] and the benefits of AWS's managed services. Amazon Keyspaces allows you to build applications that seamlessly and securely handle any amount of traffic and data [27], making it a robust choice for many use cases.

This section will explore Amazon Keyspaces (for Apache Cassandra), its features, benefits, and the use cases where it shines as a fully managed, serverless, and scalable database service.

Key features and advantages

The following are features and advantages of Amazon Keyspaces:

- **Serverless and managed**: Amazon Keyspaces eliminates the need for database management tasks, such as hardware provisioning, setup, and patching. You can focus on building applications while AWS takes care of operational tasks [47].

- **Scalability**: It provides a highly scalable database that can manage substantial amounts of data and traffic [48]. You can easily scale up or down to match the requirements of your application [47].

- **Compatibility with Apache Cassandra**: Amazon Keyspaces is compatible with the Apache **Cassandra Query Language** (**CQL**). This means you can migrate your existing Cassandra workloads to Amazon Keyspaces with minimal code changes [49].

- **Security and compliance**: It offers robust security features such as rest and transit encryption, IAM, and audit logging. Amazon Keyspaces also helps you maintain regulatory compliance [47].

Use cases

Amazon Keyspaces is well-suited for applications that require seamless scaling and high availability. Typical use cases include customer-facing applications, IoT applications, and various scenarios where data must be distributed across multiple regions while maintaining low-latency and high availability [47].

Amazon MemoryDB for Redis

Amazon MemoryDB for Redis provides a fully managed, Redis-compatible in-memory database service, ideal for applications needing rapid, real-time data access with sub-millisecond response times. This service extends Redis's capabilities, which are widely used for caching and real-time analytics, by providing a managed solution that ensures high availability and scalability across AWS environments.

In this section, we will discuss Amazon MemoryDB for Redis and explore its compatibility with Redis, high availability, performance, and use cases [50]. We will also discuss how it can benefit applications that require low-latency, real-time data storage and retrieval [51].

Key features and advantages

The following are features and advantages of Amazon MemoryDB:

- **Compatibility**: Amazon MemoryDB for Redis is fully compatible with Redis, which means you can use your existing Redis clients and code with minimal changes. It supports Redis data types and commands, making migrating existing applications to the managed service easy [52].

- **High availability**: It offers multiple AZ deployments, ensuring data redundancy and automatic failover. This helps maintain high availability and durability for your applications [53].

- **Performance**: Amazon MemoryDB for Redis efficiently manages both read-heavy and write-heavy workloads. With sub-millisecond response times, it excels in real-time and low-latency applications [54].

- **Security**: The service supports encryption at rest and in transit, and IAM to help secure your data. You can also use Amazon VPC [55] peering to isolate your MemoryDB clusters [52].

Use cases

Amazon MemoryDB for Redis is an excellent choice for use cases that require a fast and universally available in-memory database. These include caching, session management, leaderboard and counting systems, and real-time analytics for gaming, ad targeting, and e-commerce applications. [56].

Amazon Neptune

Amazon Neptune, a fully managed graph database service from AWS, excels at storing and querying data with intricate relationships. It is a powerful tool for applications that rely on highly connected data, such as social networks, recommendation engines, and knowledge graphs.

This section will explore Amazon Neptune, its features, compatibility with different graph models, scalability, and use cases. This will help you understand how this managed graph database service can be a valuable addition to your application architecture, especially for scenarios involving highly connected data and complex relationships.

Key features and advantages

The following are features and advantages of Amazon Neptune:

- **Graph database model**: Amazon Neptune is purpose-built for graph data. It supports both property graph and **Resource Description Framework (RDF)** (graph models, making it flexible for various use cases. Property graph models are often used for highly connected data with complex relationships [57], while RDF graph models are suitable for representing and querying semantic data [58].

- **Universally available and scalable**: Neptune provides high availability through multiple AZs, ensuring redundancy and automatic failover. It can also scale out [59] to accommodate growing workloads [60].

- **Support for multiple query languages**: Neptune supports popular graph query languages, like SPARQL [61] and Apache [62] TinkerPop Gremlin, allowing you to choose the query language that best suits your application [63].

- **Security**: The service offers data encryption at rest and in transit. It integrates with AWS IAM for access control and Amazon VPC for network isolation [64].

Use cases

Amazon Neptune supports applications that require advanced relationship modeling and querying, making it ideal for use cases such as social networks, fraud detection, recommendation engines, knowledge graphs, and life sciences research [65].

Amazon RDS

Amazon RDS is a managed database service that simplifies the setup, operation, and scaling of relational databases. It supports multiple database engines, including MySQL, PostgreSQL, SQL Server, MariaDB, and Oracle. Amazon RDS handles routine database tasks, allowing you to focus on your application instead of managing the database.

This section will discuss Amazon RDS and explore its key features, such as flexibility in database engines, automated management tasks, scalability, and high availability. Understanding Amazon RDS will help you make informed decisions regarding the database infrastructure for your applications, ensuring reliability and performance.

Key features and advantages

The following are the features and advantages of Amazon RDS:

- **Database engine flexibility**: Amazon RDS offers a choice of database engines, making it suitable for a wide range of applications [66]. You can choose MySQL, PostgreSQL, SQL Server, MariaDB, and Oracle. [67]

- **Automated backups and software patching**: RDS automatically performs database backups, enabling point-in-time recovery. It also manages software patching, including critical security updates [68].

- **Scalability**: Amazon RDS allows you to easily scale your database up or down based on your application's demands [69]. This ensures your database can manage traffic spikes and grow with your business [70].

- **High availability**: RDS offers high availability with automated failover to a standby instance in case of a hardware failure. This helps ensure that your application remains accessible even in the face of infrastructure issues [71].

Use cases

Amazon RDS is suitable for various use cases, including web applications, mobile apps, e-commerce platforms, and content management systems [72].

Amazon Redshift

Amazon Redshift utilizes SQL to deliver rapid query performance for analytics and **business intelligence** (**BI**). It enables the quick analysis of large datasets, making it a valuable tool for organizations that aim to make data-driven decisions efficiently.

This section will explore Amazon Redshift, its columnar storage, and substantial parallel processing capabilities. Integration with BI tools and their role in data warehousing and analytics [73]. Understanding Amazon Redshift's strengths will help you harness the power of data for your analytical workloads and data-driven decision-making processes.

Key features and advantages

The following are features and advantages of Amazon Redshift:

- **Columnar storage**: Amazon Redshift uses a columnar storage format, which is highly efficient for analytical queries. This enables rapid data retrieval and aggregation, making it well-suited for complex analytical tasks [74].

- **Massively parallel processing (MPP)**: Redshift employs MPP architecture to distribute and parallelize queries across multiple nodes, ensuring quick query execution [75], even with large datasets [76].

- **Integration with BI tools**: Redshift integrates seamlessly with popular BI tools such as Tableau, Power BI, and Amazon QuickSight, enabling easy visualization and reporting [77].

- **Data lake integration**: Redshift Spectrum allows you to query data in your Amazon S3 data lake directly from Redshift, providing a unified view of your data [78].

Use cases

Amazon Redshift excels in data warehousing and analytics, supporting tasks like ad hoc analysis, data exploration, and complex queries [48]. It finds widespread use in finance, healthcare, and e-commerce industries. [72].

Amazon Timestream

Amazon Timestream is a fully managed, serverless time-series database designed to manage high volumes of data from various sources with millisecond resolution. It is a valuable addition to the AWS database offerings, specifically catering to applications and workloads that rely on time-series data, such as IoT, DevOps, and industrial telemetry.

This section explores Amazon Timestream, highlighting its serverless architecture, high-resolution data capabilities, and built-in analytics functions [79], and seamless integration with other AWS services. Understanding Amazon Timestream's role in handling time-series data efficiently can significantly enhance your ability to monitor and analyze data with high precision, benefiting applications across various domains [1].

Key features and advantages

The following are features and advantages of Amazon Timestream:

- **Serverless and scalable**: Amazon Timestream is serverless, meaning there is no need to provide or manage servers. It automatically scales to manage fluctuating workloads, making it cost-effective and requiring minimal maintenance [80].

- **High resolution**: Timestream can capture and store data with millisecond precision, essential for time-series data, ensuring that you can monitor and analyze data with high accuracy [81].

- **Built-in analytics**: It includes built-in analytical functions for real-time data processing, including interpolation, smoothing, and aggregation, simplifying data analysis [82].

- **Integration with AWS services**: Timestream can seamlessly integrate with other AWS services, including IoT Core, Lambda, and Quicksight, to build end-to-end IoT and data analytics solutions [83].

Use cases

Organizations use Amazon Timestream to track industrial machinery performance and monitor IoT devices [84], and analyze log data. It excels in scenarios that require efficient collection, storage, and analysis of time-series data [85].

Conclusion

In this chapter, we explored AWS's extensive suite of database services, examining their features and use cases. AWS offers a diverse range of database options, including relational databases like Amazon RDS, NoSQL solutions like Amazon DynamoDB, and specialized databases such as Amazon Timestream and Amazon Neptune. These services cater to business needs, from transactional applications to complex analytical workloads.

The managed nature of these services alleviates the burden of administrative tasks, enabling organizations to focus on innovation and data-driven decision-making. AWS databases provide scalability and flexibility, supporting applications with fluctuating demands and ensuring robust security and compliance [86]. AWS's continued innovation in database technologies also empowers businesses to explore advanced data management and analytics.

Overall, the AWS database ecosystem exemplifies the transformative potential of cloud computing in modern data management. By leveraging these services, organizations can efficiently manage their data, optimize performance, and unlock new opportunities for growth and innovation.

In the next chapter, we will explore the core tools that AWS provides for developers, including **software development kits (SDKs)**, code editors, and DevOps practices. We will also discuss how these tools facilitate streamlined software development, deployment, and operations, further enhancing the capabilities of organizations in the AWS cloud.

Join our Discord space

Join our Discord workspace for latest updates, offers, tech happenings around the world, new releases, and sessions with the authors:

https://discord.bpbonline.com

CHAPTER 7

Developer Tools and DevOps: Part 1

Introduction

This chapter examines the evolving landscape of software development in cloud environments, focusing on how AWS facilitates agility, scalability, and automation throughout the software development lifecycle. It begins with an overview of serverless computing, highlighting how AWS services allow developers to concentrate on code rather than infrastructure. The discussion then shifts to **integrated development environments (IDEs)** and **machine learning (ML)** to improve code quality and automate reviews.

We examine how **continuous integration/continuous deployment (CI/CD)** pipelines are implemented using AWS CodeBuild, CodePipeline and CodeDeploy tools. We also provide security for best practices for CI/CD pipelines, ensuring robust application delivery. The chapter further explores **infrastructure as code (IaC)** using AWS CloudFormation and AWS Cloud Control API to manage scalable, repeatable infrastructure.

Advanced topics, such as artifact management, chaos engineering, and resilience testing, are introduced to demonstrate how AWS supports the development of robust and fault-tolerant applications. Finally, we explore **event-driven architectures (EDAs)** and their role in building responsive, loosely coupled systems using services like **Simple Notification Service (SNS)** and Step Functions.

By the end of this chapter, readers will understand how to use AWS developer tools and DevOps practices to streamline development, enhance security, and accelerate innovation in the cloud.

Structure

In this chapter, we will go through the following topics:

- Developer tools
- Application integration
- Containers and robotics
- Quantum technologies
- AWS developer tools overview
- Amazon CodeCatalyst
- Amazon CodeGuru
- Amazon Corretto
- AWS Cloud Control API
- AWS Cloud9
- AWS CodeArtifact
- AWS CodeBuild
- AWS CodeCommit
- AWS CodeDeploy
- AWS CodePipeline
- AWS CodeStar
- AWS Command Line Interface
- AWS Device Farm
- AWS Fault Injection Simulator
- AWS tools and SDKs
- AWS X-Ray
- Amazon CodeWhisperer

Objectives

This chapter provides a comprehensive understanding of modern software development practices in cloud environments, with a primary focus on AWS. We will explore essential tools, methodologies, and best practices for developing and deploying scalable and efficient applications. By the end of the chapter, you will understand serverless computing and its benefits, gain skills in using IDEs for enhanced coding and debugging, and learn how to integrate ML algorithms for improved code quality. You will also master artifact management, version control, and dependency management with AWS CodeArtifact, and be able to implement secure and efficient CI/CD pipelines using AWS CodeBuild, CodeCommit, and CodePipeline. Furthermore, you will become proficient in deploying IaC with AWS CloudFormation, learn advanced deployment strategies for zero-downtime releases, and gain knowledge in resilience testing through chaos engineering. Finally, you will learn to use AWS services like SNS and Step Functions to create scalable and responsive EDAs and be able to integrate DevOps practices with AWS to accelerate the **software development lifecycle (SDLC)**.

Developer tools

AWS offers a range of developer tools to enhance productivity, simplify workflows, and ensure code quality. Services like Amazon CodeGuru and the AWS **Cloud Development Kit (CDK)** help developers work more efficiently. At the same time, tools like AWS CloudShell and AWS CodePipeline provide integrated environments for efficient development processes. These tools allow developers to automate the entire development lifecycle, from code creation to deployment on a scale. Exposure to these services will equip you to harness AWS's full potential for your projects.

DevOps practices

DevOps, an essential part of modern software development, emphasizes efficient collaboration between development and operations teams to expedite software delivery. AWS offers an extensive suite of services that support DevOps practices. This section examines their capabilities and demonstrates how AWS CodePipeline, AWS CodeBuild, and AWS CodeDeploy automate tasks within the software delivery pipeline. With Amazon CodeStar, you can kick-start projects with well-architected pipelines, while the AWS CDK offers a programmatic way to define IaC, streamlining cloud infrastructure management.

Application integration

In today's interconnected world, efficient application integration is vital. This section covers services like Amazon EventBridge and AWS Step Functions, which enable efficient communication between different application components. These tools help coordinate various AWS resources and third-party services, allowing applications to respond quickly to events and messages. By using Amazon AppFlow, developers can simplify data transfers between multiple services. Amazon **Simple Queue Service (SQS)** and Amazon SNS help manage event-driven and message-based interactions efficiently.

Containers and robotics

The rise in containerization has brought about significant changes in software deployment and management. AWS offers a comprehensive ecosystem for managing containers, featuring services such as Amazon ECS, Amazon EKS, and AWS Fargate. These services allow you to run containerized applications at scale, while AWS App2Container and AWS Copilot make migrating and managing containers in the cloud easier. In addition, AWS provides tools like AWS RoboMaker for developing robotic applications, highlighting the versatility of AWS's DevOps tools across various domains.

Quantum technologies

The next technological frontier is quantum computing, and AWS is leading the way with Amazon Braket. This service gives developers access to quantum computing resources, enabling them to experiment with quantum algorithms and hardware. By providing an intuitive interface, Amazon Braket aims to democratize access to quantum computing, making it easier for developers to integrate quantum solutions into their applications. This section explores how developers can experiment with quantum computing and the future potential of this transformative technology.

Developer tools and DevOps

In the digital age, having a deep understanding of developer tools and DevOps practices is essential for accelerating cloud-powered innovation. With AWS's broad range of tools, developers are equipped to simplify workflows, automate tasks, and improve code quality. These tools support everything from collaborative coding to automated testing and deployment, ensuring your applications are strong and scalable.

Mastering these tools will enable you to build and deploy software more efficiently, collaborate more effectively with your team, and maintain a high standard of code quality throughout your projects.

To better visualize how these AWS tools interact within the DevOps pipeline, the diagram below illustrates how services like AWS CodePipeline, AWS CodeBuild, and AWS CodeDeploy integrate to simplify and automate the software delivery process. This integration fosters collaboration across development and operations teams, ensuring efficient and continuous delivery.

Figure 7.1 illustrates how AWS DevOps tools integrate across the SDLC, enabling continuous integration, delivery, and monitoring through a unified set of services:

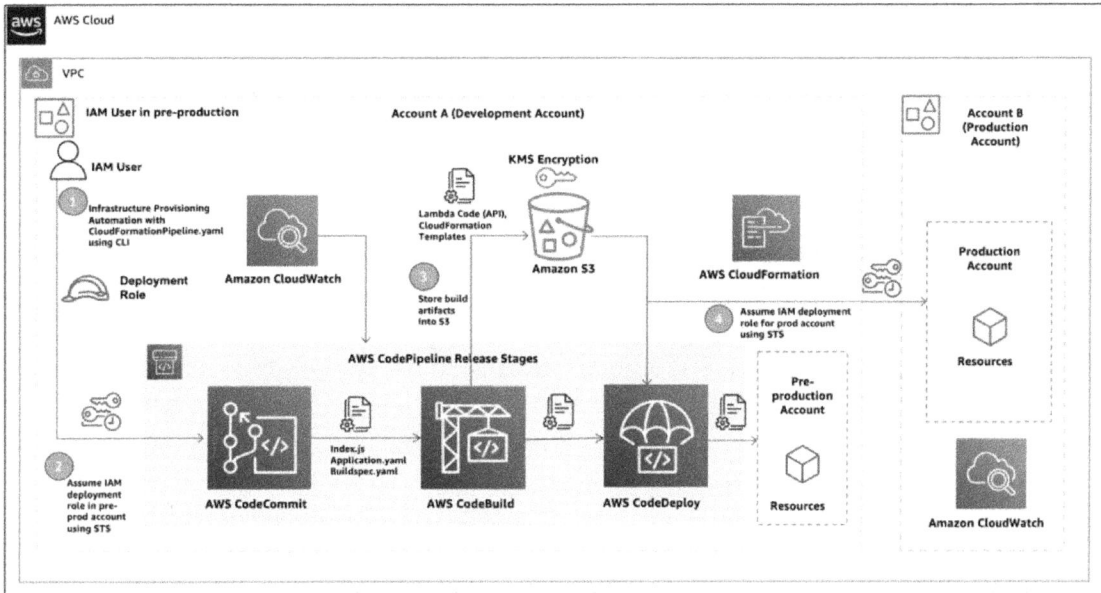

Figure 7.1: *AWS DevOps tools integrations*

AWS developer tools overview

AWS's developer tools suite provides comprehensive solutions to enhance developer productivity, simplify workflows, and ensure secure and efficient application development. Whether automating code reviews, managing CI/CD pipelines, or deploying cloud-native applications, AWS's tools enable an efficient development experience. From the real-time collaboration features of AWS Cloud9 to the AI-powered insights of Amazon CodeGuru, these tools cater to diverse development needs, helping developers build, evaluate, and deploy applications faster and more reliably.

Amazon CodeCatalyst

In the fast-paced world of cloud-based application development, AWS constantly strives to empower developers with tools and services that enhance productivity, simplify workflows, and improve code quality. Amazon CodeCatalyst is one such offering within AWS's developer tools ecosystem. It facilitates the development and deployment processes, allowing developers to focus on creating and refining software solutions [1].

Key features

Amazon CodeCatalyst integrates deeply with AWS services and is a strong and flexible IDE, creating an efficient environment for building, testing, and deploying applications. This integration simplifies resource management, enabling developers to concentrate on writing code. It also supports collaborative coding, enabling multiple developers to work on the same project simultaneously, making reviewing and iterating on code easier, as discussed:

- **AWS service integration**: CodeCatalyst integrates smoothly with AWS services, offering developers a smooth environment for building, testing, and deploying applications [2].

- **Collaborative capabilities**: It supports real-time collaborative coding, which ensures that multiple developers can work on the same project at once [3]; [4].

- **Serverless development**: Amazon CodeCatalyst enables serverless application development using AWS Lambda, freeing developers from managing server infrastructure.

- **Code insights**: The IDE provides real-time insights and recommendations, helping developers improve code quality and adhere to best practices.

Amazon CodeCatalyst is a valuable addition to the AWS developer tools portfolio. It accelerates the development process by enabling developers to create, collaborate, and refine applications more efficiently.

Amazon CodeGuru

Efficient and optimized software development remains a priority in cloud computing, and Amazon CodeGuru addresses this by combining ML with best practices to improve code quality and application performance. CodeGuru performs automated code reviews, finds code defects, and optimizes performance, reducing developers' time debugging and enhancing their applications [5].

Amazon CodeGuru integrates ML into the code review process, allowing it to learn from Amazon's extensive codebase to provide developers with actionable insights. This tool enables developers to make real-time improvements, ensuring that best practices are followed from the outset.

Key features

In the ever-evolving landscape of cloud computing, efficient and optimized software development is paramount. Amazon CodeGuru, a groundbreaking developer tool offered by AWS, addresses this imperative by using ML to enhance code quality and application performance. This section provides a detailed exploration of Amazon CodeGuru, shedding light on its features, functionalities, and the transformative impact it brings to software development, as discussed:

- **Automated code reviews**: CodeGuru Reviewer analyzes source code, finds defects, and offers suggestions for improvements, streamlining the code review process [5].

- **Code insights**: Powered by ML, CodeGuru offers insights that enhance code quality, performance, and adherence to best practices.

- **Application profiling**: The CodeGuru Profiler offers deep insights into runtime behavior, helping developers find bottlenecks and improve their applications.

Amazon CodeGuru empowers developers by automating code reviews and profiling [6], improving overall software quality and application performance.

Amazon Corretto

For Java development in the cloud, Amazon Corretto provides a robust, production-ready runtime environment that streamlines Java application management. This open-source distribution of the **Open Java Development Kit** (**OpenJDK**) delivers a high-performance, secure runtime ideal for cloud-native application developers.

Amazon Corretto integrates smoothly with AWS services, making it a strong choice for any team relying on Java. AWS fully supports it, and as a long-term supported version of OpenJDK, it ensures that Java developers can work confidently, knowing they are using a stable, secure platform with continuous updates and security patches.

Key features

One of Amazon Corretto's key strengths is its focus on performance and security. AWS emphasizes the importance of prompt updates and patches to address security vulnerabilities, ensuring that developers can build and deploy Java applications with confidence [7]. Corretto incorporates performance enhancements derived from the collaboration within the OpenJDK community, contributing to a faster and more efficient runtime environment [8], as discussed:

- **Long-term support**: Amazon Corretto is built to last with **long-term support** (**LTS**), ensuring that developers receive prompt updates and security patches.

- **Security and monitoring**: Corretto includes performance enhancements, security updates, and tools for monitoring Java applications, helping developers improve their Java runtime environment.

- **Multi-platform compatibility**: Whether you are working on Amazon EC2, AWS Lambda, or even on-premises, Corretto works across platforms to deliver consistent experience.

Amazon Corretto is an essential tool for Java developers on AWS. It offers a stable, secure, high-performance solution for running Java applications in the cloud.

AWS Cloud Control API

Cloud orchestration is a key element for modern software development. Developers need to manage and provision cloud resources smoothly, and the AWS Cloud Control API is built to simplify that process. The API simplifies resource provisioning, updates, and deletion across different AWS services, all from a unified interface by providing a programmatic interface to interact with AWS resources.

The Cloud Control API is essential in automating AWS resource management, making it ideal for teams looking to manage cloud infrastructure with code. With this service, developers can easily incorporate resource management into their CI/CD pipelines, ensuring that infrastructure and applications scale efficiently and reliably.

To visualize how the AWS Cloud Control API helps resource management and simplify cloud orchestration, the diagram below highlights its capabilities in providing a unified interface for interacting with various AWS and third-party services. This visualization underscores the API's role in automating infrastructure management within modern DevOps workflows.

Figure 7.2 illustrates how the AWS Cloud Control API simplifies cloud orchestration by providing a unified interface for managing AWS resources and integrating third-party services, enhancing the efficiency of modern DevOps workflows:

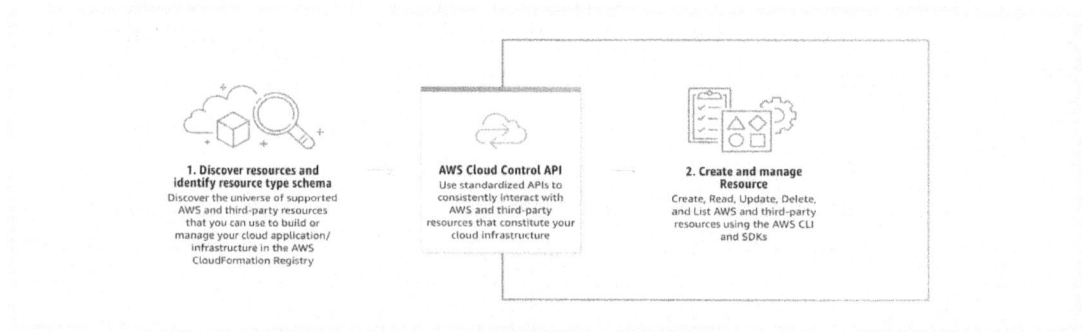

Figure 7.2: AWS Cloud Control API

Key features

The key features and capabilities are as follows:

- **Cross-service resource management**: The Cloud Control API simplifies the management of AWS resources by unifying them under a single API. This is particularly useful in complex cloud environments where multiple services must work together.

- **IaC**: The API's integration with IaC allows developers to define and manage AWS resources programmatically, helping to achieve a version-controlled and repeatable approach to infrastructure management.

- **Consistent resource schema**: The API simplifies management and accelerates cloud deployment workflows by enforcing a consistent schema across resources. This makes it easier for developers to interact with various AWS services without needing to understand each service's unique API.

Use case examples

Let us visit examples of scenarios to introduce the practical application of AWS Cloud Control API:

- **Automated resource provisioning**: DevOps teams can leverage the AWS Cloud Control API to automate the provisioning of resources, ensuring rapid and consistent deployments across development, testing, and production environments [9].

- **Multiple service workflows**: In scenarios where applications span multiple AWS services, the Cloud Control API becomes instrumental in orchestrating and managing the entire stack of resources cohesively [9].

- **IaC**: The AWS Cloud Control API is particularly beneficial in IaC scenarios, where developers define and manage infrastructure using code. Offering a unified API enables the creation and management of AWS resources in a programmatic and version-controlled manner.

- **IaC pipelines**: Integration with IaC pipelines enables the automation of resource updates and ensures that the infrastructure remains coordinated with the codebase throughout its lifecycle [10].

- **Automation and orchestration**: DevOps practices emphasize automation and orchestration. The Cloud Control API enables developers and DevOps teams to automate resource provisioning, updates, and deletion, streamlining deployment processes.

- **Multi-service applications**: In scenarios where applications span multiple AWS services, the Cloud Control API simplifies the coordination of resources. It becomes instrumental in keeping consistency and coherence across distinct parts of a distributed application.

The AWS Cloud Control API provides a powerful tool for consistently and efficiently managing resources for any DevOps team aiming to implement IaC at scale.

AWS Cloud9

AWS Cloud9 offers a strong, collaborative, fully IDE in a cloud-native world. With Cloud9, developers can write, run, and debug code directly from a browser, ending the need for complex local setups or worrying about environment configurations.

Cloud9 is designed for teams, enabling real-time collaboration and efficient access to cloud-based development resources. This cloud-based IDE allows developers to work from anywhere without losing access to the tools they need for effective and productive software development.

Key features

Here, we visit a sample of key features and capabilities of AWS Cloud9:

- **Collaborative coding**: Cloud9 allows multiple developers to work on the same project simultaneously, improving teamwork and reducing development cycles.

- **Built-in tools**: Integrated debugging and terminal tools help simplify development. Developers can run code, test functionality, and debug from within the IDE, saving time and improving workflow efficiency [11].

- **Language support**: AWS Cloud9 supports various programming languages and frameworks, ensuring it works for all cloud development projects.

Use case examples

A sample of real-life applications of AWS Cloud9 is as follows:

- **Remote development environments**: AWS Cloud9 is particularly valuable for teams distributed across separate locations. It enables developers to access a consistent and fully configured development environment from anywhere with an internet connection [12].

- **Education and training**: AWS Cloud9's collaborative nature makes it an excellent choice for educational purposes. Instructors can create shared environments for students to collaborate on coding exercises and projects, fostering a cooperative learning environment.

- **Serverless application development**: AWS Cloud9 simplifies the development experience for developers working on serverless applications. It integrates smoothly with AWS Lambda, making building, evaluating, and deploying serverless functions easier.

AWS Cloud9 is the go-to tool for teams needing a cloud-based IDE that fosters collaboration and simplifies the development workflow across languages and cloud resources.

AWS CodeArtifact

Managing dependencies and software packages is a critical task in modern development workflows. AWS CodeArtifact helps solve this problem by providing a fully managed artifact repository service that integrates smoothly with your CI/CD pipeline. By securely storing and sharing software packages in the cloud, CodeArtifact ensures that all your dependencies are managed efficiently across the development lifecycle.

For teams working in environments with complex dependencies or across multiple teams, CodeArtifact simplifies artifact management, versioning, and access control, improving collaboration while keeping a high standard of security.

Key features

AWS CodeArtifact is a fully managed artifact repository service that allows organizations to securely store, publish, and share software packages and dependencies [13]. With native integration into popular build and deployment tools, CodeArtifact simplifies the management of dependencies in the SDLC. The following are the key features and capabilities:

- **Universal package management**: CodeArtifact supports multiple package formats, such as Maven, npm, and PyPI, ensuring that it fits a wide range of development needs and supports polyglot environments.

- **Security and access control**: With deep integration into +, CodeArtifact enables fine-grained access control, ensuring only authorized users can access or publish packages.

- **Scalability**: CodeArtifact scales with your team's needs, managing increasing volumes of artifacts without sacrificing performance or reliability.

Use cases and scenarios

Let us review a sample of actual use scenarios for AWS CodeArtifact:

- **Dependency management in CI/CD pipelines**: CodeArtifact simplifies the process of managing dependencies in CI/CD pipelines, ensuring consistent and reliable builds [14].

- **Centralized artifact repository**: Organizations with multiple projects and teams receive help from a centralized repository for managing and sharing software artifacts. CodeArtifact simplifies the organization-wide use of shared packages.

- **Support for polyglot development**: By supporting various package formats, CodeArtifact facilitates polyglot development environments in which different projects may use distinct programming languages and dependencies [15].

AWS CodeArtifact is essential for teams managing complex dependencies or building software with various package formats, helping them keep track of versions and support secure access to dependencies.

AWS CodeBuild

With cloud-native development practices, building and testing software should be automated to enable faster release cycles. AWS CodeBuild delivers a fully managed build service that compiles source code, runs tests, and packages software for deployment. This service is integrated with other AWS tools to support efficient CI/CD workflows, improving the speed and reliability of your software delivery pipeline.

Whether your team is dealing with minor code updates or large-scale feature builds, CodeBuild automatically scales to meet your needs, ensuring consistent, repeatable builds across your organization.

Key features

AWS CodeBuild is a cloud-based build service that compiles source code, runs tests, and produces ready-to-deploy software artifacts [16]. It integrates smoothly with other AWS services and supports popular programming languages, enabling developers to focus on writing code rather than managing build infrastructure. The following are the key features and capabilities:

- **Fully managed service**: AWS CodeBuild automates the process of compiling source code, running tests, and packaging software, removing the need for teams to manage build infrastructure [16].

- **Support for multiple languages**: With support for a wide variety of programming languages, CodeBuild fits into almost any development pipeline, handling the build and test phases for your team, regardless of the language or framework [14].

- **Customizable build environments**: Developers can define their build environments, including build commands, environment variables, and custom tools to ensure that each build matches their project's needs [16].

Figure 7.3 shows what happens when you run a build with CodeBuild:

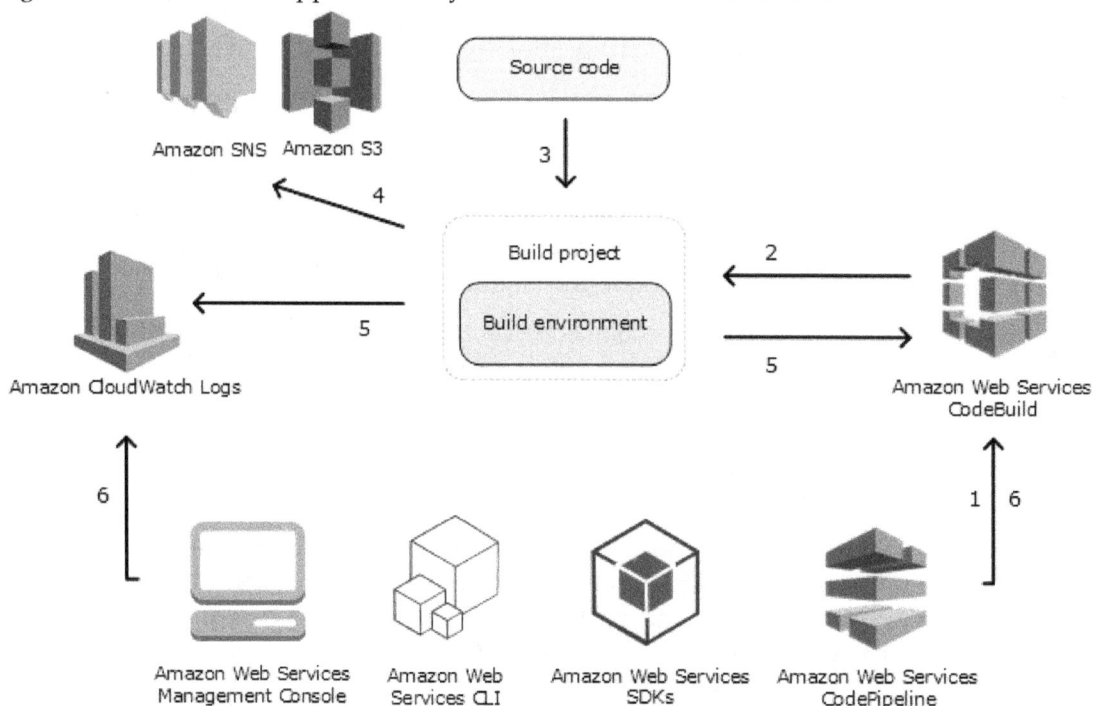

Figure 7.3: Running a build with CodeBuild

Use cases and scenarios

The use cases and scenarios are as follows:

- **CI**: CodeBuild is a key part of CI pipelines, automating the build and test phases. It integrates smoothly with AWS CodePipeline, enabling a CI workflow.

- **Scalable build processes**: With its ability to scale automatically, CodeBuild is well-suited for projects with varying build workloads. Whether managing small code changes or significant feature additions, CodeBuild adapts to the demands of the development pipeline [17].

- **Integration with source control**: CodeBuild smoothly integrates with version control systems such as AWS CodeCommit, GitHub, and Bitbucket, automatically triggering builds when changes are pushed to the repository [18].

AWS CodeBuild is the backbone of any CI/CD pipeline, ensuring that code is built, evaluated, and packaged efficiently without introducing bottlenecks in your development workflow.

AWS CodeCommit

Version control is essential for any development team to track changes, collaborate, and maintain consistency across projects. AWS CodeCommit is a fully managed source control service that provides secure and scalable hosting for Git repositories. This service helps teams keep code integrity while simplifying collaboration and streamlining development.

AWS CodeCommit provides a reliable and secure environment for version control, supporting large teams and complex projects. With integration into the broader AWS ecosystem, CodeCommit smoothly fits into DevOps workflows and automation pipelines.

Key features

AWS CodeCommit allows developers to store and version their code in the cloud, helping collaboration and ensuring a secure and accessible repository. Key aspects include [8]:

- **Secure Git repositories**: CodeCommit ensures data is encrypted in transit and at rest. It integrates with AWS IAM, allowing teams to manage permissions and access securely.

- **Scalability**: CodeCommit scales to your needs, supporting repositories of any size and accommodating growing teams and projects.

- **Integration with AWS tools**: It works smoothly with AWS CodePipeline and AWS CodeBuild, creating CI/CD pipelines that enhance workflow efficiency.

Use cases

In this section, we will go through the use cases:

- **Collaborative software development**: CodeCommit facilitates team collaboration by providing a central repository for code changes, enabling version control and efficient collaboration [19].

- **CI/CD**: Integration with AWS CodePipeline allows for the efficient implementation of CI/CD pipelines, automating code builds, testing, and deployments [20].

- **Secure code storage**: CodeCommit serves as a secure and compliant storage solution for source code, meeting the requirements of industries with stringent security and compliance standards [21].

For development teams seeking a dependable, scalable, and secure version control solution, AWS CodeCommit streamlines the process and integrates seamlessly with the AWS ecosystem, ensuring consistency across environments.

Best practices for AWS CodeCommit implementation

Now, we introduce the best practices for implementing AWS CodeCommit. We can find case studies and best practices developed from practices by AWS, its partners, and other companies delivering professional services or building products for the AWS cloud. They are beneficial, helpful, and easy to find, as follows. It is possible to generalize them as tools to keep code quality and ensure adherence to coding standards [19].

- **Branching strategies**: Adopt effective branching strategies to manage feature development, bug fixes, and releases efficiently [21].

- **Code reviews**: Leverage CodeCommit's built-in code review tools to keep code quality and ensure adherence to coding standards [19].

- **Repository structure**: Organize repositories logically, considering factors like team structure, project dependencies, and deployment pipelines [20].

AWS CodeDeploy

Software deployment can be complex, especially when managing updates across distributed systems. AWS CodeDeploy automates this process, helping teams deploy applications to various compute services with minimal downtime and fewer manual interventions. Whether deploying EC2 instances, Lambda functions, or on-premises servers, CodeDeploy streamlines the deployment process, enhancing efficiency and minimizing deployment risks.

Key features

By supporting various deployment strategies, CodeDeploy provides flexibility, enabling teams to select the approach that best suits their needs, ranging from blue/green deployments to rolling updates. The following are the key features of AWS CodeDeploy:

- **Flexible deployment strategies**: AWS CodeDeploy supports multiple deployment strategies, including in-place deployments, blue/green deployments, and canary releases. This flexibility ensures that teams can choose the most suitable approach for their application and infrastructure needs [8].

- **Multi-platform support**: CodeDeploy works across platforms, enabling deployments on EC2, Lambda, and on-premises servers, making it versatile for various application types and deployment requirements.

- **Rollback capabilities**: CodeDeploy includes automatic rollback functionality, minimizing risk by ensuring that if a deployment fails, it can quickly revert to the earlier working version, reducing downtime.

Figure 7.4 shows a high-level architecture for AWS CodeDeploy, a fully managed deployment service:

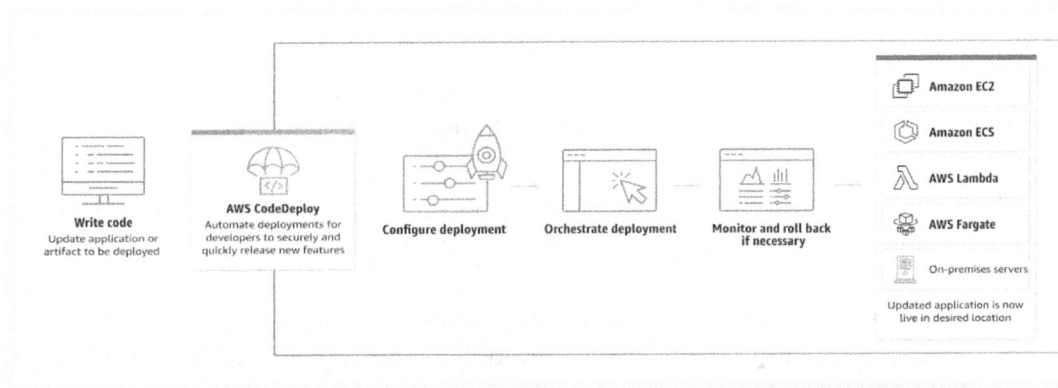

Figure 7.4: *CodeDeploy fully managed deployment service*

AWS CodeDeploy simplifies the deployment process, allowing development teams to deploy faster, with fewer issues and greater flexibility.

AWS CodePipeline

CI/CD pipelines are critical to modern development workflows, ensuring that applications are delivered quickly and reliably. AWS CodePipeline automates the entire process, from code changes to build, test, and deployment stages, integrating with AWS and third-party tools to create a fully automated pipeline.

CodePipeline enhances efficiency by automating repetitive tasks and reducing the manual overhead associated with deployment. It supports parallel and sequential stages, enabling flexibility in deployment strategies and workflows.

Key features

The key features of AWS CodePipeline are as follows [22]:

- **Automated workflows**: CodePipeline automates the flow of code changes through build, test, and deployment processes, removing manual interventions and improving the speed of application delivery [23].

- **Integration with AWS and third-party tools**: CodePipeline integrates with a wide range of AWS services, like AWS CodeBuild and AWS CodeDeploy, as well as third-party tools such as GitHub, to offer flexibility in workflows [20].

- **Parallel and sequential execution**: CodePipeline supports both parallel and sequential execution of stages, allowing teams to tailor their workflows to the needs of their applications and deployment environments [21].

Use cases of AWS CodePipeline

The following are the use cases of AWS CodePipeline:

- **Multi-environment deployments**: CodePipeline facilitates the creation of pipelines that support deploying applications to multiple environments, such as development, testing, and production.

- **Microservices architecture**: Ideal for orchestrating CI/CD workflows in microservices-based applications, allowing independent testing and deployment of individual services [24].

- **Serverless application deployments**: Well-suited for automating the deployment of serverless applications, managing the build and deployment of AWS Lambda functions and related resources.

Best practices for AWS CodePipeline implementation

The following are the best practices for AWS CodePipeline implementation:

- **Version control integration**: Integrate CodePipeline with version control systems like AWS CodeCommit or GitHub for efficient source code management [22].

- **Automated testing strategies**: Implement automated testing at each stage of the pipeline to find and address issues early in the development process [25].

- **Security best practices**: Follow AWS security best practices, including least privilege principles and encryption of sensitive data within the pipeline.

By automating the release process, AWS CodePipeline allows development teams to focus more on innovation and less on manual deployment tasks, making the entire process more efficient and dependable.

AWS CodeStar

Managing and building applications on AWS requires an integrated platform that connects development tools, code repositories, and deployment pipelines. AWS CodeStar serves as that unified platform, allowing teams to quickly setup and manage their software development activities. With built-in support for various AWS tools, CodeStar accelerates the creation of fully configured CI/CD pipelines for a smoother development experience.

Whether building a new project or managing an existing one, AWS CodeStar's simplicity and integration with AWS services make it an ideal choice for developers seeking a simplified experience.

Key features

The key features of AWS CodeStar are as follows [26]:

- **Unified development platform**: CodeStar integrates tools for coding, building, testing, and deploying applications into a single interface, simplifying the management of the SDLC.
- **Project templates**: CodeStar provides pre-configured templates for various programming languages and AWS services, making it easier to start new projects.
- **Built-in CI/CD pipeline**: Each project automatically receives a CI/CD pipeline that manages code builds, testing, and deployments, helping to simplify development operations.
- **Team collaboration**: CodeStar's integration with AWS IAM enables role-based access control, making team management easier and ensuring secure access to project resources.

Use cases

The following are the use cases of AWS CodeStar [27]; [26]:

- **Rapid prototyping**: CodeStar is beneficial for rapidly prototyping applications, allowing developers to focus on coding while it manages the underlying infrastructure.
- **Multi-language support**: This feature is ideal for projects involving multiple programming languages, providing a flexible environment for diverse development needs.
- **Serverless application development**: Suited for serverless application development, simplifying the process of building and deploying AWS Lambda functions.

Best practices for AWS CodeStar implementation

The following are the best practices for AWS CodeStar implementation:

- **Customization of templates**: Customize project templates to align with specific project requirements and coding standards [28].

- **Integration with AWS services**: Leverage integrations with other AWS services, such as AWS CodeCommit and AWS CodeBuild, to enhance the CI/CD pipeline [29].

- **Regular monitoring and optimization**: Monitor project activity and resource usage regularly, improving configurations based on project needs and changing requirements [26].

AWS CodeStar is the go-to service for teams to simplify their cloud-based application development processes, offering a unified platform for efficient collaboration and project management.

AWS Command Line Interface

The AWS CLI provides a CLI for AWS services, allowing developers to manage their AWS resources directly from a terminal. It provides a powerful and efficient way to interact with AWS services, especially for tasks that need to be automated or run on a large scale.

Key features

The AWS CLI helps teams simplify workflows, automate tasks, and save time by enabling scripting, automation, and batch operations. Its simplicity and flexibility make it a valuable tool for developers and DevOps teams. The following are the key features of the AWS CLI. [30]:

- **Cross-service commands**: The AWS CLI enables users to interact with various AWS services, providing a consistent experience regardless of the service they are using.

- **Scripting and automation**: Using the AWS CLI in scripts, developers can automate repetitive tasks, reduce manual errors, and accelerate workflows.

- **Customization and configuration**: The CLI allows users to configure it to meet their needs, including setting default regions, output formats, and security credentials.

Use cases

The use cases of AWS CLI are as follows:

- **Batch operations**: Ideal for executing batch operations, AWS CLI allows users to automate repetitive tasks and manage resources at scale [30].

- **Integration with scripts**: Suited for integration into scripts and third-party tools, enabling efficient incorporation of AWS actions into existing workflows [31].

- **Quick resource management**: Users can quickly create, configure, and manage AWS resources without accessing the AWS Management Console, offering a simplified experience [30].

Best practices for AWS CLI usage

The following are the best practices for AWS CLI usage [30]:

- **Security best practices**: Adhere to security best practices by securely managing and storing AWS CLI credentials, utilizing IAM roles, and implementing **multi-factor authentication (MFA)**.

- **Version compatibility**: Ensure compatibility by using the latest version of the AWS CLI, staying informed about updates, and checking for any breaking script changes.

- **Output formatting**: Improve output formatting for scripts by selecting proper output options, such as JSON or table format, to enhance readability and parsing [32].

AWS CLI is an essential tool for developers. It enables easy management of AWS resources, automates tasks, and improves workflow efficiency.

AWS Device Farm

Testing mobile applications across various devices ensures your app works smoothly on all platforms. AWS Device Farm is a cloud-based mobile app testing service that provides access to a wide range of real devices for testing purposes. This section explores how AWS Device Farm helps developers ensure their mobile applications work flawlessly across different devices, operating systems, and configurations.

AWS Device Farm simplifies the testing process by allowing developers to run tests in parallel on multiple devices, saving valuable time and improving the quality of the application. By providing access to real devices rather than relying on emulators, Device Farm offers a better representation of how the app will perform in real-world scenarios.

Key features

AWS Device Farm streamlines the testing process by enabling developers to run tests in parallel across multiple devices, saving valuable time and enhancing the quality of the application. By providing access to real devices rather than relying on emulators, Device Farm offers a more accurate representation of how the app will perform in real-world scenarios. The following are the key features of AWS Device Farm [33]:

- **Device compatibility testing**: AWS Device Farm allows developers to assess their mobile apps on a wide range of real devices, ensuring compatibility across multiple platforms, screen sizes, and configurations.

- **Parallel testing**: Device Farm supports parallel test execution, enabling multiple tests to run concurrently on different devices and accelerating the testing process.

- **Built-in test scripts**: The service comes with built-in support for popular test automation frameworks such as Appium, XCTest, and Espresso, simplifying the creation and execution of tests.

Use cases

The following are the cases of AWS Device Farm:

- **Automated testing**: Well-suited for automated testing scenarios, AWS Device Farm supports popular test automation frameworks such as Appium, XCTest, and Espresso [33].

- **Real device testing:** Allows developers to perform testing on real devices rather than relying solely on emulators, ensuring correct simulation of user interactions [34].

- **Performance testing**: Ideal for performance testing, developers can assess app behavior under various conditions, such as different network strengths and device specifications [33].

Best practices for AWS Device Farm usage

The following are the best practices for AWS Device Farm usage:

- **Test on real devices**: Prioritize testing on real devices to uncover issues that may not be clear in emulator-based testing [34].

- **Parallel execution planning**: Efficiently plan parallel test executions to maximize testing throughput and minimize overall testing time [33].

- **Regular test updates**: Keep test scripts updated to align with the latest features and capabilities of AWS Device Farm, ensuring the best testing performance [35].

AWS Device Farm streamlines the testing process for mobile applications, enabling developers to quickly identify issues, optimize performance, and deliver high-quality apps.

AWS Fault Injection Simulator

Ensuring the resilience of cloud-based applications is critical in today's environment, where uptime and reliability are paramount. AWS **Fault Injection Simulator** (**FIS**) provides developers and operations teams with a controlled environment for assessing the resilience of their applications by simulating various failure scenarios. This service helps teams understand how their systems behave under stress and find potential vulnerabilities before they affect real users.

AWS FIS enables chaos engineering by introducing failures into production systems to evaluate how well applications manage disruptions. This initiative-taking approach allows teams to make necessary adjustments to improve their cloud applications' fault-tolerance and resilience.

Key features

AWS FIS enables chaos engineering by introducing failures into production systems to evaluate how well applications manage disruptions. This initiative-taking approach allows teams to make necessary adjustments to improve their cloud applications' fault-tolerance and resilience. The following are the key features of the AWS FIS [36]:

- **Fault injection scenarios**: AWS FIS allows users to create and execute failure scenarios, simulating various conditions like latency, errors, and timeouts to evaluate application behavior.

- **Observability integration**: It integrates with AWS observability tools such as Amazon CloudWatch, providing insights into system performance during fault injection experiments.

- **Automation capabilities**: The service supports automation for fault injection experiments, allowing DevOps teams to schedule resilience tests regularly.

The AWS FIS enables teams to inject controlled faults, ensuring that cloud applications can withstand failures and remain dependable under various adverse conditions.

Benefits of using AWS FIS

Building resilient cloud applications requires more than a high-availability architecture; it demands proactive failure testing to uncover vulnerabilities before they impact production. AWS FIS provides a controlled, cost-effective environment for conducting realistic failure simulations, allowing teams to confirm system resilience, improve recovery strategies, and ensure business continuity. The following are key benefits of using AWS FIS:

- **Resilience validation**: The service allows teams to confirm the resilience of their applications by testing how they perform during unexpected disruptions.

- **Cost-effective testing**: The AWS FIS offers a cost-effective way to perform resilience testing without requiring complex infrastructure setup.

- **Realistic failure simulations**: By simulating real-world failure conditions, the service ensures that testing is correct and relevant, helping teams better prepare for potential issues in production.

The AWS FIS is a crucial tool for organizations seeking to enhance the resilience of their cloud-native applications and prepare for unexpected disruptions.

Practical applications

The following are examples of practical applications:

- **Chaos engineering**: Supports the principles of chaos engineering by allowing controlled injection of faults, helping organizations understand how their systems behave under adverse conditions [36].

- **Continuous resilience testing**: Helps the incorporation of continuous resilience testing into the development and deployment pipelines, ensuring ongoing evaluation of application strength [37].

Best practices for AWS Fault Injection Simulator

The following are the best practices for the AWS SDLC:

- **Start with low-impact scenarios**: Begin by injecting faults with minimal impact to understand the first response of the system before progressing to more severe scenarios [38].
- **Regularly review results**: Regularly review and analyze the results of fault injection experiments to find patterns and potential areas for improvement [36].

AWS tools and SDKs

AWS provides a comprehensive set of tools and **software development kits** (**SDKs**) that enable developers to build, deploy, and manage applications efficiently on the AWS cloud. These tools simplify interactions with AWS services, improve productivity, and foster the adoption of DevOps practices across organizations.

AWS SDKs help developers easily integrate AWS services into their applications by providing language-specific libraries and APIs, streamlining the development process. In addition, AWS Tools extend the functionality of SDKs, offering capabilities such as automation, scripting, and command line interactions with AWS services.

Key features

AWS SDKs help developers easily integrate AWS services into their applications by providing language-specific libraries and APIs, streamlining the development process. In addition, AWS Tools extend the functionality of SDKs, offering capabilities such as automation, scripting, and command-line interactions with AWS services. The following are the key features of AWS Tools and SDKs:

- **Multi-language support**: AWS SDKs support various programming languages such as Java, Python, JavaScript, .NET, and more, making it easier for developers to integrate AWS services into their applications [39].
- **Comprehensive service coverage**: AWS tools and SDKs cover a wide range of AWS services, providing developers with the necessary libraries and utilities to interact with AWS resources [24].
- **Integration with popular IDEs**: The tools and SDKs integrate smoothly with popular IDEs like Visual Studio, Eclipse, and IntelliJ IDEA, enhancing the overall development experience.

By using AWS Tools and SDKs, developers can reduce the time and effort needed to interact with AWS services and simplify their workflows.

Benefits of using AWS tools and SDKs

The following are the benefits of using AWS Tools and SDKs:

- **Efficiency and productivity**: AWS Tools and SDKs help automate repetitive tasks, provide pre-built functions, and reduce the complexity of interacting with AWS services [24].

- **Consistent development experience**: These tools offer a consistent development experience across multiple languages, ensuring that development teams working with various technology stacks can rely on the same tools and processes [40].

- **Version compatibility**: AWS SDKs maintain compatibility with the latest AWS service updates, allowing developers to take advantage of new features and improvements without worrying about version discrepancies [39].

AWS Tools and SDKs help developers build and deploy cloud-native applications faster and more reliably while ensuring consistency and productivity across development teams.

Figure 7.5 visualizes the SDKs and how they provide pre-built modules, components, packages, and tools for developers to build, evaluate, and deploy software applications:

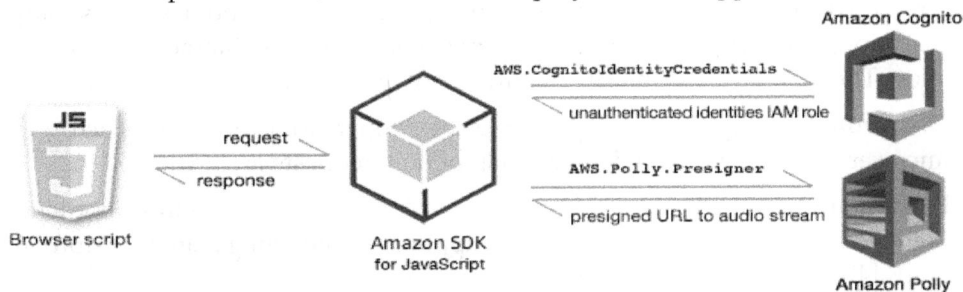

Figure 7.5: SDKs provide pre-built tools

Practical applications

In this section, we will go through the practical applications:

- **Application development**: Helps the development of cloud-native applications by providing tools and SDKs that abstract the complexities of AWS service interaction [41].

- **Automation and scripting**: Enables automation and scripting of everyday tasks, allowing DevOps teams to create efficient and repeatable workflows [39].

Best practices for using AWS tools and SDKs

The following are the best practices for using AWS tools and SDKs:

- **Regularly update SDK versions**: Stay up to date with the latest SDK versions to access new features, improvements, and security updates [40].

- **Utilize code samples and documentation**: Leverage code samples and comprehensive documentation provided by AWS to speed up development and troubleshoot issues effectively [41].

AWS X-Ray

Monitoring the performance of distributed applications can be challenging, especially as microservices architectures become more common. AWS X-Ray is a service that helps developers analyze and troubleshoot their applications' performance, offering real-time insights into system behavior. This section explores how AWS X-Ray enables developers to find performance bottlenecks, detect errors, and improve applications for improved user experiences.

Key features

AWS X-Ray uses distributed tracing to track requests as they flow through various components of an application, allowing developers to see how their services interact and find areas for optimization. The following are the key features of AWS X-Ray:

- **Distributed tracing**: AWS X-Ray enables developers to trace requests across different microservices, providing a detailed map of how requests are processed [42].

- **Performance monitoring**: The service helps find performance bottlenecks by highlighting the slowest segments of an application, enabling teams to improve critical paths [42].

- **Error detection**: AWS X-Ray automatically detects errors and exceptions, offering detailed insights into where and why issues occur in the system [43].

By offering deep insights into application behavior, AWS X-Ray helps developers ensure that their applications run efficiently and meet performance expectations.

Benefits of using AWS X-Ray

The following are the benefits of using AWS X-Ray [42]:

- **Improved debugging**: AWS X-Ray offers real-time debugging capabilities, allowing developers to pinpoint the root causes of errors and issues in their applications.

- **Enhanced performance optimization**: With detailed performance insights, developers can improve their applications, improving response times and overall user satisfaction.

- **Reduced downtime**: By detecting errors quickly and accurately, AWS X-Ray minimizes downtime and ensures that issues are resolved before they affect end-users.

Practical applications

The following are the practical applications:

- **Microservices architecture**: Particularly valuable in microservices architectures, AWS X-Ray helps developers understand the interactions between different services [42].
- **Production issues**: Simplifies the process of troubleshooting and diagnosing production issues by offering detailed insights into application behavior [40].

Best practices for using AWS X-Ray

In this section, we will go through the best practices for using AWS X-Ray:

- **Instrumentation of code**: Implement thorough instrumentation of code to capture trace data effectively and gain comprehensive insights [42].
- **Integration with AWS services**: Leverage integration with other AWS services, such as AWS Lambda and Amazon EC2, to capture traces from various components [40].

AWS X-Ray enables developers to check and troubleshoot distributed applications, ensuring their systems perform optimally and reliably.

Amazon CodeWhisperer

Amazon CodeWhisperer is an ML-powered tool that helps developers by providing real-time code suggestions and automating the code review process. Using ML, CodeWhisperer learns from large code bases and offers developers helpful suggestions that improve the quality and efficiency of their coding tasks.

Key features

CodeWhisperer enhances collaboration and accelerates the SDLC by offering real-time feedback and suggestions that help teams keep high coding standards. The following are the key features of Amazon CodeWhisperer:

- **Real-time collaboration**: CodeWhisperer facilitates real-time collaboration among developers by providing in-line comments and suggestions directly within the code.
- **Automated code reviews**: The service automates code reviews, ensuring all code adheres to predefined best practices and coding standards.
- **In-line comments and suggestions**: Developers can receive in-line suggestions while working, helping simplify the review process and improving code quality.

Figure 7.6 is a visual representation of the Amazon CodeWhisperer, the ML-powered coding companion:

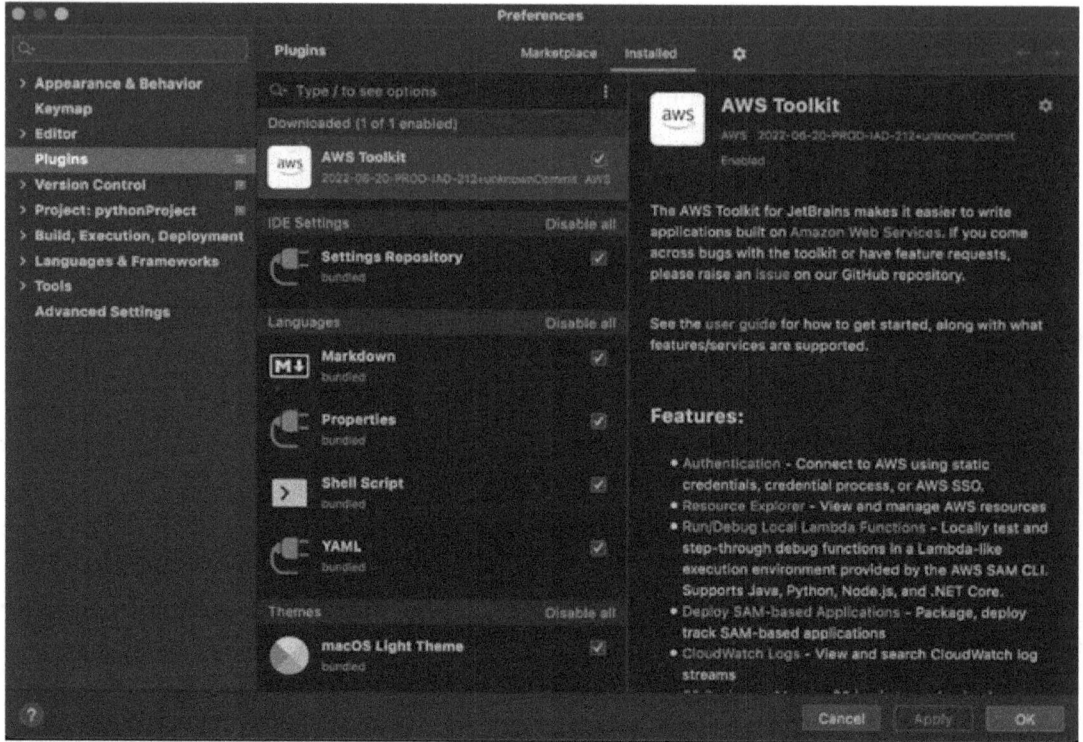

Figure 7.6: *Amazon CodeWhisperer, the ML-powered coding companion*

Benefits of using Amazon CodeWhisperer

The following are the benefits of using Amazon CodeWhisperer:

- **Accelerated code review process**: This simplifies and accelerates the code review process by automating routine checks and providing a collaborative environment for developers [44].

- **Code quality improvement**: Contributes to improved code quality by flagging potential issues and ensuring adherence to coding best practices [43].

- **Knowledge transfer**: Helps knowledge transfer among team members by promoting collaboration and shared understanding of the codebase [43].

Practical applications

In this section, we will go through the practical applications:

- **Large-scale development projects**: Particularly beneficial in large-scale development projects with distributed teams, where efficient code collaboration is crucial [43].

- **Open-source contributions**: Supports open-source contributors by providing a transparent and collaborative platform for reviewing and contributing code changes [44].

Best practices for using Amazon CodeWhisperer

In this section, we will go through the best practices for using Amazon CodeWhisperer:

- **Define clear review guidelines**: Setup clear guidelines for code reviews to ensure that the team focuses on critical aspects of code quality and functionality [43].

- **Regularly update review rules**: Regularly update and customize automated review rules to align with evolving coding standards and project requirements [44].

Amazon CodeWhisperer fosters collaboration and improves code quality across development teams by providing real-time feedback.

Conclusion

This chapter has thoroughly explored the AWS developer tools and DevOps practices that enable modern software development in the cloud. We have examined tools such as Amazon CodeWhisperer, AWS CodePipeline, and AWS X-Ray, which help enhance developer productivity, simplify workflows, and ensure application quality and reliability. AWS services like CodeBuild, CodeDeploy, and CodeCommit have also proven essential in automating the development pipeline and providing the scalability of cloud-native applications.

As we move to the next chapter, the second part of DevOps and developer tools, we will delve deeper into the advanced services and practices that drive continuous integration and deployment, exploring tools like AWS CodeStar and AWS Cloud Control API to improve the development and operational lifecycle.

Join our Discord space

Join our Discord workspace for latest updates, offers, tech happenings around the world, new releases, and sessions with the authors:

https://discord.bpbonline.com

CHAPTER 8
Developer Tools and DevOps: Part 2

Introduction

As modern cloud applications grow increasingly complex, seamless integration, automation, and scalability are critical for efficiency and reliability. AWS offers a comprehensive suite of developer Tools and DevOps services, enabling organizations to build, manage, and deploy cloud-native applications at scale. This chapter explores advanced AWS services for application integration, container orchestration, robotics, and quantum computing, enabling optimized workflows and innovation-driven development.

Structure

In this chapter, we will cover the following topics:

- AWS application integration services
- Amazon AppFlow
- Amazon EventBridge
- Amazon Managed Workflows for Apache Airflow
- Amazon MQ
- Amazon Simple Notification Service

- Amazon Simple Queue Service
- Managed message queues
- AWS Step Functions
- Amazon Elastic Container Registry
- Amazon Elastic Container Service
- Amazon Elastic Kubernetes Service
- AWS App2Container
- AWS Fargate
- AWS Copilot
- Red Hat OpenShift Service on AWS
- Managed OpenShift in the cloud
- AWS RoboMaker
- Quantum technologies in AWS
- Amazon Braket
- Developer tools and DevOps in AWS

Objectives

By the end of this chapter, you will understand the role of AWS application integration services in modern cloud architecture and explore container management solutions such as Amazon **Elastic Kubernetes Service** (EKS) and AWS **App2Container** (A2C). You will also analyze how AWS supports robotics development through AWS RoboMaker and examine AWS's quantum computing capabilities, with a focus on Amazon Braket for experimenting with quantum algorithms. Ultimately, this chapter will guide you in identifying the best practices for utilizing AWS DevOps tools to automate, optimize, and scale cloud applications efficiently.

AWS application integration services

AWS offers a comprehensive suite of services for seamless application integration, enabling organizations to build scalable, efficient, and connected applications. Integrating different software applications and systems ensures efficient data flow, real-time communication, and interoperability, streamlining business processes and enhancing overall productivity [1]. Key services include:

- **Amazon Simple Queue Service (SQS)**: SQS is a fully managed message queuing service that helps decouple application components, promoting scalability and fault-tolrance by ensuring reliable message delivery.

- **Amazon Simple Notification Service (SNS)**: SNS is a flexible messaging service that facilitates communication between distributed components, enabling seamless delivery across microservices.

- **Amazon AppFlow**: This service enables secure integration between AWS services and **software as a service (SaaS)** applications, allowing for automated data flows to and from various platforms.

- **Amazon EventBridge**: EventBridge simplifies event-driven integration by connecting application data with various AWS services and enabling real-time event processing.

These services provide a robust infrastructure to connect diverse applications, systems, and data sources, promoting business agility, enhanced decision-making, and overall system reliability.

To better illustrate how these services integrate applications and data sources seamlessly, *Figure 8.1* highlights AWS application integration services and their key functionalities:

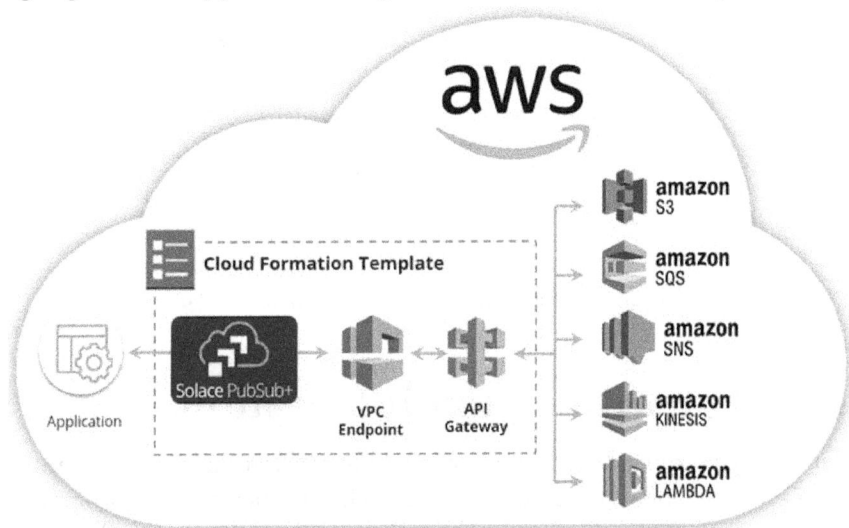

Figure 8.1: *AWS application integration services*

Application integration allows different systems and software to work together, ensuring efficient data flow and real-time communication. This process ensures smooth data exchange and real-time communication, enabling organizations to create more agile and responsive business operations [2]. Modern cloud computing enables systems to communicate and share data effectively. Key integration strategies include utilizing an **enterprise service bus (ESB)** as middleware to connect applications, leveraging API-based integration for seamless data exchange, and employing an event-driven architecture to manage real-time data responses. The significance of application integration lies in its ability to synchronize data across various systems, minimize errors, and reduce manual processes [3]. Furthermore, it enhances decision-making by providing a comprehensive data view, enabling organizations to swiftly act on the most relevant insights [4].

Asynchronous communication via SQS is crucial in microservices architectures, where services interact through the exchange of events and messages. The following figure illustrates a typical AWS microservices application, highlighting the integration services' role in supporting these architectures:

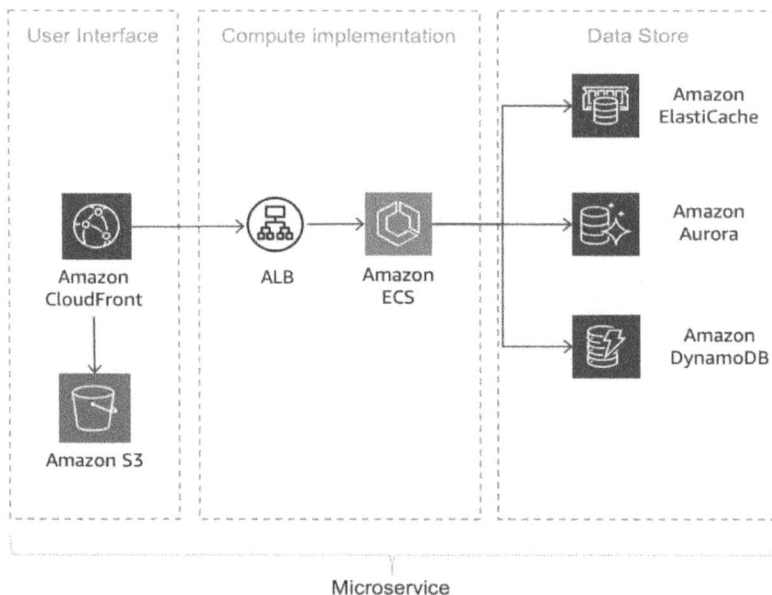

Figure 8.2: *Typical microservices application on AWS*

Significance of application integration

Application integration is crucial in modern software ecosystems as it ensures data consistency across various platforms, enhances efficiency, and facilitates better decision-making. Through seamless communication between applications, integration cuts data silos and minimizes manual tasks, ultimately driving operational efficiency [3]. Moreover, when systems work cohesively, businesses can make informed, data-driven decisions promoting agility and innovation [4].

With the growing need for dynamic, real-time capabilities, integrating applications ensures that organizations can react promptly to changes, whether scaling operations, responding to market shifts, or addressing customer demands. Organizations can achieve a unified view of their processes through integrated systems, ensuring they stay competitive in fast-moving industries [1].

Strategies for application integration

Different strategies are essential for implementing effective application integration in cloud-native environments. An ESB is a common approach. This middleware enables communication between disparate systems and services through a central hub [5]. This approach simplifies the management of communications between applications, ensuring that they interact in a standardized manner.

Another strategy involves API-based integration, where applications communicate via APIs. This approach offers flexibility, scalability, and easy data exchange across services, allowing applications to work independently while sharing necessary functionality [1]. The third strategy is adopting event-driven architectures, where systems communicate by triggering events based on specific actions or changes in the environment, thus enabling real-time responses [6].

Best practices for effective application integration

Best practices should be followed to ensure smooth and efficient integration. Standardizing data formats is efficient for compatibility between applications and guarantees the smooth flow of information [3]. Robust security measures, including encryption and authentication, are essential for safeguarding sensitive data during integration processes [4]. Additionally, adopting event-driven design principles enhances flexibility and scalability by allowing applications to interact through events rather than direct calls, which decouples components and simplifies system architecture [1].

Another best practice is decoupling components, where systems like Amazon SQS manage asynchronous communication between applications. This decoupling allows services to scale independently and promotes system reliability, making applications more adaptable to changes and failures [6].

Amazon AppFlow

Amazon AppFlow is a fully managed integration service provided by AWS. It enables secure and efficient data transfer between AWS services and various SaaS applications. As businesses increasingly rely on cloud-based applications, Amazon AppFlow helps ensure seamless data flows, supporting operational efficiency and enhancing platform decision-making capabilities.

Key features

Amazon AppFlow offers critical features that enhance its utility for organizations seeking to improve their data integration strategies [7]. These include:

- **Bidirectional data flow**: AppFlow supports bidirectional data transfer, enabling seamless data movement in both directions between AWS services and external SaaS applications. This flexibility allows organizations to integrate various systems efficiently while maintaining consistent data flows.

- **Pre-built connectors**: The service offers pre-built connectors for popular SaaS applications, including *Salesforce, ServiceNow*, and others, streamlining the integration process. These connectors simplify the connection between AWS and SaaS platforms, reducing the need for manual configurations.

- **Data mapping and transformation**: AppFlow enables automatic data mapping and transformation, ensuring compatibility between different data formats across source and destination systems. This functionality ensures that data can be transferred and processed seamlessly without format mismatches.

Use cases

Everyday use cases highlight the practical benefits of Amazon AppFlow:

- **Sales and marketing automation**: Businesses can automate the data flow between **customer relationship management (CRM)** systems, such as Salesforce, and marketing platforms. This automation streamlines sales and marketing processes, helping organizations to keep up-to-date customer data and improve marketing campaign effectiveness [8].
- **Data warehousing**: AppFlow facilitates data transfer from SaaS applications into AWS-based data warehouses, enabling powerful analytics and reporting capabilities. By moving data to centralized storage solutions, organizations can leverage AWS's analytical services to gain insights and make data-driven decisions [7].

Considerations for implementation

When implementing Amazon AppFlow, organizations must consider several key factors to ensure seamless data transfers and integration. These considerations include:

- **Security and compliance**: Ensuring the security and compliance of data transferred through Amazon AppFlow is paramount. Organizations should show proper security protocols and ensure that data transfers meet regulatory requirements, especially when dealing with sensitive or personal data [7].
- **Data mapping accuracy**: To ensure the integrity of data flows, organizations must verify and assess their data mapping configurations. Any inaccuracies in mapping could lead to inconsistencies or errors in the transferred data, thereby compromising the effectiveness of the integration.

Challenges

While Amazon AppFlow offers robust integration capabilities, specific challenges may arise during implementation:

- **Data transfer speed**: The speed at which data can be transferred between SaaS applications and AWS services depends on the volume of data and the capabilities of the SaaS application in use. Organizations need to account for potential bottlenecks and consider transfer speed when designing data integration processes [9]. Planning for these challenges will ensure that integration continues smoothly and data flows as efficiently as possible.

Amazon EventBridge

Amazon EventBridge is an AWS serverless event bus service that simplifies the development of event-driven applications. This service enhances the scalability and flexibility of cloud architectures by enabling seamless communication between different services through events.

Key features

Amazon EventBridge provides features [10]:

- **Event routing**: The service allows the creation of event rules that route events from sources to one or more targets, promoting decoupled service communication.
- **Schema registry**: EventBridge includes a schema registry, ensuring consistency and compatibility in event formats across applications.
- **Managed integration**: The service's event-driven architecture.

Use cases

Amazon EventBridge serves various use cases:

- **Microservices communication**: EventBridge facilitates communication between microservices by enabling them to publish and subscribe to events, which encourages a loosely coupled architecture [11].
- **Real-time data processing**: Organizations can use EventBridge for real-time data processing, responding to events generated by different services or applications [10].

Best practices

To maximize the effectiveness of EventBridge, follow these best practices [10]:

- **Event schema design**: Ensure event schemas are designed for clarity, extensibility, and long-term maintainability.
- **Rule filtering strategies**: Develop efficient rule filtering strategies to manage event flow and enhance event-driven workflows.

Challenges

While EventBridge offers a robust framework for event-driven applications, there are challenges:

- **Event consistency**: Ensuring consistency in event formats and schemas across diverse services and teams require comprehensive communication and documentation [11].

Amazon Managed Workflows for Apache Airflow

Amazon **Managed Workflows for Apache Airflow (MWAA)** is a fully managed service that simplifies the orchestration of complex workflows, cutting the operational overhead of managing Apache Airflow environments. This service enhances the scalability and reliability of workflows, making it ideal for orchestrating data-intensive tasks across various cloud resources. *Figure 8.3* provides an overview of Amazon MWAA's architecture:

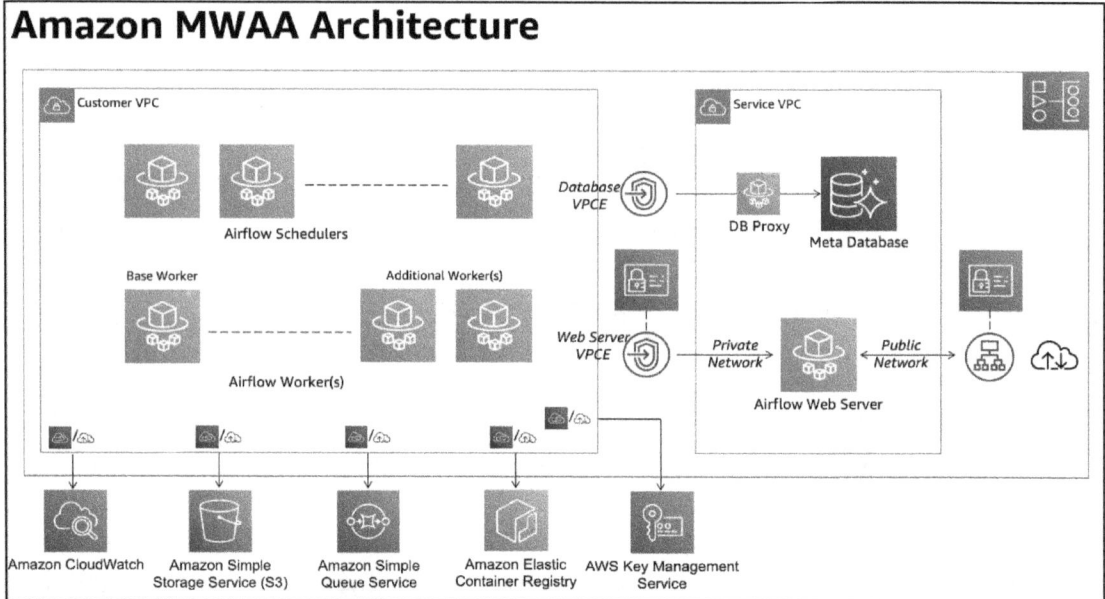

Figure 8.3: Amazon MWAA Architecture

Key features

Amazon MWAA offers different key features that make it a powerful tool for workflow automation [12]:

- **MWAA environment**: The service provides a fully managed environment, reducing the burden of infrastructure management.

- **Scalability and reliability**: MWAA automatically scales resources based on workload requirements, ensuring high-performace and reliability.

- **Integration with AWS services**: Seamless integration with various AWS services allows workflows to interact effectively with cloud resources.

Use cases

MWAA is particularly useful for the following use cases:

- **Data processing pipelines**: They help automate data workflows across diverse data sources and destinations [13].

- **ETL workflows**: MWAA efficiently orchestrates ETL tasks, streamlining data processing for analytics and reporting [12].

Best practices

To maximize the benefits of Amazon MWAA, follow these best practices [13]:

- **Environment configuration**: Configure the Airflow environment to improve performance and security.

- **Monitoring and logging**: Implement robust monitoring and logging systems to track workflow performance and promptly identify issues.

Considerations

While MWAA offers powerful capabilities, distinct factors should be considered for successful implementation:

- **Cost management**: As workflows scale, watch and manage associated costs, particularly when integrating data-intensive services [12].

- **Security configuration**: Ensure robust security practices, including proper **Identity and Access Management (IAM)** roles, data encryption, and AWS security best practices.

- **Performance optimization**: Tune task concurrency, use Spot Instances, and select the correct instance types to enhance performance and reduce costs.

- **Dependency management**: Manage dependencies effectively by utilizing MWAA's support for Python packages, ensuring they are up-to-date and compatible.

- **Compliance and governance**: Ensure the utilization of tools like AWS CloudTrail for auditing and logging, and verify that workflows adhere to relevant standards.

- **Backup and recovery**: Implement reliable backup strategies, using services like Amazon S3 for workflow definitions, and regularly evaluate recovery procedures.

- **CI/CD integration**: Incorporate MWAA workflows into **continuous integration/ continuous deployment (CI/CD)** pipelines to ensure consistency and reliability across environments.

- **Monitoring, alerts, and notifications**: Setup CloudWatch metrics, alarms, and notifications to watch workflow execution and system performance.

- **Data privacy**: Ensure data handling practices comply with privacy regulations, such as *the General Data Protection Regulation (GDPR)* and the *California Consumer Privacy Act (CCPA)*, particularly when handling sensitive data.

- **Training and documentation**: Provide comprehensive training and operational documentation to ensure the effective use and maintenance of MWAA.

- **Vendor lock-in and portability**: Consider the implications of vendor lock-in and utilize **infrastructure as code (IaC)** tools, such as AWS CloudFormation, to mitigate portability concerns.

Amazon MQ

Amazon MQ is a fully managed message broker service that simplifies the deployment and maintenance of popular messaging systems. This service supports multiple messaging protocols, including **Advanced Message Queuing Protocol (AMQP)**, **Message Queuing Telemetry Transport (MQTT)**, and **Simple Text-Oriented Messaging Protocol (STOMP)**, ensuring high compatibility with various applications and systems. By offering a managed infrastructure, Amazon MQ reduces the operational complexity typically associated with running messaging systems, allowing developers to focus on application logic.

Key features

The key features of Amazon MQ include [14]:

- **Industry standard compatibility**: Amazon MQ supports various messaging protocols, including MQTT, AMQP, and STOMP, ensuring seamless integration with different systems and applications.

- **Managed broker**: It provides a fully managed message broker, minimizing the operational overhead of keeping the infrastructure and scaling the messaging system.

Use cases

Amazon MQ excels in the following use cases:

- **Decoupled microservices communication**: It helps communication between microservices in a decoupled manner, enhancing scalability and flexibility in microservices architectures [15].

- **Event-driven architecture**: Amazon MQ supports building reliable event-driven architectures by enabling applications to respond to events and messages in a scalable, efficient way [14].

Best practices

To improve the use of Amazon MQ, the following best practices should be implemented:

- **Secure configuration**: Secure the service by using IAM roles, encryption, and access control mechanisms to protect sensitive data [14].

- **Scalability planning**: Choose the correct instance types and configure resources based on expected message throughput and processing needs to ensure the best performance [15].

Considerations

When implementing Amazon MQ, the following factors should be considered:

- **Message retention and cleanup**: Set the right retention policies and cleanup processes to manage storage costs and keep system efficiency [14].

Amazon Simple Notification Service

SNS is a fully managed messaging service that enables the decoupling of microservices, distributed systems, and serverless applications. This section examines the features, use cases, and best practices related to Amazon SNS.

Key features

The following are the key features of Amazon SNS [16]:

- **Publish-subscribe model**: Amazon SNS adheres to a publish-subscribe messaging paradigm, enabling message producers to send messages to multiple subscribers simultaneously.

- **Wide range of message protocols**: The service supports various message protocols, including HTTPS, email/SMTP, SMS, and application-specific protocols, ensuring flexibility in message delivery.

Use cases

The following are the use cases of Amazon SNS [16]:

- **Event-driven architecture**: Amazon SNS is crucial in building event-driven architecture, facilitating communication and coordination between loosely coupled components.

- **Mobile application notifications**: The service enables the sending of push notifications to mobile devices, thereby enhancing user engagement with mobile applications.

Best practices

The following are Amazon SNS's best practices [16]:

- **Topic organization**: Organize topics effectively to reflect the structure of your application, making it easier to manage and control message distribution [17].

- **Message filtering**: Implement message filtering to control which subscribers receive specific messages based on their preferences or attributes.

Considerations

One efficiency consideration is message retention. Details of which are as follows:

- **Message retention**: Understand the default message retention periods and adjust them based on your application's requirements to avoid message loss [17].

Integration with other AWS services

Amazon SNS integrates with other AWS services to enhance various aspects of application development and deployment. Notable integrations include:

- **Amazon SQS**: Enables asynchronous communication by allowing SNS messages to be sent to SQS queues [18].

- **AWS Step Functions**: Helps coordinate distributed applications using SNS to trigger state transitions in Step Functions [19].

Amazon Simple Queue Service

SQS is a fully managed message queuing service that helps with decoupled components in a distributed system. This section examines features, use cases, and best practices related to Amazon SQS. *Figure 8.4* illustrates the basic architecture of Amazon SQS:

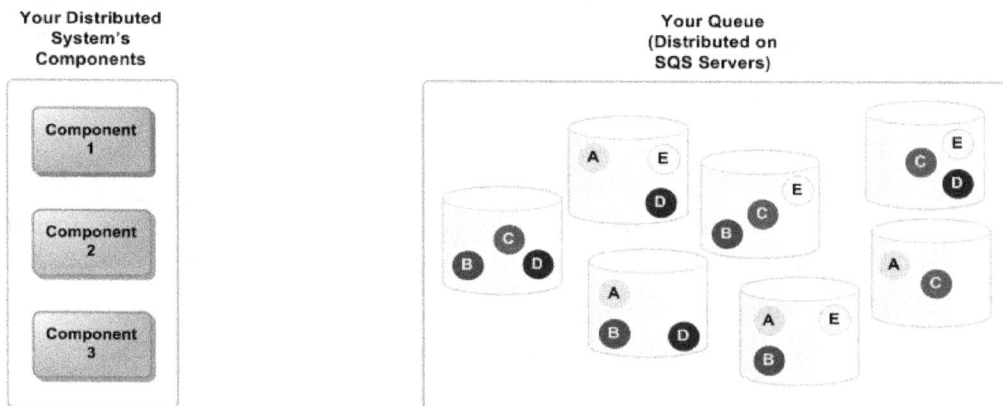

Figure 8.4: Amazon Simple Queuing Service basic architecture

Key features

Amazon SQS provides different key features that enhance its utility in distributed systems. [20]:

- **Scalability and elasticity**: The service automatically scales to manage variable message volumes, ensuring reliable delivery even during workload fluctuations.
- **Message retention**: SQS enables users to define the retention period for messages, offering flexibility in managing how long messages remain in the queue.

Use cases

Amazon SQS is beneficial in various scenarios, including:

- **Load leveling**: SQS helps smooth out traffic spikes by acting as a buffer, decoupling the rate at which messages are produced and consumed [21].
- **Task decoupling**: SQS facilitates task decoupling in microservices architectures, enabling components to communicate asynchronously.

Best practices

To improve the use of Amazon SQS, follow these best practices:

- **Visibility timeout**: Adjust the visibility timeout to prevent duplication by hiding a message from other consumers while processing.
- **Dead-letter queues**: Implement dead-letter queues to capture undeliverable messages after a predefined number of attempts and analyze their failure [20].

Considerations

While Amazon SQS offers best-effort ordering, it is efficient to design systems that can manage potential out-of-order message delivery [20].

Integration with other AWS services

SQS seamlessly integrates with various AWS services, enhancing its capabilities and applications in different scenarios. Notable integrations include:

- **Amazon S3**: SQS can be used to trigger events in response to changes in an S3 bucket, enabling event-driven architectures [20].
- **AWS Lambda**: Leverage SQS to trigger serverless functions in AWS Lambda, allowing for the seamless execution of compute workloads [18].

Managed message queues

Managed message queues are essential components of modern cloud architecture. They offer a scalable and reliable way to decouple system components. This section discusses the role of managed message queues and their importance in distributed systems.

Overview

Managed message queues, such as *Amazon SQS, Azure Queue Storage*, and *Google Cloud Pub/Sub*, provide a robust solution for enabling asynchronous communication in distributed systems. These queues help streamline message handling by ensuring scalability, reliability, and efficient decoupling between system components.

Advantages

Managed message queues offer advantages that enhance the performance and reliability of distributed systems:

- **Scalability**: These queues scale automatically to manage changing workloads, ensuring consistent performance as demand fluctuates [22].

- **Reliability**: By offloading the tasks of message storage and delivery to managed services, message processing reliability greatly improves.

- **Decoupling**: Managed message queues help the decoupling of producers and consumers, supporting asynchronous communication and reducing the interdependencies between components [23].

Use cases

Managed message queues are pivotal in different use cases:

- **Microservices architectures**: These queues enable microservices to communicate asynchronously, avoiding direct dependencies between services.

- **Event-driven systems**: In these systems, managed message queues facilitate the smooth transfer of events across components, enabling real-time processing.

Best practices

To maximize the efficiency of managed message queues, adhere to the following best practices:

- **Message retention**: Configure retention policies based on application needs, striking a balance between storage costs and the time-sensitive nature of messages.

- **Error handling**: Implement robust error-managing mechanisms, including the use of dead-letter queues, to manage messages that do not process [20].

Integration with AWS services

Managed message queues integrate seamlessly with different AWS services, enhancing their capabilities in various scenarios. Key integrations include:

- **AWS Lambda**: Use managed message queues to trigger AWS Lambda functions, enabling serverless, event-driven architectures.
- **Amazon EC2**: Integrate with EC2 instances to allow communication between different components of a distributed application [20].

AWS Step Functions

AWS Step Functions is a fully managed service that enables developers to coordinate and automate the execution of serverless workflows using visual workflows. This section explores AWS Step Functions capabilities, use cases, and benefits in application integration.

Overview

AWS Step Functions simplifies building scalable and resilient applications by allowing developers to design workflows using a visual interface. Workflows in Step Functions are represented as state machines, where each state is a step in the workflow.

Key features

The following are the key features of AWS Step Functions [19]; [24]:

- **Visual workflow design**: Step Functions provides a visual workflow designer, allowing developers to design, visualize, and change workflows easily.
- **Coordination of microservices**: It excels in coordinating microservices, enabling seamless communication and task execution across distributed applications.
- **Error handling**: Step Functions include built-in error management capabilities, allowing for the definition of error states and automatic retribution.

Figure 8.5 illustrates AWS Step Functions microservice orchestration, combining Lambda functions to build a web-based application:

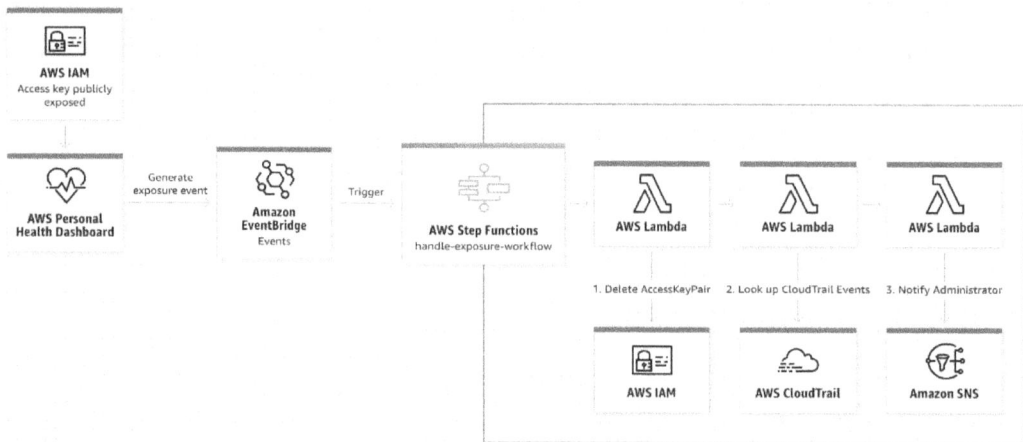

Figure 8.5: AWS Step Functions Microservice Orchestration

Use cases

The following are the use cases of AWS Step Functions [19]:

- **Order processing workflows**: Step Functions can orchestrate order processing workflows, coordinating tasks such as payment processing, inventory management, and shipping.

- **Data processing pipelines**: It is ideal for building data processing pipelines, where different steps in the pipeline are executed based on the success or failure of earlier steps.

- **Media processing workflows**: Step Functions can coordinate media processing tasks, such as video transcoding and image recognition, in a scalable and efficient manner.

Benefits

The following are the benefits of using AWS Step Functions [19]:

- **Simplified workflow management**: The visual designer allows developers to easily manage complex workflows, thereby reducing the complexity of application integration.

- **Scalability**: Step Functions scale automatically based on the workload, ensuring that workflows execute reliably under varying conditions.

- **Cost efficiency**: Step Functions pay-as-you-go pricing model ensures cost efficiency, with charges based on the number of state transitions.

The benefits of using AWS Step Functions are as follows [19]:

- **Simplified workflow management**: Developers can manage complex workflows with ease using the visual designer, reducing the complexity of application integration[95].

- **Scalability**: Step Functions scale automatically based on the workload, ensuring that workflows execute reliably under varying conditions.

- **Cost efficiency**: Step Functions pay-as-you-go pricing model ensures cost efficiency, with charges based on the number of state transitions.

Integration with other AWS services

AWS Step Functions seamlessly integrates with various AWS services, including AWS Lambda, AWS Fargate, and Amazon SageMaker, enabling developers to utilize multiple functionalities within their workflows.

Amazon Elastic Container Registry

Amazon **Elastic Container Registry (ECR)** is a fully managed container registry service that enables developers to store, manage, and deploy Docker container images efficiently. This section explores Amazon ECR's features and role in the containerization ecosystem.

Amazon ECR simplifies containerization by offering a secure and scalable repository for Docker images, supporting the entire lifecycle of containerized applications.

Key features

The following are the key features of Amazon ECR [25]; [26]:

- **Secure and private repositories**: ECR provides private repositories where container images are securely stored and accessed only by authorized users and systems.

- **Integration with AWS services**: It integrates seamlessly with AWS services, such as Amazon **Elastic Container Service** (**ECS**) and Kubernetes, facilitating containerized application deployment.

- **Scalability**: ECR scales with the development team's needs, efficiently managing the storage and retrieval of large container images.

Use cases

The following are the key features of Amazon ECR [25]; [26]:

- **Secure and private repositories**: ECR provides private repositories where container images are securely stored and accessed only by authorized users and systems.

- **Integration with AWS services**: It integrates seamlessly with AWS services, such as Amazon ECS and Kubernetes, facilitating containerized application deployment.

- **Scalability**: ECR scales with the development team's needs, efficiently managing storage and retrieval of large numbers of container images.

Figure 8.6 shows AWS Container options by layer:

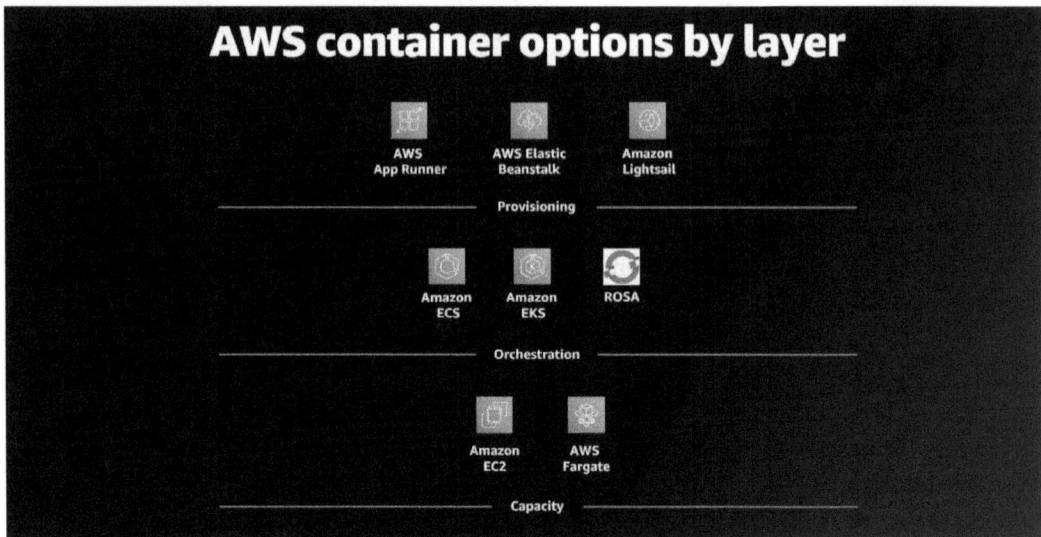

Figure 8.6: AWS containers

Benefits

The benefits of using Amazon ECR are as follows [25]:

- **Ease of use**: Integrating AWS services and Docker tools simplifies usage for novice and experienced container developers.
- **Cost efficiency**: ECR follows a pay-as-you-go pricing model, charging users based on storage and data transfer for container images.
- **Comprehensive security**: ECR provides fine-grained access control, integrating with AWS IAM to securely manage container image repositories.

Integration with DevOps workflow

Amazon ECR plays a pivotal role in DevOps workflows by integrating containerized applications into deployment pipelines. Its compatibility with CI/CD tools ensures a smooth transition from development to production.

Amazon Elastic Container Service

Amazon ECS is a fully managed service for container orchestration that simplifies the deployment and management of containerized applications. This section highlights ECS's features, architecture, and use cases, emphasizing its role in scaling these applications.

Amazon ECS enables users to run, stop, and manage Docker containers across clusters. It abstracts infrastructure complexities, allowing developers to focus on scaling applications without managing the underlying resources.

Key features of Amazon ECS

The key features of Amazon ECS include [27]:

- **Scalability**: ECS automatically scales containers based on application load, ensuring efficient resource utilization.
- **Integration**: Thereby improving load balancing.
- **Task definitions**: Developers define applications through task definitions, specifying Docker images, CPU, memory, and container links.

Amazon ECS architecture

Amazon ECS orchestrates Docker containers on EC2 instances or AWS Fargate, AWS's serverless compute engine for containers. The architecture revolves around clusters, tasks, and services. Clusters group EC2 instances or Fargate tasks, while tasks are discrete units of work defined by task definitions. ECS services manage tasks' lifecycle, ensuring high availability and scalability [27].

Components of Amazon ECS

Amazon ECS architecture includes:

- **Clusters**: Logical groups of EC2 instances or Fargate tasks where containers are deployed.
- **Tasks**: Units of work defined by task definitions that specify Docker images, resource allocations, and dependencies.
- **Services**: Ensure high availability and scalability by managing task lifecycles and adjusting based on demand [27].

Scalability and integration

ECS scales containers dynamically in response to workload demands. Integrated with AWS Auto Scaling and ELB, ECS distributes traffic across containers, improving performance in microservices and batch processing environments [28].

Operational simplicity and its benefits

ECS abstracts infrastructure complexities, streamlining operations. It improves resource use, integrates with AWS IAM for secure container management, and supports CI/CD pipelines for automated testing and deployment, enabling rapid innovation [27].

To better understand Amazon ECS's architecture and key components, *Figure 8.7* illustrates how the service orchestrates containerized applications across managed clusters, leveraging EC2 instances or AWS Fargate for scalable deployment:

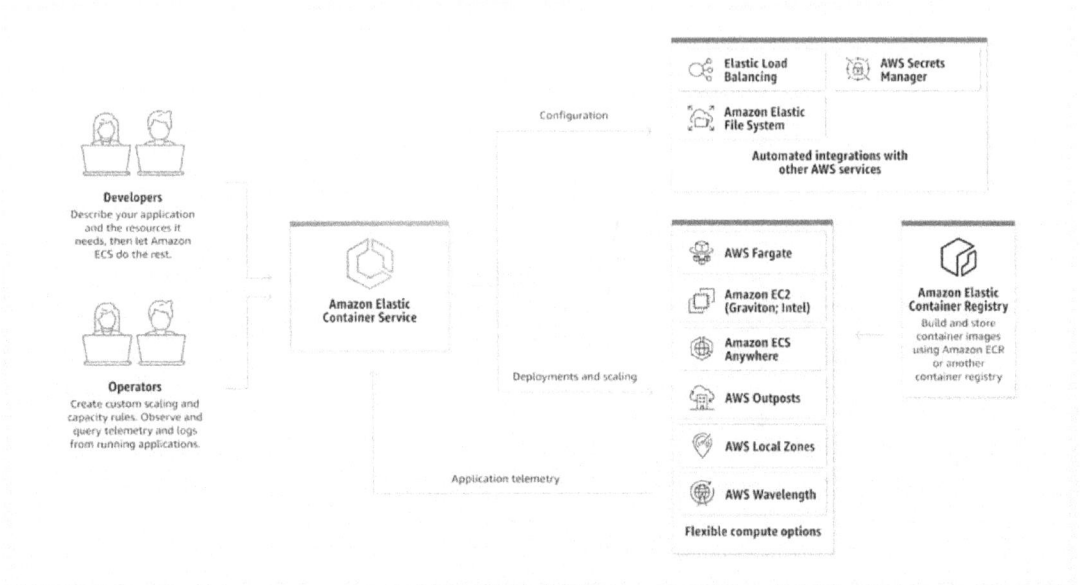

Figure 8.7: *Amazon ECS*

Amazon ECS architecture core components

ECS architecture includes:

- **Clusters**: Logical groupings of container instances or Fargate tasks.
- **Tasks**: Units of work based on task definitions, ensuring seamless execution across ECS clusters.
- **Services**: Manage the lifecycle and scaling of tasks to keep availability [27].

Use cases of Amazon ECS

ECS is ideal for:

- **Microservices architecture**: Efficient orchestration and scaling of microservices.
- **Batch processing**: Scaling containerized applications dynamically in response to workload demands.
- **CI/CD**: ECS integrates with CI/CD pipelines for automated testing and deployment [28].

Benefits

Key benefits of ECS include [27]:

- **Cost efficiency**: ECS improves resource utilization, charging users only for the compute resources they consume.

- **Security**: Integrated with AWS IAM for secure container management and access control.

- **Operational simplicity**: ECS abstracts infrastructure management, enabling developers to focus on building applications.

Integration with DevOps workflow

Amazon ECS integrates seamlessly with DevOps tools, enhancing the deployment and management of containerized applications in CI/CD pipelines.

Amazon Elastic Kubernetes Service

Amazon EKS is a fully managed Kubernetes service provided by AWS. It offers a simplified yet powerful platform for deploying, managing, and scaling containerized applications using Kubernetes.

Overview

Amazon EKS is a fully managed Kubernetes service by AWS that simplifies container orchestration and scaling for Kubernetes-based applications. This section discusses EKS's features, architecture, use cases, and its role in modern containerized applications.

Amazon EKS abstracts the complexity of Kubernetes control plane management, providing a scalable solution for running containerized applications with Kubernetes orchestration.

Key features

Amazon EKS delivers a fully managed Kubernetes environment, simplifying container orchestration while ensuring scalability, security, and deep integration with AWS services. Designed for organizations leveraging Kubernetes, EKS automates infrastructure management, optimizes performance, and enhances reliability, enabling seamless deployment of containerized applications across hybrid and multi-cloud environments.

The key features are as follows [29]:

- **Scalability**: Automatically adjusts to workload demands, ensuring efficient use of resources.

- **Seamless AWS integration**: EKS integrates with other AWS services, such as IAM and VPC, for enhanced security and networking.

- **Flexibility**: Supports Kubernetes tooling and AWS-specific integrations, providing operational flexibility.

Amazon EKS architecture

EKS architecture is built on essential components:

- **Control plane**: Managed by AWS, the control plane includes components such as the API server, scheduler, and controller manager.

- **Worker**: Nodes execute containerized applications and communicate with the control plane.

- **Clusters**: EKS clusters group worker nodes utilizing AWS infrastructure, such as EC2 instances or AWS Fargate, for scalable deployments.

- **Use cases of Amazon EKS**: EKS supports various deployment strategies [29].

- **Microservices architecture**: Scalable orchestration for managing containerized microservices.

- **Hybrid deployments**: Orchestrates applications across on-premises and cloud environments.

- **Multi-region deployments**: Supports multi-region setups for enhanced availability.

Refer to *Figure 8.8* for a visualization of an Amazon EKS use case example:

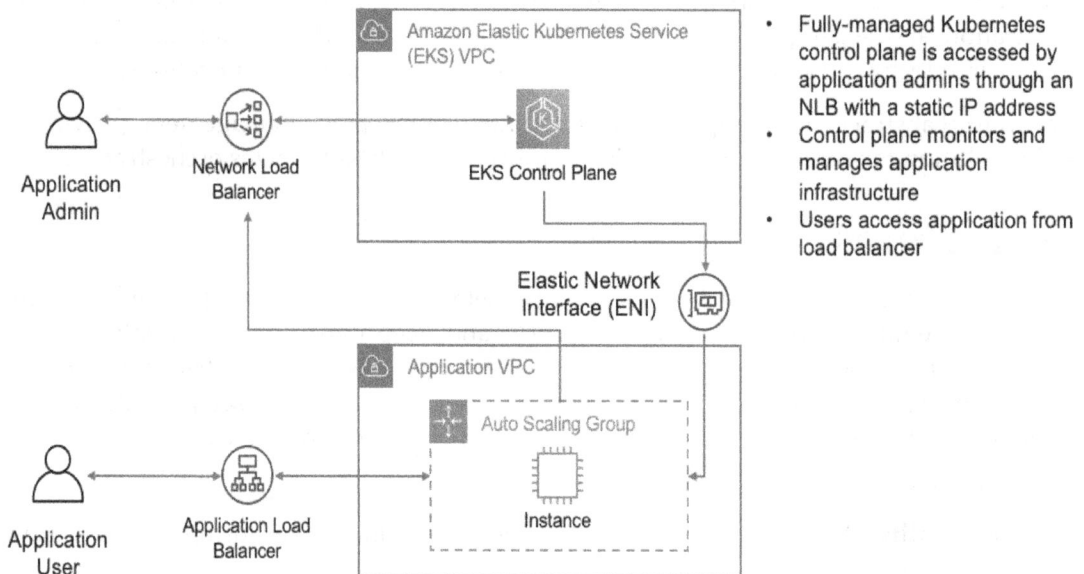

Figure 8.8: Amazon EKS use case

Benefits

Key benefits include [29]:

- **Operational efficiency**: Automates setup, scaling, and management of Kubernetes clusters.
- **Security**: Integrated with AWS IAM and VPC for secure, isolated networking.
- **Flexibility**: Supports both standard Kubernetes tools and AWS integrations, providing users with a broad range of options.

Integration with DevOps workflow

EKS integrates seamlessly with DevOps pipelines, enhancing CI/CD practices and accelerating the deployment of containerized applications.

Modern DevOps workflows rely on automation, scalability, and seamless orchestration to accelerate software delivery. Amazon EKS enhances DevOps practices by integrating with popular CI/CD tools, IaC frameworks, and monitoring solutions, enabling the efficient, scalable, and cost-effective deployment of containerized applications.

To fully leverage the power of Kubernetes in cloud-native environments, Amazon EKS integrates with essential DevOps tools and practices. The following features illustrate how EKS enhances automation, scalability, monitoring, and cost efficiency within modern CI/CD pipelines and operational workflows:

- **Continuous integration**: Works with Jenkins, GitLab CI/CD, and AWS CodePipeline to automate builds and deployments.
- **Continuous deployment**: EKS automates deployments using Helm and AWS CodeDeploy, ensuring consistent updates.
- **IaC**: Integrates with AWS CloudFormation and Terraform, ensuring consistent environments.
- **Monitoring and logging**: Works with Amazon A to Z and AWS X-Ray to provide visibility and initiative-taking troubleshooting.
- **Scalability and high availability**: Supports Auto Scaling and multi-region deployments, ensuring fault-tolrance and reduced downtime.
- **Cost optimization**: EKS reduces costs with dynamic scaling, AWS Spot Instances, and cost management tools like AWS Cost Explorer.
- **Summary**: Amazon EKS streamlines the management of Kubernetes clusters by automating key tasks, improving operational efficiency, and integrating seamlessly with the AWS ecosystem. This service accelerates the deployment lifecycle for containerized applications, helping with high availability, scalability, and security. [29].

AWS App2Container

AWS A2C is a service that simplifies the process of containerizing legacy applications, enabling organizations to modernize and migrate their applications to cloud-native architectures. This section examines the capabilities of AWS A2C, its use cases, and the benefits it provides for modern application development.

AWS A2C is designed to convert existing applications into containerized environments without requiring significant code changes. It packages an application and its dependencies into containers, allowing users to deploy them in container orchestration environments such as Amazon ECS or Amazon EKS.

Key features

The following are the key features of AWS A2C (AWS, AWS A2C, 2023):

- **Automated containerization**: A2C automatically scans applications and packages them into Docker containers, making the process more efficient and less error-prone.

- **Support for Java and .NET**: The service supports both Java and .NET applications, enabling organizations with legacy systems to migrate to the cloud.

- **Integration with AWS services**: Once the application is containerized, users can integrate it seamlessly with Amazon ECS, EKS, or AWS Fargate for orchestration.

Use cases

The following are everyday use cases for AWS A2C:

- **Legacy application modernization**: Organizations can use A2C to modernize legacy applications, enabling them to move from monolithic architectures to containerized solutions.

- **Cloud migration**: A2C accelerates the process of migrating applications to the cloud, particularly for organizations moving from on-premises data centers to AWS.

- **Microservices conversion**: A2C helps organizations transition to microservices architecture by breaking down legacy monolithic applications into manageable, containerized services.

Benefits

The benefits of using AWS A2C [17] are as follows:

- **Simplified containerization**: A2C automates the containerization process, reducing the complexity of manually configuring and packaging legacy applications.

- **Accelerated cloud migration**: A2C helps expedite cloud migration by providing a streamlined approach to containerization, making it easier to migrate workloads to AWS.

- **Scalability**: Once containerized, applications can be easily scaled using AWS container services, ensuring they perform reliably under varying workloads.

Integration with DevOps workflows

AWS A2C integrates seamlessly into DevOps workflows, allowing developers to incorporate containerization into their CI/CD pipelines. This integration streamlines the development-to-production cycle, improving the efficiency of application deployment.

AWS Fargate

AWS Fargate is a serverless compute engine for containers that cuts the need to manage servers. This section discusses how Fargate simplifies container management and provides a scalable solution for running containers in a serverless environment.

Overview

Fargate allows developers to run containers without worrying about the underlying infrastructure. It automatically manages provisioning, scaling, and the compute resources needed to run containers, enabling teams to focus on application logic rather than infrastructure management.

Key features

The key features of AWS Fargate include [30]:

- **Serverless architecture**: Fargate abstracts infrastructure management, enabling developers to focus on writing code rather than managing servers.

- **Automatic scaling**: Fargate automatically scales the number of containers based on demand, ensuring optimal resource utilization.

- **Integration with AWS services**: Seamless integration with Amazon ECS, Amazon EKS, and AWS Lambda enables users to run containers in various configurations, enhancing workflows.

Use cases

The main use cases are as follows [30]:

- **Microservices architecture**: Fargate simplifies microservices management by allowing independent scaling of individual services.

- **Batch processing**: Fargate can run containerized batch jobs that scale automatically based on workload.

- **CI/CD pipelines**: Integrating Fargate with CI/CD pipelines enables automation of testing, building, and deployment processes.

Benefits

The benefits of AWS Fargate include:

- **Operational simplicity**: With no need to manage infrastructure, Fargate reduces the operational complexity associated with running containers.

- **Cost efficiency**: Fargate offers a pay-per-use pricing model, where users only pay for the compute resources their containers use.

- **Scalability and flexibility**: Fargate scales containers based on demand, ensuring applications can manage traffic spikes and fluctuating workloads.

Integration with DevOps workflow

AWS Fargate seamlessly integrates into DevOps workflows, enabling the management and scaling of containerized applications without manual intervention. It works with services like AWS CodePipeline and ECS, helping teams automate their development, testing, and deployment processes [30].

AWS App2Container and AWS Fargate integration

When combined, AWS A2C and AWS Fargate offer a comprehensive solution for containerizing and deploying applications:

- **Seamless containerization**: A2C prepares applications for deployment on Fargate with minimal configuration.

- **Serverless deployment**: Fargate manages all infrastructure management, providing a fully serverless deployment experience.

- **Enhanced efficiency**: This integration streamlines container lifecycle management, optimizing resource utilization and minimizing operational overhead.

Benefits

Integrating the AWS A2C with AWS Fargate delivers multiple advantages:

- **Serverless container orchestration**: Fargate automates the entire container orchestration process, freeing developers from managing infrastructure.

- **Resource optimization**: Fargate scales resources automatically based on application demand, enhancing performance and cost efficiency.

- **Simplified operations**: The combination of A2C and Fargate simplifies the containerization and deployment process, making operations more efficient.

Use cases

The A2C and Fargate integration is ideal for:

- **Microservices architecture**: Perfect for deploying individual services independently and efficiently.
- **Application modernization**: Helps migrate legacy applications to cloud-native environments, enhancing scalability and cost-effectiveness.

AWS Copilot

AWS Copilot is a powerful CLI that streamlines the deployment, management, and execution of containerized applications on Amazon ECS and AWS Fargate. This section discusses the capabilities, key features, and benefits of using AWS Copilot to streamline the development and deployment of containerized applications.

Overview

AWS Copilot provides a streamlined, opinionated approach to deploying containerized applications. It allows developers to quickly create production-ready environments for their applications without requiring deep knowledge of AWS services. Copilot automates the necessary AWS infrastructure setup, enabling developers to focus on writing code and building features.

Key features

The following are the key features of AWS Copilot [31]:

- **Application scaffolding**: Copilot automatically generates the necessary AWS infrastructure components, such as load balancers, security groups, and Auto Scaling settings, for deploying containerized applications.
- **Multiple environment support**: AWS Copilot enables the creation and management of applications across multiple environments, including development, staging, and production, ensuring a seamless deployment process for each stage of development.
- **Integrated CI/CD**: Copilot offers built-in integration with Amazon CodePipeline and GitHub Actions, simplifying automated build and deployment workflows.
- **Environment configuration**: Copilot enables users to define environment-specific settings for their containerized applications, including resource allocation and environment variables.

Use cases

Everyday use cases for AWS Copilot are as follows:

- **Microservices deployment**: Copilot is well-suited for deploying microservices applications, where different services can be deployed and scaled independently across multiple environments.

- **Rapid development and deployment**: For teams seeking to develop and deploy containerized applications rapidly, Copilot streamlines the entire process, enabling developers to push code to production quickly without manual configuration.

- **Cloud-native migration**: Organizations seeking to migrate their containerized applications from on-premises or other cloud environments to AWS can seamlessly transition to Copilot.

Benefits

The benefits of using AWS Copilot are as follows [31]:

- **Simplified application deployment**: Copilot streamlines the deployment of containerized applications by automating much of the setup, making it easier for developers to deploy their applications quickly and reliably.

- **Best practice defaults**: The service implements AWS best practices for security, scalability, and cost efficiency, ensuring that applications are deployed securely and optimized for optimal performance.

- **Faster time to market**: With automated infrastructure setup and integration with CI/CD tools, Copilot accelerates the development cycle, enabling teams to release applications more quickly.

Integration with DevOps workflows

AWS Copilot integrates smoothly into DevOps workflows by providing a simplified yet powerful toolset for managing containerized applications in AWS. It enables automated deployment through continuous integration and delivery pipelines, making it an ideal choice for organizations looking to streamline their DevOps processes and keep a consistent, repeatable deployment flow.

AWS App2Container and AWS Copilot integration

Combining AWS A2C with AWS Copilot delivers a robust solution for containerizing and deploying legacy applications into scalable, serverless environments.

As organizations modernize their legacy applications, they require efficient tools that automate containerization and deployment while minimizing complexity. The integration of AWS A2C and AWS Copilot provides a comprehensive solution for transitioning traditional applications into cloud-native, scalable environments without disrupting existing workflows.

The combination of AWS A2C and AWS Copilot empowers organizations to modernize legacy applications with minimal disruption. The following key features highlight how these tools work together to automate containerization, simplify deployment, and integrate seamlessly with modern DevOps workflows:

- **Seamless migration and deployment**: A2C prepares legacy applications by generating Docker images, and AWS Copilot simplifies the deployment process, ensuring a streamlined CI/CD pipeline and environment setup.

- **Simplified container management**: A2C automates containerization, and Copilot handles deployment and scaling with minimal configuration, enabling developers to focus on application logic.

- **End-to-end DevOps integration**: Integrates with AWS CodePipeline, enabling automated CI/CD and supporting agile DevOps workflows.

Benefits

Organizations leveraging AWS A2C and Copilot gain a streamlined approach to modernization. By automating containerization, deployment, and scaling, these tools enhance operational efficiency and accelerate cloud adoption while ensuring cost optimization through AWS's flexible pricing model:

- **Accelerated modernization**: Quickly migrate legacy applications to containerized environments, reducing the manual work in modernizing legacy systems.

- **Operational efficiency**: A2C and AWS Copilot simplify container management and deployment, reducing operational complexity.

- **Cost efficiency**: With AWS's pay-as-you-go pricing model, organizations pay only for the resources they use, improving cost management.

Use cases

AWS A2C and Copilot cater to businesses aiming for a seamless transition to containerized environments. Whether modernizing legacy applications or integrating with DevOps pipelines, these tools simplify deployment, management, and scaling, making cloud adoption more accessible and efficient:

- **Legacy application modernization**: Easily containerize and migrate traditional applications to modern cloud-native architectures.

- **CI/CD integration**: Simplify the integration of containerized applications into CI/CD workflows, enhancing DevOps practices.

Red Hat OpenShift service on AWS

The **Red Hat OpenShift Service on AWS (ROSA)** is a fully managed Kubernetes service that combines the power of Red Hat OpenShift with the scalability of AWS infrastructure. This section delves into the capabilities, benefits, and use cases of ROSA for organizations seeking a streamlined, enterprise-grade platform for deploying and managing containerized applications on AWS [32].

Overview

ROSA is designed to offer a seamless integration of Red Hat OpenShift's container orchestration capabilities with AWS's cloud infrastructure. By providing a fully managed Kubernetes environment, ROSA simplifies the deployment, scaling, and management of containerized applications while using the operational benefits of OpenShift's enterprise features, such as integrated CI/CD pipelines and enhanced security [32].

Key features

As organizations embrace containerized application development, they require a fully managed, enterprise-grade Kubernetes solution that simplifies deployment and operations. ROSA bridges the gap between Kubernetes flexibility and enterprise-ready features, offering a seamless cloud-native experience [32], as follows:

- **Enterprise-grade Kubernetes**: ROSA combines Kubernetes's flexibility and power with Red Hat OpenShift's added capabilities, such as integrated logging, monitoring, and CI/CD tools.

- **Fully managed service**: ROSA manages the installation, configuration, and management of OpenShift clusters, allowing teams to focus on developing applications without worrying about the underlying infrastructure.

- **Seamless integration with AWS**: ROSA integrates with AWS services like Amazon RDS, Amazon S3, and AWS IAM to provide a robust platform for cloud-native application deployment.

- **Enhanced security and compliance**: Red Hat OpenShift's security features, such as **role-based access control (RBAC)**, automated patching, and security updates, are integrated into ROSA, ensuring that your applications follow enterprise security standards.

Benefits

Businesses seeking faster deployment cycles and operational efficiency benefit from ROSA's fully managed infrastructure. By combining automated scaling, built-in security, and deep AWS integration, ROSA enables teams to focus on building and deploying applications rather than managing clusters [32], as follows:

- **Faster time to market**: ROSA accelerates application development and deployment with integrated CI/CD workflows, automated scaling, and simplified management.

- **Operational efficiency**: By offloading the management of Kubernetes clusters and infrastructure to AWS, ROSA reduces the operational burden on DevOps teams, allowing them to focus on building and deploying applications.

- **Scalability and flexibility**: ROSA leverages AWS's elastic compute resources to scale containerized applications dynamically, ensuring high availability and best performance under varying workloads.

- **Security and compliance**: ROSA offers built-in enterprise security features, including network isolation, IAM integration, and automated updates, ensuring that applications meet stringent compliance and security requirements.

Use cases

ROSA is designed for modern application development, supporting various use cases, from microservices architecture to hybrid cloud strategies. With its integrated CI/CD pipelines, scalability, and cross-cloud compatibility, ROSA provides an optimized environment for enterprises to accelerate their digital transformation initiatives [32].

ROSA provides a flexible and scalable platform to address various modern application development needs. The following use cases highlight how organizations can leverage ROSA to support containerized workloads, enhance deployment strategies, and drive operational efficiency across hybrid and cloud-native environments:

- **Microservices architecture**: ROSA supports the deployment and management of microservices, enabling teams to break down applications into more minor, independently deployable services.

- **Hybrid cloud deployments**: ROSA is ideal for hybrid cloud environments, allowing organizations to run containerized applications both on-premises and on AWS, seamlessly integrating with on-premises infrastructure.

- **CI/CD pipelines**: With built-in CI/CD capabilities, ROSA enables automated testing, integration, and deployment of containerized applications in fast-moving environments.

Integration with AWS services

ROSA integrates tightly with various AWS services, enhancing the management and deployment of containerized applications [32]:

- **Amazon RDS and Amazon EFS**: ROSA can easily integrate with Amazon RDS for relational database services and Amazon EFS for scalable storage, making it suitable for applications with diverse data storage needs.

- **Amazon CloudWatch**: Integration with CloudWatch enables monitoring and logging of containerized applications, providing insights into performance, errors, and system health.

- **AWS IAM**: ROSA uses AWS IAM to manage resource access, providing fine-grained control over who can access OpenShift resources within the AWS cloud environment.

Managed OpenShift in the cloud

Managed OpenShift in the cloud offers a fully managed Kubernetes platform designed to accelerate the development and deployment of containerized applications. This service combines the power of Red Hat OpenShift with the scalability of public cloud providers like AWS, allowing organizations to focus on application development while leaving the management of the underlying infrastructure to the provider [24].

Overview

Managed OpenShift in the cloud provides organizations with a streamlined approach to deploying, managing, and scaling containerized applications. With OpenShift's powerful Kubernetes orchestration and enterprise-grade features, teams can use an integrated platform that simplifies container management, scaling, and security. Whether it is an on-demand service or a private cloud deployment, managed OpenShift offers a robust platform that integrates seamlessly with a wide range of cloud-native tools and services [24].

Key features

Organizations leveraging Managed OpenShift in the cloud gain access to a fully integrated Kubernetes solution designed for enterprise-scale application deployment. With enhanced security, automation, and cloud-native integrations, OpenShift simplifies the complexities of managing containerized workloads while ensuring flexibility and efficiency [24].

Managed OpenShift in the cloud offers powerful features designed to simplify Kubernetes operations while addressing enterprise demands for security, scalability, and operational efficiency. The following key features demonstrate how OpenShift enables organizations to deploy and manage containerized applications across diverse cloud environments confidently:

- **Enterprise-Grade Kubernetes**: Managed OpenShift brings Kubernetes orchestration with added security, scalability, and enterprise capabilities, making it ideal for organizations with complex application needs.

- **Simplified application deployment**: OpenShift's native tools for automated deployment, CI/CD pipelines, and monitoring streamline the process of getting applications up and running in the cloud.

- **Integrated security features**: The platform offers built-in security features, including RBAC, automated patching, and vulnerability scanning, to protect applications in production.

- **Cloud-native integrations**: Managed OpenShift integrates seamlessly with cloud services like storage, networking, and identity management tools, enabling flexible, cloud-native application architectures.

Benefits

By offloading infrastructure management, organizations can focus on innovation rather than operational challenges. Managed OpenShift delivers scalability, security, and automation, enabling businesses to streamline development workflows, maintain compliance, and optimize performance across dynamic cloud environments [24], as discussed:

- **Reduced operational overhead**: By outsourcing the management of Kubernetes clusters and OpenShift components, development teams can focus on building applications rather than managing infrastructure.

- **Scalability and flexibility**: Managed OpenShift in the cloud dynamically scales resources based on application load, ensuring high availability and performance.

- **Simplified CI/CD**: With built-in CI/CD capabilities, OpenShift accelerates the development cycle, automating testing, integration, and deployment pipelines.

- **Enhanced security and compliance**: Managed OpenShift in the cloud integrates with IAM and provides comprehensive logging, monitoring, and auditing features that help meet stringent security and compliance requirements.

Use cases

Businesses adopting modern cloud strategies require platforms that support scalable architecture, hybrid deployments, and DevOps automation. Managed OpenShift caters to diverse workloads, from microservices-driven applications to hybrid cloud integrations and fully automated CI/CD pipelines, making it a preferred solution for enterprises embracing cloud-native development [24].

By adopting managed OpenShift in the cloud, organizations can unlock a wide range of benefits that go beyond simplified container management. The following benefits illustrate how OpenShift accelerates development, optimizes resources, and strengthens security while reducing operational complexity:

- **Microservices deployment**: Managed OpenShift is ideal for organizations transitioning to a microservices architecture. It supports the deployment and management of microservices at scale.

- **Hybrid Cloud solutions**: Managed OpenShift offers seamless integration with public and private cloud environments, enabling hybrid cloud strategies and allowing organizations to run applications across diverse cloud platforms.

- **DevOps and CI/CD pipelines**: Managed OpenShift simplifies the adoption of DevOps practices by integrating CI/CD pipelines directly into the platform, ensuring smooth and consistent deployment processes.

Integration with AWS services

Managed OpenShift in the cloud integrates with various AWS services, enhancing its capabilities and extending its use for different application needs [24].

Managed OpenShift in the cloud supports diverse use cases across industries and workloads. The following examples highlight how organizations leverage OpenShift to modernize their application architectures, implement hybrid cloud strategies, and streamline DevOps practices:

- **Amazon EC2 and Amazon S3**: These services are often integrated with managed OpenShift for compute and storage solutions, ensuring that applications can scale dynamically while utilizing secure, reliable cloud storage.

- **AWS IAM**: Integrated with AWS IAM, Managed OpenShift ensures secure access control for cloud resources and provides robust identity and permissions management.

- **Amazon CloudWatch**: Managed OpenShift integrates with Amazon CloudWatch for monitoring, enabling organizations to track application performance metrics, logs, and health status in real-time.

AWS RoboMaker

AWS RoboMaker simplifies the development, testing, and deployment of robotics applications in the cloud. It provides comprehensive tools for building intelligent robots, including simulation environments, fleet management, and integration with the **Robot Operating System (ROS)**. RoboMaker supports a streamlined workflow, from development and simulation to deployment [33].

Key features and capabilities

AWS RoboMaker equips developers with a comprehensive suite of tools for building, testing, and deploying robotics applications on a scale. By offering realistic simulation environments, fleet management solutions, and deep integration with ROS, RoboMaker accelerates the development lifecycle of intelligent robots, as follows:

- **Simulation environments**: AWS RoboMaker provides realistic testing scenarios before deploying applications to physical robots [33].

- **Fleet management**: It provides tools for efficiently managing and scaling robot fleets.

- **ROS integration**: Seamlessly integrates with ROS, allowing compatibility with widely used robotic frameworks [33].

Figure 8.9 illustrates AWS RoboMaker's simulation service to visualize how it helps cloud-based robotic development. It highlights how realistic simulations refine and evaluate robotic applications before deploying them to physical robots.

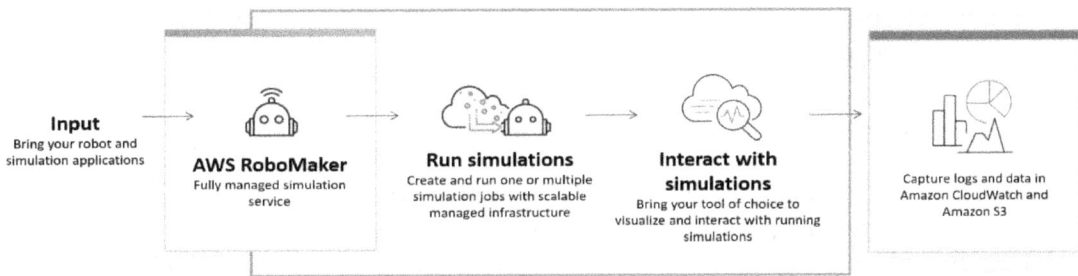

Figure 8.9: *AWS RoboMaker cloud-based simulation service*

Workflow

RoboMaker's workflow covers:

- **Development**: Use the **integrated development environment** (**IDE**) to build and debug applications.

- **Simulation**: Test applications in virtual environments to refine robot behavior.

- **Deployment**: Deploy tested applications to physical robots using RoboMaker [33].

Integration with AWS services

Seamless integration with AWS services enhances robotics applications' scalability, storage, and automation. AWS RoboMaker leverages cloud-native capabilities to manage robotics infrastructure efficiently, ensuring secure data storage and scalable deployments [33], as follows:

- **Amazon S3**: Store simulation data and model files.

- **AWS CloudFormation**: Provision infrastructure for robotics applications.

Use cases

AWS RoboMaker is widely adopted across industrial automation, research, and education, providing a cloud-powered solution for robotics innovation. Organizations leverage RoboMaker to enhance operational efficiency, streamline development, and enable cutting-edge research in **artificial intelligence** (**AI**) driven robotics, as follows:

- **Industrial automation**: Automating tasks like material handling and inspection.

- **Research and education**: Supporting robotic research and educational purposes [33].

Quantum technologies in AWS

Quantum technologies represent a significant leap forward in computing, harnessing the principles of quantum mechanics to enable robust computation. AWS helps the adoption of quantum computing through services like Amazon Braket, providing access to diverse quantum processors and tools to experiment with quantum algorithms [34].

Key concepts

Understanding the fundamental principles of quantum computing is crucial for leveraging its computational advantages. AWS provides resources to explore key concepts in quantum mechanics, including qubits, quantum gates, and entanglement, which form the foundation of quantum algorithms and computation [34].

The foundational concepts of quantum computing provide the basis for understanding how this emerging technology differs from classical computing. AWS enables users to explore these critical principles underpinning quantum algorithms and their unique capabilities:

- **Qubits and quantum gates**: Qubits exist in multiple states simultaneously, enabling complex computations.

- **Entanglement**: Qubits influence each other across distances, a fundamental property of quantum systems.

Amazon Braket

Amazon Braket serves as AWS's gateway to quantum computing, offering a unified environment for designing, testing, and executing quantum algorithms. It provides researchers and developers access to multiple quantum processors and hybrid computing resources, enabling real-world experimentation with quantum mechanics.

By bridging classical and quantum computing, Amazon Braket enables users to explore next-generation computational models and push the boundaries of problem-solving in optimization, cryptography, and materials science.

Amazon Braket offers a comprehensive set of features that allow users to experiment with quantum computing in a practical and scalable environment. The following capabilities illustrate how Amazon Braket empowers organizations to explore quantum workflows using AWS's managed services:

- **Quantum processors**: Access to multiple quantum processors for varied algorithm testing.

- **Quantum tasks**: Execute quantum tasks by selecting processors and algorithms.

- **Hybrid quantum-classical computing**: Combines quantum and classical computing for complex problem-solving [34].

Integration with AWS services

AWS seamlessly integrates quantum computing with its existing cloud infrastructure, enabling businesses to store, process, and analyze data generated by quantum computing.

Organizations can enhance efficiency and extend quantum computing capabilities to broader applications by combining quantum resources with AWS services [34].

The integration of Amazon Braket with other AWS services extends the value of quantum computing by enabling efficient data storage, processing, and event-driven automation. The following services exemplify how quantum tasks can interact with AWS's broader cloud ecosystem:

- **Amazon S3**: Store quantum data and results.

- **AWS Lambda**: Execute serverless functions triggered by quantum tasks.

Use cases

Quantum computing has the potential to revolutionize industries by tackling problems beyond the reach of classical computing. AWS Braket enables researchers, scientists, and businesses to experiment with quantum algorithms, optimize computations, and explore novel applications in fields such as cryptography, materials science, and AI [34]:

- **Quantum algorithm development**: For refining and testing algorithms.

- **Exploring quantum capabilities**: Testing quantum computing applications without dedicated infrastructure.

Challenges

Despite its transformative potential, quantum computing faces several technical and practical challenges. Issues such as error rates, resource optimization, and quantum decoherence require ongoing hardware and algorithm development advancements. AWS provides tools and research support to address these challenges, helping users maximize the benefits of quantum computing [34]:

- **Error correction**: Quantum computing's susceptibility to errors requires effective strategies.

- **Resource allocation**: Optimal quantum processor and task configuration are key to success.

Developer tools and DevOps in AWS

AWS developer tools and DevOps services empower development teams by automating software delivery, optimizing infrastructure management, and enhancing operational efficiency. These tools are designed to streamline **continuous integration and continuous delivery (CI/ CD)**, infrastructure provisioning, and deployment automation, allowing developers to focus on innovation rather than manual configurations [35] [36]. The following key areas highlight how AWS accelerates modern DevOps workflows:

- **CI/CD**: Integrating AWS CodeCommit and AWS CodePipeline streamlines code management and automation [37]; [38].

- **Cloud Development Kit (CDK)**: AWS CDK promotes IaC, making it easier to define cloud infrastructure [39].

- **DevOps automation**: Tools like AWS CodeDeploy and AWS Fargate simplify deployment and management [40]; [30].

Integrating AWS tools into DevOps and cloud development workflows boosts efficiency, security, and scalability. These tools provide seamless solutions for application management, fostering rapid deployment and innovation.

Conclusion

This chapter revolved around AWS developer tools, DevOps solutions, application integration services, container management, robotics, and quantum technologies. These services empower developers to innovate, collaborate, and deploy applications with speed, scalability, and reliability. AWS supports the entire **software development lifecycle (SDLC)**, making it a cloud provider and a comprehensive ecosystem for code creation, collaboration, deployment, and monitoring.

The evolution of cloud computing, with AWS at the forefront, highlights its role in shaping the future of technology. From traditional development to quantum computing, AWS provides the tools necessary to navigate this transformative landscape.

Next, we will explore AWS's powerful analytics and **machine learning (ML)** tools, including Amazon Redshift, Athena, AWS Glue, and SageMaker. The next chapter will equip you with the skills to harness data and ML, driving innovation and insights in your applications.

Join our Discord space

Join our Discord workspace for latest updates, offers, tech happenings around the world, new releases, and sessions with the authors:

https://discord.bpbonline.com

CHAPTER 9
End-user, Front-end, and Mobile

Introduction

In the dynamic landscape of cloud computing, empowering end-users and enabling seamless front-end interactions is critical for modern applications, especially across web and mobile platforms. **Amazon Web Services (AWS)** offers a range of tools and services to enhance **user experience (UX)** and development agility. This chapter explores the essential AWS services, with a focus on AWS **end-user computing (EUC)**, front-end web development, and mobile application integration. It also examines how they contribute to the development of robust, user-centric applications.

Structure

In this chapter, we will cover the following topics:

- End-user, front-end, and mobile
- End-user computing
- Front-end web and mobile
- Amazon Simple Email Service
- Reflecting further

Objectives

In this chapter, readers will explore how AWS empowers EUC through services such as Amazon AppStream 2.0 and Amazon WorkSpaces, providing flexible and secure computing environments. To build responsive, scalable, and secure applications, this course will examine front-end web and mobile services using AWS tools, including **Application Programming Interface (API)** Gateway, Location Service, Pinpoint, and **Simple Email Service (SES)**. The chapter will also cover AWS Amplify and AppSync, simplifying web and mobile development by providing real-time data synchronization and API management. Using AWS Device Farm, quality assurance best practices will ensure that applications perform optimally across a diverse range of devices and platforms.

This chapter will equip readers with the knowledge to empower end-users, build secure APIs, integrate location-based services, streamline mobile development, and ensure top-quality testing and performance for web and mobile applications.

End-user, front-end, and mobile

In the dynamic landscape of cloud computing, empowering end-users and helping seamless interaction with front-end applications, particularly in the web and mobile spaces, are key factors. This chapter examines the multifaceted aspects of EUC and the intricacies of front-end web and mobile services provided by AWS.

End-user computing

In today's increasingly remote and digital-first world, the need for robust, flexible, and scalable EUC solutions has never been greater. AWS provides a comprehensive suite of services to meet organizational needs, helping secure and provide high-performance access to applications and desktops regardless of user location. In this section, we will explore key AWS offerings in EUC and examine how these solutions drive productivity, security, and efficiency.

Amazon AppStream 2.0

One of the key components explored in this chapter is Amazon AppStream 2.0, an innovative service that transforms EUC. It enables the secure streaming of desktop applications to various devices, ensuring a consistent and responsive UX. As we navigate through the details of AppStream 2.0, we will uncover its applications across diverse use cases, from educational institutions to enterprise scenarios, highlighting its role in enhancing accessibility and flexibility for end-users.

Amazon WorkSpaces Family

The exploration of EUC is incomplete without a comprehensive look at the Amazon WorkSpaces Family. This suite of services provides cloud-based desktop solutions, enabling organizations to deliver a personalized, secure, and scalable desktop experience to their users. We will dissect the features of various WorkSpaces options, shedding light on how they cater to different user requirements and scenarios.

In *Figure 9.1*, you will find a high-level architecture showing standard EUC technologies such as **virtual desktop infrastructure (VDI)**, **desktop as a service (DaaS)**, and **application as a service (AaaS)**:

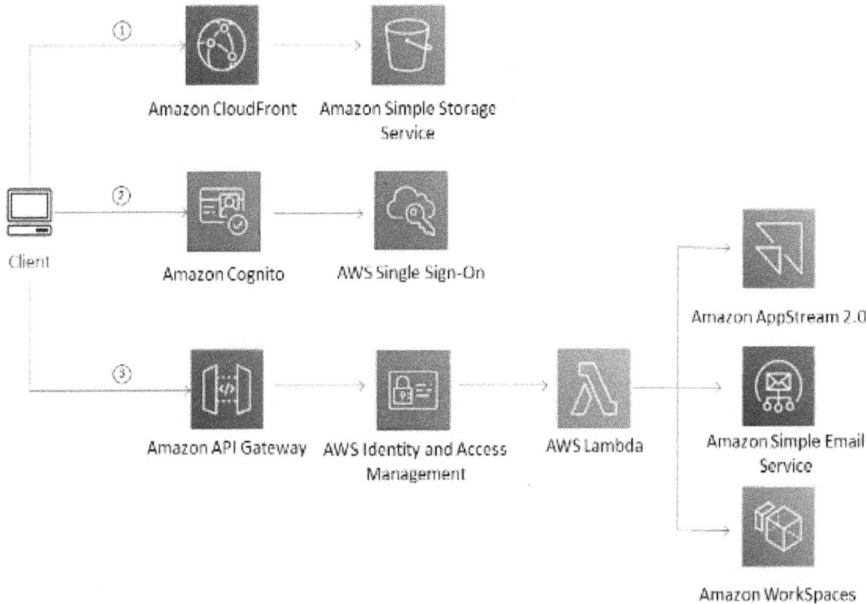

Figure 9.1: AWS EUC services

Front-end web and mobile

In an increasingly mobile and interconnected world, delivering high-quality, responsive, and engaging front-end web and mobile experiences is invaluable. AWS offers a rich portfolio of services that empower developers to build, manage, and scale applications easily. This section will explore key services that enable seamless integration, communication, and location-based functionality designed to improve front-end application development.

Amazon API Gateway

Transitioning to front-end web and mobile services, our journey begins with Amazon API Gateway. This service serves as a gateway for creating, publishing, and managing APIs, facilitating seamless integration of applications. The chapter will navigate through the functionalities of API Gateway, emphasizing its role in building robust, scalable, and secure APIs that drive innovation in the front-end ecosystem.

Amazon Location Service

Geospatial applications are gaining prominence, and Amazon Location Service takes center stage in this section. We will explore how this service simplifies the integration of location-based features into applications, opening new possibilities for developers to create context-aware and location-aware UX.

Amazon Pinpoint

Communication is essential for user engagement, and Amazon Pinpoint is a tool for improving customer interactions. Our exploration will uncover how Pinpoint enables personalized and targeted communication across multiple channels, including email, SMS, and mobile push notifications.

Amazon Simple Email Service

Email communication is still a cornerstone in the digital landscape. Amazon SES is centered on stage as we discuss its role in sending transactional and marketing emails on a large scale. We will unravel the features of SES that ensure deliverability, reliability, and compliance in email communication strategies.

AWS Amplify

AWS Amplify offers a comprehensive framework for developers building scalable and secure full-stack applications. We will enter the Amplify ecosystem, exploring how it simplifies the development process for web and mobile applications by providing a unified set of tools and services.

AWS AppSync

The chapter concludes its exploration of front-end web and mobile services with a detailed look at AWS AppSync. As a fully managed service, AppSync helps develop responsive and collaborative applications by enabling real-time data synchronization. We will examine its role in building GraphQL APIs and integrating with diverse data sources.

AWS Device Farm

Quality assurance is paramount in the world of mobile applications. AWS Device Farm is our destination in this chapter, providing a comprehensive testing environment for web and mobile applications. We will explore how Device Farm enhances the testing process, ensuring the reliability and functionality of applications across a myriad of devices.

This chapter provides a comprehensive examination of AWS user-centric and front-end services. From empowering end-users with innovative computing solutions to providing developers with robust tools for crafting engaging front-end experiences, this chapter sets the stage for a comprehensive understanding of AWS services across the end-user, front-end, and mobile segments.

End-user computing

EUC refers to the technologies, policies, and processes that enable users to securely access the applications, desktops, and data they need, often from remote locations and on various devices [1]. In modern IT environments, where remote and hybrid work is increasingly common, EUC is crucial for keeping productivity and business continuity. By allowing employees to work from anywhere using laptops, tablets, or phones, a well-designed EUC strategy ensures that staff have immediate access to the digital tools they need, without compromising security or compliance [1] [2]. In essence, EUC empowers organizations to support flexible work styles (e.g., **work-from-home (WFH) and bring-your-own-device (BYOD)**) in a safe and scalable manner, making it a foundational part of cloud-era IT strategy.

AWS's secure, scalable, and flexible EUC solutions

Cloud providers like AWS have adopted EUC by offering fully managed services that deliver desktops and applications securely and elastically from the cloud. AWS EUC services enable organizations to quickly provision virtual desktops and stream applications to users on demand, with AWS handling the infrastructure management. These services are built with security in mind—data remains encrypted and centralized in AWS, rather than residing on user devices and they can seamlessly scale from a few users to thousands as business needs evolve [3] because AWS EUC solutions are device-agnostic and delivered over the internet, employees can work from any supported device or location, enjoying the same access to tools and information for maximum flexibility. [3]. In short, AWS provides a robust platform to implement EUC, ensuring that end-users receive a responsive, secure, and scalable experience. At the same time, IT keeps control and agility in managing those resources.

Key AWS EUC services

AWS offers different specialized services to meet EUC needs, each addressing distinct aspects of EUC:

- **Amazon WorkSpaces**: A fully managed DaaS solution that delivers persistent cloud-hosted desktops to users. With Amazon WorkSpaces, organizations can provide Windows or Linux virtual desktops that employees access from anywhere on any supported device without needing to deploy or keep on-premises VDI infrastructure [4]. This service provides a secure and reliable desktop experience over the cloud, ending the hassle of managing physical PCs for each user.

- **Amazon AppStream 2.0**: A fully managed application streaming service that enables users to run desktop applications directly in a web browser, cutting the need for local installations. Applications are hosted on AWS, and only the interactive streaming visuals are delivered to the user's device [3] is allows organizations to centrally manage complex or resource-intensive apps and securely stream them to any compatible device. Amazon AppStream 2.0 is ideal for delivering software to diverse user environments (for example, 3D design tools for Chromebooks or Macs) and converting traditional software into a **software-as-a-service** (**SaaS**) model without requiring rewriting.

- **AWS WorkLink**: A managed service for secure mobile access, providing one-click, remote access to internal websites and web apps from employees' smartphones without a VPN. Amazon WorkLink [5] renders internal web content in a secure container on AWS and streams it to the mobile device, ensuring that no sensitive corporate data is ever stored or cached on the phone's cloud. This provides field workers and remote staff with instant access to internal corporate portals or web-based tools, as if they were on the company network, while keeping strong security isolation.

Common EUC use cases

The flexibility and security of cloud-based EUC make it applicable to a variety of scenarios across industries:

- **Enterprise workforce**: Large companies use EUC services to support distributed teams and global offices. Instead of shipping laptops or keeping regional data centers, an enterprise can onboard new employees or contractors in minutes by provisioning cloud desktops (via WorkSpaces) pre-loaded with corporate applications. This ensures all users get a consistent, secure environment without the hassle of managing physical hardware [3]. EUC solutions also help when scaling up teams quickly or integrating acquisitions, as IT can deliver standardized work environments on demand.

- **Education**: Schools and universities leverage EUC to provide students and faculty access to specialized software and lab environments from anywhere. For example, Amazon AppStream 2.0 enables students to run high-performance applications (like engineering, graphic design, or STEM software) on low-cost devices through a browser, effectively turning any internet-connected computer into a powerful virtual lab [6]. This is invaluable for remote learning programs, computer labs, or BYOD initiatives in education, as it ensures that every student can use required applications without needing expensive workstations.

- **Remote and hybrid workforce**: In today's remote work era, EUC solutions enable employees to WFH or on the go while keeping access to internal systems secure. Organizations can rapidly setup virtual desktops for teleworkers and provide them with the same applications they would have in the office, all delivered through the cloud. AWS EUC services allow companies to onboard remote workers quickly and give them the tools and data access needed to do their jobs effectively, all while keeping sensitive data within the secure cloud environment [1] This capability proved critical for business continuity during events like the *COVID-19* pandemic, when hundreds of millions suddenly had to work from personal devices and locations outside the office [1]. Even in regular times, a remote or hybrid work policy backed by EUC enables employees to be productive from anywhere, while the organization keeps complete control over the work environment.

Benefits of cloud-based EUC

Adopting EUC in a cloud computing model yields different vital benefits for organizations and end-users alike:

- **Security**: Cloud EUC significantly enhances data security by centralizing applications and information in the cloud rather than on endpoint devices. Only screen updates (in pixels) and user input travel between the cloud and the device, so no sensitive data is stored on laptops, tablets, or phones [1]. This reduces the risk of data loss or theft (for example, if a device is lost or stolen) and enables IT to enforce security policies in a single, centralized location, such as encryption, access control, and backups.

- **Accessibility**: EUC enhances accessibility by enabling authorized users to access their desktops or apps from anywhere and on almost any device. Whether an employee is on a home PC, a tablet while traveling, or a shared computer, they can log into their cloud-hosted workspace and find the same applications and data ready to use [7]. This work-from-anywhere capability not only boosts user productivity and flexibility but also ensures that work is not tied to a specific physical machine or office, making the organization more resilient and agile.

- **Simplified IT management**: From an IT perspective, cloud EUC streamlines the management of user computing environments. Instead of updating and troubleshooting hundreds of individual PCs, administrators can keep a golden image or a set of applications in the cloud and deploy updates centrally. AWS EUC services allow apps and desktops to be managed in one place, reducing the complexity of software distribution, patching, and hardware refresh cycles [1]. Scaling up or down is also easier—new users can be added with a click, and resources can be right-sized or turned off when not needed, resulting in more efficient use of IT resources and lower costs over time.

In summary, EUC in the cloud is a game-changer for organizations looking to provide secure, anywhere access to work resources. AWS suite of EUC services exemplifies how the cloud can deliver desktops and applications as an on-demand utility with robust security, global accessibility, and simplified management—ultimately empowering end-users and IT departments alike. Companies can enhance workforce agility and productivity by using AWS EUC solutions, such as WorkSpaces, AppStream 2.0, and WorkLink, while keeping strict control over data and compliance in a cloud-first environment [3].

Amazon AppStream 2.0

In the ever-evolving landscape of cloud computing, EUC is a critical area focusing on delivering a seamless and flexible computing experience to end-users. Amazon AppStream 2.0, a service offered by AWS, takes center stage in this section. This service revolutionized application delivery, offering responsive and secure streaming across various devices.

Amazon AppStream 2.0 overview

Amazon AppStream 2.0 is a fully managed application streaming service that enables users to securely stream desktop applications to their devices. It eliminates the need for users to install and run applications locally, providing a dynamic and scalable solution for enterprises and educational institutions [8].

Key features and capabilities

Amazon AppStream 2.0 offers many powerful features that enhance its functionality, making it a versatile choice for businesses and educational institutions. Below, we examine the key features that enable AppStream 2.0 to deliver a seamless, secure, and scalable application streaming experience across various platforms and devices.

To fully understand the impact of Amazon AppStream 2.0, it is essential to explore its features that make it a powerful cloud-based application streaming solution. By leveraging AWS's scalable infrastructure, AppStream 2.0 delivers high-performance applications to users regardless of their device or location. The following key capabilities illustrate how AppStream 2.0 enhances accessibility, security, and performance for businesses, educational institutions, and other organizations that need flexible, on-demand application streaming.

Amazon AppStream 2.0 is designed to address the challenges of delivering desktop applications to diverse users across multiple devices. Its core features focus on improving accessibility, strengthening security, and ensuring scalable performance for various use cases. The following capabilities demonstrate how AppStream 2.0 enables organizations to deliver reliable, high-performance application streaming in a secure and flexible cloud environment:

- **Application streaming**: AppStream 2.0 enables real-time application streaming, ensuring that users can access and use resource-intensive applications without requiring powerful local hardware.

- **Security and isolation**: The service prioritizes security by isolating each user session, ensuring data privacy, and preventing interactions between streaming sessions. This is important for keeping a secure computing environment.

- **Cross-platform compatibility**: AppStream 2.0 supports various devices, including Windows and Mac computers, Chromebooks, and multiple tablets. This cross-platform compatibility enhances its versatility and user accessibility.

- **Dynamic scaling**: The service allows dynamic scaling based on the number of users, ensuring best performance during peak usage periods and cost-efficiency during periods of lower demand.

The significance of AWS cloud capabilities extends beyond traditional business applications. As shown in *Figure 9.2*, AWS built a highly secure data lake and a global-scale analytics environment to help forecast the spread and risk of COVID-19. This exemplifies the scalability, resilience, and security of AWS services such as Amazon AppStream 2.0 in real-world crisis management.

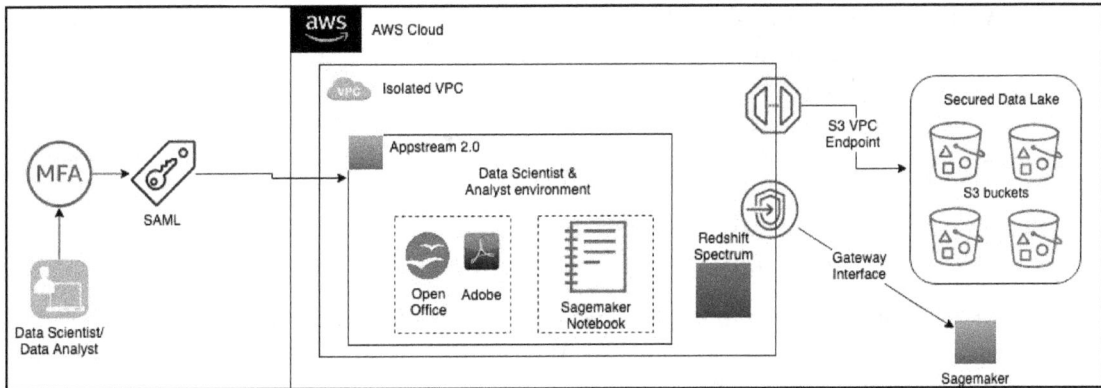

Figure 9.2: Data Lake solution for the COVID-19 risk study

Use cases

Diverse industries and segments have adopted Amazon AppStream 2.0, providing tailored solutions that cater to the needs of enterprises and educational institutions. The key use cases where AppStream 2.0's secure, scalable, and dynamic capabilities bring significant value to organizations are as follows:

- **Enterprise applications**: AppStream 2.0 enables enterprises to centrally manage and stream resource-intensive applications to end-user devices, thereby reducing the need for extensive local computing resources [9].

- **Educational institutions**: The service helps deliver software applications to students without complex local installations, streamlining the learning process in educational settings [10]. Amazon AppStream 2.0 presents a transformative solution in EUC, offering a flexible, secure, and scalable approach to application delivery. As we explore its features, capabilities, and real-world applications, it becomes clear that AppStream 2.0 is not merely a technological advancement but a strategic tool for organizations aiming to enhance UX and streamline application management in an increasingly digital world.

Amazon WorkSpaces Family

In the cloud-driven EUC landscape, the Amazon WorkSpaces Family is prominent, offering a comprehensive solution for virtualized desktops. This section examines the intricacies of Amazon WorkSpaces, its features, capabilities, and the broader implications it has for providing a flexible and secure computing environment to end-users.

Amazon WorkSpaces overview

Amazon WorkSpaces is a cloud-based service that provisions and manages virtual desktops. It enables users to access their desktop environment from various devices, promoting flexibility and mobility in today's dynamic work environments [11].

Key features and capabilities

To better understand Amazon Workspaces' transformative potential, let us examine its core features, which enhance usability, security, and performance for end-users [11]:

- **Virtual desktop provisioning**: WorkSpaces simplifies creating and managing virtual desktops, allowing organizations to provision desktop environments for their users without complex on-premises infrastructure.

- **Customizable compute resources**: Users can customize the compute resources of their WorkSpaces, ensuring that each virtual desktop meets the individual user's performance requirements, from standard office applications to graphics-intensive tasks.

- **Security and compliance**: The service strongly emphasizes security, featuring encryption, **multi-factor authentication** (**MFA**), and integration with AWS **Key Management Service** (**KMS**). This ensures that sensitive data stays secure in transit and at rest.

- **Cross-device accessibility**: WorkSpaces supports access from a variety of devices, including computers, tablets, and zero clients, providing users with a consistent desktop experience regardless of their device.

Use cases

Amazon WorkSpaces addresses various workplace scenarios. The following are the key cases where this service can have a significant impact on the workplace:

- **Remote work environments**: WorkSpaces enables remote work by allowing users to access their desktops from any location, fostering collaboration and productivity outside the traditional office setting [12].

- **Bring your device policies**: Organizations can implement BYOD policies seamlessly, as WorkSpaces ensures a uniform and secure desktop experience regardless of the device used by the end-user [13].

Amazon WorkSpaces Family presents a transformative solution in EUC, offering a flexible, customizable, and secure approach to virtual desktop provisioning. As organizations continue to adopt cloud technologies to enhance workforce mobility and productivity, WorkSpaces is a testament to the distinct role cloud-based EUC solutions play in the modern workplace.

Figure 9.3 highlights the architecture of the Amazon WorkSpace automation solution, which streamlines virtual desktop deployment and management:

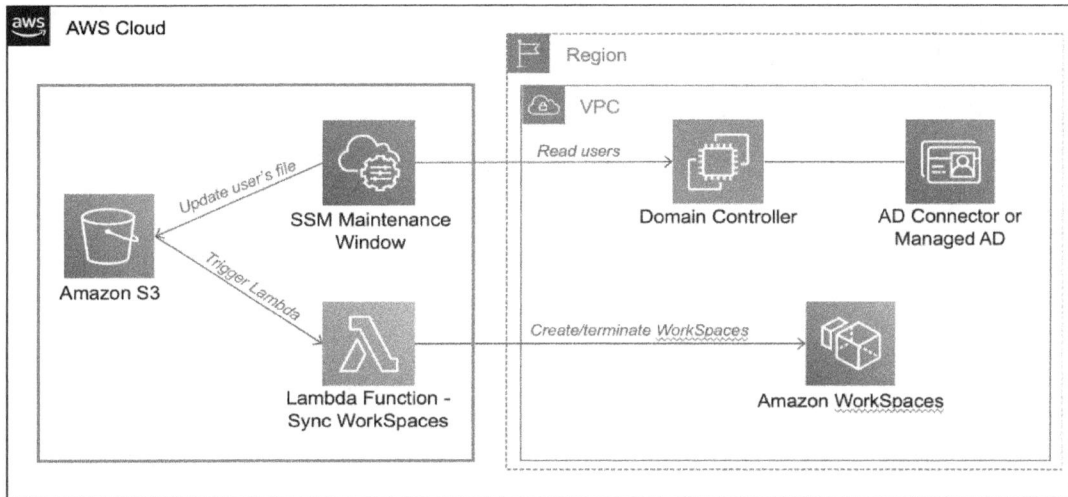

Figure 9.3: *Amazon WorkSpaces automation solution architecture*

Front-end web and mobile

AWS provides a suite of robust services that empower developers to build, deploy, and manage front-end and mobile applications with efficiency and scalability. The following figure illustrates how AWS front-end services interact with the back-end, highlighting the layered architecture that supports dynamic, user-centric applications.

Amazon API Gateway

In the dynamic landscape of web and mobile development, efficient management and deployment of APIs play a fundamental role. Amazon API Gateway, a fully managed service, takes center stage in this context, providing developers with tools to create, publish, and secure APIs. This section examines the intricacies of Amazon API Gateway, its key features, and its importance in modern application development.

Refer to the following figure:

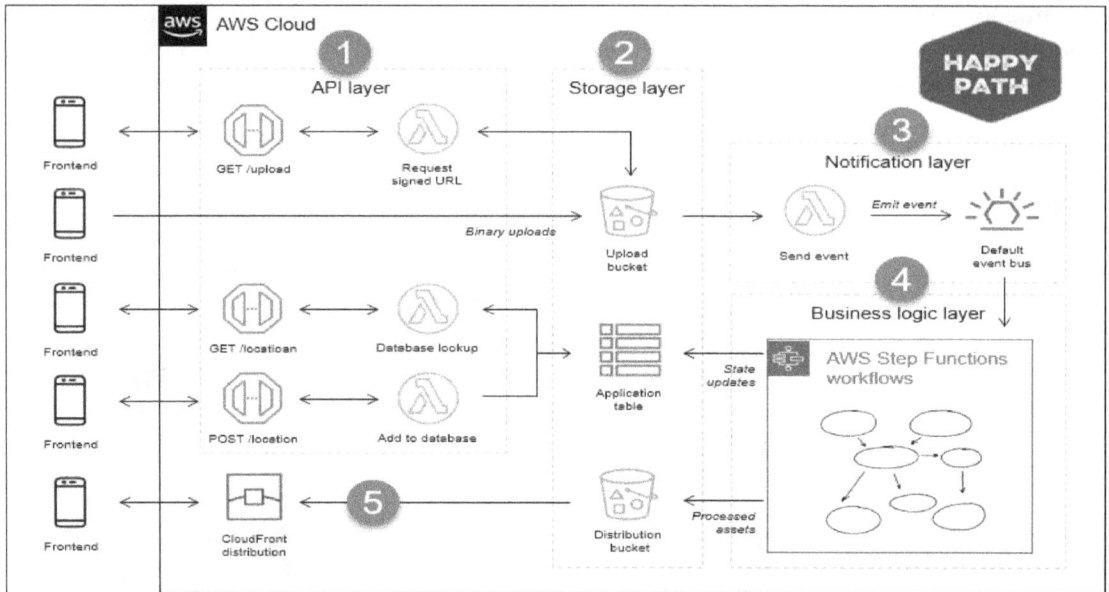

Figure 9.4: Front-end and back-end application interactions

Amazon API Gateway overview

Amazon API Gateway is a scalable and fully managed service that simplifies the creation, deployment, and management of APIs. Whether for web applications, mobile applications, or back-end services, API Gateway allows seamless communication between diverse applications and services [14].

Key features and capabilities

In the dynamic landscape of web and mobile development, efficient management and deployment of APIs are crucial. Amazon API Gateway, a fully managed service, takes center stage in this context, providing developers with tools to create, publish, and secure APIs. This section examines the intricacies of Amazon API Gateway, its key features, and its importance in modern application development [14]:

- **API creation and deployment**: API Gateway helps create RESTful APIs, WebSocket APIs, and other types of APIs, providing a unified platform for developers to build and deploy their application interfaces.

- **Scalability**: The service scales automatically to manage different traffic levels, which is key for applications with fluctuating demand.

- **Security and access control**: API Gateway supports various authentication mechanisms, including AWS **Identity and Access Management (IAM)**, OAuth, and custom authorizers. This ensures that APIs are secure and accessible only to authorized users.

- **Monitoring and analytics**: Integrated monitoring and analytics tools help developers gain insights into API usage, performance, and error rates, helping them find and address issues proactively.

Use cases

The following scenarios highlight the versatility of Amazon API Gateway and its integral role in supporting modern application architecture:

- **Microservices architecture**: API Gateway is instrumental in implementing microservices architecture by acting as the entry point for various microservices, enabling efficient communication and orchestration [15].

- **Serverless architecture**: In serverless architecture, API Gateway seamlessly integrates with AWS Lambda, allowing developers to build serverless applications easily [16].

Amazon API Gateway plays a key role in modern application development, providing a unified and scalable platform for creating, deploying, and managing APIs. As organizations strive for agility and flexibility in their application architectures, API Gateway is a testament to the innovative capabilities that cloud-based API management services bring to the forefront of web and mobile development.

The following figure illustrates AWS front-end computing layers, detailing the architecture components that power efficient, responsive UXs:

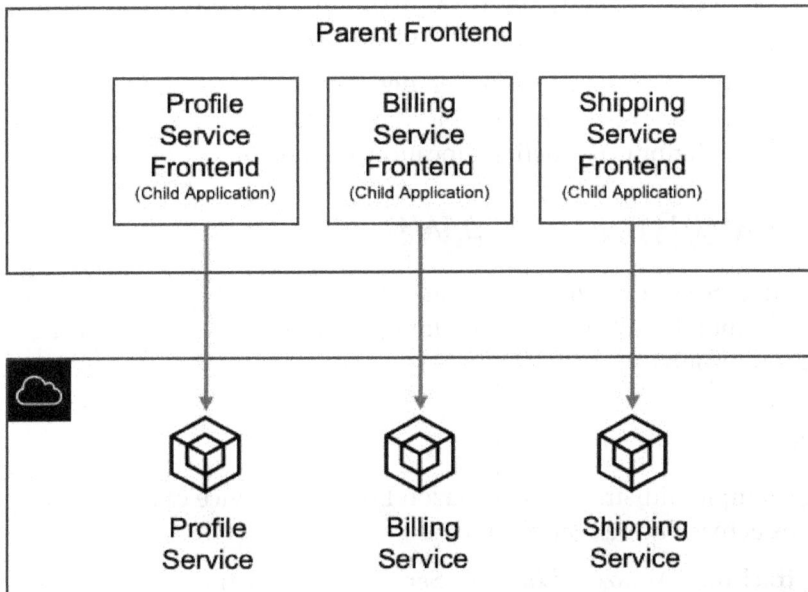

Figure 9.5: AWS front-end computing layers

Amazon Location Service

Geospatial data has become integral to modern applications, especially those in the realm of location-based services. Amazon Location Service is a fully managed service that enables developers to incorporate location-based features into their applications without the complexity of managing infrastructure. In this section, we detail Amazon Location Service's capabilities and applications.

Amazon Location Service overview

Amazon Location Service enables developers to add location-based services such as maps, places, and geofencing to their applications. Leveraging data from top-tier providers, it offers a scalable and cost-effective solution for integrating location-based features into applications [17].

Key features and capabilities

The following features of Amazon Location Service provide developers with powerful tools to build engaging and responsive applications [17]:

- **Maps**: Amazon Location Service provides high-quality, customizable maps that developers can integrate into their applications. These maps include points of interest and terrain details.

- **Places**: Developers can incorporate location-based information into places, making it easier for users to find and explore nearby points of interest. This feature enhances UX in travel, e-commerce, and social networking applications.

- **Geofencing**: Geofencing allows developers to create virtual boundaries around specific geographic areas. This feature enables applications to trigger events or notifications when users enter or exit a defined location, enhancing UX personalization.

Integration with other AWS services

Amazon Location Service seamlessly integrates with other AWS services, fostering interoperability within the AWS ecosystem. Integration with AWS IAM ensures secure access control to location resources.

Use cases

The following examples illustrate how Amazon Location Service can improve operations and user interactions across different applications:

- **Asset tracking**: Amazon Location Service helps with real-time tracking of assets, which is valuable in scenarios such as planning and supply chain management [18].

- **Fleet management**: Applications related to fleet management can leverage geofencing capabilities to improve routes, watch vehicle locations, and enhance overall operational efficiency [19].

Amazon Location Service appears to be a transformative tool for developers looking to enhance their applications with location-based features. This service enables developers to create engaging and personalized experiences for end-users across diverse areas by providing access to high-quality maps, location data, and geofencing capabilities.

Amazon Pinpoint

In the ever-evolving digital communication landscape, engaging users successfully is paramount for the success of applications. Amazon Pinpoint, a fully managed AWS service, plays a crucial role in enabling developers to understand, segment, and target their audience with personalized and timely messages. In this section, we explore Amazon Pinpoint's features and functionalities.

Amazon Pinpoint overview

Amazon Pinpoint is a versatile service designed to help developers communicate with end-users in targeted ways across various channels, including email, SMS, and mobile push notifications. It provides analytics and insights that empower developers to refine their communication strategies and enhance user engagement [20].

Key features and capabilities

The following are the key features of Amazon Pinpoint that equip developers to build effective, multi-channel communication strategies [20]:

- **User engagement analysis**: Amazon Pinpoint provides detailed analytics on user engagement, offering developers insights into user behavior, preferences, and interactions with the application. This data-driven approach enables the optimization of communication strategies.

- **Multi-channel communication**: The service supports a range of communication channels, including email, SMS, and push notifications. This multi-channel capability enables developers to reach users through their preferred communication channels, thereby increasing the efficiency of their messages.

- **Personalization**: Amazon Pinpoint enables developers to create personalized messages based on user attributes and behavior. This personalization enhances UX and fosters a connection with the application.

- **Journey orchestration**: Developers can design customer journeys by defining communication workflows based on user actions and interactions. This feature ensures that users receive relevant messages at distinct stages of their interaction with the application.

Integration with other AWS services

Amazon Pinpoint seamlessly integrates with other AWS services, enhancing its capabilities and extending its reach within the AWS ecosystem. Integration with Amazon **Simple Notification Service** (**SNS**) and AWS IAM ensures secure and efficient communication [13].

Use cases

Here are practical ways organizations can use Amazon Pinpoint to drive user engagement:

- **Marketing campaigns**: Amazon Pinpoint is instrumental in orchestrating targeted marketing campaigns, delivering personalized promotions, and analyzing campaign performance [21].
- **User onboarding**: Developers can use the service to guide users through onboarding processes by sending prompts and relevant information, thereby enhancing the overall UX [22].

Amazon Pinpoint is a valuable tool for developers looking to enhance user engagement through targeted and personalized communication. By offering a range of communication channels, robust analytics, and the ability to create personalized customer journeys, Amazon Pinpoint empowers developers to build applications that resonate with their audience, contributing to the success of their digital initiatives.

Amazon Simple Email Service

Email communication remains a cornerstone of engaging end-users, and Amazon SES is a cloud-based solution provided by AWS to help with scalable and cost-effective email sending. This section explores Amazon SES features and functionalities, exploring its reliable and secure email communication capabilities.

Amazon SES overview

Amazon SES streamlines the process of sending transactional and marketing emails. It provides a reliable infrastructure for email delivery that is scalable to meet the demands of businesses of all sizes. By leveraging AWS cloud infrastructure, SES ensures high deliverability rates while offering flexibility and better cost [23].

Key features and capabilities

The following key features make Amazon SES an efficient choice for handling email communication needs [23]:

- **Email sending**: Amazon SES enables developers to send various email types, including transactional and marketing emails. Its robust infrastructure ensures reliable delivery and easy integration with applications and systems.

- **Deliverability**: With features like dedicated IP addresses, content filtering, and bounce and complaint tracking, Amazon SES prioritizes high deliverability rates. This is relevant for ensuring that emails reach the intended recipients' inboxes.

- **Content personalization**: Developers can personalize email content using dynamic variables, allowing for customizing messages based on user attributes or behaviors. This personalization enhances user engagement and the overall efficiency of email campaigns.

- **Integration with AWS ecosystem**: Amazon SES seamlessly integrates with other AWS services, such as AWS Lambda and Amazon S3. This integration enhances SES capabilities, allowing developers to build comprehensive and automated email workflows.

Security and compliance

Amazon SES prioritizes security and compliance, implementing measures to protect against spam, phishing, and other email-related threats. Features like **DomainKeys Identified Mail (DKIM)** and **Sender Policy Framework (SPF)** authentication contribute to the security of email communications.

Use cases

Here are typical applications of Amazon SES that highlight its versatility:

- **Transactional emails**: Amazon SES is well-suited for sending transactional emails, such as order confirmations, password resets, and other personalized communications [24].

- **Marketing campaigns**: Developers can use Amazon SES for marketing campaigns, ensuring that promotional emails reach a broad audience reliably [25].

Amazon SES is a robust solution for businesses and developers looking to setup reliable and scalable email communication. Focusing on deliverability, security, and integration with the broader AWS ecosystem, SES offers a comprehensive platform for both transactional and marketing email needs. Its flexibility and cost savings make it a valuable tool for organizations looking to enhance their email communication strategies.

AWS Amplify

AWS Amplify is a comprehensive set of tools and services designed to streamline building scalable and feature-rich front-end applications in the ever-evolving web and mobile application development landscape. This section examines the functionalities and benefits of AWS Amplify, as well as its role in streamlining the development lifecycle.

AWS Amplify overview

AWS Amplify is a development platform for building and deploying full-stack web and mobile applications. Focusing on providing developers with a seamless experience, Amplify integrates with popular frameworks and services to create modern, serverless applications. [26].

Key features and capabilities

The following features make AWS Amplify an invaluable tool for developers to build efficient and scalable applications [26]:

- **Front-end framework agnostic**: AWS Amplify supports React, Angular, and Vue.js front-end frameworks. This framework agnosticism enhances developer flexibility, allowing them to use the tools with which they are most comfortable.

- **Authentication and authorization**: Amplify simplifies user authentication and authorization processes, offering built-in authentication workflows and support for social identity providers. This streamlines the implementation of secure user access controls.

- **API management**: With Amplify, developers can easily manage REST and GraphQL APIs. The platform streamlines the creation and integration of APIs, enabling developers to efficiently connect their applications to various data sources.

- **Continuous integration/continuous deployment (CI/CD)**: It is integral to modern application development. AWS Amplify integrates popular CI/CD tools, automating web and mobile application build, test, and deployment processes.

Figure 9.6 illustrates the typical Amplify architecture within an AWS Region, highlighting its integration capabilities and streamlined structure for deploying robust applications across AWS:

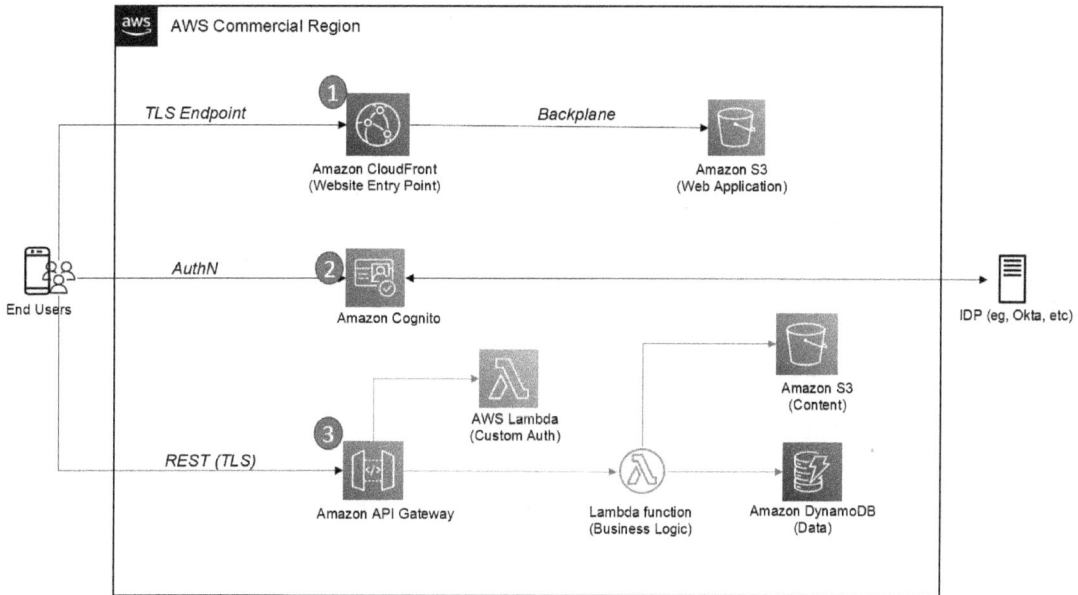

Figure 9.6: Common Amplify Architecture in an AWS Region

Serverless functionality

AWS Amplify promotes serverless architecture, allowing developers to focus on building features without managing the underlying infrastructure. Serverless functions enhance application functionality and scalability [27].

Scalability and performance

Amplify applications benefit from the scalability and performance optimizations provided by AWS services. This ensures that applications can manage varying workloads and deliver a responsive UX [28].

AWS Amplify is a versatile and powerful toolset for developers venturing into front-end web and mobile application development. Amplify accelerates the development lifecycle with its flexibility, integration capabilities, and focus on simplifying complex tasks. Whether managing authentication, integrating APIs, or implementing serverless functions, Amplify provides a cohesive platform that aligns with the modern demands of building responsive and scalable applications.

Introduction to AWS AppSync

AWS AppSync is a powerful service that simplifies building scalable and interactive applications in the dynamic realm of front-end web and mobile development. This section examines the functionalities and features of AWS AppSync, highlighting its role in efficiently synchronizing and communicating data between applications and back-end services.

AWS AppSync overview

AWS AppSync is a managed service that enables developers to create flexible and scalable APIs for applications by controlling the heavy lifting of securely connecting to data sources such as AWS DynamoDB, Lambda, or HTTP data sources. It plays a relevant role in simplifying data fetching, updates, and real-time data synchronization across various platforms [29].

Key features and capabilities

The following key features highlight AWS AppSync's extensive functionality for front-end application developers [29]:

- **GraphQL as a service**: AWS AppSync utilizes GraphQL, a powerful query language for APIs, providing a flexible and efficient way to request and deliver data. This enables clients to order only the needed data, reducing over-fetching and improving performance.

- **Real-time data synchronization**: One of AppSync's standout features is its support for real-time data synchronization. This enables developers to build applications that receive real-time back-end updates, thereby enhancing the overall UX.

- **Offline data access**: AppSync includes features for offline data access, allowing applications to remain functional even when there is no internet connection. This is particularly valuable for mobile applications that need to provide a seamless UX in various network conditions.

- **Data source integration**: The service seamlessly integrates with various data sources, including AWS DynamoDB, AWS Lambda, and HTTP data sources. This flexibility allows developers to use different back-end services based on their application requirements.

Serverless functionality

AWS AppSync's serverless architecture cuts the need for developers to manage servers. This serverless approach enables automatic scaling based on demand, ensuring the best performance under varying workloads [30].

AWS AppSync appears as an asset for developers in the front-end web and mobile development space, offering a robust and scalable solution for building APIs [31]. Whether enabling real-time data synchronization, supporting offline access, or seamlessly integrating with various data sources, AppSync empowers developers to create responsive and feature-rich applications. Its adoption of GraphQL as a service further enhances its capabilities, providing a modern and efficient approach to data communication in the cloud.

AWS Device Farm

In the ever-evolving landscape of front-end web and mobile development, ensuring the seamless functionality of applications across various devices and platforms is paramount [32]. AWS Device Farm is a comprehensive testing service that enables developers to enhance the quality and reliability of their applications by conducting tests on a diverse range of real devices. This section provides an in-depth exploration of AWS Device Farm, elucidating its features, advantages, and the significant role it plays in enhancing the end-UX.

AWS Device Farm overview

AWS Device Farm is a cloud-based mobile application testing service that enables developers to run tests on many real devices, ensuring their applications perform optimally across different devices, screen sizes, and operating systems. This service supports Android and iOS platforms, offering a more efficient solution for testing applications on real devices in the AWS Cloud [33].

Key features and capabilities

The following features underscore AWS Device Farm's extensive support for mobile application testing, highlighting how it improves testing accuracy and efficiency [33]:

- **Real device testing**: AWS Device Farm provides access to a vast collection of real devices, allowing developers to execute tests on actual hardware rather than relying solely on emulators. This ensures a more correct representation of the application's behavior in real-world scenarios.

- **Parallel testing**: The service supports parallel testing, enabling developers to execute tests concurrently on multiple devices. This accelerates the testing process, saving time and resources.

- **Appium and Selenium compatibility**: Device Farm is compatible with popular testing frameworks, including Appium and Selenium, providing flexibility for developers who prefer these frameworks for their testing processes.

- **Remote access**: During testing, developers can remotely access and interact with devices in real-time. This feature is incomparable for diagnosing issues and gaining insights into the application's behavior on specific devices.

- **Built-in test reports**: Device Farm generates detailed test reports, including logs, screenshots, and videos of the test execution. This comprehensive feedback enables developers to identify and resolve issues efficiently.

Figure 9.7 illustrates an example of web applications hosted in a private network using AWS Device Farm, highlighting the practical application of this testing environment within secure configurations:

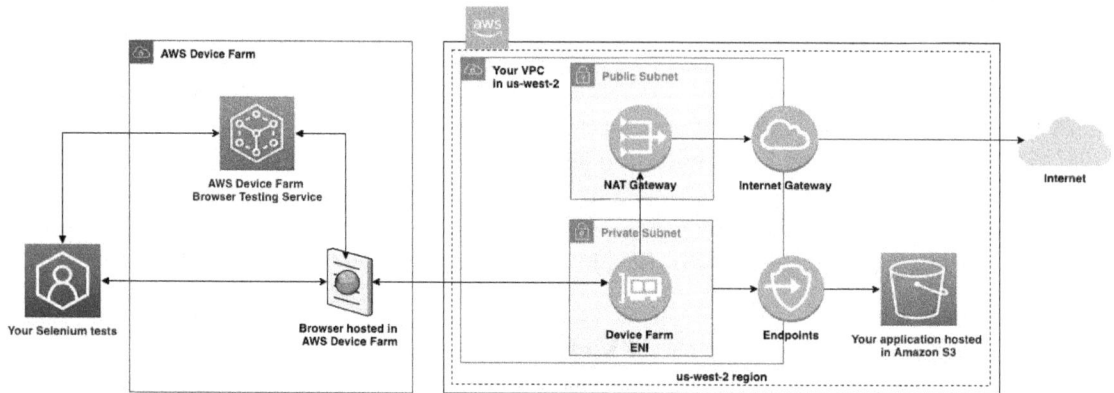

Figure 9.7: Web applications using AWS Device Farm

AWS Device Farm is a valuable tool for front-end web and mobile development developers. It provides a robust testing environment on real devices. By offering a diverse array of devices, supporting parallel testing, and integrating seamlessly with popular testing frameworks, Device Farm empowers developers to identify and rectify issues early in the development lifecycle [34]. The service's ability to generate comprehensive test reports further facilitates a streamlined testing process, contributing to the delivery of high-quality and reliable mobile applications to end-users.

Reflecting further

Chapter 10, End-user, Front-end, and Mobile, provides a detailed exploration of AWS services essential for delivering seamless and innovative UXs. These services are vital in transforming application development, deployment, and usage.

End-user computing

Within the Amazon AppStream 2.0 and Amazon WorkSpaces Family, we explored the future of EUC. The ability to stream resource-intensive applications and provide virtual desktops on demand not only enhances user flexibility but also ensures data security and compliance. This becomes particularly important in the evolving remote work landscape, where organizations seek scalable solutions for delivering a consistent and secure computing experience to their workforce [8] [11] [35].

Front-end web and mobile

The journey through Amazon API Gateway highlighted its defining role as a fully managed service for creating, publishing, and securing APIs at any scale. The service bridges back-end services and front-end applications, helping ensure seamless communication and integration. Amazon Location Service introduced a geospatial dimension, enabling developers to build location-aware applications. Amazon Pinpoint and Amazon SES underscore the significance of targeted communication, with Pinpoint providing personalized engagement across multiple channels and SES ensuring reliable and scalable email communication [14] [17] [20] [23].

The trifecta of AWS Amplify, AWS AppSync, and AWS Device Farm showcases AWS's commitment to simplifying front-end development. AWS Amplify streamlines the development process, allowing developers to build scalable and secure cloud-powered web and mobile apps. AWS AppSync simplifies application development by enabling real-time data synchronization and offline data access, which is relevant for responsive and user-friendly applications. AWS Device Farm facilitates continuous testing, ensuring that applications function seamlessly across a myriad of devices, browsers, and operating systems [36] [29] [33] [37].

Conclusion

In conclusion, this chapter has unraveled the diverse aspects of AWS services catering to EUC and front-end development. The flexibility, scalability, and user-centric design embedded in these services position AWS as a pioneer in the cloud computing landscape. In continuation, these services are not merely tools but enablers of innovation, playing a significant role in shaping the future of user interactions, mobile experiences, and front-end development.

As technology advances, AWS stays at the forefront, continually refining and expanding its services to meet the evolving demands of the digital landscape. This chapter serves as a testament to the integral role AWS plays in empowering developers and organizations to create innovative applications that redefine the boundaries of UXs.

The next chapter will examine DevOps and **infrastructure as code (IaC)**, highlighting AWS tools and services that enhance automation, configuration management, and deployment workflows.

Join our Discord space

Join our Discord workspace for latest updates, offers, tech happenings around the world, new releases, and sessions with the authors:

https://discord.bpbonline.com

CHAPTER 10
Applications for Business

Introduction

In the fast-paced world of cloud computing, businesses continually seek innovative solutions to enhance agility, reduce operational costs, and improve customer experience. *Chapter 10, Applications for Business,* explores various **Amazon Web Services** (**AWS**) business applications, cloud monetary management tools, media services, and blockchain technologies. These AWS services enable organizations to centralize governance, drive innovation, and adhere to industry standards while maintaining operational efficiency and effectiveness.

This chapter highlights how AWS tools transform business processes, making collaborating and managing resources easier and enhancing customer and employee experiences.

Structure

This chapter will cover the following topics:

- Business applications
- Cloud Financial Management
- Media services
- Amazon Elastic Transcoder

- AWS Elemental MediaTailor
- Amazon Managed Blockchain

Objectives

By the end of this chapter, you will understand how AWS business applications enhance workplace efficiency and collaboration by streamlining communication, project management, and customer engagement. You will gain insight into **Cloud Financial Management (CFM)** practices using AWS tools that improve cost allocation, budgeting, and resource use. Additionally, you will explore how AWS media services help create, process, and deliver multimedia content across various platforms. This chapter will explore AWS blockchain solutions and their role in enabling businesses to develop decentralized applications, ensuring transparency, security, and trust in digital transactions.

Business applications

AWS business applications help seamless collaboration, improve productivity, and streamline organizational operations. These tools offer significant value by addressing communication challenges, enhancing project management, and providing tools for customer engagement. This section will examine key AWS business applications, their associated challenges, best practices, and real-world use cases.

Figure 10.1 illustrates an application that utilizes RDS Database fleet management through a voice command infrastructure:

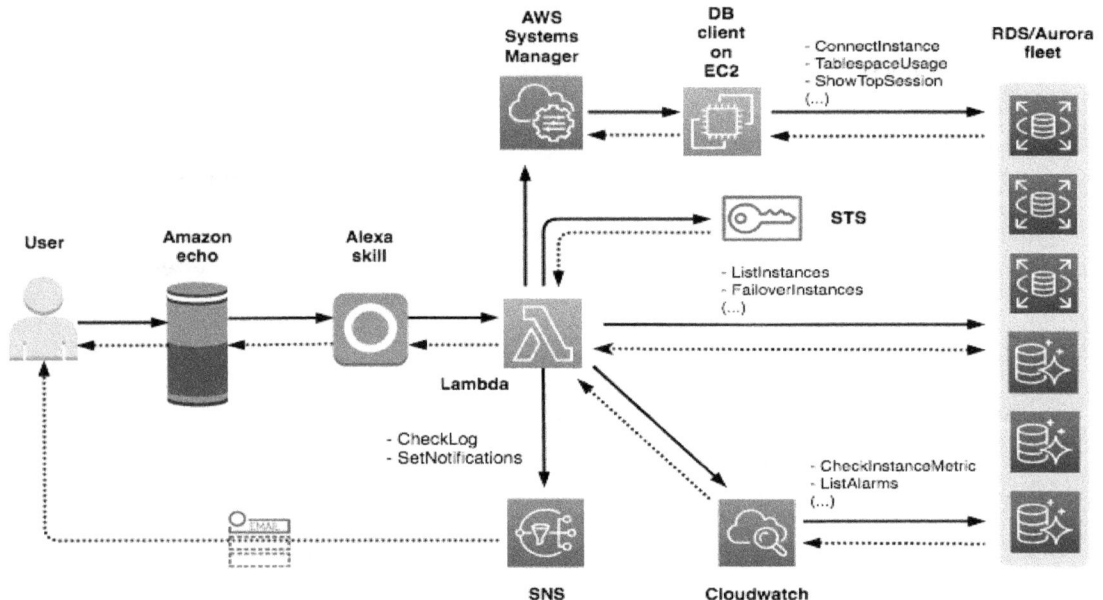

Figure 10.1: Fleet management through voice commands

Challenges in business applications

Modern enterprises encounter numerous challenges in implementing efficient business applications, including communication barriers and inefficiencies. Addressing these challenges is crucial for organizations to enhance productivity, promote collaboration, and optimize their operations.

Before organizations can fully benefit from AWS business applications, they must address several obstacles hindering digital transformation and collaboration. The following challenges highlight the typical issues enterprises face when attempting to modernize their workflows and improve operational efficiency:

- **Fragmented communication**: Different businesses struggle with siloed communication channels, leading to inefficiencies and delays.

- **Manual processes**: Traditional workflows often require manual intervention, leading to errors and hindering scalability.

- **Lack of integration**: Disconnected tools and applications can lead to lost productivity and a suboptimal **user experience (UX)**.

Alexa for Business

Alexa for Business integrates the Amazon Alexa virtual assistant into organizational environments to streamline daily tasks and increase workplace productivity. Since its launch in 2017, this voice-activated assistant has revolutionized workplace efficiency by providing intuitive automation for tasks ranging from scheduling meetings to controlling office devices [1].

Key features

Among the features offered by Amazon Alexa for business, we selected:

- **Voice-activated meetings and conferencing**: Alexa for Business allows users to schedule, reschedule, cancel meetings, check room availability, and even start or join virtual meetings, all with voice commands. This reduces administrative friction and improves productivity by automating mundane meeting tasks [2].

- **Voice-controlled devices**: With seamless integration into smart devices like Echo and third-party hardware, Alexa enables users to control office devices, such as lights, thermostats, and projectors, via voice commands. In healthcare settings, this touchless functionality helps ensure hygiene and operational efficiency [2].

- **Customizable skills**: Organizations can develop custom Alexa skills tailored to their specific needs, expanding their utility from essential meeting management to automating business-specific processes like generating reports or tracking project deadlines [2].

Challenges

Integrating Alexa for Business into existing infrastructure can pose challenges, especially for companies with complex workflows and fragmented systems. Different businesses may struggle with adoption, as they need to ensure that Alexa can integrate seamlessly with existing tools, such as project management platforms or communication apps. Additionally, privacy and security concerns arise when voice-activated devices manage sensitive company data, requiring robust safeguards.

Benefits

Alexa for Business enhances productivity by automating scheduling, simplifying communication, and enabling hands-free control of office environments. Employees can focus on higher-value tasks while Alexa manages routine administrative work. The system's voice-activated nature reduces the time spent on manual operations, boosting overall workplace efficiency. Moreover, custom skills make Alexa adaptable to various business processes, allowing it to fit seamlessly into the organization's operational flow.

Use case

A multinational firm integrates Alexa for Business across its offices to streamline scheduling, room management, and communication. Employees use Alexa to manage conference room bookings and join meetings by simply using voice commands, eliminating the need for separate scheduling software. Additionally, Alexa controls smart devices, such as adjusting room temperatures and lighting, improving workplace comfort and efficiency. The system also automates the generation of weekly reports, reducing manual labor.

Wrap up

Alexa for Business enables organizations to streamline operations and foster a more efficient and collaborative work environment. Integrating Alexa into daily workflows allows businesses to automate mundane tasks, simplify communication, and promote a more productive environment. Its flexibility, security features, and seamless integration with other AWS services make Alexa a valuable tool for modern organizations looking to enhance workplace efficiency.

Amazon Chime

Amazon Chime is a secure and scalable communication service that simplifies online meetings, video conferencing, and business collaboration. Launched in 2017, Chime integrates seamlessly with other AWS services to enhance communication efficiency across teams, whether they are remote or in the office [3].

Key features

Amazon Chime's key features are as follows:

- **Online meetings and video conferencing**: Amazon Chime offers HD video and audio, delivering a near-face-to-face meeting experience. The platform also provides real-time chat and content-sharing features to foster collaboration during virtual meetings [4].
- **Unified communications**: Chime combines voice, video, and messaging into a single platform. This enables teams to easily switch between communication methods, improving connectivity and efficiency regardless of location [5].
- **Security and compliance**: Security is a top priority for Amazon Chime, which uses encryption and access controls to ensure that only authorized users can join meetings. The platform follows industry regulations, making it ideal for businesses with strict compliance needs [3].

Challenges

Coordinating seamless communication across different time zones and regions can significantly challenge rapidly growing organizations. Traditional email and messaging apps often lack real-time, dynamic communication support, crucial for making quick decisions. Furthermore, keeping secure and compliant communication channels while scaling is a constant concern.

Benefits

Amazon Chime enhances remote team collaboration by offering a unified communication solution. With HD video, voice calls, and chat all on one platform, teams can easily collaborate without switching between tools. The platform's integration with AWS services ensures that communication stays secure and scalable, helping businesses keep smooth workflows as they grow.

Use case

A tech startup with teams across continents adopts Amazon Chime to streamline communication. By utilizing Chime's high-definition video capabilities, teams can conduct effective virtual meetings. Chime's unified platform enables the startup's team members to transition seamlessly between video, voice calls, and chat, enhancing collaboration. The startup also integrates Chime with AWS **Simple Storage Service** (**S3**) for document sharing and AWS **Key Management Service** (**KMS**) for data security, ensuring secure and efficient communication [5].

Wrap up

Amazon Chime empowers businesses to enhance collaboration, reduce communication friction, and scale their remote operations efficiently. By offering unified communication features with robust security and seamless integration with the AWS ecosystem, Chime is an invaluable tool for businesses seeking to enhance productivity and maintain reliable, secure communication channels.

Amazon Chime software development kit

The Amazon Chime **software development kit** (**SDK**) enables businesses to integrate real-time communication features, such as video and audio calls, into their applications. Built on Amazon Chime's scalable and secure infrastructure, the SDK allows developers to incorporate seamless communication tools, such as video conferencing and audio calls, into custom applications, offering a robust solution for various business needs [6].

Key features

Effective communication is a cornerstone of success in the fast-paced and interconnected business landscape. Amazon Chime addresses this need by offering comprehensive tools that streamline virtual meetings, enhance collaboration, and ensure a secure communication environment, as follows:

- **Real-time communication**: The SDK allows for seamless audio and video calls within applications, enabling one-to-one or multiparty video calls, conferencing, and content-sharing to create an engaging communication experience [7].

- **Customizable user interface**: Developers can tailor the **user interface** (**UI**) to suit their application's look and feel, ensuring the communication tools blend seamlessly with the application and enhancing UX [6].

- **Scalable infrastructure**: Built on AWS's highly scalable infrastructure, the SDK adjusts automatically to accommodate growing user counts and variable usage patterns, ensuring the best performance even during demand surges [8].

Challenges

Developing seamless, real-time business communication platforms requires the integration of complex video and audio technologies. Some solutions offer inconsistent performance, resulting in poor video quality and user dissatisfaction. Integrating high-quality communication tools into applications usually involves managing scalability and ensuring service reliability during peak demand [7].

Use case

A healthcare startup integrates Amazon Chime SDK into its telemedicine platform to provide real-time video consultations between patients and doctors. The company enhances patient engagement and workflow efficiency by embedding high-quality video and audio features and customizing the interface to include patient records and appointment scheduling. As the user base grows, Chime SDK's scalability ensures the platform can manage increased demand during flu season while maintaining a reliable service for all users.

Wrap up

The Amazon Chime SDK is essential for businesses that want to integrate seamless, real-time communication into their applications. By offering easy integration, customizable UIs, and scalable infrastructure, companies can deliver high-quality communication experiences that evolve with their needs. Whether in healthcare, education, or customer service, Chime SDK is a flexible and reliable solution for real-time communication across various industries [7].

Amazon Connect

Amazon Connect is a cloud-based contact center service that enables businesses to deliver personalized customer service. By offering omnichannel [9]. Effective communication and integration with AWS services, including Amazon Connect, facilitates efficient handling of customer interactions [3].

Key features

With a focus on simplicity and flexibility, Amazon Connect empowers businesses to build scalable and personalized customer service solutions [10]:

- **Omnichannel communication**: Amazon Connect enables seamless communication across multiple channels—voice, chat, and email—creating a unified customer experience. This flexibility enhances customer satisfaction by allowing interactions through the preferred communication mode [8].

- **Natural language processing**: By integrating Amazon Lex, Amazon Connect utilizes **natural language processing (NLP)** to automate responses to common customer queries. This reduces the need for human intervention, improving response times and enabling support agents to focus on more complex tasks [3].

- **Scalability and flexibility**: Amazon Connect's infrastructure scales automatically, adjusting to demand spikes, ensuring businesses can manage fluctuating call volumes without manual intervention [8].

Challenges

Retail businesses frequently encounter challenges in managing fluctuating customer support demands, particularly during peak periods such as the holiday season. These challenges include inefficient response times, resource allocation, and service quality during peak demand.

Benefits

Amazon Connect enables businesses to deliver efficient, scalable, personalized customer service. Its omnichannel communication [9], **artificial intelligence** (**AI**) driven NLP and automatic scaling features reduce operational strain, ensure a seamless customer experience, and help businesses meet high demand without sacrificing performance.

Use case

A global retail business integrates Amazon Connect to handle customer inquiries during the holiday season surges. They implement omnichannel support to provide voice, chat, and email communication options, automate common queries using NLP-powered bots, and scale their support team during peak times to ensure efficient handling of increased demand [3].

Wrap up

Amazon Connect transforms customer service by offering seamless communication, AI-driven automation, and scalable support. It helps businesses manage fluctuations in demand, improve response times, and ensure high customer satisfaction. Its integration with AWS services and scalability make it an ideal solution for companies looking to improve their customer service operations.

Amazon Honeycode

Amazon Honeycode is a no-code service enabling businesses to rapidly create custom web and mobile applications. It empowers teams without the technical ability to automate workflows and streamline processes. By leveraging Honeycode's visual interface and automation features, businesses can quickly and efficiently develop applications tailored to their specific needs [11].

Key features

Honeycode's visual interface and powerful automation capabilities allow businesses to develop apps without writing a single line of code. Amazon Honeycode provides a no-code solution that enables companies to build custom applications with minimal effort. By cutting the need for traditional programming, Honeycode empowers users to automate workflows and enhance team collaboration, as discussed:

- **No-code application development**: Honeycode provides a simple visual interface that enables business users to create applications without writing code. This feature empowers teams to build solutions for managing tasks, projects, and workflows without requiring developer resources [3].

- **Database and logic building blocks**: Honeycode includes built-in tools for designing workflows and automating processes, such as task assignments and project tracking.

This functionality allows users to create data-driven applications that can efficiently manage and manipulate information [11].

- **Real-time collaboration**: With real-time collaboration, Honeycode allows multiple users to work on applications simultaneously. This enhances team productivity, enables quick updates, and ensures that everyone stays aligned [3].

Challenges

Different teams struggle with fragmented project management systems, leading to inefficiencies, missed deadlines, and poor communication. Despite utilizing software tools, businesses often encounter challenges such as scattered information and difficulty tracking progress across teams.

Benefits

Honeycode enhances team collaboration by enabling real-time updates and seamless task management. It is a no-code interface that simplifies application development, while its powerful automation tools reduce administrative burdens. As a result, teams can focus on key tasks, improve efficiency, and enhance overall productivity.

Use case

A marketing firm uses Honeycode to streamline project management. They developed a custom task management app that enables project managers to assign tasks, set deadlines, and monitor progress. The app integrates real-time collaboration and automated notifications to ensure the on-time completion of tasks, improving team alignment and productivity [11].

Wrap up

The Amazon Honeycode revolutionizes project management by providing a no-code platform for creating customized applications. With real-time collaboration and automated workflows, Honeycode enables businesses to enhance efficiency, promote teamwork, and meet deadlines. It empowers teams to automate repetitive tasks, allowing them to focus on high-value activities and fostering a more transparent and productive work environment.

Amazon Pinpoint

Amazon Pinpoint is a versatile service that empowers businesses to engage and keep customers through personalized, multi-channel communication. With its robust analytics and seamless integration with AWS services, companies can create impactful interactions across multiple platforms, including email, SMS, and push notifications [12].

Key features

With features tailored for targeted communication, analytics, and user engagement, Pinpoint empowers businesses to create personalized and impactful interactions with their audience. Effective customer engagement requires a robust communication strategy. Amazon Pinpoint enables businesses to craft personalized, multi-channel messaging experiences, ensuring targeted and impactful interactions with their audience, as discussed:

- **Multi-channel messaging**: Pinpoint supports multi-channel messaging, enabling businesses to communicate with customers across various channels, including email, SMS, push notifications, and voice messages. This approach ensures that companies can engage customers on their preferred platforms [13].

- **Personalization and targeting**: Pinpoint enables businesses to tailor user messages based on their behavior, preferences, and demographics. This personalization increases engagement and customer satisfaction by delivering relevant content to the right audience [13].

- **Analytics and user insights**: Pinpoint provides powerful analytics that track user interactions, measure campaign effectiveness, and offer deep insights into customer behavior. These insights help businesses improve their engagement strategies and improve outcomes [5].

Challenges

Businesses often struggle with delivering relevant messages to the right customers, managing multi-channel engagement, and measuring the effectiveness of their campaigns. Without the right tools, campaigns can become inefficient, leading to lower customer engagement [14].

Benefits

Pinpoint allows businesses to engage customers more effectively by using multi-channel communication, personalization, and real-time analytics. With automation capabilities, companies can streamline their messaging workflows, improve customer engagement, and drive higher conversion rates.

Figure 10.2 summarizes what Amazon Pinpoint offers marketers and developers as one customizable tool to deliver customer communications across channels, segments, and campaigns at scale:

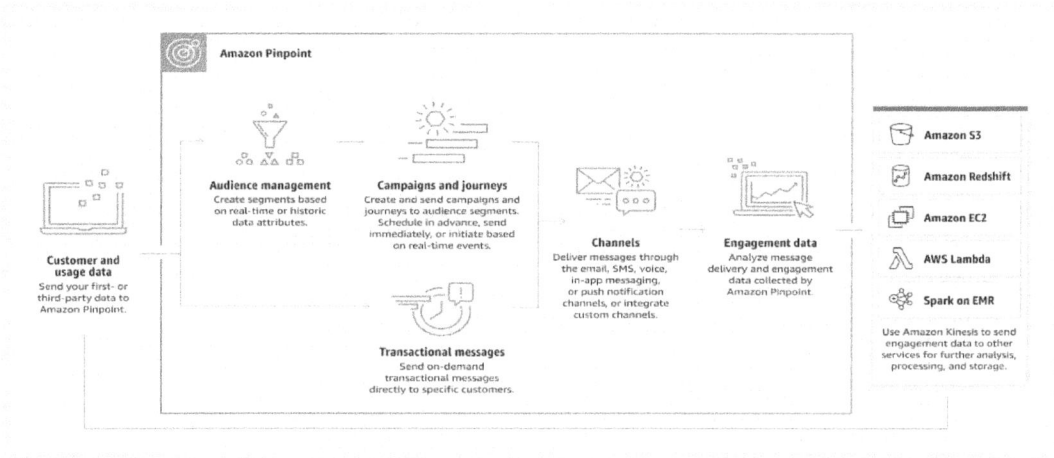

Figure 10.2: Amazon Pinpoint customizable tool

Use case

An e-commerce company uses Amazon Pinpoint to personalize email, SMS, and push notification campaigns. By analyzing customer behavior, they tailor messages, such as unique offers for loyal customers and onboarding emails for new users. Pinpoint's real-time analytics enable them to refine campaigns, enhance customer engagement, and improve campaign performance [13].

Wrap up

Amazon Pinpoint helps businesses enhance customer engagement by offering multi-channel communication, real-time analytics, and targeted messaging. By automating and optimizing campaigns, companies can improve customer satisfaction and increase conversion rates, all while maintaining flexibility and scalability within the AWS ecosystem.

Amazon Simple Email Service

Amazon **Simple Email Service** (**SES**) is a cloud-based email-sending service designed to simplify the delivery of transactional and marketing emails. Its scalable infrastructure ensures high deliverability, making it a vital tool for businesses that aim to enhance customer email communication [15].

Key features

By integrating seamlessly with the AWS ecosystem and offering various sending options, SES stands as a valuable tool for businesses looking to streamline their email communication processes and enhance their overall customer engagement [16]. Amazon SES offers a scalable and reliable email-sending solution, enabling enterprises to manage transactional and marketing emails efficiently. Its integration with AWS services enhances deliverability, security, and analytics, as discussed:

- **Scalability and deliverability**: SES offers reliable email delivery, adapting to business needs whether for startups or large enterprises. This scalability ensures that businesses can manage large volumes of email without compromising delivery [16] [17].

- **Email-sending options**: SES offers multiple sending options, such as SMTP or APIs, allowing businesses to integrate email functionality seamlessly into applications or marketing platforms [17].

- **Content personalization and customization**: Businesses can personalize their emails with dynamic content and attachments based on user attributes, improving customer engagement and communication effectiveness [17].

Challenges

Sending high volumes of transactional and promotional emails can overwhelm internal systems. Without a scalable solution, businesses risk delivery issues, delays, or miscommunication [18].

Benefits

SES allows businesses to efficiently manage large email volumes, offering high deliverability rates, content personalization, and deep integration with other AWS services. By improving workflows and monitoring performance, businesses can improve engagement and campaign success [17].

Use case

An e-commerce company integrates SES to automate order confirmations, shipping updates, and promotional emails. By segmenting their customer base, the company sends targeted email offers, improving engagement and driving conversions. SES's analytics help improve future campaigns by analyzing open rates, click-through rates, and other key metrics [17].

Wrap up

Amazon SES is an effective tool for managing email communications, whether for transactional messages or marketing campaigns. Its scalability, security, and integration capabilities make it an essential part of the AWS ecosystem, allowing businesses to perfect email workflows and drive higher customer engagement [17].

Amazon WorkDocs

Amazon WorkDocs is a fully managed, secure content creation, storage, and collaboration service designed to help organizations collaborate on documents securely [19].

Key features

Amazon WorkDocs empowers teams to securely create, store, and share documents in a collaborative environment [20]. Efficient document management is critical for modern organizations. Amazon WorkDocs offers a secure and collaborative environment for teams to create, store, and manage documents with real-time collaboration features, as discussed:

- **Secure document storage and sharing**: WorkDocs offers cloud-based document storage with granular access controls, ensuring secure sharing and collaboration within teams [21]. Sensitive documents are accessible only by authorized personnel, promoting compliance with data protection regulations [22].
- **Real-time collaboration**: Multiple users can edit and comment on documents simultaneously, with version history and change tracking features. This supports teams working on dynamic projects with frequent updates [23].
- **Integration with productivity tools**: WorkDocs integrates with tools like *Microsoft Office*, allowing teams to use familiar applications while collaborating in a cloud-based environment [22]. This integration simplifies adoption and enhances workflow efficiency.

Challenges

Organizations that handle sensitive data face the challenge of managing secure, collaborative workflows while adhering to stringent regulatory requirements. Traditional document management systems can lack the flexibility, scalability, and security necessary for modern business needs [22].

Benefits

Amazon WorkDocs enhances team collaboration by allowing real-time document editing and comments. Its secure document sharing and integration with AWS tools, such as **Identity and Access Management (IAM)** and KMS, ensure compliance and data protection, making it suitable for businesses in regulated industries [21].

Use case

A law firm struggling with document versioning and review delays uses WorkDocs to securely store and collaborate on legal documents. By using real-time collaboration and version control, the team ensures that everyone works with the most recent document versions. Additionally, WorkDocs compliance features help meet regulatory requirements [22].

Wrap up

Amazon WorkDocs provides businesses with a secure and collaborative document management solution. Its real-time collaboration features, integration with productivity tools, and robust security options make it ideal for organizations needing to meet compliance standards while fostering productivity.

Amazon WorkMail

Amazon WorkMail is a fully managed, secure email and calendaring service designed for businesses to manage communications effectively while adhering to compliance and security standards [24].

Key features

With features designed for compliance, security, and collaboration, WorkMail is an ideal choice for organizations looking to streamline communication while maintaining data protection standards, as discussed:

- **Email and calendar management**: Amazon WorkMail provides a feature-rich email experience with integrated calendar functionality, making it easy to manage meetings, emails, and appointments [17]. It ensures seamless internal and external communication [25].

- **Security and compliance**: Amazon WorkMail emphasizes security with encryption, secure access controls, and anti-malware protection. It meets various compliance standards, offering a secure environment for handling sensitive business communications. WorkMail is particularly valuable for organizations that need to follow regulations such as *Health Insurance Portability and Accountability Act* (*HIPAA*), the *General Data Protection Regulation* (*GDPR*), and the *International Organization for Standardization* (*ISO*) [24].

- **Integration with productivity tools**: Amazon WorkMail integrates seamlessly with *Microsoft Outlook*, allowing users to access their emails, calendars, and contacts using a familiar interface. This integration improves the UX and ensures that organizations can continue using the tools their teams are comfortable with [22].

Challenges

For organizations, especially in regulated industries, keeping email communication that is both secure and compliant can be complex. Ensuring the protection of sensitive information from unauthorized access while helping collaboration stay a key challenge [24].

Benefits

Amazon WorkMail simplifies corporate communication by offering secure email and calendar management, encrypted communication, and integration with productivity tools like Microsoft Outlook. With built-in compliance features and robust security, WorkMail is especially suitable for businesses that require stringent data protection [22].

Use case

A healthcare organization adopts Amazon WorkMail for secure email communication. WorkMail's encryption and compliance features help the organization adhere to HIPAA regulations, while integration with Microsoft Outlook ensures that the team can efficiently manage emails and schedules [25].

Wrap up

Amazon WorkMail is a comprehensive, secure, and scalable email solution ideal for businesses in regulated industries. By offering encryption, compliance capabilities, and seamless integration with productivity tools, WorkMail helps streamline communication while ensuring data protection and regulatory compliance.

AWS Supply Chain

AWS Supply Chain is a comprehensive suite of services that improve various aspects of the supply chain process. By integrating **machine learning** (**ML**), **Internet of Things** (**IoT**), and cloud storage, AWS enhances visibility, forecasting, and efficiency across supply chains, helping organizations streamline their operations [26].

Key components

AWS Supply Chain ML, IoT, and cloud storage technologies to deliver improved visibility, forecasting, and efficiency throughout the supply chain. Managing supply chains requires a combination of predictive analytics, real-time monitoring, and automation. AWS Supply Chain leverages cloud and AI technologies to enhance visibility, forecasting, and operational efficiency, as discussed:

- **Amazon Forecast**: Amazon Forecast uses historical data to generate the right demand forecasts, helping businesses improve inventory management and supply chain processes [27].

- **Amazon Connect**: Amazon Connect enables businesses to improve communication within the supply chain by providing an omnichannel contact center for seamless interaction with customers, suppliers, and internal teams [26].

- **AWS IoT Core**: AWS IoT Core provides real-time monitoring and control of assets in the supply chain, ensuring full visibility into the transportation and condition of goods [28].

- **Amazon Simple Storage Service**: Amazon S3 offers scalable, secure storage for managing supply chain data, enabling businesses to create data lakes and analytics solutions for informed decision-making [26].

Challenges

Effective management of inventory, ensuring real-time asset tracking, and seamless communication across a dynamic supply chain can be complex. The need for data-driven insights, scalability, and integration across diverse tools is critical.

Benefits

AWS Supply Chain delivers enhanced visibility, optimized inventory management, and improved communication. By using ML and IoT, organizations can automate processes, reduce costs, and make data-driven decisions that enhance operational efficiency [27].

Figure 10.3 shows a reference architecture for an IoT-enabled supply chain consisting of a retailer and a manufacturer:

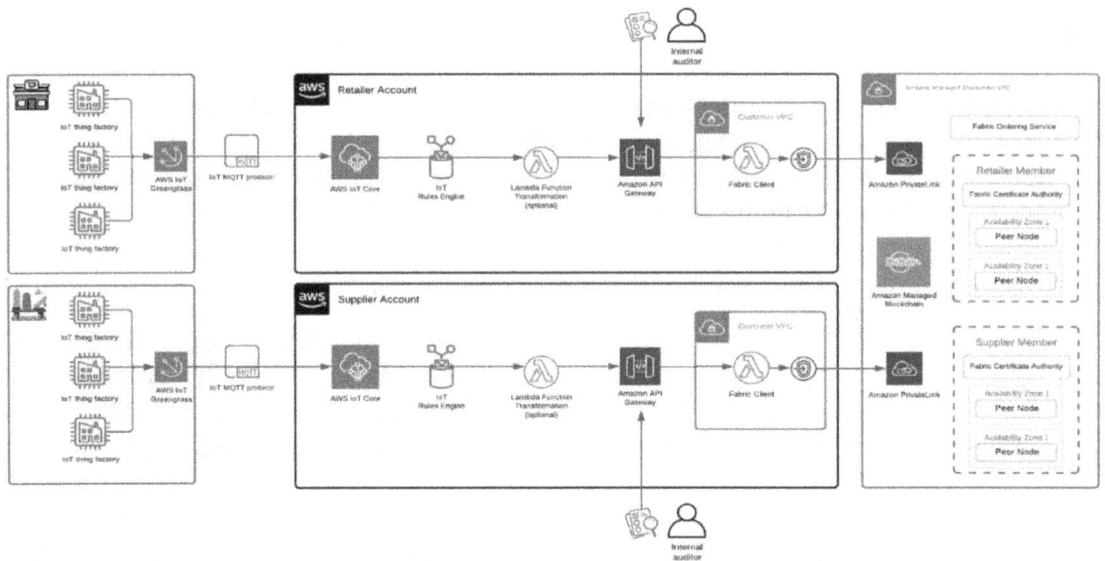

Figure 10.3: IoT-enabled supply chain reference architecture

Use case

A retail business integrates AWS Supply Chain components to improve inventory management and delivery. The company successfully enhances operational efficiency and customer satisfaction by using Amazon Forecast for demand forecasting, AWS IoT Core for asset tracking, and Amazon Connect for customer communication [27].

Wrap up

AWS Supply Chain empowers organizations to improve operations by integrating ML, IoT, and cloud storage. This suite of services helps businesses streamline their supply chain, improve decision-making, and remain competitive in a rapidly evolving marketplace.

AWS Wickr

AWS Wickr is a secure communication platform that ensures end-to-end encryption for messaging, file sharing, and voice/video calls. Its design aims to help businesses keep confidentiality while enhancing collaboration across distributed teams [29].

Key features

Designed to ensure end-to-end encryption for messages, files, and voice and video calls. The following is a sample of AWS Wickr's features:

- **End-to-end encryption**: Wickr uses end-to-end encryption for all communication forms, including text, files, and calls, ensuring privacy and protecting sensitive business data [30].
- **Secure file sharing**: With Wickr's secure file sharing feature, businesses can collaborate on documents with granular access controls to protect sensitive information [29].
- **Voice and video calls**: Wickr supports encrypted voice and video calls, providing secure, real-time communication for teams, both internally and with external partners [30].

Challenges

In industries with high data sensitivity, keeping confidentiality during communication is paramount. The challenge lies in ensuring security across both internal and external channels [29].

Figure 10.4 shows the Wickr secure messaging protocol. It is open and documented, allowing the community to inspect it. The source code we use in Wickr clients to implement the protocol is available for audit and review.

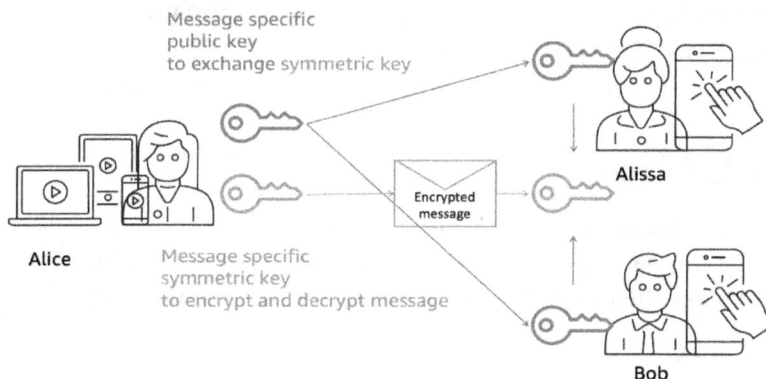

Figure 10.4: *The Wickr secure messaging protocol*

Benefits

AWS Wickr ensures confidential communication, regulatory compliance, and efficient remote collaboration. Its encryption and data protection features meet industry standards, making it ideal for businesses in regulated sectors [29].

Use case

A financial services firm integrates AWS Wickr for internal communication and secure file sharing, ensuring confidentiality and compliance with industry regulations such as HIPAA and GDPR. Wickr also supports secure collaboration with external partners, keeping ambitious standards of data protection throughout [29].

Wrap up

AWS Wickr provides businesses with a secure platform for messaging, file sharing, and real-time communication, enabling teams to collaborate confidently while ensuring compliance with industry regulations. Its robust encryption guarantees confidentiality, making it ideal for highly regulated sectors.

Cloud Financial Management

As organizations increasingly migrate their workloads to the cloud, managing costs, improving resources, and keeping financial accountability have become critical priorities. CFM is a strategic approach that enables businesses to control cloud expenditures, accurately forecast budgets, and ensure cost efficiency while scaling operations. AWS offers a comprehensive suite of financial management tools designed to help organizations monitor, analyze, and optimize their cloud spending.

In this section, we will explore AWS services that support cost tracking, budgeting, forecasting, and resource allocation. These tools empower businesses to align cloud costs with operational goals, ensuring financial transparency and efficiency. From AWS Budgets and AWS **Cost and Usage Report** (**CUR**) to AWS Savings Plans, we will examine how AWS helps organizations make informed financial decisions and maximize their return on cloud investments.

Amazon EC2 Spot Instances

Amazon EC2 Spot Instances offer businesses a cost-effective way to run applications flexibly, while also reducing cloud computing costs. This section explores how EC2 Spot Instances can help businesses manage their financial resources effectively in cloud computing environments [31]; [32].

Key features of Amazon EC2 Spot Instances

In this section, we explore the key features, benefits, and practical applications of EC2 Spot Instances, focusing on their role in cloud monetary management. Cost-effective cloud computing solutions are crucial for businesses seeking to optimize their resources. Amazon EC2 Spot Instances provide an affordable alternative to On-Demand Instance pricing, offering flexibility for scalable workloads, as discussed:

- **Cost savings**: EC2 Spot Instances allow businesses to bid on unused EC2 capacity at reduced prices. These instances provide substantial cost savings compared to On-Demand Instances, but with the risk of termination when the market price rises [33].

- **Flexible workloads**: Spot Instances are ideal for workloads that can tolerate interruptions, such as batch processing and data analysis. These workloads receive help from cost savings during periods of excess ability [34].

- **Integration with Auto Scaling**: Spot Instances integrate seamlessly with Auto Scaling groups, enabling businesses to automatically adjust capacity based on fluctuating workloads, ensuring performance is even during interruptions [33].

Figure 10.5 introduces CFM on AWS Architecture [35]:

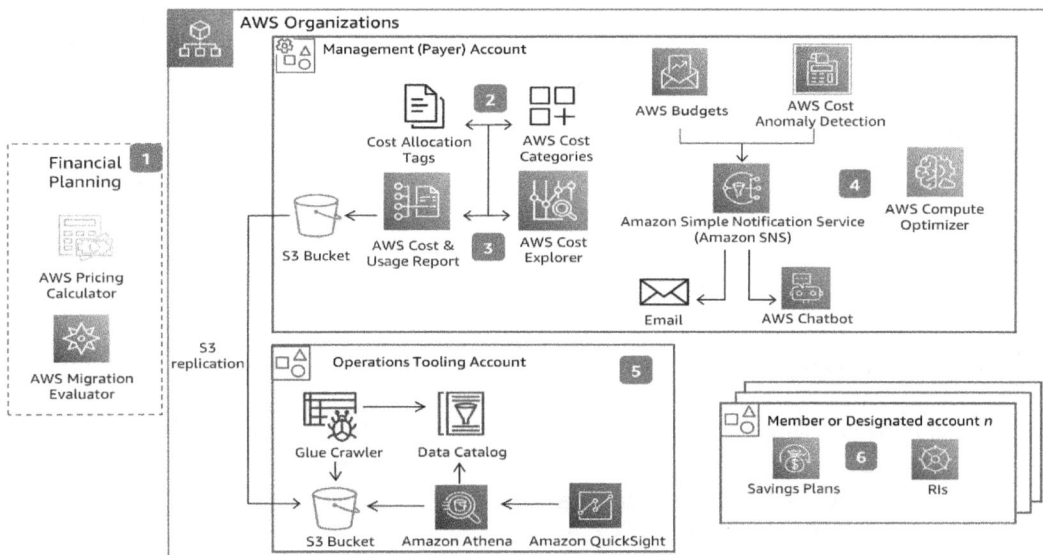

Figure 10.5: *CFM on AWS Architecture*

Challenges

The primary challenge of Spot Instances lies in the potential for interruptions. Businesses must plan for terminations and design applications that can manage these interruptions effectively.

Benefits

With careful consideration of use cases, fault-tolrance, and automation, organizations can receive help from the flexibility and cost-effectiveness that Spot Instances bring to cloud monetary management. Spot Instances offer other benefits like:

- **Optimized cost-performance ratio**: Spot Instances provide a higher cost-performance ratio, offering businesses more computational power for a fixed budget [33].

- **Scalability and flexibility**: Spot Instances provide a scalable, flexible ability that adapts to dynamic workload demands, reducing resource waste and aligning usage patterns with needs [34].

- **Diverse use cases**: Spot Instances support a wide range of use cases, including batch processing, **high-performance computing** (**HPC**), and testing environments, offering businesses a versatile, cost-effective solution [33].

Use case

A company can use Spot Instances for batch processing tasks, such as data transformation, receiving help from cost savings during periods of excess capacity. Similarly, development teams can use Spot Instances for scalable testing environments, perfect for spending during development phases [34].

Wrap up

Amazon EC2 Spot Instances offer businesses a powerful and flexible cloud resource, providing substantial cost savings and the ability to scale applications efficiently. By planning for fault-tolrance, integrating automation, and monitoring resource usage, businesses can maximize the potential of Spot Instances while minimizing costs [34].

AWS Budgets

AWS Budgets provides businesses with a powerful tool to take control of their cloud spending, helping them manage costs and usage efficiently. By offering customizable budgeting, real-time alerts, and forecasting capabilities, AWS Budgets supports organizations in aligning cloud expenditures with financial goals [36].

Key features of AWS Budgets

This section covers the features, benefits, and applications of AWS Budgets, showing how this tool can contribute to more precise cost management within the AWS ecosystem. Monitoring cloud costs is crucial for financial control and resource optimization. AWS Budgets provides businesses with real-time cost tracking, alerts, and forecasting tools to manage expenses effectively. We start by introducing a sample of AWS Budgets key features as follows:

- **Customizable budgeting**: AWS Budgets enable businesses to setup personalized budgets based on specific AWS services, accounts, or cost categories. This flexibility allows businesses to align their cloud spending with their financial goals [37].

- **Real-time alerts and notifications**: AWS Budgets provides real-time alerts when costs exceed predefined thresholds. These alerts can go through email or SNS, helping businesses take immediate corrective actions [36].

- **Forecasting capabilities**: With built-in forecasting, AWS Budgets predicts future spending based on historical data. This feature helps businesses adjust their strategies to avoid overspending [37].

Benefits

AWS Budgets is a fundamental tool for businesses looking to exert precise control over their AWS spending. Beyond cost tracking, AWS Budgets ensures financial accountability across organizations by offering precise spending insights, improving resource allocation, and enforcing budgetary discipline. We list other relevant benefits as follows:

- **Cost predictability**: AWS Budgets improves financial predictability by providing insights into current and future cloud costs. Organizations can reduce unexpected expenses and improve budget allocation [37].

- **Resource optimization**: By configuring AWS Budgets for various cost categories, businesses can distribute resources efficiently, ensuring spending aligns with financial constraints [37].

- **Financial accountability**: With transparent budget tracking and real-time alerts, AWS Budgets fosters a culture of financial accountability. Each department can watch and manage its usage, encouraging responsible resource usage in AWS organizations [36].

Use case

A retail company uses AWS Budgets to manage its departmental budgets, ensuring each team stays within budgetary constraints while meeting operational goals [37].

Wrap up

AWS Budgets offers businesses a comprehensive solution for managing AWS spending. With its ability to customize budgets, send real-time alerts, and forecast future spending, AWS Budgets helps businesses keep financial control and align cloud usage with organizational goals [38].

AWS Cost and Usage Report

The AWS CUR provides detailed insights into AWS consumption, enabling businesses to optimize their cloud costs. This service allows organizations to manage expenses with precision by offering granular data on resource usage and associated costs [39].

Key features

This section discusses the features and functionalities of AWS CUR, showing how it helps inform decision-making and enhances cost optimization within the AWS ecosystem. Understanding cloud spending patterns is key to improving costs and efficiency. AWS CUR offers detailed insights into AWS resource usage, allowing businesses to make informed financial decisions. The following are the key features of AWS CUR:

- **Granularity and customization**: AWS CUR offers granular insights with data available at hourly or daily intervals. Businesses can customize reports to track specific services, usage patterns, and costs, aligning the data with their needs for more exact financial planning [40].

- **Custom reporting**: AWS CUR allows businesses to configure reports based on criteria like service type, region, and tags, helping organizations get a detailed breakdown of resource use and billing [41].

Benefits

The AWS CUR provides businesses with invaluable insights into their AWS consumption, empowering them to improve cloud spending effectively. The granular data and customizable reporting features of AWS CUR empower businesses to track expenses, distribute costs efficiently, and improve resource usage to enhance cloud spending strategies. Other benefits include:

- **Granular cost insights**: AWS CUR provides detailed cost breakdowns, enabling businesses to track the financial implications of their resources at the granular level. This insight helps improve resource allocation and improve budget predictability [39].

- **Resource optimization**: With CUR, organizations can find underutilized resources and make informed decisions about scaling resources up or down based on actual usage [41].

- **Showback and chargeback**: For complex organizations, CUR allows for correct cost allocation across departments or projects, promoting financial accountability and transparency [39].

Use cases

It serves as a vital tool for businesses looking to gain control over their cloud spending and enhance financial accountability. AWS CUR supports businesses by providing transparency into cost allocation, facilitating budgetary planning, and enabling data-driven decision-making for enhanced financial management, as discussed:

- **Budgetary planning**: CUR helps organizations create exact budgets by providing detailed usage and cost data, ensuring financial projections align with actual consumption [41].

- **Cost allocation**: For enterprises with multiple departments or teams, CUR facilitates precise cost allocation, promoting transparency and accountability [40].

- **Resource-specific analysis**: Organizations can analyze the costs associated with various AWS services (e.g., compute, storage, data transfer), enabling targeted cost optimization [41].

Best practices

By offering granular cost breakdowns, customizable reports, and detailed usage patterns, AWS CUR enables organizations to make data-driven decisions, reduce unnecessary expenditures, and align their resource allocation with financial goals. We share the best practices for improving the use of AWS CUR as follows:

- **Regular review and analysis**: Proactively reviewing CUR reports helps organizations spot opportunities for optimization and adjust resource allocation to meet business goals [39].

- **Collaboration across teams**: Sharing CUR insights with technical, finance, and operational teams ensures alignment with budgetary goals and effective resource optimization strategies [41].

Wrap up

The AWS CUR offers invaluable insights, enabling businesses to make data-driven decisions that improve cloud spending. With customizable reports and granular data, AWS CUR empowers organizations to align their resource allocation with financial goals, enhancing financial accountability and efficiency [40].

AWS Cost Explorer

AWS Cost Explorer helps businesses manage and improve their AWS costs by providing insights into spending patterns. This tool allows users to visualize costs, forecast future expenditures, and distribute budgets more effectively [42].

Key features

AWS Cost Explorer is a powerful tool for visualizing, understanding, and managing AWS costs and usage. In this section, we explore the features and functionalities of AWS Cost Explorer, highlighting how it contributes to CFM by providing businesses with a detailed and interactive way to explore their cloud spending patterns. We present relevant features of the service as follows:

- **Cost allocation and optimization**: AWS Cost Explorer enables businesses to break down costs by resource, service, or department, making it easier to improve resource allocation and reduce wasteful spending [42].

- **Forecasting and cost prediction**: With built-in forecasting, the tool predicts future costs based on historical usage patterns, helping businesses adjust their budgets proactively and avoid unexpected cost spikes [42].

- **Visualization and custom reports**: Cost Explorer offers customizable reports with filters such as service type, account, and date range. These visualizations empower businesses to check trends and track usage in real-time [42].

Benefits

With regular monitoring and initiative-taking analysis, AWS Cost Explorer helps businesses keep control over their cloud budgets and drive long-term cost savings. The relevant benefits of ASW CUR are as follows:

- **Cost allocation and optimization**: By analyzing detailed cost drivers, businesses can find inefficiencies and opportunities for optimization. This granular approach supports better decision-making and reduces unnecessary spending [42].

- **Forecasting and budgeting**: AWS Cost Explorer helps businesses forecast costs and set budgets, ensuring financial plans align with expected cloud expenditures [42].

- **Insights into cost drivers**: The tool allows businesses to understand which services or accounts contribute most to their costs, making it easier to improve usage and control spending [42].

Use cases

The tool's ability to distribute costs across departments and identify cost drivers enables businesses to make data-driven decisions, reducing expenses and improving resource utilization. The following use cases give us the tool in real-life scenarios:

- **Cost allocation across departments**: Organizations with multiple teams can use Cost Explorer to track and distribute costs across departments, fostering transparency and accountability [42].

- **Cost optimization in multi-account environments**: Cost Explorer helps businesses with multiple AWS accounts find inefficiencies and improve resource usage across all accounts [42].

- **Tracking Reserved Instances usage**: Businesses can use Cost Explorer to check **Reserved Instance** (**RI**) use, ensuring that they are fully using their long-term commitments and adjusting as necessary [42].

Best practices

A list of the best practices for obtaining the best results with AWS Cost Explorer is as follows:

- **Regular monitoring and analysis**: Consistently check spending trends using AWS Cost Explorer to find anomalies early and adjust budgets to stay on track [42].

- **Collaborative decision-making**: Share insights from Cost Explorer across teams, including finance, IT, and operations, to align efforts on cost optimization [42].

- **Setting custom alerts**: Setup real-time custom alerts to check when costs exceed predefined thresholds, enabling immediate corrective action [42].

Wrap up

AWS Cost Explorer serves as a key tool for businesses looking to perfect their AWS spending. It provides detailed cost analysis, forecasting, and resource allocation capabilities, helping organizations control their cloud costs and make data-driven decisions to drive long-term savings [42].

Reserved Instance Reporting

RIs offers businesses significant savings by committing them to a one or three-year term for AWS services. This section examines how RI Reporting enables businesses to track and optimize the utilization of RIs, ensuring maximum cost efficiency and alignment with resource demands.

Key features and benefits

AWS RIs provide businesses with significant discounts (up to 75%) in exchange for committing to a one or three-year term of usage. By paying in advance for RIs, organizations can significantly reduce the cost of their AWS resources, especially for predictable and steady-state workloads [43]. The key features that help RIs' implementations to meet those goals:

- **Cost savings**: RIs provide significant discounts in exchange for long-term commitments. RI Reporting helps businesses ensure they are maximizing their savings by tracking actual usage and finding underutilized resources [43].

- **Financial forecasting**: RI Reporting offers insights that help businesses forecast future costs more accurately. By aligning RI purchases with actual usage, companies can predict their cloud expenditures, avoiding unexpected expenses [43].

- **Alignment with cloud usage**: RI Reporting ensures that RIs align with actual resource demand. This improves the cost-performance ratio by keeping the right balance between on-demand and reserved ability [43].

Use cases

By analyzing RI usage patterns, businesses can improve their reservations, ensuring they match the required resource ability [43]. We list cases that show the scenario:

- **Improving RI usage**: Businesses can use RI Reporting to find and adjust underutilized RIs, ensuring they are taking full advantage of their reservations [43].

- **Cost planning for long-term projects**: For long-term projects requiring steady resource usage, RI Reporting helps businesses track usage against forecasts, ensuring that reserved resources align with project demands [43].

- **Managing RI expiry and renewals**: RI Reporting enables businesses to track end dates and renew or adjust reservations proactively, avoiding the higher costs associated with On-Demand Instances after RIs expire [43].

Best practices

RIs stand for a strategic investment for businesses with predictable workloads, such as development, testing, and production environments. You will find a list of best practices for operating Ris as follows:

- **Regularly review RI use**: Businesses should regularly assess their RI usage and adjust reservations based on changing requirements to avoid unnecessary costs [43].

- **Collaboration between teams**: Finance and technical teams should collaborate to align RI usage with the business's overall cloud strategy, ensuring that cost-saving opportunities are fully realized [43].

- **Integrating RI data with financial forecasting**: By integrating RI usage data into financial forecasting processes, businesses can create more exact budgets for their cloud services. RI Reporting provides the data required to predict future costs and make informed decisions about cloud resource use [43].

Wrap up

RI Reporting is a crucial tool for optimizing cloud spending. By tracking usage and aligning RIs with actual resource demand, businesses can maximize savings and avoid overcommitting to their abilities. Initiative-taking RI management ensures long-term cost-efficiency in the cloud [43].

AWS Savings Plans

AWS Savings Plans offer a flexible, cost-effective pricing model designed to help businesses reduce their cloud expenditure. By committing to a specific level of usage for one or three years, companies can unlock significant savings, up to 72% compared to On-Demand pricing, while keeping flexibility across instance types and regions [44].

Key features

As cloud computing continues to transform the way businesses manage and scale their infrastructure, improving cloud costs has become a top priority for organizations of all sizes. To meet this growing demand, AWS introduced Savings Plans as a flexible, cost-effective pricing model designed to help businesses reduce their cloud expenditure while keeping the agility they need to adapt to changing workloads.

Cloud cost optimization is essential for long-term financial planning. AWS Savings Plans offer a flexible pricing model that allows businesses to reduce expenses while keeping workload agility. Among the key features provided by AWS Cost Savings, you will find [44]:

- **Definition and flexible pricing model**: Savings Plans provide businesses with the opportunity to commit to consistent usage in exchange for savings. Unlike RIs, which are tied to specific configurations, Savings Plans provide broader flexibility, covering different instance types, families, and regions [45]; [46].

- **Usage flexibility**: Businesses can switch between instance families, sizes, and operating systems, allowing them to adapt their cloud infrastructure without losing the benefits of their savings [47].

- **Commitment period**: With one or three-year terms, businesses can achieve significant cost savings for predictable usage patterns while receiving help from predictable billing [45].

Advantages

Savings Plans are the evolution of AWS's pricing models. Initially introduced to offer customers a choice that provided more flexibility than RIs, they allow businesses to make predictable cost savings by committing to consistent usage of AWS services for one or three years.

AWS Savings Plans go beyond simple discounts by providing organizations with predictable billing, usage flexibility, and the ability to scale cloud resources without compromising financial efficiency, as discussed:

- **Cost savings**: Savings Plans provide significant savings, especially for companies with steady or variable workloads that would otherwise pay full On-Demand pricing [45].

- **Predictable billing**: The commitment to consistent usage helps businesses forecast and budget more effectively, reducing financial surprises [45].

- **Usage flexibility**: This model ensures businesses can adapt to evolving workloads without sacrificing cost benefits [47].

Managing AWS Savings Plans

To thoroughly improve Savings Plans, businesses can use various AWS tools that help manage usage, watch trends, and maximize cost savings.

To fully leverage cost savings, businesses can integrate AWS Savings Plans with CFM tools, such as AWS Cost Explorer and AWS Budgets, ensuring efficient resource allocation, as discussed:

- **AWS Cost Explorer**: Cost Explorer offers detailed insights into Savings Plans usage, helping businesses track usage patterns and adjust as needed to maximize savings [47].

- **AWS Budgets**: AWS Budgets enables businesses to track and set alerts for Savings Plans-related costs, ensuring they meet their financial goals [47].

- **Custom reporting with CUR**: The AWS CUR provides detailed data to integrate with BI tools for deeper analysis [45].

Best practices

To ensure the most effective use of Savings Plans, businesses should adhere to the following best practices that improve both cost savings and use:

- **Regular analysis and adjustment**: Regular reviews of Savings Plans usage ensure that businesses are improving their cloud expenditures [45].

- **Collaboration between teams**: Finance and technical teams must collaborate to align Saving Plans with infrastructure needs, ensuring cost-effectiveness [46].

- **Forecasting and long-term planning**: Using AWS tools like Cost Explorer and AWS Budgets for forecasting ensures businesses stay prepared for growth or usage fluctuations [47].

In *Figure 10.6* you can see the four pillars of CFM:

See	Save	Plan	Run
Measurement & accountability	Cost optimization	Planning & forecasting	Cloud financial operations
Account & tagging strategy	Cost aware architecture, design & service selection	Budgeting & forecasting variable cloud usage	Secure executive sponsorship
Cost reporting & monitoring processes	Match capacity with demand	POC based cost estimation	Partnership between Finance & Technology organizations
Cost show/chargeback	Choose the right pricing model	Business case/value articulation	Invest in people, governance & tools
Efficiency/value KPIs	Identify resource waste	Strategic fit	Celebrate accomplishments

Figure 10.6: The four pillars of CFM

Use cases

A *Gartner* report [48] This flexibility is one of the main drivers for businesses transitioning to Savings Plans over RIs. The report notes that organizations that previously had rigid cloud resource needs were increasingly receiving help from Savings Plans flexibility, especially in industries where scalability and changing demands are the norm. Use case examples of Savings Plans flexibility are as follows:

- **Predictable workloads**: Savings Plans are ideal for businesses with steady-state workloads, such as production applications or database management systems [45].

- **Hybrid workload**: Organizations that need resources across multiple regions or instance types can balance their usage with Savings Plans, receiving help from savings while meeting dynamic needs [47].

- **Startups and growing businesses**: Startups can lock in savings as they scale, ensuring cloud costs stay manageable [46].

Wrap up

AWS Savings Plans provide businesses with a flexible and cost-effective way to manage cloud spending, offering significant savings, flexibility, and predictable billing. By utilizing tools such as AWS Cost Explorer and AWS Budgets, businesses can effectively monitor and optimize their usage, ensuring that their cloud infrastructure aligns with their financial goals. [45].

Media services

Figure 10.7 serves as a pivotal guide for understanding how AWS Media Services meets the diverse requirements for multimedia processing. This diagram encapsulates the interconnected components and workflows that enable scalable, efficient, and cost-effective media solutions, aligning with AWS's commitment to delivering seamless multimedia experiences. Comprehensive visualization provides insights into how AWS services, such as Amazon Elastic Transcoder, AWS Elemental MediaLive, and Amazon S3, collaborate to support end-to-end media processing, storage, and delivery.

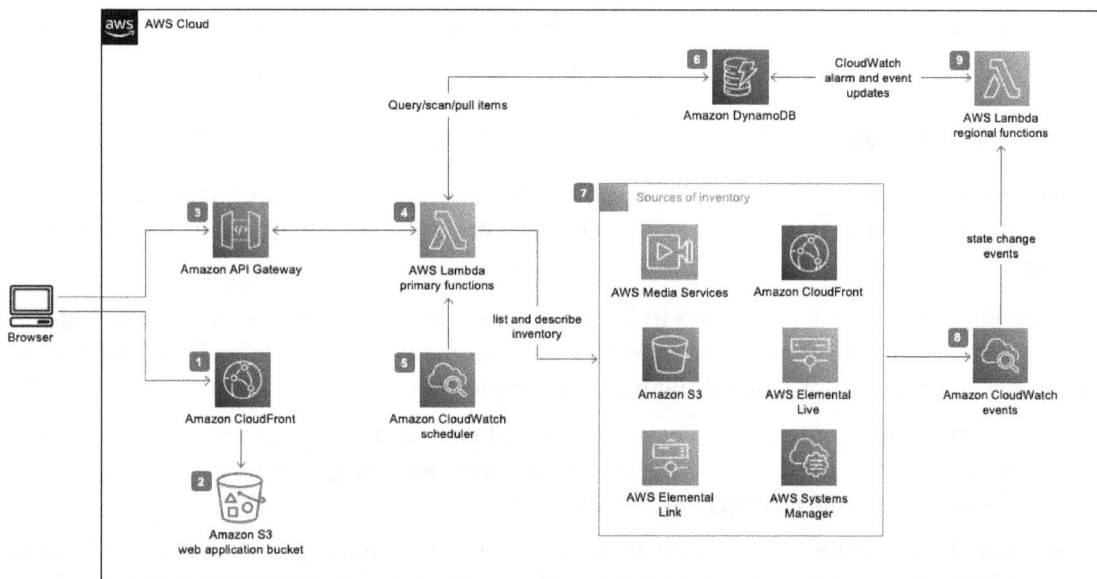

Figure 10.7: *Media Services Application Mapper on AWS*

Amazon Elastic Transcoder

In the ever-evolving digital content landscape, efficient and scalable media transcoding is crucial for delivering high-quality multimedia experiences. Amazon Elastic Transcoder, a part of AWS Media Services, addresses this need by providing a comprehensive solution for transcoding media files into various formats. This section delves into the intricacies of Amazon Elastic Transcoder, exploring its features, use cases, and the advantages it offers in the realm of media processing.

Key features

Amazon Elastic Transcoder is a fully managed media transcoding service that enables the conversion of media files from their source format into versions improved for various devices and playback scenarios [49].

High-quality media transcoding is crucial for delivering content across multiple platforms. Amazon Elastic Transcoder enables businesses to convert and improve media files for seamless playback on various devices. The key features of the service are as follows:

- **Elastic scalability**: Amazon Elastic Transcoder automatically scales based on the volume of transcoding jobs, ensuring the best performance and responsiveness to varying workloads [49].

- **Customizable presets**: Users can choose from a selection of predefined transcoding presets or create custom presets to tailor the output to specific requirements, such as resolution, bitrate, and codec settings [50].

- **Thumbnail generation**: The service can generate thumbnails from the input video at specified intervals, enhancing the ability to create engaging and visually appealing content [51].

Use cases of Amazon Elastic Transcoder

The service supports a wide range of input and output formats, enabling users to transcode media files into formats compatible with web browsers, mobile devices, smart TVs, and other platforms [52].

Amazon Elastic Transcoder supports industries that require adaptive streaming, multi-device content delivery, and user-generated media processing, ensuring optimized media playback and audience engagement. The following are examples of the service's application:

- **Multi-device content delivery**: Amazon Elastic Transcoder is crucial in preparing media content for delivery to various devices, ensuring a seamless and optimized viewing experience across various platforms.

- **DASH and HLS**: The service supports popular streaming protocols like **Dynamic adaptive streaming over HTTP (DASH)** and **HTTP Live Streaming (HLS)**, enabling the delivery of adaptive bitrate streaming for an enhanced streaming experience [53].

- **User-generated content processing**: Content platforms that involve user-generated media can use Amazon Elastic Transcoder to efficiently process and format content uploaded by users.

Best practices for effective usage

Seamless integration with Amazon S3 allows users to store input and output files, simplifying the management of media assets throughout the transcoding process [54]. Amazon Elastic Transcoder can couple with Amazon CloudFront to ensure low-latency and high-performance delivery of transcoded media files to end-users globally [49].

To maximize efficiency, businesses should improve transcoding settings, integrate storage with Amazon S3, and leverage Amazon CloudFront for low-latency content delivery, as discussed:

- **Optimal preset choice**: Careful consideration of transcoding presets is crucial for achieving the right balance between file size, quality, and compatibility with target devices [52].

- **Cost optimization**: Understanding the cost structure and improving transcoding configurations based on the specific needs of the project is essential for the cost-effective usage of Amazon Elastic Transcoder [53].

Wrap up

Amazon Elastic Transcoder stands as a powerful tool in the AWS Media Services suite, empowering businesses to deliver high-quality multimedia content efficiently and on a large scale. By understanding its features, use cases, and integration possibilities, organizations can unlock the full potential of this service, enhancing their capabilities in the ever-expanding digital content landscape.

Amazon Interactive Video Service

The growing demand for engaging, interactive video content has placed a spotlight on services that simplify live streaming while incorporating real-time features. Amazon **Interactive Video Service (IVS)** addresses this need by offering a managed service for live video streaming, complete with interactive capabilities. This section discusses the features, use cases, and benefits of Amazon IVS in the live streaming domain.

Key features

Today, Amazon IVS is a significant player in the modern digital landscape, particularly in the creation of interactive and engaging video content. Among the key features offered by IVS, we find the following:

- **Low-latency**: Designed to minimize delays, making it suitable for events requiring immediate interaction [53].

- **Scalable infrastructure**: Automatically adjusts to audience size, accommodating a variety of event scales [52].

- **Streamlined live streaming**: Simplifies live video delivery by managing infrastructure, enabling businesses to focus on content creation and audience interaction.

- **Real-time interaction**: Features such as live chat, polls, and **question and answer (Q&A)** enhance engagement during broadcasts [49].

Use cases of Amazon IVS

Live events and webinars: Ideal for events that require active audience participation, such as live Q&As and polls.

AWS IVS enables real-time engagement through low-latency streaming. Various industries use IVS for live events, gaming, online education, and interactive broadcasting, as discussed:

- **Gaming and esports**: Low-latency capabilities make it a preferred choice for gaming streams, ensuring minimal delays.

- **Online education and training**: Supports interactive workshops, live classes, and training sessions.

Best practices for implementation

IVS offers integration with AWS services through the IVS Player SDK, ensuring smooth integration of video streams into apps, delivering consistent playback quality, and AWS Elemental Media Services, which adds advanced features like content protection, ad insertion, and transcoding. Other best practices for IVS implementation include:

- **Enhancing viewer engagement**: Use interactive features strategically to match content goals and audience expectations.

- **Leveraging analytics**: Regularly analyze performance data to improve content and UX.

Wrap up

Amazon **Kinesis Video Streams (KVS)** empowers businesses to harness the power of video data for a wide array of applications, from enhancing security and surveillance to enabling real-time analytics and ML. As an integral part of the AWS ecosystem, Amazon KVS exemplifies AWS's commitment to providing scalable and innovative solutions for handling video data in the cloud.

Amazon Kinesis Video Streams

Amazon KVS provides a robust solution for processing and analyzing video streams in the cloud. Designed to manage real-time video data ingestion and storage, it supports applications ranging from ML to surveillance and live streaming.

Key features

Real-time video ingestion enables the ingestion of real-time video data from cameras, connected devices, and mobile applications [55]. Other key features include:

- **Scalable and flexible**: Adapts to changing workloads, managing concurrent video streams with ease [52].
- **AWS integration**: Builds end-to-end pipelines with tools like Amazon Kinesis Data Analytics and Amazon S3 [53].

Use cases

Success cases, like those listed below, benefit from secure and durable storage. It ensures reliable storage of video streams, supporting applications like analytics, ML, and playback [49], as discussed:

- **Video analytics and ML**: Powers applications like object detection, facial recognition, and sentiment analysis.
- **Security and surveillance**: Helps scalable monitoring and analysis for multi-camera setups.
- **Live streaming and content delivery**: Supports high-quality live broadcasts for events, gaming, and interactive streaming.

Best practices for effective usage

For the effective deployment of Amazon Kinesis, AK Data Analytics, which performs real-time analytics on streaming data, enabling actionable insights [49]. Also, Amazon Rekognition adds advanced image and video analysis, including object detection and activity tracking [53]. Other best practices include:

- **Improving cost and performance**: Configure storage, resolution, and throughput settings based on specific needs [52].
- **Ensuring security**: Implement encryption and access controls to safeguard video data.

Wrap up

Amazon KVS shows the power of video data for applications ranging from analytics to live streaming. Integrating seamlessly with the AWS ecosystem enables businesses to derive actionable insights and enhance their digital workflows.

Amazon Nimble Studio

Amazon Nimble Studio stands out as an innovative service in AWS's media services portfolio. It transforms how studios and creators approach animation, **visual effects** (**VFX**), and interactive media production. This section highlights its features, applications, and benefits in the media and entertainment industry.

Key features

This section highlights the features, applications, and benefits of Amazon Nimble Studio in the media and entertainment industry. A sample of the key features is as follows:

- **Virtual studio in the cloud**: Provides a cloud-based virtual studio, enabling creative professionals to collaborate on content creation from anywhere.

- **End-to-end production**: Offers comprehensive tools for content production, including virtual workstations, scalable storage, and integration with popular creative applications [49].

- **Collaborative workflows**: Help team collaboration, allowing artists and contributors to work simultaneously on projects.

- **Elastic rendering**: Scales giving resources based on project requirements, reducing processing times [52].

Use cases of Amazon Nimble Studio

IAM is essential when discussing Amazon Nimble Studio success cases. These services enhance security by allowing administrators to set fine-grained permissions for resources. Other examples include:

- **Animation and VFX**: This function supports the production of high-quality animation and VFX, enhancing collaboration and productivity.

- **Remote media collaboration**: Enables geographically dispersed teams to collaborate effectively, addressing the challenges of remote production.

- **Interactive media and gaming**: Provides a platform for creating visually stunning and interactive gaming experiences, integrating with popular gaming engines [53].

Best practices for practical usage

To maximize the efficiency of Amazon Nimble Studio, creative teams should adopt the best practices that enhance performance, security, and scalability. A studio can achieve seamless workflows and cost-effective operations by integrating AWS storage solutions and optimizing workstation configurations. Key best practices include:

- **Amazon S3 and Amazon FSx for Lustre**: Tools to integrate Amazon Nimble with Amazon S3 for scalable storage and Amazon FSx for Lustre for high-performance file systems. Among the best practices to improve the use of Amazon Nimble are:

  o **Optimizing workstation configurations**: Select the optimal instance types and GPU configurations for maximum performance.

o **Implementing secure collaboration**: Configure access controls, encrypt data, and regularly audit permissions.

Wrap up

Amazon Nimble Studio is a transformative service for the media and entertainment sector. It enables seamless collaboration, scalability, and flexibility in content creation workflows. It addresses the evolving needs of creative professionals, offering a robust platform for cloud-enabled media production.

AWS Elemental Appliances and Software

AWS Elemental Appliances and Software [56] is a comprehensive suite of solutions designed to revolutionize video processing and delivery workflows. This section explores its key components, features, and applications, illustrating its critical role in delivering high-quality, scalable, and efficient video content across various platforms.

Key components and features

AWS Elemental includes the following key features to reinforce its role in delivering high-quality, scalable, and efficient video content across various platforms:

- **Elemental Live**: Real-time video and audio processing software that ensures high-quality live streaming by encoding and packaging content for various devices [56].

- **Elemental Server**: An on-premises video processing solution for file-based video transcoding, creating on-demand assets improved for different screens [52].

- **Elemental Conductor**: A centralized management tool for coordinating multiple Elemental Live and Server instances, streamlining control and monitoring [53].

- **Complete video processing solution**: Provides a comprehensive solution for video processing, encompassing encoding, transcoding, packaging, and delivery.

- **Scalability and flexibility**: Built to scale and adapt to varying project demands and audience sizes [56].

Use cases of AWS Elemental Appliances and Software

AWS Elemental Appliances and Software design aims to meet the evolving demands of video content providers, broadcasters, and live streaming platforms. Whether powering high-profile live events or enabling seamless on-demand video streaming, AWS Elemental solutions deliver industry-leading performance, scalability, and flexibility. The following are key use cases showing its capabilities:

- **Live event streaming**: Enables real-time encoding and packaging of video content for global audiences during live events, ensuring a seamless viewing experience [52].

- **On-demand video processing**: Empowers content providers to transcode and package video files, improving them for delivery across various platforms [56].

- **Multiscreen video delivery**: Creates adaptive bitrate streams, ensuring best video quality tailored to device and network conditions [53].

Best practices for practical usage

AWS Elemental MediaPackage enhances live or on-demand content delivery by packaging and originating video for diverse devices, and AWS Elemental MediaLive facilitates real-time video encoding, enabling high-quality live streaming to global viewers [56]. To achieve success in every MediaPackage implementation, AWS recommends the following best practices:

- **Improving video workflows**: Use the suite's scalability and flexibility to align resources with project requirements and dynamic workloads.

- **Implementing security measures**: Protect video assets by employing encryption protocols and robust access controls throughout the processing pipeline [52].

Wrap up

AWS Elemental Appliances and Software is a cornerstone in the video processing landscape, offering a comprehensive suite of tools to meet the needs of content creators and distributors. With its focus on scalability, flexibility, and integration with other AWS services, it enables efficient and high-quality video content delivery.

AWS Elemental MediaConnect

AWS Elemental MediaConnect ensures secure, high-quality live [56] video transport between sources and destinations. It supports real-time workflows for seamless content transmission, critical for live streaming and media production.

Key features

AWS Elemental MediaConnect provides a reliable and scalable solution for live video transport, addressing the growing need for secure, high-quality media distribution. The service design aims to simplify content workflows while keeping low-latency, making it an essential tool for broadcasters and content providers, as discussed:

- **Secure transport**: Protects live video with encryption and secure network protocols.

- **Hub-and-spoke model**: Simplifies workflow management with flexible, scalable connections between sources and destinations [53].

- **Live video transport**: Transmits live video efficiently and securely, forming an essential part of workflows.

- **Low-latency**: Keeps minimal delays and high quality for real-time applications [56].

Use cases of AWS Elemental MediaConnect

AWS Elemental MediaConnect enables media companies, broadcasters, and live event organizers to distribute high-quality video content seamlessly. Supporting cloud-based and hybrid workflows enhances the efficiency and security of live video transport, as discussed:

- **Live event broadcasting**: Ensures uninterrupted transmission of live video feeds for global events [52].
- **Contribution and distribution**: Helps with video transport from remote locations to studios and affiliates.
- **Cloud-based workflows**: Connects on-premises sources with cloud resources for seamless media processing.

Best practices for effective usage

To maximize the benefits of AWS Elemental MediaConnect, organizations should adopt industry best practices that enhance security, improve workflows, and improve reliability, as discussed:

- **AWS Elemental MediaLive**: Enhances live video workflows by offering real-time processing capabilities.
- **AWS Elemental MediaPackage**: Prepares live video streams for diverse devices and platforms efficiently.
- **Improving transport workflows**: Strategically positioned hubs to improve manageability and reduce complexity.
- **Ensuring security**: Configure encryption and access controls to protect video streams [56].

Wrap up

AWS Elemental MediaConnect is a reliable, secure solution for live video transport. Its integration capabilities and focus on high-quality transmission make it an ideal choice for diverse live video production and distribution workflows.

AWS Elemental MediaConvert

AWS Elemental MediaConvert provides scalable, file-based video transcoding to ensure compatibility across devices and delivery platforms. It supports diverse media workflows while keeping high quality and efficiency [57].

Key features and components

AWS Elemental MediaConvert offers advanced video processing capabilities, enabling content providers to deliver high-quality media across multiple platforms. Automating resource scaling and supporting various formats ensures efficiency and flexibility in file-based video transcoding, as discussed:

- **File-based video transcoding**: Converts video files to various formats, ensuring compatibility with multiple devices and platforms.

- **Scalability and elasticity**: Processes single files or millions of files effortlessly, adapting to changing workloads [56].

- **Wide format support**: Manages a broad range of input and output formats for streaming, broadcasting, and on-demand delivery [52].

- **Automated resource scaling**: Dynamically adjusts resources based on transcoding requirements, improving performance and cost-efficiency [53].

Use cases of AWS Elemental MediaConvert

AWS Elemental MediaConvert plays a crucial role in modern media workflows, enabling broadcasters, streaming services, and content creators to efficiently prepare video content for various platforms and audiences, as discussed:

- **Multiscreen video delivery**: Enables content providers to deliver optimized videos for smartphones, tablets, and smart TVs.

- **OTT streaming**: Powers **over-the-top (OTT)** streaming services by transcoding content into formats suited for internet-based viewing.

- **Broadcast workflows**: Prepares video content for live events and scheduled broadcasts, meeting industry standards efficiently.

Best practices for effective usage

To maximize the capabilities of AWS Elemental MediaConvert, organizations should follow best practices that improve transcoding performance, enhance video quality, and streamline content delivery:

- **AWS Elemental MediaPackage**: Prepares transcoded videos for delivery to various devices, streamlining workflows.

- **AWS Elemental MediaLive**: Combines with MediaLive for end-to-end live video workflows, enhancing both services.

- **Improving transcoding settings**: Select codecs, resolutions, and bitrates based on specific use cases to balance quality and file size.

- **Utilizing automated workflows**: Implement job templates and pre-configured settings to streamline processes and minimize errors.

Wrap up

AWS Elemental MediaConvert offers a flexible, scalable solution for file-based video transcoding. Its integration with other AWS services enhances its capabilities, making it an essential part of efficient media processing [57].

AWS Elemental MediaLive

AWS Elemental MediaLive provides real-time video encoding for broadcast and multiscreen delivery, supporting diverse live video workflows with scalability and resilience.

Key features

The key features are as follows:

- **Live video encoding**: Encodes live video streams in real-time, making it essential for broadcasting live events, 24/7 channels, and OTT content delivery.

- **Scalability and resilience**: Adjusts resources automatically to meet demand, ensuring efficiency and cost-effectiveness [58].

- **Wide format support**: Supports various input and output formats, codecs, and resolutions to deliver high-quality video streams across platforms [52].

- **Channel configuration**: Allows users to manage channels with customizable settings, input sources, and output destinations [53].

Use cases

AWS Elemental MediaLive design aims to meet the demands of modern live video workflows, providing broadcasters and content creators with the tools needed for seamless, high-quality streaming experiences. Whether delivering breaking news, live sports, or continuous 24/7 broadcasting, MediaLive ensures reliability and flexibility in video encoding, as discussed:

- **Live events streaming**: Powers live events such as sports, concerts, and news broadcasts, ensuring smooth streaming experiences [52].

- **24/7 channel broadcasting**: Supports continuous 24/7 channel operations for broadcasters and content providers [53].

- **OTT content delivery**: Helps with encoding for internet-based live content delivery, aligning with the demands of modern media consumption.

Best practices for practical usage

Implementing best practices that enhance video quality and security and ensure uninterrupted streaming is essential to maximizing the performance and reliability of AWS Elemental MediaLive, as discussed:

- **AWS Elemental MediaPackage**: Prepares and protects live video streams for seamless delivery to various devices and platforms.

- **AWS CloudTrail**: Monitors and audits MediaLive API activity for enhanced security and compliance [58].

- **Improving video quality**: Select the optimal codecs, bitrates, and resolutions to strike a balance between quality and bandwidth usage.

- **Implementing redundancy**: Configure backup inputs and redundant outputs to ensure reliability during live streams.

Wrap up

AWS Elemental MediaLive stands out as a versatile solution for live video encoding, supporting a range of broadcasting scenarios. Its integration with other AWS services enhances its capabilities, making it an essential tool for content providers and broadcasters.

AWS Elemental MediaLive

AWS Elemental MediaLive provides real-time video encoding for broadcast and multiscreen delivery, supporting diverse live video workflows with scalability and resilience.

Key features

The key features are as follows:

- **Live video encoding**: Encodes live video streams in real-time, supporting live events, 24/7 channels, and OTT content delivery.

- **Scalable architecture**: Adjusts resources dynamically to meet workload demands, ensuring efficiency and reliability [56].

- **Wide format support**: Supports different codecs, resolutions, and formats, enabling delivery to varied platforms [52].

- **Customizable channels**: Users can define input sources, output destinations, and encoding settings to meet specific workflow needs [53].

Use cases

AWS Elemental MediaLive is essential for broadcasters, content creators, and media platforms that require real-time video encoding for live events and continuous streaming. Its robust architecture ensures high-quality video content delivery with minimal latency, making it ideal for large-scale media operations, as discussed:

- **Live events**: Helps encode sports, concerts, and news broadcasts, providing smooth and reliable streaming [52].

- **24/7 broadcasting**: Enables broadcasters to maintain continuous, high-quality channel operations.
- **OTT streaming**: Powers deliver OTT content, ensuring compatibility with internet-based streaming platforms [53].

Best practices for practical usage

AWS Elemental MediaLive should improve by using the best practices that improve quality, resilience, and efficiency to ensure seamless video streaming and enhance performance, as follows:

- **AWS Elemental MediaPackage**: Processes and protects streams for seamless device delivery.
- **AWS CloudTrail**: Tracks API activity for monitoring and compliance.
- **Improve quality settings**: Adjust bitrate and codec settings to match device and bandwidth conditions.
- **Build redundancy**: Configure backup sources and outputs for uninterrupted streaming.

Wrap up

AWS Elemental MediaLive is a cornerstone for live video encoding, offering flexibility, scalability, and seamless integration with AWS services. Its features and best practices empower broadcasters and content providers to deliver high-quality live streaming experiences.

AWS Elemental MediaPackage

AWS Elemental MediaPackage streamlines video content delivery by dynamically packaging live and on-demand video streams for various devices and platforms. Its capabilities ensure flexibility and high-quality streaming experiences for a diverse audience.

Key features

The key features are as follows:

- **Dynamic video packaging**: AWS Elemental MediaPackage prepares and protects video streams for delivery to multiple devices by dynamically packaging content into various formats.
- **Scalable architecture**: Resources scale automatically to meet demand, ensuring reliability and high-performance during peak loads [59].
- **Multiple streaming formats**: Supports various formats, including HLS, DASH, and **Common Media Application Format (CMAF)**, to accommodate different devices and platforms.

- **Digital rights management (DRM)**: Integrates DRM to protect content, ensuring secure distribution and protection.

- **Customizable channels**: Users can define packaging configurations to tailor delivery to specific requirements [52].

Use cases

AWS Elemental MediaPackage offers a robust solution for efficiently delivering video content across various platforms. By dynamically packaging live and on-demand streams, it ensures seamless playback experiences, reducing complexity for content providers, as follows:

- **Multiscreen video delivery**: Prepares video for devices such as smartphones, tablets, and smart TVs, reaching audiences with diverse preferences.

- **Live event streaming**: Supports real-time packaging and low-latency delivery for live broadcasts such as sports and entertainment events [53].

- **Video-on-demand (VoD) streaming**: VoD dynamically packages content for streaming platforms, offering on-demand libraries, and ensuring efficient delivery.

Best practices for practical usage

AWS Elemental MediaPackage should integrate strategically with complementary AWS services and improve based on audience needs to maximize performance, security, and efficiency, as discussed:

- **AWS Elemental MediaLive**: Combines with MediaLive to enable seamless workflows for live streaming, from content encoding to packaging and delivery.

- **AWS CloudTrail**: Monitors API activity for enhanced security and compliance, providing detailed logs for auditing purposes [58].

- **Fine-tuning packaging configurations**: Adjust video quality, bitrate, and packaging formats according to audience and content requirements for optimal delivery.

- **Leveraging content delivery networks (CDN) integration**: Utilize CDNs to enhance scalability and minimize latency, thereby ensuring a seamless streaming experience.

Wrap up

AWS Elemental MediaPackage is indispensable for the secure, efficient, and scalable delivery of video content. Its robust feature set, wide-ranging use cases, and seamless integration with AWS services empower broadcasters, media companies, and streaming platforms to effectively meet the demands of modern streaming.

AWS Elemental MediaStore

AWS Elemental MediaStore offers optimized storage for media workflows, providing the performance and low-latency required for efficient content delivery. It ensures durable and scalable storage tailored to the demands of modern media operations.

Key features and components

AWS Elemental MediaStore provides a purpose-built storage solution specifically designed for media applications, ensuring high-performance retrieval and low-latency access to content. It combines the scalability of object storage with the responsiveness needed for media streaming workflows, as follows:

- **Durable storage**: Provides multiple **Availability Zones (AZs)** replication to safeguard against data loss.
- **HTTP-based API**: Enables easy integration into media workflows for efficient asset retrieval.
- **Byte-range requests**: Supports partial file access, which is crucial for efficient media streaming [52].
- **Optimized media storage**: AWS Elemental MediaStore's purpose is to store and deliver media assets with low-latency access and high reliability.
- **Scalable architecture**: The service replicates objects across multiple AZs, ensuring durability and availability [60].

Use cases

AWS Elemental MediaStore plays a critical role in media workflows by providing highly available and optimized storage for streaming and on-demand applications, as follows:

- **Content delivery**: Ensures seamless and responsive delivery of media content by providing low-latency access to stored assets.
- **Live streaming**: Offers real-time storage and retrieval of live streaming content, meeting the stringent requirements of live broadcasts [53].
- **VoD applications**: Supports scalable and durable storage for on-demand video libraries, ensuring reliable access to content even during high-demand periods.

Best practices for practical usage

To maximize efficiency and ensure the best performance, AWS Elemental MediaStore should be integrated with other AWS services and configured strategically, as follows:

- **Amazon CloudFront**: Integrates with CloudFront to use its global edge locations, improving content delivery performance.

- **AWS Elemental MediaLive and MediaPackage**: Works seamlessly with other AWS Media Services to enable end-to-end workflows, from encoding to delivery [58]; [59].

- **Multiple AZ configuration**: Configure storage across multiple AZs to enhance durability and reduce the risk of data loss.

- **CDN integration**: Pair with a CDN, such as CloudFront, to reduce latency and optimize global content delivery.

Wrap up

AWS Elemental MediaStore is crucial for efficiently storing and delivering media assets. Its robust features, seamless integration with AWS services, and scalability make it ideal for live streaming, VoD applications, and content delivery scenarios.

AWS Elemental MediaTailor

AWS Elemental MediaTailor empowers content providers to deliver personalized and targeted advertisements while ensuring seamless integration into media workflows. Using server-side ad insertion, MediaTailor provides a consistent and engaging viewing experience across all devices [61].

Key features and components

AWS Elemental MediaTailor provides a server-side ad insertion solution that enhances content monetization while ensuring a smooth and uninterrupted viewing experience. By dynamically stitching targeted advertisements into live and on-demand video streams, it cuts buffering issues associated with client-side ad insertion and supports seamless ad integration across devices, as follows:

- **Personalized ad delivery**: AWS Elemental MediaTailor enables targeted ad delivery by stitching ads into video streams on the server-side. This ensures a seamless viewing experience for audiences on smart TVs, tablets, and smartphones.

- **Scalable ad insertion**: The service supports dynamic ad insertion, scaling resources to meet the demands of diverse audience sizes and complex workflows [56].

- **Server-side ad insertion**: Inserts ads directly into the video stream, ending buffering and playback disruptions common with client-side solutions.

- **Targeted Ad delivery**: Helps personalize ads through integrations with AWS Elemental MediaPackage and **Ad Decision Server** (**ADS**), improving ad placement based on viewer profiles [52].

Use cases

AWS Elemental MediaTailor enables content providers to enhance video monetization strategies while keeping the best viewer experience, as follows:

- **Enhanced monetization**: Maximizes revenue potential by delivering ads aligned with viewer interests, improving ad relevance and engagement.

- **Consistent viewer experience**: Ensures smooth transitions between content and ads, enhancing overall audience satisfaction.

Best practices for practical usage

To achieve the best results with AWS Elemental MediaTailor, organizations should integrate it with other AWS services and improve ad workflows effectively, as follows:

- **AWS Elemental MediaPackage**: Seamlessly integrates with MediaPackage to deliver low-latency, high-quality video streams with embedded ads.

- **ADS**: This product supports existing ad decisioning workflows and ensures compatibility with industry standard ADS solutions for precise ad targeting.

- **Viewer profile management**: Develop comprehensive viewer profiles to enhance ad targeting and ensure the delivery of relevant content.

- **Collaborative ad campaign planning**: Work closely with advertisers to align ad content with audience preferences, improving campaign outcomes [61].

Figure 10.8 summarizes how to configure advanced features in AWS Elemental MediaTailor. A holistic view of an OTT streaming solution with MediaTailor, various origin types, an ADS connection, and media types served through a CDN.

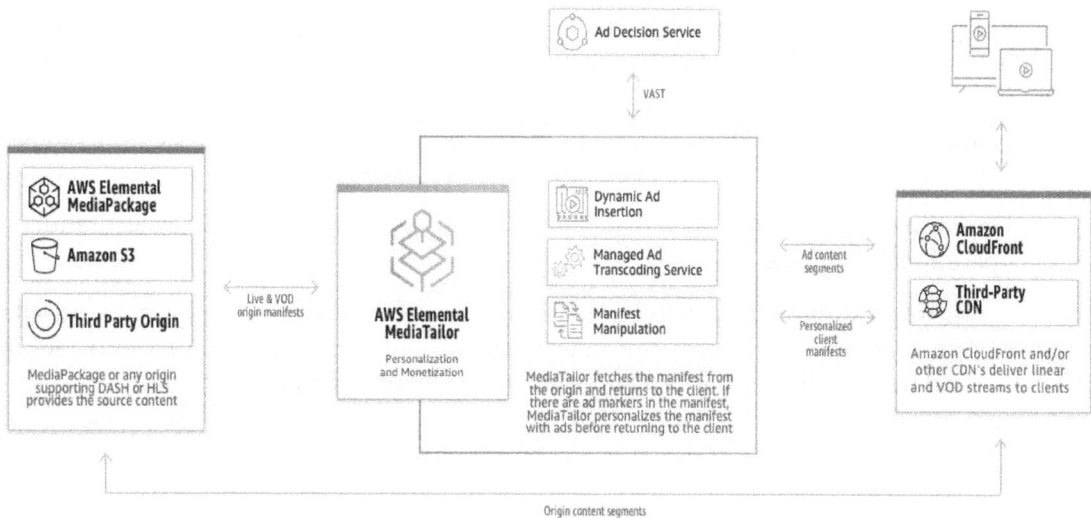

Figure 10.8: Configuring AWS Elemental MediaTailor

Wrap up

AWS Elemental MediaTailor revolutionizes the delivery of advertisements in the digital age. Its capabilities for server-side ad insertion and targeted ad delivery enable content providers to increase monetization, enhance viewer engagement, and improve ad campaign performance.

Amazon Managed Blockchain

Amazon Managed Blockchain (**AMB**) simplifies the creation and management of scalable blockchain networks. By utilizing this service, businesses can focus on developing innovative applications without the complexities of setting up manual blockchain infrastructure [62].

Key features

AMB provides a fully managed service that streamlines blockchain network deployment, enabling businesses to leverage the benefits of decentralized technology easily. With support for popular frameworks, built-in automation, and enterprise-grade security, organizations can build scalable blockchain applications without the complexity of managing the infrastructure, as discussed:

- **Scalable blockchain networks**: It supports frameworks like Hyperledger Fabric and Ethereum, enabling businesses to build secure, decentralized networks without requiring specialized skills.

- **Fully managed infrastructure**: Manages the setup, configuration, and maintenance of blockchain networks, allowing organizations to focus on application development [63].

- **Decentralized trust**: Helps transparent and tamper-resistant data sharing among network participants.

- **Operational efficiency**: Automates monitoring and maintenance tasks, reducing operational overhead.

Figure 10.9 illustrates how blockchain can enhance the security and transparency of digital identities. The diagram emphasizes the integration of AMB into applications that require immutable and decentralized data structures for secure identification systems [62].

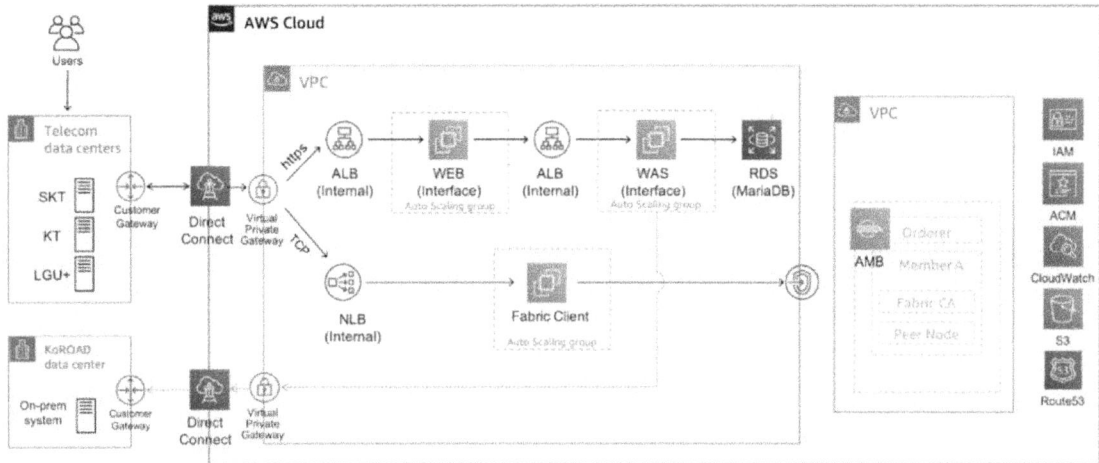

Figure 10.9: Digital ID using AMB

Use cases

AMB offers businesses a secure and scalable platform for building blockchain-powered solutions that enhance transparency, security, and efficiency, as discussed:

- **Supply chain management**: Enhances transparency and traceability across supply chains by securely recording every transaction and movement of goods.

- **Financial transactions**: Ensures secure, immutable transaction records for financial institutions, reducing risks and streamlining audits.

Best practices

To maximize the benefits of AMB, businesses should adopt best practices that ensure the best scalability, security, and efficiency, as follows:

- **Amazon Aurora and RDS**: Enables hybrid solutions by integrating blockchain networks with traditional databases for comprehensive application functionality.

- **Scalability**: Dynamically scales as participant numbers or transaction volumes increase, accommodating business growth.

- **Network planning**: Define members, policies, and permissions during network setup to ensure security and performance.

- **Compliance**: Leverage AWS tools for encryption and compliance monitoring to secure blockchain data and meet regulatory requirements.

Wrap up

AMB is a testament to AWS's commitment to providing accessible and scalable blockchain solutions. This service allows businesses to explore innovative applications across various industries by simplifying the complexities associated with blockchain infrastructure, promoting transparency, security, and efficiency.

Amazon Quantum Ledger Database

Amazon **Quantum Ledger Database** (**QLDB**) provides a fully managed ledger database that guarantees immutability and cryptographic verification of transaction logs. This centralized ledger solution ensures reliable and tamper-proof records for diverse business applications.

Key features

Amazon QLDB design aims to provide businesses with a transparent, immutable, and cryptographically verifiable ledger for tracking transactions. With high scalability, low-latency, and seamless AWS integration, QLDB ensures data integrity and trustworthiness for applications requiring secure record-keeping, as follows:

- **Cryptographic verifiability**: Ensures data integrity using cryptographic hash chains.
- **Scalable performance**: Delivers high-throughput and low-latency for large-scale applications.
- **Transparent and immutable**: Maintains a complete history of all data changes, ensuring an auditable and verifiable record.
- **Centralized ledger model**: Combines the integrity of blockchain with the performance of traditional databases [64].

Use cases

Amazon QLDB is ideal for applications that require a reliable and tamper-proof record of transactions, enhancing trust and transparency across industries, as follows:

- **Supply chain traceability**: Recording every step in the supply chain ensures transparency and reduces the risk of fraud.
- **Regulatory compliance**: Provides immutable logs for industries like healthcare and finance, aiding compliance and audit readiness.

Best practices

To fully leverage QLDB's capabilities, organizations should follow best practices that enhance security, efficiency, and performance, as follows:

- **Seamless AWS integration**: Works with IAM, KMS, and CloudTrail to enhance security, access control, and monitoring capabilities.
- **Flexibility and scalability**: It adapts to a variety of application needs, from transactional databases to complex integrity-reliant systems.
- **Efficient data modeling**: Enhance ledger structures to ensure fast and reliable query performance.
- **Security controls**: Implement fine-grained access permissions and regular monitoring to protect ledger integrity.

Wrap up

AMB and Amazon QLDB highlight AWS's commitment to delivering scalable and secure solutions for blockchain and ledger-based applications. By simplifying the complexities of blockchain infrastructure and ensuring the integrity of transactional records, these services enable businesses to innovate confidently and meet the demands of modern applications.

Conclusion

This chapter highlighted the transformative potential of AWS services, spanning business applications, economic management, media solutions, and blockchain technologies. Each service offers organizations the tools to innovate, enhance efficiency, and address the complexities of modern digital operations.

As we transition to *Chapter 11, Analytics and Machine Learning,* the focus shifts toward real-world implementation strategies and case studies. These examples demonstrate how the principles and services discussed thus far create robust, scalable, and impactful cloud-based solutions.

Join our Discord space

Join our Discord workspace for latest updates, offers, tech happenings around the world, new releases, and sessions with the authors:

https://discord.bpbonline.com

CHAPTER 11

Analytics and Machine Learning

Introduction

In the ever-evolving landscape of cloud computing, the integration of analytics and **machine learning (ML)** has appeared as a transformative force, empowering businesses to extract meaningful insights from vast datasets and deploy intelligent solutions. This chapter explores a range of AWS services serving analytics and ML needs, offering a comprehensive suite for data-driven decision-making and innovative **artificial intelligence (AI)** applications.

This chapter will guide you through the intricacies of each of these services, offering insights into their functionalities, use cases, and practical applications. From analytics to ML, AWS provides a comprehensive suite of tools that cater to businesses' diverse needs, enabling them to explore the scope of data-driven decision-making and AI.

Structure

This chapter will cover the following topics:

- Analytics
- Machine learning

Objectives

By the end of this chapter, you will have a solid understanding of the foundational and advanced concepts underlying AWS analytics and ML services and their contributions to modern cloud-native architectures. You will explore key analytics tools, including Amazon Athena, QuickSight, Redshift, and AWS Glue, gaining insight into their roles in data querying, visualization, warehousing, and **extract, transform, and load** (ETL) processes. You will also learn how AWS supports real-time data processing through services like Amazon Kinesis and **Managed Streaming for Apache Kafka** (**MSK**) and collaborative analytics with AWS Clean Rooms and Data Exchange. At the forefront of Rekognition and learning, you will examine the AWS ML lifecycle using tools such as Amazon SageMaker, Bedrock, and Rekognition, and discover how pre-built and customizable models can be used to automate tasks, drive intelligence, and enhance application functionality. The chapter also provides real-world use cases and architectural patterns, enabling you to design, deploy, and scale analytics and AI-driven applications across diverse industries.

Analytics

In the dynamic landscape of cloud computing, analytics plays a pivotal role in extracting meaningful insights from vast datasets. This section examines various AWS services designed for analytics, offering users powerful tools to process, analyze, and visualize data efficiently.

The architecture in *Figure 11.1* illustrates how various AWS services integrate to support a modern analytics workflow. It highlights how raw data from diverse sources is ingested, transformed, stored, and queried, showing the end-to-end journey from data collection to insight generation in a scalable and cloud-native environment.

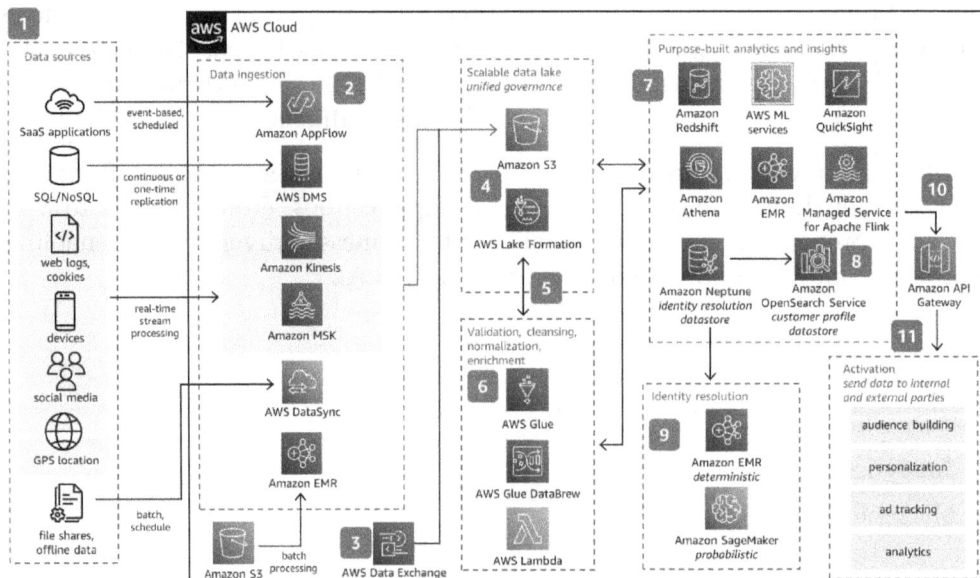

Figure 11.1: Example analytics architecture

Amazon Athena

Amazon Athena stands out as a serverless query service. It allows users to analyze data stored in Amazon S3 using SQL queries, enabling on-the-fly analysis without complex data transformations or managing infrastructure [1].

Amazon CloudSearch

Amazon CloudSearch is a fully managed search service designed to simplify the application implementation of search functionality. It offers fast, scalable, and full-text search capabilities, making it an asset for applications that require robust search functionality [2].

Amazon DataZone

Amazon DataZone offers a secure environment for data sharing and collaboration in life sciences. It aims to advance genomics and biomedical research by providing a safe space for researchers to collaborate on sensitive data [3].

Amazon Elastic MapReduce

Amazon **Elastic MapReduce (EMR)** is a cloud-based data processing platform that manages large datasets using popular frameworks, including Apache Spark and Apache Hadoop. EMR enables scalable and cost-effective data processing, making it a fundamental tool for big data analytics [4].

Hosted Hadoop framework

AWS offers a hosted Hadoop framework as part of its analytics services. This framework enables users to deploy and manage Hadoop clusters faultlessly, providing a scalable and reliable environment for distributed data processing [5].

Amazon FinSpace

Tailored for the financial industry, Amazon FinSpace streamlines data management, analytics, and collaboration. It addresses the unique challenges of financial data workflows and offers a comprehensive solution for financial analytics [6].

Amazon Kinesis

Amazon Kinesis is a suite of services that helps process streaming data in real-time at scale. It enables applications to ingest, buffer, and process streaming data easily, making it vital to real-time analytics scenarios [7].

Amazon Managed Stream for Apache Kafka

Amazon MSK is a fully managed Kafka service that simplifies the deployment, scaling, and management of Apache Kafka clusters. It provides a reliable and scalable platform for streaming data and supports various analytics and data processing applications [8].

Amazon OpenSearch Service

Amazon OpenSearch Service is a managed service for Elasticsearch that offers powerful search and analytics capabilities. It simplifies the deployment and operation of Elasticsearch clusters, making it easier for users to build scalable search applications [9].

Amazon QuickSight

Amazon QuickSight is a fast, cloud-powered business analytics service that enables users to create interactive dashboards and visualizations. QuickSight makes it easy to derive insights from data, enhancing the decision-making process [10].

Amazon Redshift

Amazon Redshift is a fully managed data warehouse service that is optimized for high-performance analysis. It allows users to run complex queries on large datasets, making it a cornerstone of data warehousing and analytics [11].

AWS Clean Rooms

In compliance with data privacy, AWS Clean Rooms offers a secure and isolated environment for analyzing sensitive data. It addresses the need for secure data processing in compliance with regulatory requirements [12].

AWS Data Exchange

AWS Data Exchange is a marketplace for discovering and subscribing to third-party datasets. It promotes data collaboration and accessibility, providing a platform for users to find and use valuable external data [13].

AWS Data Pipeline

AWS Data Pipeline is a web service that orchestrates and automates the movement and transformation of data between various AWS services. It simplifies the creation, scheduling, and management of data pipelines [14].

AWS Glue

AWS Glue is a fully managed ETL service that automates data preparation for analysis. It provides a serverless environment for running ETL jobs, making data integration more efficient [15].

Figure 11.2 illustrates the ingestion layer within a data architecture built on AWS Glue. It describes how source systems provide raw data to the analytics pipeline, highlighting Glue's role in orchestrating data extraction and transformation before it reaches storage or query layers. This foundational step enables precise, prompt, and scalable analytics.

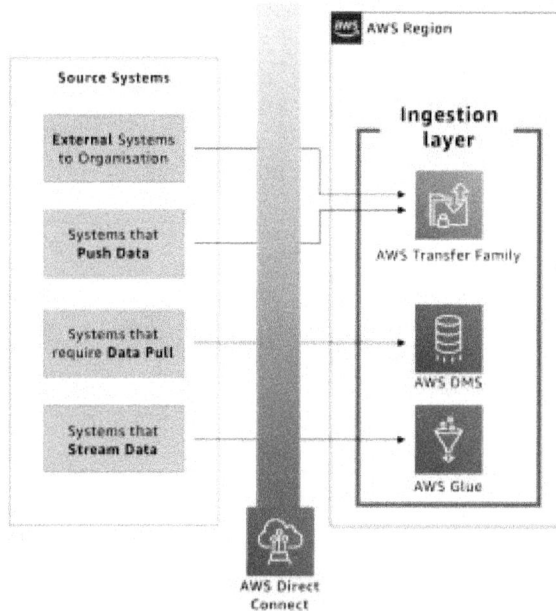

Figure 11.2: Ingestion layer against source systems

AWS Lake Formation

AWS Lake Formation plays a significant role in modern data lake architecture by simplifying the creation of secure, well-governed, and highly scalable data lakes. As enterprises generate increasingly large and diverse datasets, the need for unified data storage, access control, and governance becomes critical. Lake Formation addresses this challenge by automating the complex manual steps in setting up data lakes, such as ingesting data from multiple sources, cleaning and classifying data, defining access policies, and enabling secure analytics. It empowers organizations to move faster from raw data to actionable insights while ensuring compliance with internal and external data regulations.

Designed for building, securing, and managing data lakes, AWS Lake Formation streamlines the process of organizing and analyzing diverse datasets. It offers data ingestion, security, and access control tools in a data lake environment [16].

Figure 11.3 illustrates the governance and transformation layer within AWS Lake Formation architecture. It shows how raw data is cleansed, cataloged, secured, and made query-ready within the data lake, enabling controlled access and compliance across analytical workloads. This step ensures the data lake stays scalable and trustworthy for enterprise use.

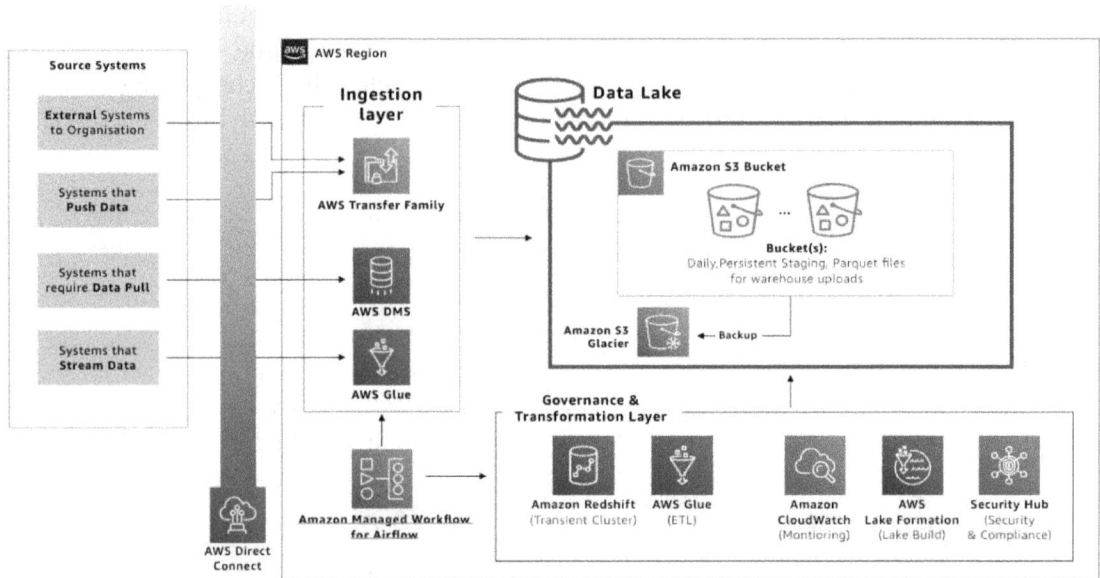

Figure 11.3: *The governance and transformation layer prepares data in the lake*

This section has provided an overview of AWS analytics services, highlighting the breadth and depth of tools available for processing, analyzing, and visualizing data. As we delve into the specifics of each service, you will gain a deeper understanding of how to use these tools for various analytics use cases.

In the expansive domain of ML, AWS offers a comprehensive suite of services satisfying diverse needs, from building custom models to seamlessly integrating pre-trained solutions.

Machine learning

In the AWS ecosystem, ML provides an end-to-end platform for designing, training, deploying, and managing intelligent applications. Whether users are building custom models or using pre-trained APIs, AWS offers scalable tools that support a wide range of use cases—from fraud detection and recommendation systems to **natural language processing** (**NLP**) and image recognition. The platform is designed to accommodate a range of skill levels, enabling data scientists, developers, and non-technical users to build and run ML workflows. With integrated support for frameworks like TensorFlow, PyTorch, and Apache MXNet and robust services like Amazon SageMaker, AWS accelerates the entire ML lifecycle, transforming raw data into actionable, real-world predictive insights.

Amazon augmented AI

Amazon **Augmented AI (A2I)** empowers developers to create custom ML workflows with human review. By integrating human intelligence into the model's decision-making process, A2I ensures the reliability and accuracy of ML predictions [17].

Figure 11.4 illustrates the core infrastructure and components of AWS's ML stack, highlighting the diverse services and tools that support scalable, secure, and production-ready ML workflows across various industries:

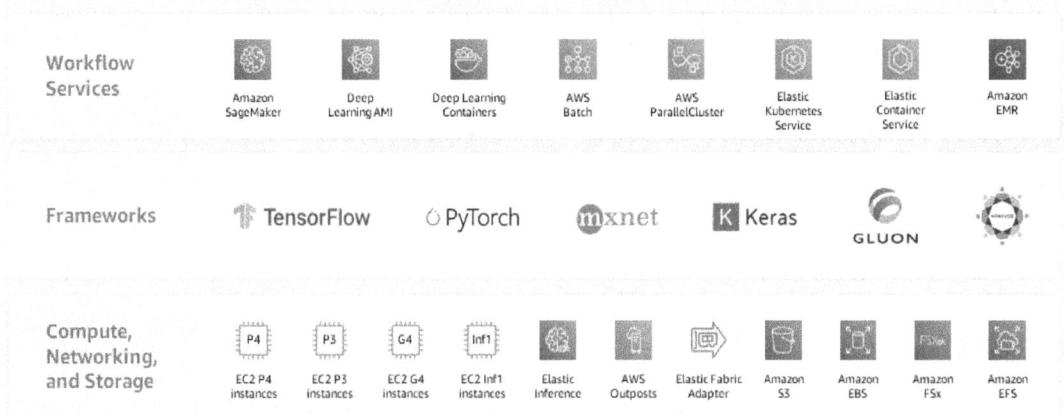

Figure 11.4: *AWS ML infrastructure*

Amazon Bedrock

Amazon Bedrock is a foundational service that simplifies the end-to-end ML process. Bedrock streamlines the lifecycle development from data preparation and model training to deployment, enabling efficient and scalable development of ML applications [18].

Amazon CodeGuru

Amazon CodeGuru enhances code quality by providing automated code reviews. This ML-powered service finds and recommends improvements in code, optimizing performance and reliability [19].

Amazon Comprehend

Amazon Comprehend facilitates NLP tasks by extracting insights and relationships from text. With support for multiple languages, understanding enables developers to build applications with advanced language understanding capabilities [20].

Amazon DevOps Guru

Amazon DevOps Guru leverages ML to find operational issues and anomalies. By analyzing operational data, it automates problem detection and offers actionable insights to enhance application reliability [21].

Amazon Elastic Inference

Amazon Elastic Inference complements ML instances with cost-effective inference acceleration. Elastic Inference improves deep learning inference by attaching low-cost GPU-powered inference acceleration to Amazon EC2 instances [22].

Deep learning inference acceleration

AWS offers deep learning inference acceleration to enhance the performance of ML models. This service includes purpose-built hardware solutions, such as AWS Inferentia, designed to deliver high-throughput and low-latency inference [23].

Amazon Forecast

Amazon Forecast is a fully managed forecasting service that uses ML to generate correct predictions. Forecast automates the forecasting process with minimal effort, whether for demand forecasting or financial planning [24].

Amazon Fraud Detector

Amazon Fraud Detectors use ML to detect and prevent online fraud. By analyzing historical data and building custom models, Fraud Detector enhances security measures to protect against fraudulent activities.[25].

Amazon HealthLake

Amazon HealthLake is a HIPAA-eligible service designed for healthcare providers to store, transform, and analyze health data securely. It uses ML for NLP, enabling structured data extraction from unstructured medical information [26].

Amazon Kendra

Amazon Kendra is an intelligent search service powered by ML. It enables organizations to build powerful search capabilities into their applications, making it easy for users to discover relevant information [27].

Amazon Lex

Amazon Lex streamlines the process of building conversational interfaces using natural language understanding. This service powers chatbots and **interactive voice response (IVR)** systems, enhancing user interactions through ML [28].

Amazon Lookout for Equipment

Amazon Lookout for Equipment uses ML to detect abnormal equipment behavior. Analyzing sensor data finds early signs of equipment failure, enabling preventive maintenance and minimizing downtime [29].

Amazon Lookout for Metrics

Amazon Lookout for Metrics is a service that uses ML to detect anomalies in metrics. It automates monitoring key performance indicators and provides prompt alerts for unusual patterns or deviations [30].

Amazon Monitron

Amazon Monitron offers an end-to-end solution for equipment monitoring. By combining sensors, a gateway, and ML algorithms, Monitron enables the prediction of equipment failures before they occur [31].

Amazon Omics

Amazon Omics is a comprehensive service for analyzing genomic data on a large scale. Leveraging ML enables researchers to derive meaningful insights from genomic information, advancing scientific discoveries in life sciences [32].

Amazon Personalize

Amazon Personalize is an ML service that helps create personalized user recommendations. Personalize fits product recommendations, content, and more by analyzing user behavior [33].

Amazon Polly

Amazon Polly transforms text into lifelike speech using ML. With support for multiple languages and various voices, Polly enables developers to add natural-sounding speech to applications [34].

Amazon Rekognition

Amazon Rekognition is a powerful image and video analysis service that uses ML. It can find objects, people, text, scenes, and activities, making it a valuable tool for content analysis and security applications [35].

Amazon SageMaker

Amazon SageMaker is a fully managed ML service that covers the end-to-end ML workflow. It simplifies model-building, training, and deployment, allowing developers to focus on creating robust ML applications [36].

Amazon SageMaker Ground Truth

Amazon SageMaker Ground Truth is a data labeling service that uses ML to reduce labeling costs and improve annotation accuracy. It streamlines the process of creating high-quality training datasets for ML [36].

Figure 11.5 shows the cross-validation process using Amazon SageMaker:

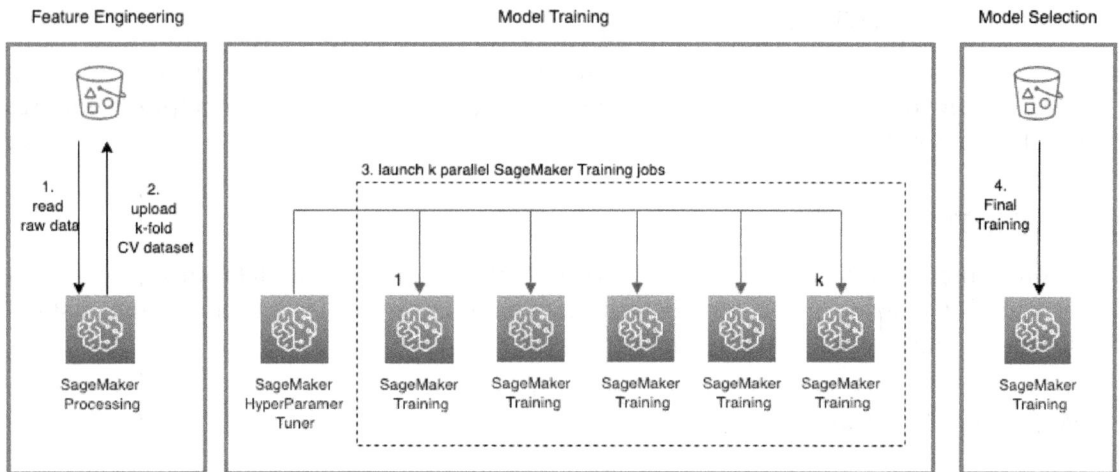

Figure 11.5: Cross-validation with Amazon SageMaker

Amazon Textract

Amazon Textract is a fully managed **Optical Character Recognition** (**OCR**) service powered by ML. It extracts text, forms, and tables from scanned documents, automating the data extraction [37].

Amazon Transcribe

Amazon Transcribe provides **automatic speech recognition** (**ASR**) services using ML. It converts spoken language into written text, enabling applications to transcribe audio content accurately and reliably [38].

Amazon Translate

Amazon Translate is a neural machine translation service that supports translating text between languages. Leveraging ML, translate provides correct and natural-sounding translations for various applications [39].

Apache MXNet on AWS

AWS supports Apache MXNet, an open-source deep learning framework. With AWS infrastructure, developers can use MXNet's scalability and flexibility to build and deploy ML models [40].

AWS Deep Learning AMIs

AWS offers Deep Learning **Amazon Machine Images** (**AMIs**), a collection of deep learning frameworks that simplify setting up a deep learning environment on EC2 instances.

AWS Deep Learning Containers

AWS Deep Learning Containers provide pre-configured Docker images for deep learning applications. These containers offer a consistent and reproducible environment for running ML workloads [23].

AWS DeepComposer

AWS DeepComposer is an ML enabled keyboard that allows developers to create music using generative AI models. It shows the creative possibilities of combining ML with music composition [41].

AWS DeepLens

AWS DeepLens is a deep learning-enabled video camera that helps develop computer vision applications. It offers a direct approach to learning and implementing deep learning models in real-world scenarios [42].

AWS DeepRacer

AWS DeepRacer is an autonomous 1/18th scale race car designed for reinforcement learning. Developers can use DeepRacer to enhance their understanding of ML concepts through an interactive, competitive racing environment [43].

AWS Inferentia

AWS Inferentia is a custom-built chip designed to accelerate deep learning inference workloads. With high-throughput and low-latency, Inferentia enhances the performance of ML models [44].

AWS Panorama

AWS Panorama is an ML appliance that brings computer vision capabilities to on-premises cameras. It enables the local analysis of video feeds, opening possibilities for applications in industrial automation and beyond [45].

PyTorch on AWS

AWS supports PyTorch, an open-source deep learning framework. With AWS infrastructure, developers can use PyTorch's flexibility and efficiency to build and deploy ML models [46].

TensorFlow on AWS

AWS provides robust support for TensorFlow, an open-source ML framework. Developers can harness AWS's scalability and power to build and train ML models using TensorFlow [47].

TensorFlow on AWS

Amazon CodeWhisperer is a service that uses ML to help developers write code more efficiently. Providing context-aware suggestions enhances the coding experience and accelerates development workflows [48]. Refer to the following figure:

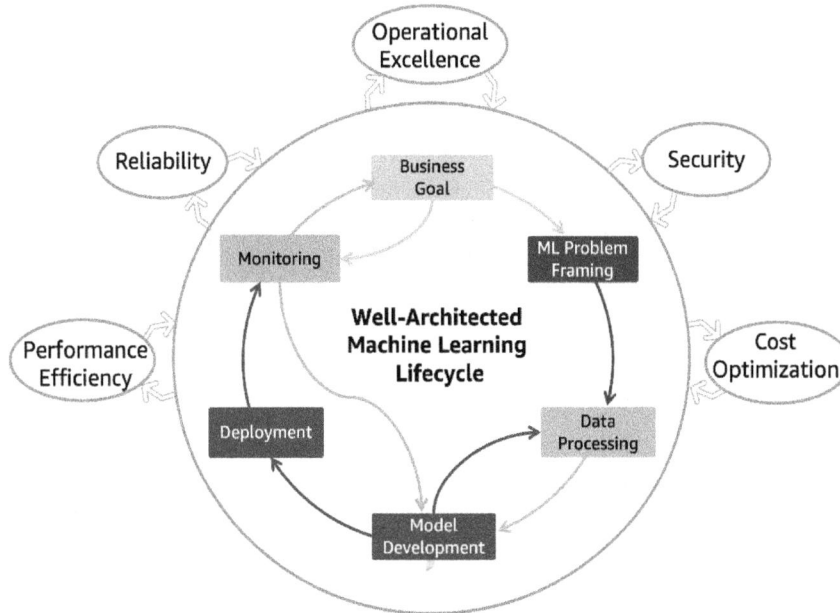

Figure 11.6: *AWS Well-Architected ML Lens*

Holistic vision

This chapter has delved into the multifaceted scopes of analytics and ML, unraveling a tapestry of AWS services designed to empower businesses with data-driven insights and intelligent automation. From the seamless query capabilities of Amazon Athena to the advanced ML models helped by Amazon SageMaker, this chapter explores the expansive landscape of AWS offerings in analytics and ML.

In the analytics domain, AWS offers a comprehensive suite of services tailored to the diverse needs of organizations managing vast datasets. Amazon Athena, a standout in this category, offers a serverless query service that enables on-the-fly analysis of data stored in Amazon S3 [1]. Complementing this, Amazon QuickSight helps with intuitive and interactive data visualization, empowering users to derive actionable insights from their analytics [10].

Amazon EMR is a stalwart in the evolving big data landscape. It offers a cloud-based platform for processing large datasets using popular frameworks such as Apache Spark and Apache Hadoop [8]. Simultaneously, Amazon Redshift is a powerful data warehousing solution, allowing organizations to analyze vast datasets quickly and efficiently [11].

As organizations grapple with data management challenges, AWS offers solutions such as AWS Glue and AWS Lake Formation, which streamline data integration, transformation, and data lake formation [15]. These services contribute to setting up a robust analytics foundation within AWS, fostering an environment where data becomes a strategic asset [16].

The second part—ML, delved into the dynamic landscape of ML, where AWS offers an extensive array of services to cater to the evolving needs of developers and data scientists. Amazon SageMaker is a cornerstone at the forefront, offering end-to-end ML workflow capabilities that simplify the model-building, training, and deployment processes [36].

Within the ML spectrum, specialized services such as Amazon Comprehend [20] Amazon Rekognition brings NLP and computer vision capabilities to the forefront [35]. These services empower developers to integrate ML into applications without requiring extensive technical ability.

Amazon Personalize takes center stage in recommendation engines and personalization, providing developers with tools to create individualized user experiences based on their behavior [33]. Simultaneously, services like Amazon Forecast use ML to generate right predictions, providing an asset for demand forecasting and financial planning businesses [24].

As the chapter unfolds, it becomes clear that AWS is not merely providing tools but fostering an ecosystem where ML becomes an accessible and integral part of the development process. The array of services, including deep learning inference acceleration, supports developers in improving the performance of their ML models [49].

Conclusion

In conclusion, this chapter encapsulates AWS's holistic vision of democratizing analytics and ML. The seamless integration of services, spanning from the granular analytics of Amazon Athena to the intricate ML models of Amazon SageMaker, reflects a commitment to simplifying complex processes and empowering users across the spectrum of technical ability.

The journey through analytics and ML within AWS shines innovation, efficiency, and scalability. AWS's commitment to customer-centric solutions is clear in the diverse range of services that cater to the unique needs of businesses, regardless of their size or industry. As organizations navigate the data-intensive landscape, the tools and services explored in this chapter become beacons, guiding them toward a future where data is not just a resource but a strategic advantage. In the next chapter, the focus will shift towards the understanding of AWS services that underpin networking, IoT, and satellite communication within cloud environments.

Join our Discord space

Join our Discord workspace for latest updates, offers, tech happenings around the world, new releases, and sessions with the authors:

https://discord.bpbonline.com

CHAPTER 12

Management and Governance

Introduction

Managing cloud environments requires robust governance and meticulous oversight to ensure optimal performance, security, and scalability. AWS services are designed for management and governance. From real-time monitoring with Amazon CloudWatch to infrastructure orchestration through AWS CloudFormation, this chapter covers foundational tools that equip organizations with control and operational efficiency within AWS.

Structure

This chapter will cover the following topics:

- Amazon CloudWatch overview
- AWS Personal Health Dashboard
- AWS Proton
- AWS Resilience Hub
- AWS Service Catalog
- AWS Trusted Advisor

Objectives

This chapter aims to provide readers with a comprehensive understanding of AWS services that underpin networking, IoT, and satellite communication within cloud environments. Readers will explore how Amazon VPC facilitates secure, isolated cloud networks, and how tools like AWS Direct Connect, Global Accelerator, and Transit Gateway extend and optimize network performance across hybrid and Global Infrastructure. The chapter introduces service meshes and discovery mechanisms such as AWS App Mesh and Cloud Map, illustrating how microservices can communicate securely and efficiently at scale. In the IoT domain, the chapter equips readers to understand the architectural and operational roles of AWS IoT Core, Greengrass, SiteWise, FleetWise, TwinMaker, and Device Defender—each contributing to scalable, secure, and real-time device interaction. Emphasis is placed on lifecycle management, deployment strategies, and analytics through services like AWS IoT Device Management, IoT 1-Click, and IoT Analytics. Additional focus is given to education and event-driven architecture via AWS IoT EduKit and AWS IoT Events, offering practical insights into adoption, automation, and prototyping. Finally, the chapter introduces AWS Ground Station as a modern interface for satellite data acquisition, integrating orbital systems into cloud-native workflows. By the end of this chapter, readers will understand how AWS services support advanced connectivity, edge intelligence, and distributed systems, positioning these technologies within broader enterprise and research contexts.

Amazon CloudWatch overview

Amazon CloudWatch is a central monitoring service within AWS that enables real-time collection, analysis, and response to operational data. It helps businesses gain insights into their AWS infrastructure, improve performance, and address issues proactively.

Core functionality

CloudWatch provides a platform to track AWS resources, applications, and services. Users can collect metrics, access logs, and setup alarms, gaining real-time visibility into resource utilization and operational health.

Key features and use cases

CloudWatch monitors key AWS components, including EC2 instances, Auto Scaling groups, and **Elastic Load Balancing** (**ELBs**). It helps businesses optimize performance, manage costs, and enhance operational efficiency.

Deployment strategies

Businesses should use structured deployment strategies to maximize CloudWatch's potential. This includes setting up custom dashboards, configuring alarms, utilizing CloudWatch Logs for troubleshooting, and optimizing overall monitoring and operations.

The accompanying diagram illustrates the flow of metrics and logs from AWS resources to Amazon CloudWatch, highlighting its role in real-time monitoring and alerting.

The following figure illustrates how metrics and logs flow from various AWS resources to Amazon CloudWatch, emphasizing its role in real-time monitoring, alerting, and visualization:

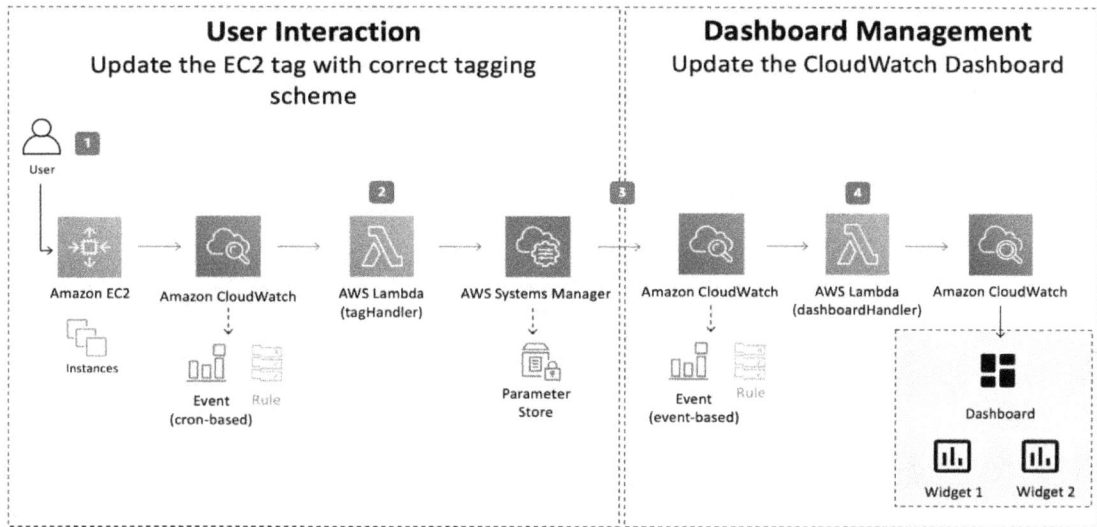

Figure 12.1: *Architecture of a typical monitoring setup using Amazon CloudWatch*

Amazon Managed Grafana

Amazon Managed Grafana offers a centralized platform for visualizing operational data, making it easier for organizations to manage and analyze cloud resources. This fully managed service streamlines deployment, scales effortlessly, and reduces operational overhead. IT teams use it to create interactive dashboards that deliver actionable insights.

Security and compliance

Amazon Managed Grafana prioritizes security. It includes features like encryption, access controls, and AWS **Identity and Access Management (IAM)** integration, so organizations can deploy it confidently while adhering to compliance standards.

Deployment strategies

Organizations can improve Amazon Managed Grafana by implementing structured deployment strategies. Best practices include configuring data sources, designing effective dashboards, and optimizing performance to enhance visibility and inform decision-making.

The following figure shows the seamless integration of Amazon Managed Grafana with various AWS data sources, emphasizing its role in creating customizable dashboards for data visualization and analytics:

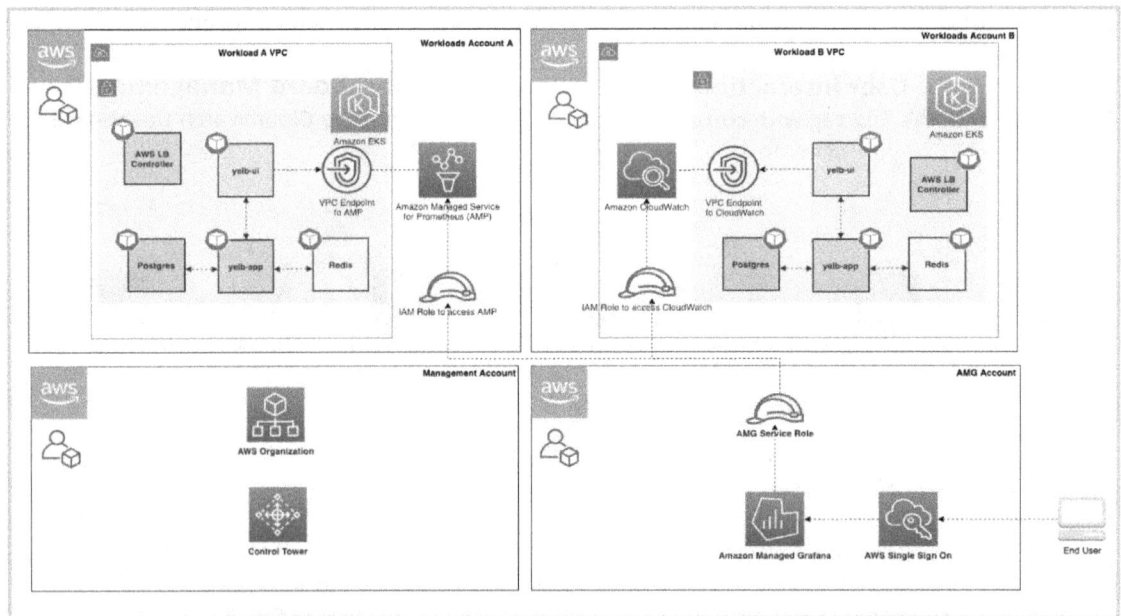

Figure 12.2: Typical deployment architecture of Amazon Managed Grafana

Amazon Managed Service for Prometheus

Amazon Managed Service for Prometheus (**AMP**) offers a scalable monitoring solution for cloud environments. As businesses adopt cloud technologies, efficient monitoring and alerting tools are essential for maintaining stability. AMP simplifies Prometheus deployment, providing real-time observability for AWS infrastructure.

Key capabilities and integration

AMP facilitates easy metric collection and analysis, integrating with AWS services like Amazon CloudWatch and Amazon Managed Grafana. It helps monitor system performance, ensuring high availability and optimal resource use.

Applications and best practices

AMP supports various use cases, including application performance monitoring, resource optimization, and compliance tracking. AWS Documentation and Whitepapers, such as *Enhance Observability with Amazon Managed Service for Prometheus*, offer best practices for maximizing AMP's capabilities.

Business benefits

AMP enhances operational efficiency by facilitating the rapid detection and resolution of issues. With real-time insights, IT teams can reduce risks, minimize downtime, and align monitoring with the industry's best practices.

The following illustration provides a visual overview of the key components and interactions within the AMP ecosystem, highlighting its seamless integration with AWS resources, applications, and the Prometheus toolkit for enhanced cloud observability:

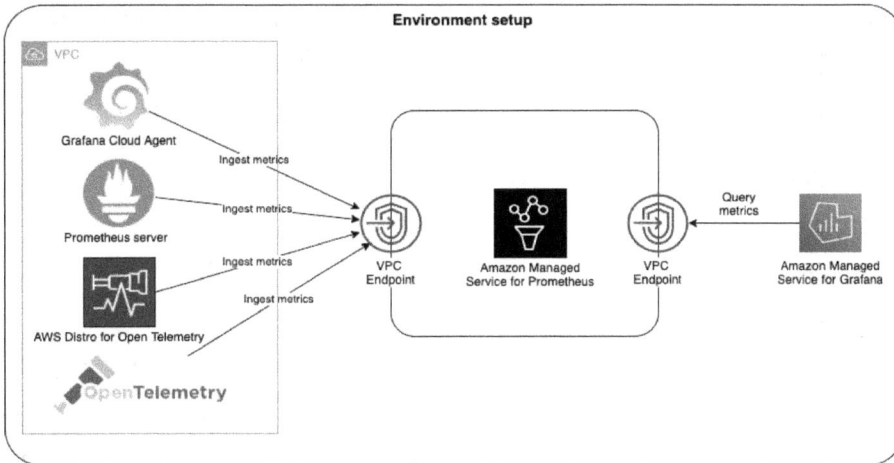

Figure 12.3: AMP ecosystem

AWS Chatbot

Effective communication is crucial for cloud governance. AWS Chatbot enhances operational awareness and response by integrating with collaboration platforms. It allows teams to receive real-time alerts, execute commands, and manage AWS resources directly in chat tools like Slack and Amazon Chime.

Figure 12.4 shows AWS Chatbot integration. This illustration highlights the role of AWS Chatbot. In managing cloud alerts and executing AWS commands through chat-based interfaces.

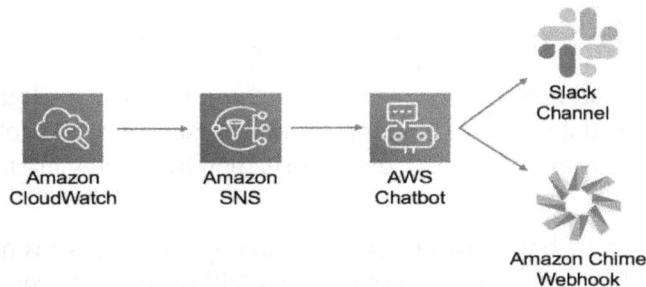

Figure 12.4: AWS Chatbot in action

Use cases and best practices

Integrating AWS Chatbot with Amazon CloudWatch automates alert delivery and system notifications. For more strategies on optimizing AWS Chatbot, refer to the whitepaper, *Effective Cloud Management with AWS Chatbot*.

Business impact and future adoption

AWS Chatbot centralizes AWS notifications in workplace chat apps, improving team collaboration and operational efficiency. It enhances cloud management workflows by providing real-time alerts and enabling command execution.

The following figure illustrates how AWS Chatbot integrates into messaging platforms to enhance real-time communication, simplify cloud operations, and empower teams to manage AWS resources collaboratively and efficiently:

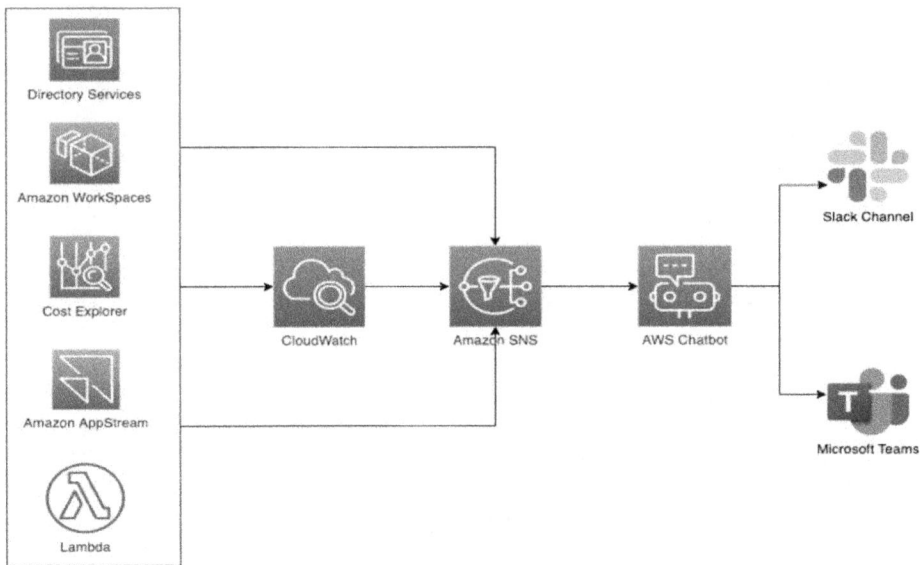

Figure 12.5: AWS Chatbot in action

AWS services for cloud management

AWS offers various cloud management services, including Amazon CloudWatch monitoring and AWS Chatbot for collaboration. These tools enable organizations to optimize performance, enhance security, and ensure regulatory compliance, thereby gaining greater control over their AWS environments.

In summary, the AWS Chatbot is crucial for cloud management. It is a central communication hub that enhances collaboration and responsiveness within AWS environments.

ChatOps for AWS

ChatOps integrates communication tools with AWS services, enabling teams to collaborate, execute commands, and receive real-time alerts.

Key features and integration

By using AWS Chatbot with tools like Slack and Amazon Chime, ChatOps enables automated responses and command execution. Incorporating AWS Lambda into these workflows automates routine tasks, increasing efficiency in managing AWS resources.

Business impact

Adopting ChatOps streamlines communication and task execution, leading to faster response times and improved operational efficiency. This supports the goal of a more collaborative cloud management environment.

In conclusion, ChatOps represents a transformative approach to integrating communication and operations within AWS environments. Organizations can foster collaboration, streamline workflows, and elevate cloud resource management efficiency by seamlessly incorporating chat platforms and AWS services. Embracing ChatOps represents a strategic move towards achieving a more agile, responsive, and collaborative cloud management paradigm.

Figure 12.6 showcases a practical example of ChatOps using Amazon Lex integrated with AWS Control Tower, highlighting how conversational interfaces can automate complex provisioning tasks in multi-account environments:

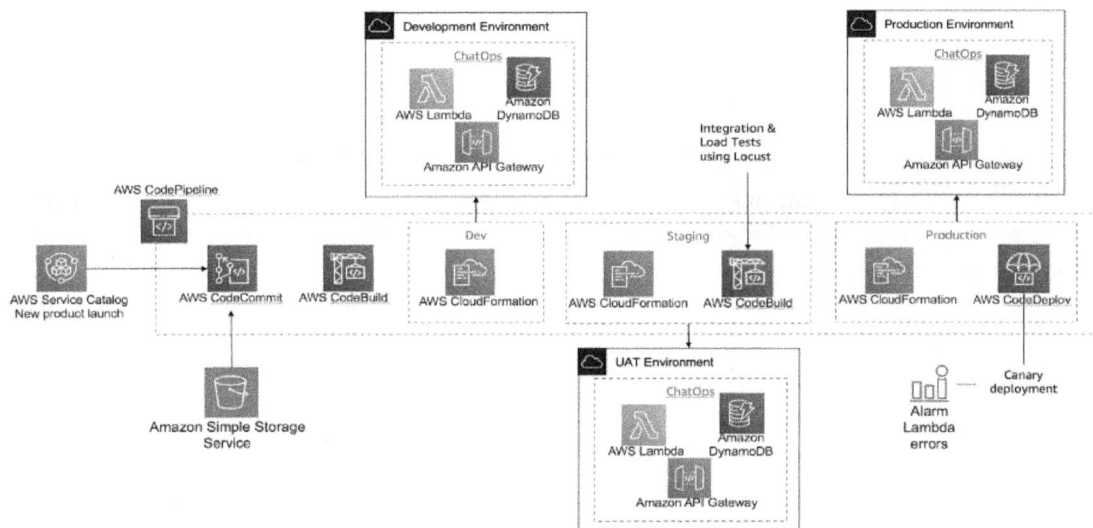

Figure 12.6: *AWS ChatOps in action*

Applications

Businesses that leverage ChatOps report benefits such as quicker incident response, faster troubleshooting, reduced downtime, and improved team collaboration.

ChatOps effectively merges communication and operations in AWS environments, streamlining workflows and enhancing cloud resource management. Embracing this approach leads to a more agile and responsive cloud management strategy.

AWS CloudFormation

AWS CloudFormation helps organizations manage **infrastructure as code (IaC)** by automating the provisioning and management of AWS resources. Users define infrastructure using declarative templates, which ensures consistency and scalability. Key concepts include stacks, templates, and change sets to automate deployments and reduce manual work.

Best practices

AWS Documentation provides thorough guidance on implementing CloudFormation. *Mitch Tulloch's* book *AWS CloudFormation: Getting Started Guide* offers template design strategies and advanced use cases, making it valuable for beginners and experienced users. Exploring AWS Documentation for real-world examples, reference architectures, and case studies enhance understanding and showcases the effective use of CloudFormation.

Business advantages

CloudFormation streamlines deployment processes, maintains infrastructure consistency, and reduces configuration drift. Automating infrastructure provisioning aligns with efficiency, cost control, and agility business goals. Adopting CloudFormation leads to improved resource governance, enhanced cost management, and a faster time-to-market for applications.

The following diagram outlines the standard AWS CloudFormation process, demonstrating how templates, modules, and StackSets automate and share infrastructure deployments across accounts and regions:

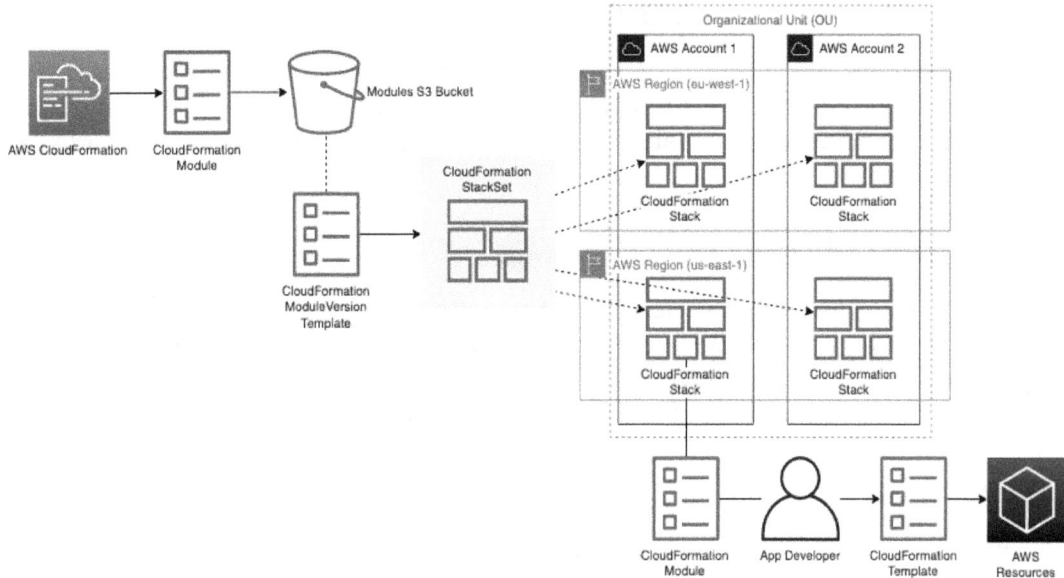

Figure 12.7: *AWS CloudFormation*

Use cases

AWS offers reference architecture and sample templates demonstrating CloudFormation's capabilities across various industries. These resources support organizations in implementing scalable and secure cloud deployments.

In conclusion, AWS CloudFormation is crucial for managing IaC in AWS. It equips users with the knowledge to utilize CloudFormation effectively, highlighting its foundations, validation, examples, and business benefits.

AWS CloudTrail

AWS CloudTrail provides capabilities for tracking activity, monitoring security, and ensuring compliance in AWS environments. It logs and analyzes API calls, helping organizations detect anomalies, investigate security events, and maintain an audit trail of resource interactions.

Key features

CloudTrail records API activity and changes to AWS resources, storing logs in Amazon S3 for analysis. To ensure accuracy, it supports multi-region logging, data event tracking, and log file validation. This detailed logging is essential for enhancing security and compliance.

Integration with AWS services

CloudTrail integrates seamlessly with other AWS services to improve governance. It pairs with Amazon CloudWatch for real-time alerts, AWS Security Hub for security insights, and AWS Lambda for automated anomaly responses, creating a comprehensive monitoring and response ecosystem.

Deployment strategies

Organizations should configure CloudTrail for optimal security monitoring, compliance tracking, and forensic analysis. Best practices involve enabling multi-region trails, integrating with Amazon CloudWatch, and encrypting logs with AWS **Key Management Service (KMS)**. Regular log reviews help identify unauthorized access attempts.

Use cases for AWS CloudTrail

AWS CloudTrail is utilized for security incident response, regulatory compliance tracking, and operational troubleshooting. It enables organizations to monitor changes, ensure accountability, and maintain an auditable history of actions within AWS environments. The diagram illustrates how AWS CloudTrail captures events from AWS services and securely stores them in Amazon S3.

AWS CloudTrail is valuable for security analysis, tracking resource changes, and compliance auditing. It tracks API calls, logs resource changes, and delivers logs to Amazon S3. These logs are critical for demonstrating compliance with regulations. Additionally, CloudTrail helps organizations identify and respond to security incidents. It can be configured to meet specific security and compliance needs, fostering a robust governance framework.

AWS Command Line Interface

The AWS **Command Line Interface (CLI)** is a unified tool for interacting with various AWS services from the command line. It provides administrators and developers with efficient access to AWS services, supports automated infrastructure management, and streamlines operational workflows. The CLI is designed to offer a consistent experience across multiple AWS services, which reduces users' learning curve.

Key features

AWS CLI offers a unified interface for command line interactions with AWS services. It simplifies tasks like launching EC2 instances, configuring Amazon S3 buckets, and managing AWS Lambda functions. CLI supports profile-based authentication, automation through scripting, and integration with AWS SDKs.

Integration with AWS services

The AWS CLI integrates with AWS CloudFormation, Amazon S3, and AWS Systems Manager, enabling effective infrastructure management, automated deployments, and command execution across multiple environments. It also interacts with Amazon DynamoDB, AWS CloudFormation, and AWS IAM.

Deployment strategies

Organizations should configure the AWS CLI with credential profiles, automate repetitive tasks through shell scripts, and enforce security best practices with IAM policies. Using AWS CLI alongside IaC tools like AWS CloudFormation enhances automation and consistency.

Use cases

Organizations use the AWS CLI for infrastructure provisioning, automated backups, security audits, and continuous deployment pipelines. It enables engineers to streamline cloud management tasks, reducing manual efforts and enhancing operational efficiency.

AWS Compute Optimizer

AWS Compute Optimizer analyzes cloud workloads and provides recommendations for optimizing compute resources, enhancing cost efficiency, and improving performance. Resource optimization is essential for operational efficiency and cost-effectiveness in cloud management. AWS Compute Optimizer provides critical insights and recommendations for optimizing compute resources.

Key features

This **machine learning (ML)** powered service evaluates EC2 instances, Auto Scaling groups, and AWS Lambda functions to recommend optimal configurations. Recommendations focus on reducing over-provisioning, improving resource utilization, and achieving an optimal balance between performance and cost. By analyzing resource usage patterns, the Compute Optimizer identifies opportunities for improvement, enabling users to balance performance and cost effectively.

Integration with AWS services

AWS Compute Optimizer integrates with Amazon CloudWatch to monitor resource utilization and AWS Cost Explorer to analyze costs, helping organizations align performance optimization with financial efficiency.

Deployment strategies

Organizations should regularly review Compute Optimizer recommendations to adjust instance sizes, modify Auto Scaling policies, and optimize workloads. Integrating Compute Optimizer with Amazon CloudWatch enables teams to gain insights into resource performance, facilitating informed decisions about scaling resources.

Use cases

AWS Compute Optimizer has everyday use cases, including optimizing EC2 workloads, reducing cloud spending through instance rightsizing, and improving application performance. It helps organizations enhance resource efficiency by aligning compute resources with actual demand, empowering informed decisions on resizing and changing instances.

AWS Config

AWS Config provides continuous oversight of resource configurations, ensuring compliance and security in cloud infrastructure. This fully managed service tracks change, evaluates compliance, and automates corrective actions to maintain governance.

Key features

AWS Config continuously records configuration changes, offers an inventory of AWS resources, and enables automated compliance checks through AWS Config Rules, ensuring organizations adhere to best practices and regulations.

Integration with AWS services

AWS Config integrates with AWS CloudTrail for auditing, AWS Security Hub for centralized security management, and AWS Lambda for automated remediation of non-compliant resources. This integration facilitates effective governance by linking configuration monitoring with security controls.

Deployment strategies

Organizations should define custom AWS Config Rules, enable periodic compliance assessments, and integrate with AWS Systems Manager for operational control. Automating remediation with AWS Lambda ensures real-time policy enforcement.

Use cases

AWS Config is commonly used for security compliance audits, troubleshooting misconfigurations, and monitoring infrastructure drift. It helps organizations maintain control over resource configurations and quickly remediate non-compliance, enhancing security and governance.

AWS Control Tower

AWS Control Tower simplifies the management of multiple AWS accounts by providing a centralized service that automates account setup, enforces policies, and ensures compliance.

Key features

It offers an automated landing zone for multi-account setups, **service control policies** (**SCPs**) for enforcing security guidelines, and pre-configured guardrails for compliance management.

Integration with AWS services

AWS Control Tower integrates with AWS Organizations for central governance, AWS **Single Sign-On** (**SSO**) for user authentication, and AWS Security Hub for security compliance monitoring.

Deployment strategies

Leverage the Account Factory to automate new account creation, customize SCPs to fit internal policies, and integrate tools like AWS Config for ongoing compliance validation, enhancing overall governance.

Use cases

AWS Control Tower helps organizations manage complex multi-account environments by ensuring centralized compliance, enforcing security, and streamlining account provisioning. It enables scaling operations while maintaining regulatory alignment and best security practices.

Business implications

Deploying AWS Control Tower improves governance, enhances security, and boosts operational efficiency. Its centralized management reduces complexity, allowing organizations to focus on innovation and growth.

AWS Distro for OpenTelemetry

AWS Distro for OpenTelemetry (**ADOT**) is crucial for gaining visibility into the performance of distributed systems. It standardizes observability data collection, providing real-time insights into application behavior and infrastructure performance.

ADOT is an open-source version of the OpenTelemetry project, designed for cloud-native environments. It generates, collects, and correlates traces and metrics, offering insights into application interactions.

Key features

ADOT supports application tracing and metric collection across various programming languages and integrates with OpenTelemetry SDKs. The OpenTelemetry Collector aggregates, processes, and forwards telemetry data.

Integration with AWS services

ADOT integrates with AWS X-Ray for distributed tracing, Amazon CloudWatch for metrics, and AWS Lambda for serverless monitoring. This unified solution enhances performance diagnostics and troubleshooting, giving businesses comprehensive insights into their AWS workloads.

Deployment strategies

Organizations should use ADOT with existing monitoring frameworks to track distributed transactions and identify latency issues. Establishing clear observability goals and optimizing tracing configurations will enhance effectiveness.

Common use cases

Typical use cases for ADOT include application performance monitoring, real-time analytics for microservices, and improved DevOps workflows. By adopting OpenTelemetry, organizations can monitor request flows, detect anomalies, and proactively resolve issues to improve user experience.

Business implications

Implementing ADOT enhances observability and decision-making. Detailed performance insights enable organizations to address issues proactively, optimize resource usage, and improve user experience.

ADOT standardizes observability practices across applications and services. Adopting open standards ensures compatibility with other tools, simplifying the management of distributed systems.

AWS Launch Wizard

AWS Launch Wizard simplifies and automates application deployment on AWS, ensuring adherence to best practices for security, performance, and cost efficiency. It streamlines infrastructure provisioning, making it essential for effective cloud operations.

AWS Launch Wizard delivers a structured and automated approach to deploying complex enterprise applications in the cloud. The following key features highlight how it supports consistent, scalable, and secure infrastructure provisioning aligned with AWS architectural best practices.

Key features

The key features are as follows:

- **Guided workflows**: Offers workflows for deploying Microsoft SQL Server, SAP, and other enterprise applications.
- **Automation**: Automates infrastructure sizing, configuration, and provisioning to reduce complexity and optimize deployments.

Integration with AWS services

Integrates with AWS CloudFormation for customization, AWS Systems Manager for operational management, and AWS IAM for **role-based access control (RBAC)**. This integration establishes a comprehensive strategy for managing an efficient application infrastructure.

Deployment strategies

Organizations should use AWS Launch Wizard for structured deployments. Custom deployment parameters can align with security policies, and monitoring solutions can further enhance outcomes.

Use cases

AWS Launch Wizard is ideal for deploying database-driven applications and SAP environments. It accelerates rollout while ensuring scalability, resilience, and compliance.

Business implications

Adopting the AWS Launch Wizard results in significant time and resource savings. Automation minimizes deployment errors, accelerates time-to-market, and enables IT teams to focus on strategic initiatives.

AWS CloudTrail

AWS CloudTrail provides essential logging and monitoring for AWS accounts, improving governance and compliance.

Overview

CloudTrail records AWS API calls, capturing key information like the caller's identity, timestamps, and request parameters. This functionality supports operational and risk auditing for AWS accounts.

Key features

CloudTrail offers a comprehensive view of account activity, recording resource changes and identifying who made changes and when.

Integration with AWS services

Integrates with Amazon S3 and AWS CloudWatch for secure log storage and alerts based on specific events. This integration enhances monitoring and accountability within AWS environments.

Security and compliance

AWS CloudTrail enhances security and ensures compliance by detecting unusual activity, aiding troubleshooting, and meeting regulatory requirements. It records API calls, which helps trace actions in an AWS environment.

Business implications

Adopting AWS CloudTrail increases transparency, accountability, and security for organizations. CloudTrail logs benefit forensic analysis, compliance reporting, and auditing, providing a more secure AWS environment that aligns with industry best practices.

Further reading

Refer to the official AWS Documentation for a deeper understanding of AWS CloudTrail. Internal references offer technical insights, while external sources, such as case studies, provide real-world examples of security implementations utilizing AWS CloudTrail.

AWS CloudTrail event flow

Figure 12.8 depicts how AWS CloudTrail captures and delivers logs of API activity across AWS services, storing them securely in Amazon S3 for auditing, compliance, and monitoring purposes:

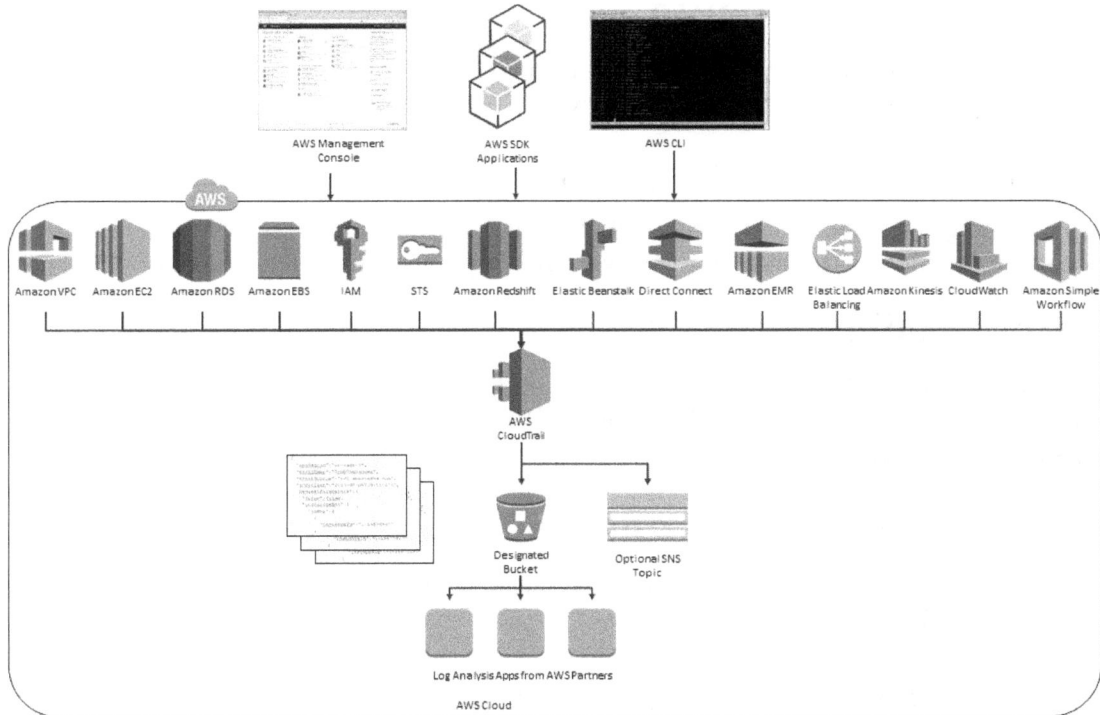

Figure 12.8: AWS CloudTrail diagram

AWS Managed Services

AWS Managed Services (**AMS**) simplifies and streamlines cloud operations for users by offloading daily management tasks. This allows organizations to focus on innovation. AMS supports a wide range of AWS services, providing a holistic management solution.

Key features

AMS automates operational tasks, including change requests, monitoring, patch management, and backup services. It includes components such as the Control Tower and landing zones, which enhance understanding of its architecture.

Integration with AWS services

AMS integrates seamlessly with various AWS services, including AWS Organizations, AWS Config, and AWS CloudTrail, improving governance, security, and compliance.

Security and compliance

AMS prioritizes security and compliance through automated security practices, regular patching, and adherence to the AWS Well-Architected Framework.

Business implications

Implementing AMS improves operational efficiency, scalability, and governance. It shifts the focus from routine tasks to strategic initiatives, enhancing business agility and competitiveness.

Further reading

Consult the official AWS Documentation to understand AMS comprehensively. Internal references offer technical insights, while external sources provide perspectives on successful AMS implementations.

AWS Management Console Mobile Application

The AWS Management Console Mobile Application allows users to manage their AWS resources anywhere.

Overview and core functionalities

This Console Mobile Application extends the AWS Management Console experience to devices, enabling users to monitor resource health, respond to alarms, and access critical operational metrics.

Key features and interface

The AWS Management Console Mobile Application provides an intuitive interface for viewing and interacting with AWS resources. Key features include real-time status monitoring, easy resource navigation, and command execution, offering a clear understanding of the application's capabilities.

Security considerations

Security is crucial for mobile usage. This section covers the security measures in the AWS Management Console Mobile Application, such as **multi-factor authentication** (**MFA**), data encryption in transit, and best practices for securing AWS resource access on mobile devices.

Practical benefits and use cases

The mobile application provides significant benefits for users who need to access AWS resources on the go. Real-world use cases demonstrate how it enhances operational efficiency, accelerates issue resolution, and facilitates prompt decision-making.

Integration with AWS services

The application integrates seamlessly with various AWS services. Users can interact with services such as Amazon EC2, Amazon S3, and AWS Lambda through the app, enhancing their overall management experience.

Business implications

From a business perspective, the AWS Management Console Mobile Application boosts operational agility and responsiveness. It helps AWS users stay connected and manage resources effectively, even when they are away from their desks.

Further reading

Readers are encouraged to explore the AWS Documentation and user testimonials to gain more insights into the AWS Management Console Mobile Application's usability and benefits.

AWS OpsWorks

AWS OpsWorks simplifies the deployment and management of cloud applications. This section outlines the features, benefits, and practical aspects of using AWS OpsWorks.

Overview and core functionality

AWS OpsWorks automates code deployment, infrastructure configuration, and application lifecycle management. It allows users to define application architecture and deploy across multiple instances efficiently.

Key features and components

Gain insights into AWS OpsWorks' key features, including stacks, layers, and instances, which enable the creation of scalable and maintainable application architectures.

Deployment strategies and flexibility

Explore various deployment strategies AWS OpsWorks supports, such as time-based and load-based deployments. OpsWorks also offers flexibility with custom Chef and Puppet recipes for application customization.

Integration with other AWS services

OpsWorks integrates smoothly with other AWS services, enhancing their functionality. This section explains how it integrates with Amazon **Relational Database Service (RDS)**, ELB, and Auto Scaling services.

Security considerations

Security is vital in application management. This section addresses AWS OpsWorks' security features, including IAM integration, encryption, and securing sensitive information.

Practical benefits and use cases

Explore the practical benefits and use cases of AWS OpsWorks, from automating tasks to managing complex applications, highlighting their efficiency and scalability.

Business implications

Utilizing AWS OpsWorks increases operational efficiency, cost savings, and enhanced reliability. This section discusses how it aligns with business objectives for consistent application deployment.

Further reading

For deeper insights into AWS OpsWorks, readers are encouraged to consult AWS resources and documentation.

AWS Organizations

AWS Organizations is a foundation service in cloud management and governance, providing a comprehensive framework for structuring and managing the AWS environment. This section explores AWS Organizations' features, benefits, and strategic considerations for efficient resource management in cloud infrastructures.

Overview and core functionality

AWS Organizations simplifies the complexity of managing multiple AWS accounts within an organization [1]. This section provides an in-depth overview of how organizations offer a hierarchical and scalable structure, enabling administrators to manage permissions, apply policies, and combine billing across accounts.

Key features and components

Readers will gain insights into the key features of AWS Organizations, including the **organizational units (OUs)**, SCPs, and the primary account. Understanding these components is crucial for designing an organizational structure that aligns with business needs and regulatory requirements.

Policy-based management

This section examines how AWS Organizations facilitates policy-based management through SCPs. Readers will understand how SCPs help enforce security and compliance standards across the organization, ensuring consistent and controlled resource deployment.

Consolidated billing and cost allocation

AWS Organizations simplifies billing and cost allocation by combining charges across all linked accounts. This section outlines the benefits of combined billing and explains how organizations can utilize this feature to gain insights into cost distribution and optimize resource allocation.

Strategic considerations for implementation

Strategic considerations are crucial for the successful implementation of AWS Organizations. This section provides practical guidance on structuring OUs, defining SCPs, and aligning the organizational hierarchy with business units, thereby enhancing the agility and efficiency of resource management.

Integration with other AWS services

AWS Organizations seamlessly integrates with other AWS services, enhancing its capabilities. This section explores how AWS Organizations can be integrated with AWS IAM, AWS SSO, and other services to create a unified and secure cloud environment.

Real-world deployment strategies

Readers will gain insights into real-world deployment strategies for AWS Organizations. Practical examples demonstrate how organizations can structure their accounts, apply policies, and utilize AWS Organizations to manage resources efficiently, ensuring scalability and effective governance.

Business implications

From a business standpoint, AWS Organizations enhance operational efficiency, facilitate cost management, and promote regulatory compliance. This section discusses how adopting organizations align with business goals and foster a streamlined and secure cloud environment.

Further reading

For readers seeking a deeper understanding of AWS Organizations, exploring AWS Documentation [1] is recommended. Internal references offer technical insights, while external references, such as case studies and best practice guides, offer practical perspectives on improving AWS Organizations for specific use cases.

AWS Personal Health Dashboard

In the cloud management and governance landscape, the AWS **Personal Health Dashboard** (**PHD**) is a crucial tool, offering real-time insights into the operational status of AWS resources. This section explores the features, benefits, and practical applications of the AWS PHD, providing readers with a comprehensive understanding of its role in ensuring operational excellence.

Overview and core functionality

The AWS PHD is a centralized service that offers a personalized view of the health of AWS resources [2]. This section provides an in-depth overview of how PHD aggregates information from multiple AWS services, presenting it in a combined and easily accessible format for users.

Key features and components

Readers will gain insights into the key features of the AWS PHD, including the ability to view alerts, remediation guidance, and integration with AWS Support. Understanding these components is essential for effectively leveraging PHD to monitor and maintain the health of AWS resources.

Proactive monitoring and alerting

This section examines how the AWS PHD facilitates proactive monitoring by delivering real-time alerts about events that may impact AWS resources. Readers will understand how to interpret these alerts and take preemptive actions to ensure the continuity of operations.

Integration with AWS Support

AWS PHD seamlessly integrates with AWS Support, enhancing its capabilities. This section discusses how users can use integration to access detailed support information, including status updates, upcoming maintenance events, and proactive recommendations.

Use cases and practical applications

Real-world use cases demonstrate how organizations can benefit from the AWS PHD. Examples include identifying and mitigating issues before they impact operations, minimizing downtime, and optimizing resource utilization for improved efficiency.

Customization and user preferences

PHD allows users to customize their dashboard based on their preferences and priorities. This section guides readers through tailoring alerts, setting preferences, and configuring notifications, ensuring a personalized and efficient monitoring experience.

Strategic considerations for implementation

Strategic considerations are vital for effectively implementing the AWS PHD. This section offers practical guidance on aligning PHD with organizational goals, setting up custom alerts, and integrating them into existing monitoring workflows.

Business implications

From a business standpoint, the AWS PHD contributes to operational resilience, minimizing the impact of potential issues on business operations. This section discusses how proactive monitoring with PHD aligns with business continuity and risk management strategies.

Further reading

For readers seeking a deeper understanding of AWS PHD, exploring AWS Documentation [3] is recommended. Internal references offer technical insights, while external references, such as case studies and best practice guides, offer practical perspectives on maximizing the benefits of PHD.

AWS Proton

In the dynamic realm of cloud management and governance, efficient application deployment is a cornerstone of operational success. AWS Proton is a comprehensive service that streamlines the deployment and management of containerized and serverless applications. This section provides a detailed exploration of AWS Proton, shedding light on its functionalities, benefits, and strategic implications for businesses.

Overview and core functionality

AWS Proton is introduced as a fully managed service designed to automate and streamline the deployment of containerized and serverless applications [4]. This section delves into the fundamental principles and core functionalities that underpin Proton's role in simplifying the application deployment lifecycle.

Key features and components

Readers gain insights into AWS Proton's key features and components, including its ability to create and manage environments, define service templates, and help collaboration among development teams. Understanding these elements is crucial for effectively harnessing Proton's capabilities.

Service templates and environments

This section explores the concept of service templates in Proton, elucidating how they serve as blueprints for defining the infrastructure and configurations of applications. Additionally, managing environments is discussed, emphasizing how Proton ensures consistency across different deployment stages.

Collaboration and governance

Proton is positioned as a collaborative tool for development teams. The section outlines how Proton helps collaboration by providing a centralized platform for defining, managing, and sharing service templates. Governance mechanisms within Proton to ensure adherence to organizational policies are also discussed.

Proton in action on the deployment of workflows

Real-world examples and use cases prove how AWS Proton runs in practical scenarios. The section walks through deployment workflows, showcasing how Proton automates the provisioning of infrastructure, deployment of code, and management of application configurations.

Integration with AWS services

AWS Proton seamlessly integrates with other AWS services, enhancing its capabilities. This section examines how Proton integrates with AWS IAM, AWS CloudFormation, and AWS CodePipeline, offering readers a comprehensive understanding of its interoperability within the AWS ecosystem.

Best practices for proton implementation

Strategic considerations for implementing AWS Proton are discussed, providing readers with guidance on optimizing Proton for their specific use cases. Best practices cover service template design, environment management, and using Proton for containerized and serverless applications.

Business implications

From a business perspective, the deployment efficiency provided by AWS Proton translates into a faster time-to-market for applications. This section examines how Proton aligns with business goals, promoting agility, minimizing manual intervention, and reducing deployment-related challenges.

Further reading

To delve deeper into AWS Proton's technical intricacies and best practices, readers are encouraged to explore AWS Documentation [5]. Internal references provide insights into Proton's features, while external references, such as case studies and success stories, offer practical perspectives on its real-world implementation.

AWS Resilience Hub

Ensure the resilience of cloud infrastructures is paramount in the dynamic landscape of cloud management and governance. The AWS Resilience Hub is critical, providing organizations with tools and insights to enhance their resilience against disruptions. This section provides an in-depth examination of the AWS Resilience Hub, its key features, and its role in improving the strength of cloud environments.

Overview

The AWS Resilience Hub is introduced as a comprehensive service designed to help organizations manage and enhance the resilience of their cloud-based applications [6]. This section highlights the importance of resilience in cloud infrastructure, laying the groundwork for a detailed examination of the tool's capabilities.

Key features and functionality

This section delves into the key features of the AWS Resilience Hub, highlighting its ability to aggregate and visualize resilience-related information across multiple AWS accounts and regions. It also discusses the hub's role in centralizing disaster recovery, fault-tolrance, and overall system stability insights.

Integration with AWS Organizations

Insights are provided on how the AWS Resilience Hub seamlessly integrates with AWS Organizations, allowing organizations to extend their resilience management across an entire organization. This integration enhances the tool's scalability and adaptability to diverse cloud architectures.

Resilience dashboard

A detailed exploration of the Resilience Hub dashboard is undertaken, elucidating how it offers a centralized view of an organization's resilience posture. This includes discussions on the dashboard's capabilities for checking the health of critical resources, finding vulnerabilities, and ensuring compliance with resilience best practices.

Automated insights and recommendations

The section examines how the AWS Resilience Hub utilizes automated insights and recommendations to identify areas for improvement within organizations. Practical examples illustrate how these automated features contribute to proactive resilience management.

Real-time monitoring and alerting

Readers learn how the AWS Resilience Hub helps with real-time monitoring and alerting, ensuring organizations respond swiftly to potential disruptions. This includes discussing the tool's capabilities for detecting anomalies and providing actionable alerts.

Business continuity and disaster recovery

The role of the AWS Resilience Hub in supporting business continuity and disaster recovery strategies is emphasized. Case studies and practical examples demonstrate how organizations utilize the tool to maintain uninterrupted operations in the face of unforeseen events.

Business implications

From a business standpoint, deploying AWS Resilience Hub is positioned as a strategic investment in long-term operational resilience. This section discusses how organizations ensure the continuous availability and reliability of critical applications for business value.

Further reading

Readers are encouraged to explore the AWS Resilience Hub documentation for a more comprehensive understanding of the tool's technical intricacies [6]. Internal references offer detailed insights, while external case studies and success stories provide practical perspectives on resilience management.

AWS Service Catalog

The AWS Service Catalog is pivotal in providing organizations with a standardized and efficient approach to managing IT services in cloud management and governance. This section delves into the intricate details of the AWS Service Catalog, exploring its features, benefits, and strategic implications for businesses.

Overview and core functionality

AWS Service Catalog is introduced as a service that allows organizations to create, govern, and manage a catalog of IT services. This section provides a foundational understanding of the core functionalities underpinning the Service Catalog's role in **IT service management (ITSM)** [7].

Key features and components

Readers are guided through the key features and components of the AWS Service Catalog, including the concept of portfolios, products, and constraints. Understanding these elements is crucial for establishing a well-organized and well-governed catalog of IT services.

Portfolios and products

This section examines how the AWS Service Catalog enables organizations to group and manage related products within portfolios. It sheds light on creating portfolios that align with organizational structures and include products within them.

Constraints and governance

AWS Service Catalog provides mechanisms for governance through the imposition of constraints. The section discusses how constraints can be defined to control the use of specific resources or configurations, ensuring compliance with organizational policies and standards.

Integration with AWS services

Service Catalog seamlessly integrates with other AWS services. This section examines how the Service Catalog interacts with AWS IAM, AWS CloudFormation, and AWS Lambda, providing readers with insights into its interoperability within the AWS ecosystem.

End-user experience

The end-user experience is a crucial aspect of the AWS Service Catalog. This section outlines how end-users can browse and launch products from the catalog, highlighting the self-service nature of the Service Catalog and its role in empowering teams.

Lifecycle management

AWS Service Catalog helps the entire lifecycle of IT services. From product creation to versioning and updates, this section provides a comprehensive understanding of how the Service Catalog ensures the smooth evolution of IT services over time.

Best practices for implementation

Strategic considerations for implementing the AWS Service Catalog are discussed, providing readers with guidance on designing efficient catalogs, defining practical constraints, and improving the end-user experience.

Business implications

From a business perspective, the AWS Service Catalog contributes to cost efficiency, standardization, and compliance. This section examines how the Service Catalog aligns with business goals, providing a structured approach to ITSM that promotes consistency and governance.

Further reading

Readers are encouraged to explore the AWS Documentation for a more profound insight into the technical intricacies and best practices of the AWS Service Catalogue [7]. Internal references offer insights into the Service Catalog's features, while external references, such as case studies, provide practical perspectives on its real-world implementation.

AWS Service Management Connector

The AWS Service Management Connector is a key cloud management and governance facilitator. It seamlessly integrates AWS services with the popular ITSM platform ServiceNow. This section explores the comprehensive features, integration capabilities, and strategic advantages the AWS Service Management Connector brings to organizations.

Overview and integration

The AWS Service Management Connector is introduced as a bridge connecting AWS services and ServiceNow. This section provides a high-level overview of its purpose and significance in ITSM [8].

Seamless AWS ServiceNow integration

Readers are guided through the seamless integration capabilities of AWS Service Management Connector with ServiceNow. This includes the bi-directional communication that allows AWS resources to be provisioned, watched, and managed directly from the ServiceNow platform.

Key features and functionality

This section examines the key features of the AWS Service Management Connector, highlighting its ability to streamline workflows, enhance visibility, and foster collaboration between AWS and ServiceNow users. It highlights incident management, change management, and service catalog integration features.

Use cases and benefits

Real-world use cases and benefits illustrate how organizations can utilize the AWS Service Management Connector to enhance their ITSM processes. Examples may include faster incident resolution, improved change management, and enhanced reporting capabilities.

Governance and compliance

AWS Service Management Connector is crucial in ensuring governance and compliance by providing a standardized and controlled way to interact with AWS resources from ServiceNow. This section explores the governance features that support regulatory compliance and security best practices.

Implementation of best practices

Strategic considerations for implementing AWS Service Management Connector are discussed, providing readers with guidance on configuration, setup, and ongoing management. Best practices for keeping secure and efficient integration are emphasized.

Business implications

From a business standpoint, AWS Service Management Connector contributes to operational efficiency, collaboration, and a unified approach to ITSM. This section examines how the connector aligns with business objectives, promoting an integrated and streamlined ITSM environment.

Further reading

For readers seeking a deeper technical understanding, AWS Documentation is recommended [8]. Internal references provide insight into the technical intricacies of the AWS Service Management Connector, while external case studies and success stories offer practical perspectives on its real-world impact.

AWS Systems Manager

AWS Systems Manager stands out as a versatile and robust solution in the intricate landscape of cloud management. This section examines its comprehensive capabilities, highlighting its role in providing operational insights and management across AWS environments.

Overview and core functionality

AWS Systems Manager has been introduced as a unified interface for centralizing operational data and automating tasks. This section provides an overview of its core functionality, emphasizing its role in simplifying resource and application management at scale [9].

Operational insights and visibility

Readers are guided through how AWS Systems Manager provides operational insights and visibility into their infrastructure. The service's ability to aggregate and visualize data, including patch compliance, instance inventory, and operational health, is highlighted.

Key features and use cases

This section delves into the key features of AWS Systems Manager, including capabilities such as Run Command, State Manager, and Automation. Real-world use cases demonstrate how organizations can utilize these features for patch management, configuration management, and automated responses to operational issues.

Automation and orchestration

This paper thoroughly explores AWS Systems Manager's automation and orchestration capabilities. It includes insights into how automation workflows can be created to streamline operational tasks and ensure resource management consistency and efficiency.

Security and compliance

AWS Systems Manager is pivotal in maintaining security and compliance by providing a centralized platform for managing and enforcing security policies. This section outlines the security features, including integration with AWS IAM and compliance reporting.

Integration with other AWS services

We explore the seamless integration of AWS Systems Manager with other AWS services. Examples may include integration with Amazon CloudWatch for enhanced monitoring and AWS IAM for secure access control.

Real-world deployment strategies

Practical deployment strategies are offered, providing guidance on best practices for configuring AWS Systems Manager to meet specific organizational needs. Insights into creating automation documents, managing patch baselines, and improving operational tasks are discussed.

Business implications

From a business perspective, AWS Systems Manager enhances operational efficiency, optimizes costs, and improves security. This section examines how the service aligns with broader business objectives, enabling organizations to maintain a proactive and well-managed AWS environment.

Further reading

To delve deeper into the technical intricacies of AWS Systems Manager, readers are encouraged to explore AWS Documentation [9]. Internal references offer detailed insights, while external case studies and best practices provide a broader understanding of the service's applications.

AWS Trusted Advisor

In the complex AWS management and governance landscape, AWS Trusted Advisor emerges as a proactive and indispensable tool for enhancing AWS environments. This section explores its comprehensive capabilities, offering insights into its role as a guidance system for best practices, cost optimization, and improved security.

Overview and core functionality

AWS Trusted Advisor is introduced as a cloud service that offers best practices and recommendations to improve AWS environments across various pillars, including cost optimization, performance, security, and reliability [10]. The section overviews its core functionality, emphasizing its role in delivering actionable insights for improving AWS resources.

Best practices and recommendations

Readers are guided through the key best practices and recommendations AWS Trusted Advisor provides. This includes insights into cost-saving opportunities, performance improvement suggestions, security enhancements, and reliability optimizations.

Pillars of evaluation

This section explores the pillars across which AWS Trusted Advisor evaluates AWS environments. It includes comprehensively examining each pillar, providing practical examples of the checks performed, and offering the corresponding recommendations.

Automation and integration

The role of AWS Trusted Advisor in automating issue identification and providing recommendations is highlighted. Integration possibilities with AWS CloudWatch and IAM are explored, demonstrating how organizations can leverage automation for a proactive approach to managing AWS resources.

Cost optimization strategies

This document thoroughly examines cost optimization strategies recommended by AWS Trusted Advisor. It includes insights into rightsizing instances, utilizing reserved instances, and identifying idle resources to optimize costs.

Security and compliance

We explored the proactive security checks performed by AWS Trusted Advisor. Readers learn how the service identifies potential security vulnerabilities and compliance gaps, enabling organizations to strengthen their security posture.

Real-world implementation

Practical implementation strategies are provided, guiding organizations to utilize AWS Trusted Advisor to enhance their AWS environments effectively. This includes creating custom notification settings, implementing automated checks, and integrating recommendations into existing workflows.

Business implications

From a business standpoint, AWS Trusted Advisor contributes to cost efficiency, enhanced performance, and fortified security. This section examines how organizations can align their AWS management strategies with the recommendations provided by Trusted Advisor to achieve optimal outcomes.

Further reading

To delve deeper into the technical intricacies of AWS Trusted Advisor, readers are encouraged to explore AWS Documentation [10]. Internal references offer detailed insights, while external case studies and best practices provide a broader understanding of the service's applications.

AWS Well-Architected Tool

In AWS management and governance, the AWS Well-Architected Tool is a guiding blueprint for organizations seeking to build robust, scalable, and efficient cloud architectures. This section explores the tool's functionalities, its significance in the cloud landscape, and its contribution to the Well-Architected Framework.

Overview

The AWS Well-Architected Tool is introduced as a service that enables organizations to review and improve their cloud architecture by following AWS's best practices [11]. This section emphasizes the tool's role in aligning architecture with the five pillars of the Well-Architected Framework: operational excellence, security, reliability, performance efficiency, and cost optimization.

Pillar-specific evaluation

The section delves into each pillar of the Well-Architected Framework, providing insights into the specific considerations and best practices assessed by the tool. This includes discussions on operational practices, security measures, reliability strategies, performance optimization, and cost-saving opportunities.

Aligning with best practices

The AWS Well-Architected Tool guides readers in aligning cloud architecture with industry best practices. It includes a detailed examination of how the tool finds areas for improvement and provides actionable recommendations to enhance the overall architecture.

Risk mitigation and security

The tool's role in risk identification and mitigation was explored, explicitly focusing on security considerations. This section gives practical examples of how the Well-Architected Tool helps organizations enhance their security posture by finding vulnerabilities and suggesting remediation steps.

Performance optimization

Provided are insights into how the Well-Architected Tool evaluates performance efficiency. This includes discussions on resource use, load balancing, and other considerations aimed at improving the overall performance of cloud architecture.

Real-time evaluation

This section discusses the Well-Architected Tool's real-time evaluation capabilities. It includes insights into how organizations can use the tool iteratively throughout the lifecycle of their applications to ensure continuous alignment with best practices.

Actionable recommendations

We offer a detailed examination of the tool's actionable recommendations, including strategies for implementing changes based on the tool's insights to drive improvements in cloud architecture.

Business implications

From a business perspective, the AWS Well-Architected Tool is positioned as a proactive measure to ensure that cloud architecture is functional and improved for long-term success. This section examines how adherence to the Well-Architected Framework enhances organizational resilience and agility.

Further reading

Readers are encouraged to explore AWS Documentation for the Well-Architected Tool [11]. Internal references provide detailed insights, while external case studies and success stories offer a broader understanding of how organizations have benefited from adopting the Well-Architected Framework.

Conclusion

This chapter explored the broad spectrum of AWS management and governance services that enable organizations to maintain visibility, control, and efficiency. [12] We demonstrated how each contributes to operational excellence in their cloud environments, from foundational tools like AWS CloudWatch and AWS CloudTrail to advanced services such as AWS Systems Manager, AWS Organizations, and AWS Trusted Advisor [13], compliance, and cost optimization. These services support day-to-day operations and play a pivotal role in enforcing security policies, automating administrative tasks, and aligning cloud usage with business objectives. The real-world scenario presented in this chapter illustrates how a financial services firm successfully implemented a comprehensive governance framework using AWS, underscoring the importance of a unified approach to cloud governance.

In the next chapter, we will focus on cost optimization and billing, diving into the financial management tools AWS offers to help organizations [1]. Forecast spending, manage budgets, and optimize cloud costs. Understanding how to govern cloud usage from an operational and financial perspective completes the strategic foundation necessary for scaling responsibly in the cloud.

Join our Discord space

Join our Discord workspace for latest updates, offers, tech happenings around the world, new releases, and sessions with the authors:

https://discord.bpbonline.com

CHAPTER 13

Migration and Transfer

Introduction

Migrating workloads, applications, and data to the cloud is critical for organizations seeking scalability, cost efficiency, and operational resilience. AWS provides migration and transfer services that enable businesses to transition from on-premises infrastructure to the cloud with minimal risk, downtime, and complexity. These services facilitate diverse migration scenarios, including infrastructure modernization, database replication, large-scale data transfers, and legacy system re-platforming [1], [2].

Historically, cloud migrations were primarily manual, time-consuming, and fraught with operational risks. Modern migration strategies leverage automation, real-time replication, and intelligent workload optimization to streamline transitions while ensuring business continuity. AWS supports these efforts through purpose-built tools designed to assess, plan, execute, and track cloud migrations with precision [3], [4].

This chapter will help you understand the key AWS migration and transfer services. It details methodologies, best practices, and real-world use cases illustrating how businesses can execute seamless, secure, and efficient cloud transitions.

Structure

This chapter will cover the following topics:

- AWS Application Migration Service
- AWS Application Discovery Service
- AWS Database Migration Service
- AWS DataSync
- AWS Mainframe Modernization
- AWS Migration Hub
- AWS Transfer Family
- Migration Evaluator

Objectives

By the end of this chapter, you will understand the strategic role of AWS migration and transfer services in cloud adoption. You will be able to assess the readiness of the infrastructure [5]. Using AWS Application Discovery Service and implementing automated, low-risk workload migrations with AWS **Application Migration Service** (**MGN**) [3]. The chapter will also guide you through using AWS **Database Migration Service** (**DMS**) [6]. You will explore AWS Mainframe Modernization approaches to transition legacy systems to cloud-native architectures for low-downtime relational database migration and AWS DataSync for secure, high-speed transfers between on-premises and AWS storage, manage and watch migration projects using AWS Migration Hub, [7] [8] [9], and conduct secure file transfers via AWS Transfer Family using standard protocols such as **SSH File Transfer Protocol** (**SFTP**), **File Transfer Protocol over SSL** (**FTPS**), and **File Transfer Protocol** (**FTP**) [12]. Finally, you will analyze migration feasibility and cost efficiency with **AWS Migration Evaluator** [12], and apply best practices to streamline, secure, and improve migration processes across diverse workloads [9].

AWS Application Migration Service

AWS MGN automates the lift-and-shift migration of applications from on-premises environments to AWS with minimal downtime and risk. It replaces older migration services, such as AWS **Server Migration Service** (**SMS**), by offering continuous data replication, automated conversion, and real-time monitoring [7], [10].

Key features

The following features show how AWS MGN streamlines and secures the migration process, minimizing operational disruptions and accelerating time to value:

- **Agentless migration**: Drops the need to install migration agents on source servers, reducing operational overhead and security risks [11].

- **Continuous data replication**: **Change data capture** (**CDC**) to ensure real-time synchronization between the source and AWS target environments, thereby reducing downtime during cutover [12].

- **Automated machine conversion**: Converts on-premises workloads into AWS-native instances, streamlining deployment [12].

- **Testing and validation**: Provides a controlled test environment to confirm performance before final migration [13].

- **Bandwidth optimization**: Reduces data transfer costs by compressing and improving replication traffic [14].

User scenarios

To better understand AWS MGN's real-world applications, consider the following user scenarios, which show its practical impact across various industries and workloads.

Scenario 1: Migrating an e-commerce platform.

One example involves a large e-commerce company using a monolithic on-premises web application. Seeking greater scalability and cost efficiency, the company starts a migration to AWS using AWS MGN, which enables the following process:

1. Continuous replication synchronizes on-premises and AWS environments.
2. The team performs pre-cutover testing in AWS.
3. The final cutover is executed with near-zero downtime.

Outcome: Improved scalability, reduced infrastructure costs by 30%, and enhanced disaster recovery capabilities [15].

Scenario 2: Financial services CRM migration.

A financial institution must migrate a legacy CRM system to AWS without disrupting customer service or compromising compliance. Using AWS MGN, the IT team enabled continuous data replication while preserving service availability throughout the migration. After evaluating the replicated environment and confirming performance benchmarks, the institution transitioned its CRM system to the cloud easily and seamlessly.

Outcome: Reduced licensing costs, improved customer experience, and enhanced compliance readiness [16].

Best practices

Organizations should follow the best practices before migrating to AWS MGN to ensure a smooth and secure transition. These guidelines can reduce risk, improve visibility, and maximize migration efficiency:

- Conduct a pre-migration assessment using the AWS Application Discovery Service to analyze dependencies and estimate resource requirements [17].

- Utilize staggered migration waves to minimize the impact on mission-critical applications and keep business continuity during cutover [18].

- Monitor migration progress and infrastructure health using AWS CloudWatch alerts to detect and resolve issues [19] quickly.

Case study

Accelerating enterprise migration with AWS MGN.

A *Deloitte* led migration initiative examined a global enterprise undergoing cloud transformation across multiple business units. The company aimed to migrate hundreds of legacy applications to physical and virtual infrastructure in various data centers. Traditionally, these workloads needed extensive manual intervention, posing timelines, downtime, and staff overhead challenges.

By adopting AWS MGN, the enterprise automated the lift-and-shift process, enabling near real-time replication of source systems and reducing manual reconfiguration tasks. Teams could confirm and incrementally cut over workloads, using predefined waves based on business criticality.

Results: The Deloitte study reported that organizations using AWS MGN achieved migration speeds that were 50% faster than those using traditional manual rehosting strategies. Furthermore, teams experienced greater consistency in cutover execution, minimized operational risk, and shortened project timelines [20].

AWS Application Discovery Service

The AWS Application Discovery Service helps assess on-premises environments before migration by gathering insights into infrastructure, performance, and dependencies [21].

Key features

Before starting cloud migration, it is essential to understand the current application and infrastructure landscape thoroughly. The AWS Application Discovery Service provides automated tools to uncover critical system data and dependencies, enabling more informed planning and decision-making. Key features include:

- **Agentless data collection**: Gathers server configurations, **operating system (OS)** details, and network dependencies without deploying agents [22].
- **Application dependency mapping**: Finds interdependencies between applications, databases, and middleware [23].
- **Performance insights**: Analyzes CPU, memory, and network usage to optimize workload migration planning [24].

User scenarios

Organizations across various industries use the Application Discovery Service to mitigate migration risks, streamline decision-making processes, and improve outcomes. The following example highlights its practical application:

Scenario 1: Data centre consolidation.

A multinational corporation evaluates over 5,000 physical and virtual servers before merging its data centers.

Outcome: Found redundant systems, resulting in a 40% reduction in infrastructure costs [25].

Best practices

To maximize the value of AWS Application Discovery Service and ensure a smooth migration experience, organizations should follow recommended strategies that enhance discovery accuracy, streamline workflows, and reduce migration risks. The following practices serve as essential guidelines for effective implementation:

- Use AWS Migration Hub strategy recommendations to define migration paths [26].
- Enable automated discovery for VMware environments [27].

Case study

A 2023 *Forrester* report examined a global insurance provider that integrated AWS Application Discovery Service into its pre-migration strategy. Facing growing costs and performance limitations in its on-premises infrastructure, the company started a migration involving over 300 applications. By using automated discovery and dependency mapping:

- The IT team reduced manual discovery efforts by 70%.
- Migration sequencing was fine-tuned to avoid unexpected application outages.
- The company found legacy systems that could be retired, further accelerating its modernization efforts.

Result: The company achieved a 35% reduction in post-migration performance issues and a 25% decrease in migration time. Forrester concluded that early visibility enabled by discovery tools was a decisive factor in the project's success [28].

AWS Database Migration Service

AWS DMS simplifies and accelerates database migration to AWS, resulting in minimal downtime and disruption. It supports homogeneous migrations (e.g., Oracle to Oracle) and heterogeneous migrations (e.g., SQL Server to Amazon Aurora), ensuring data integrity and consistency [6].

Key features

AWS DMS provides capabilities designed to simplify and accelerate database migration to the cloud. The following features ensure dependable, efficient, and secure migrations with minimal disruption to ongoing business operations:

- **Continuous data replication**: Uses CDC to replicate live database updates in near real-time [29].
- **Automated schema conversion**: AWS **Schema Conversion Tool** (**SCT**) helps cross-engine migrations [8].
- **Minimal downtime**: Ensures business continuity by replicating changes as the source database stays operational [9].
- **Support for multiple database engines**: Supports MySQL, PostgreSQL, SQL Server, Oracle, and Amazon Redshift [30].

User scenarios

Scenario 1: Migrating an on-premises Oracle database to Amazon RDS.

A financial services company migrates a transactional Oracle database to Amazon RDS for Oracle, reducing operational overhead and improving resilience.

Outcome: 50% reduction in database administration efforts, 30% cost savings on infrastructure [31].

Scenario 2: SQL Server to Amazon Aurora migration.

A SaaS company migrates from SQL Server to Amazon Aurora PostgreSQL to improve cost and performance.

Outcome: Ended SQL Server licensing costs, achieving a 35% improvement in query performance [14].

Best practices

To maximize the effectiveness of your database migration strategy, it is important to apply best practices that address schema compatibility, data validation, and operational continuity. The following recommendations aim to reduce migration risk and enhance post-migration performance:

- **Use AWS SCT for schema validation and conversion**: The AWS SCT helps identify compatibility issues between source and target databases, automatically converting schemas and allowing developers to focus on business logic [7].

- **Enable CDC for minimal downtime and faster cutover**: CDC ensures near real-time synchronization between the source and target databases, enabling the migration of workloads with minimal service interruption [10].

- **Perform data validation using AWS DMS validation tools**: DMS offers built-in validation capabilities that compare source and target datasets, helping you verify accuracy and completeness after the migration [11].

Case study

A Forrester study examined a multinational e-commerce enterprise with multiple on-premises data centers and legacy relational databases. With rising licensing costs, complex backup routines, and scalability challenges, the company migrated its mission-critical databases to AWS using AWS DMS.

Approach:

The team used AWS SCT to convert their Oracle schema into Amazon Aurora PostgreSQL format. They enabled CDC to keep the new environment synchronized with the legacy system throughout the migration period. After performing rigorous validation using DMS tools, the team executed a final cutover with near-zero downtime.

Outcome:

The migration timeline was shortened by 45% compared to earlier manual approaches. The company reported a 60% reduction in database administration efforts, significant improvements in application responsiveness, and projected annual infrastructure cost savings of over $1.2 million [10].

AWS DataSync

AWS DataSync helps with high-speed, secure data transfers between on-premises storage and AWS storage services, including Amazon S3, Amazon EFS, and Amazon FSx [12].

Key features

AWS DataSync provides features that simplify data movement from on-premises storage to AWS, ensuring efficient, secure, and scalable file transfers. The following key capabilities are designed to accelerate migration projects while preserving data integrity and reducing operational overhead:

- **Accelerated data transfers**: This method uses purpose-built agents and parallel processing to transfer data up to 10 times faster than traditional tools, such as rsync or FTP.

- **Incremental sync**: Only modified or new files are transferred, minimizing bandwidth consumption and transfer time [14].

- **Encryption and data integrity checks**: Transfers are encrypted in transit and confirmed with checksums to guarantee data is complete and secure [15].

- **Support for multiple storage solutions**: Compatible with a wide range of **network attached storage** (**NAS**), **storage area networks** (**SAN**), and file servers, offering flexibility for diverse IT environments [16].

User scenarios

AWS DataSync supports different use cases across industries that require secure and high-throughput data movement.

Scenario 1: Large-scale media file migration.

A global media and entertainment company must migrate petabytes of archived video content and raw production footage from its on-premises storage system to Amazon S3. The migration aimed to reduce dependency on local infrastructure and enhance content accessibility for post-production teams across regions.

Outcome: AWS DataSync completed the transfer 50% faster than legacy tools, improved data availability, and reduced long-term storage costs by using Amazon S3 Glacier for archiving [17].

Scenario 2: Retail inventory data synchronization.

A multinational retail chain with distributed data centers faced challenges in keeping correct real-time inventory records. The company deployed AWS DataSync to replicate sales and inventory data across regions, synchronizing data from point-of-sale systems to Amazon FSx for Windows File Server.

Outcome: This resulted in a 35% improvement in stock tracking accuracy, enabling regional inventory systems to stay synchronized with headquarters in real-time [18].

Best practices

Applying proven AWS DataSync strategies can improve transfer performance, reduce costs, and ensure long-term efficiency:

- **Use AWS Direct Connect for large-scale data transfers**: Leverage AWS Direct Connect to create a dedicated network link that improves speed, security, and reliability during massive file migrations [26].

- **Schedule off-peak incremental syncs**: To improve costs. Running sync jobs during off-peak hours minimizes the cost impact of data transfer and reduces interference with production workloads [20].

- **Enable Amazon S3 Lifecycle rules for long-term storage optimization**: Use S3 Lifecycle policies to automatically transition data to cost-effective storage classes, such as S3 Glacier or S3 Intelligent-Tiering [21].

Case study

A Deloitte report profiled a multinational pharmaceutical company undergoing a digital transformation initiative. The firm needed to migrate vast volumes of clinical trial data from local research centers to AWS to enhance collaboration, improve regulatory compliance, and help with disaster recovery.

Approach:

Using AWS DataSync, the IT team installed agents across six global research sites, enabling secure and continuous data transfers to Amazon S3. With support for incremental sync and scheduled jobs, they reduced network congestion and kept consistent updates.

Outcome:

The company reported a 45% decrease in manual IT intervention related to file movement and synchronization. Compliance reports were generated faster, research teams gained access to shared datasets faster, and data security improved significantly. The switch to AWS storage also lowered infrastructure costs and increased scalability across research workflows [22].

AWS Mainframe Modernization

AWS Mainframe Modernization offers a structured migration framework for transitioning legacy mainframe applications to cloud-native architectures [12].

Key features

Modernizing mainframe workloads requires flexibility and a well-defined strategy. AWS Mainframe Modernization provides two tailored paths—rehosting and refactoring—designed to accelerate the transition from legacy environments to cloud-native architectures, as discussed:

- **Rehosting (lift-and-shift)**: Migrates mainframe workloads directly to Amazon EC2 with minimal modifications, enabling faster time-to-cloud [24].

- **Refactoring for cloud-native services**: Deconstructs monolithic legacy applications into a microservices architecture using AWS Lambda, Amazon DynamoDB, and other serverless technologies [25].

- **Automation and DevOps integration**: Supports integration with CI/CD pipelines using tools like AWS CodePipeline and CodeDeploy, enhancing the agility of modernized workloads [26].

User scenarios

Organizations across various sectors have successfully transitioned away from mainframe systems by utilizing AWS's modernization tools. The examples below illustrate how AWS Mainframe Modernization delivers performance, cost savings, and innovation.

Scenario 1: Banking system modernization.

A global financial institution's COBOL-based transaction system running on an aging mainframe faced scalability limitations and high operational costs. The bank adopted a rehosting strategy using AWS Mainframe Modernization to address these challenges. **Outcome**: The migration to Amazon EC2 cut infrastructure costs by 50%, and the system now supports scalable transactions, handling double the earlier volume with ease [27].

Scenario 2: Insurance claims processing automation.

An insurance company's legacy claims platform struggled with latency and maintenance inefficiencies. The organization refactored its monolithic mainframe application using AWS Lambda and Amazon DynamoDB.

Outcome: This resulted in a 40% improvement in claims processing speed and a 35% reduction in overall maintenance costs, streamlining both internal workflows and customer service [28].

Best practices

AWS recommends different strategies to maximize the value of AWS Mainframe Modernization initiatives. These practices help reduce risk and improve outcomes during migration and post-modernization operations:

- **Use AWS Migration Evaluator for cost-benefit analysis**: Evaluate financial and technical feasibility before initiating rehosting or refactoring [7].
- **Refactor gradually instead of all at once**: Reduce migration risks by incrementally transforming legacy components into cloud-native microservices [32].
- **Leverage AWS DevOps tools for automated deployment**: Use tools like AWS CodeBuild and CodeDeploy to automate infrastructure provisioning, application deployment, and testing [25].

Case study

A *McKinsey* report examined the transformation journey of a leading logistics provider with over 20 years of mainframe-based operations. The organization looked to simplify the complexity of its legacy systems, which were costly to keep and hindered rapid innovation.

Approach:

The company used AWS Mainframe Modernization to migrate its mission-critical scheduling system to Amazon EC2. Then, using AWS Lambda and Amazon Aurora, it gradually refactored submodules, including billing, route planning, and reporting, into microservices.

Outcome:

The enterprise achieved a 50% reduction in deployment cycles, enabling more frequent software releases and operational improvements. Application performance improved due to elasticity and automation, resulting in a 45% decrease in ongoing infrastructure costs. The modernization project also enabled the company to introduce AI-driven logistics features previously impossible on the mainframe [33].

AWS Migration Hub

AWS Migration Hub provides centralized tracking of migration projects, offering a unified view of application dependencies, real-time migration progress, and integration with various AWS migration tools. It enables large-scale migrations to be checked and orchestrated effectively across teams and workflows [23].

Key features

This section outlines the core functionalities of AWS Migration Hub that support planning, visibility, and operational control during migration:

- **Unified migration dashboard**: Monitors application status, dependencies, and migration readiness [23].
- **Integration with AWS migration services**: Works with AWS DMS, AWS MGN, and AWS SMS to offer a centralized view [34].
- **Customizable workflows**: Enable phased or wave-based migration strategies tailored to organizational goals [35].

User scenarios

Real-world examples show the effectiveness of AWS Migration Hub across various industries and complex migration scenarios.

Scenario 1: Large-scale data center consolidation.

A global retailer aimed to shut down six regional data centers and move all workloads to AWS within 12 months. Using AWS Migration Hub:

1. The IT team watched hundreds of applications and dependencies across multiple AWS accounts.
2. They created migration waves and tracked each through the dashboard.
3. Downtime was minimized by coordinating DMS and MGN progress through a centralized interface.

Outcome: 30% reduction in infrastructure costs and 99.9% migration uptime [36].

Scenario 2: Multi-application migration for enterprises.

A financial institution must migrate over 200 interdependent applications while ensuring service continuity. Migration Hub provided:

- Real-time dependency visualization.

- Progress metrics across AWS services.

Outcome: 40% fewer migration errors and optimized scheduling and resource allocation [45].

Best practices

To maximize the effectiveness of AWS Migration Hub, consider the following practices before and during migration:

- Conduct migration readiness assessments to decide the scope and feasibility [37].

- Utilize AWS Migration Evaluator for financial modeling and **total cost of ownership** (**TCO**) analysis [38].

- Leverage AWS CloudWatch for proactive performance and error monitoring [48].

Case study

A Deloitte analysis found that 90% of enterprises using AWS Migration Hub reported reduced project delays, improved dependency tracking, and increased stakeholder alignment. Using Migration Hub's unified dashboard, IT teams experienced faster decision-making, improved planning, and better communication across departments, especially for migrations involving multiple application owners and business units [39].

AWS Transfer Family

AWS Transfer Family delivers secure, managed file transfer capabilities that support SFTP, FTPS, and FTP protocols. It enables the seamless migration of legacy file exchange workflows to AWS without requiring changes to client-side applications or server-side integrations [40].

Key features

This section presents the core capabilities of AWS Transfer Family that enable high-security, scalable file transfer solutions:

- **No need for self-managed FTP servers**: AWS manages infrastructure, patching, and availability [41].

- **Direct integration with Amazon S3 and EFS**: Provides scalable, elastic storage for incoming and outgoing files [42]; [43].

- **End-to-end encryption and access controls**: Uses Identity and Access Management (**IAM**), VPC endpoints, and audit logging to ensure secure data handling [44].

User scenarios

These scenarios show how AWS Transfer Family helps file-based workflows across various industries.

Scenario 1: Secure financial data exchange.

A multinational bank migrated its internal file-sharing system to AWS Transfer Family to meet stringent compliance requirements:

- SFTP-based workflows were replicated with no change to client-side tools.
- Access was controlled using IAM and integrated with corporate identity providers.

Outcome: Improved regulatory compliance and reduced manual intervention for file handling [45].

Scenario 2: Automated media backup to Amazon S3.

A media production company needed to automate backups of large video files from on-premises editing systems to the cloud:

- Transfer Family was used to schedule and authenticate secure transfers via FTPS.
- Amazon S3 Lifecycle rules were applied to move content to lower-cost storage tiers.

Outcome: 40% faster backup completion and a 35% reduction in operational overhead costs [46].

Best practices

Follow these guidelines to ensure secure, cost-efficient, and universally available file transfer workflows:

- Implement IAM-based access control to enforce the principle of least privilege [47].
- Enable S3 Lifecycle policies to archive or transition files to cost-effective storage classes [48].
- Monitor and audit all transfer activity using AWS CloudTrail logs [49].

Case study

A Forrester report revealed that companies using AWS Transfer Family experienced a 45% decrease in security incidents associated with file transfers. Automating compliance checks, removing manual FTP infrastructure, and seamlessly integrating with IAM and S3 were the primary drivers of improved outcomes [59].

Migration Evaluator

AWS Migration Evaluator helps enterprises assess the feasibility of cloud migration by offering automated insights on cost savings, workload right-sizing, and TCO comparisons between on-premises and AWS environments.

Initially launched as TSO Logic, the tool was purchased by AWS in 2019 and later rebranded as AWS Migration Evaluator to reflect its deeper integration into the AWS ecosystem. While the underlying capabilities remained focused on infrastructure discovery and cost analysis, the rebranding signaled a shift toward tighter alignment with AWS migration services and a streamlined experience for cloud planning. The new name highlights its core function—evaluating AWS migrations' feasibility and **return on investment (ROI)** while emphasizing automation, scalability, and AWS-native reporting dashboards. The transition also brought enhancements in usability, expanded data sources, and improved integration with tools like AWS Migration Hub and AWS Application Discovery Service.

Key features

This section highlights the capabilities that make Migration Evaluator essential for migration planning and business case justification:

- **Automated infrastructure discovery**: Collects a detailed inventory of compute, storage, and usage metrics [39].

- **TCO analysis**: Compares current IT spend with projected AWS costs based on usage patterns [39].

- **Workload right-sizing**: Suggests the best AWS services and instance types for migration targets [7].

Case study

A *PricewaterhouseCoopers (PwC)* study reported that a global financial institution used AWS Migration Evaluator to accelerate cloud adoption by 50%. By collecting telemetry from over 2,000 servers, the tool has achieved $1.2 million in potential annual savings by reducing overprovisioned compute resources and combining underutilized databases. These insights supported executive buy-ins and helped align cloud strategy with financial targets [64].

Conclusion

AWS Migration and transfer services provide structured, automation-driven tools that streamline cloud adoption while minimizing risk and downtime. This chapter explores methodologies for workload migration, database replication, large-scale data transfer, and mainframe modernization, equipping organizations with best practices for executing efficient and cost-effective migrations [50], [32].

Migration is only the first step. Organizations must adhere to AWS's Well-Architected Framework to maximize operational resilience, ensuring workloads are secure, high-performing, and cost-optimized. *Chapter 14, AWS Well-Architected Framework,* examines the six key pillars of the Well-Architected Framework and how businesses can continually enhance their AWS environments for long-term success [46].

CHAPTER 14

AWS Well-Architected Framework

Introduction

This chapter will teach the AWS Well-Architected Framework, a comprehensive guide for designing secure, high-performing, resilient, and efficient cloud environments. We will cover the framework's core principles and best practices, drawing from the knowledge and insights presented in the previous 13 chapters of this book.

Examining the Well-Architected Framework, we must reflect on the foundational pillars guiding its design and objectives. Developed by AWS, the framework serves as a tool for architects, developers, and cloud practitioners to design, evaluate, and optimize their workloads and architectures on AWS [1].

Structure

In this chapter, we will cover:

- Understanding the framework
- Understanding AWS Well-Architected lenses
- Ensuring robust protection in cloud environments
- Deepening the focus on protection

- Putting the framework into practice
- Reliability pillar
- Diving deeper into building resilient systems
- Reliability in action
- Performance efficiency lens
- Media streaming service case study

Objectives

By the end of this chapter, you will understand how the AWS Well-Architected Framework serves as a foundation for building secure, high-performing, resilient, and efficient cloud architectures. You can identify and apply the six pillars of the framework—operational excellence, security, reliability, performance efficiency, cost optimization, and sustainability—to real-world use cases. You will learn how AWS services align with each pillar and how to use the AWS Well-Architected Tool and AWS Architecture Center to evaluate and optimize cloud workloads. This chapter will also prepare you to implement architectural best practices that support long-term scalability, governance, and innovation in AWS environments.

Understanding the framework

At its core, the AWS Well-Architected Framework comprises the best practices and guidelines developed through years of collaboration with customers across various industries and use cases. It offers a comprehensive approach to cloud architecture, focusing on key areas such as security, reliability, performance efficiency, cost optimization, and operational excellence.

Purpose and development

The framework helps organizations create architectures that align with their business goals while adhering to fundamental principles. By offering a structured methodology and a set of best practices, AWS enables customers to design resilient, scalable, cost-effective, and operationally efficient solutions [2].

Core pillars of the Well-Architected Framework

At the heart of the AWS Well-Architected Framework lies a structured set of foundational principles—referred to as **pillars**—that guide architects and engineers in designing cloud-native systems that are robust, scalable, and aligned with business objectives. These six pillars form the basis for evaluating and improving architecture across operational, technical, and strategic dimensions. Each pillar addresses a critical aspect of system design, from securing sensitive data and maintaining high availability to controlling costs and promoting environmental sustainability. The following is an overview of these core pillars and their impact on best practices in cloud architecture:

- **Security**: Security is essential in any cloud architecture. The Well-Architected Framework emphasizes the importance of robust security controls, encryption, **Identity and Access Management (IAM)**, and compliance measures to safeguard data and resources against unauthorized access, breaches, and cyber threats.

- **Reliability**: Reliability ensures systems operate consistently and predictably under varying conditions. The framework encourages the implementation of fault-tolerant architectures, redundancy mechanisms, automated recovery processes, and comprehensive monitoring to mitigate the impact of failures and ensure uninterrupted service delivery.

- **Performance efficiency**: Performance efficiency focuses on optimizing resource utilization, minimizing latency, and maximizing throughput to meet the demands of dynamic workloads. The framework advocates using scalable architecture, caching strategies, load balancing, and performance-tuning techniques to deliver optimal user experiences and cost-effective performance.

- **Cost optimization**: Cost optimization involves efficiently utilizing cloud resources to minimize operational expenses without compromising performance or reliability. The Well-Architected Framework promotes the adoption of cost-effective architectures, reserved instances, usage-based pricing models, and monitoring tools to optimize spending and maximize **return of investment (ROI)**.

- **Operational excellence**: Operational excellence encompasses the ability to manage and evolve cloud environments through automation, monitoring, and continuous improvement practices. The framework advocates implementing DevOps principles, **infrastructure as code (IaC)**, automated testing, and documentation to streamline operations, enhance agility, and drive innovation.

- **Sustainability**: Sustainability emphasizes the importance of designing and operating environmentally conscious and resource-efficient systems. The Well-Architected Framework advocates for integrating sustainable practices into cloud architectures, such as optimizing energy usage across data centers, selecting energy-efficient resources, and reducing the overall carbon footprint. By promoting renewable energy sources and enhancing resource utilization, the framework fosters the development of green technologies and solutions that positively contribute to environmental stewardship while maintaining system efficiency and performance.

AWS services coming together

In the previous chapters, we explored a wide range of AWS services, tools, and best practices for improving cloud architecture, migration, governance, and management. As we now transition to discussing the AWS Well-Architected Framework, we will integrate insights from those chapters to illustrate how each component supports the framework's core principles.

For example, AWS **Application Migration Service (MGN)**, AWS **Database Migration Service (DMS)**, and AWS DataSync—covered in *Chapter 13, Migration and Transfer*—are key to enabling smooth migration and workload transfer to the cloud, a crucial element in building well-architected solutions. Likewise, AWS CloudTrail, AWS Config, AWS Control Tower, and AWS Systems Manager—discussed earlier—are vital in ensuring security, compliance, and operational excellence across AWS environments.

Best practices

This chapter serves as the culmination of our journey through AWS cloud computing. Here, we synthesize the principles, tools, and best practices from earlier chapters, applying them within the framework of the AWS Well-Architected Framework. By following the framework's core principles, organizations can design cloud solutions that are resilient, scalable, and optimized for security, performance, cost, and operational efficiency.

Join us as we explore real-world scenarios and uncover the practical application of the AWS Well-Architected Framework, highlighting how it enables the creation of efficient and resilient cloud environments.

The following illustration shows the six pillars of the Well-Architected Framework, as described by *Jeff Barr* on July 9, 2020, in the AWS Well-Architected Tool:

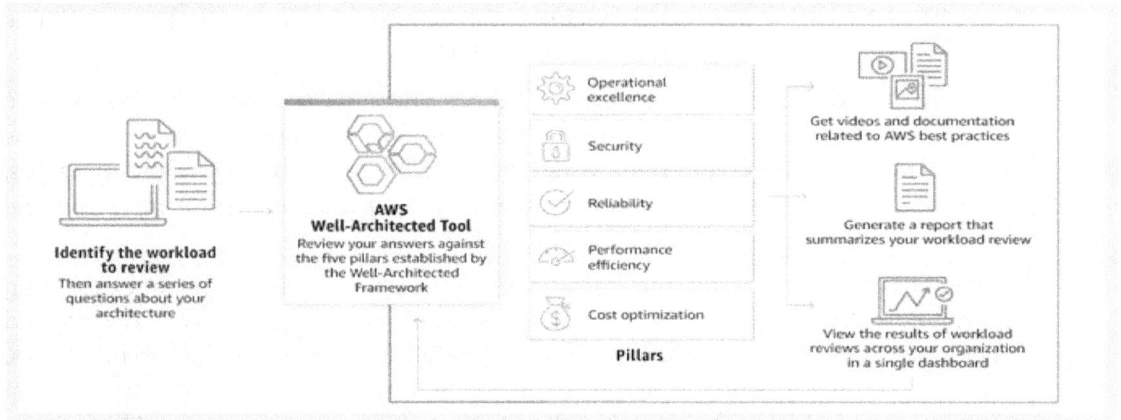

Figure 14.1: The six pillars of the Well-Architected Framework

The AWS Well-Architected Framework offers specific lenses that guide organizations through key architectural areas, enabling them to explore aspects of their cloud environments in greater detail. Each lens focuses on key considerations and best practices tailored to address specific architectural concerns within the broader context of the Well-Architected Framework [2].

The AWS Well-Architected custom lens lifecycle provides a structured framework for defining, reviewing, and evolving architecture best practices tailored to specific organizational needs. It guides teams through creating, publishing, updating, and governing custom lenses to align with internal standards while leveraging the strengths of the broader Well-Architected Framework.

Understanding AWS Well-Architected lenses

AWS Well-Architected lenses extend the foundational AWS Well-Architected Framework by providing additional, tailored guidance for specific technology domains, industries, or types of applications. These lenses are essential tools to help cloud architects build secure, high-performing, resilient, and efficient application infrastructure. Each lens provides a set of best practices, checklists, and detailed guidance that reflect the latest industry standards in a particular area, ensuring that all aspects of a solution are well-designed.

Figure 14.2 illustrates this lifecycle, highlighting the iterative stages of managing and effectively operationalizing custom lenses:

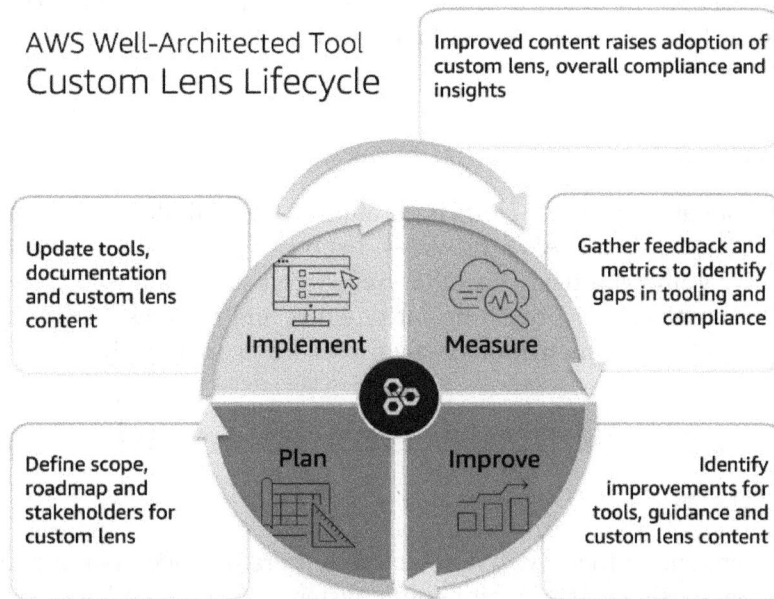

Figure 14.2: *The AWS Well-Architected custom lens lifecycle*

Importance and usage of Well-Architected lenses

Well-Architected lenses are crucial in meeting the distinct needs of industries or technologies that the general AWS Well-Architected Framework may not fully address.

They provide:

- **Deep dives into specific areas**: Each lens focuses on challenges and solutions, providing profound technical advice beyond the general advice in the main framework.

- **Contextual best practices**: Lenses adapt the five pillars of the Well-Architected Framework to specific contexts, ensuring that the advice is relevant and directly applicable to scenarios or industries.

- **Enhanced focus on compliance and security**: Different lenses are tailored to industries with stringent regulatory requirements, providing guidance that helps achieve compliance while harnessing the flexibility and efficiency of the AWS cloud.

- **Optimization opportunities**: They help identify specific opportunities for improvement and optimization within technology stacks or business domains.

Applications for Well-Architected lenses

Architects utilize these lenses during the application development, design, migration, and optimization phases to ensure their AWS environments align with best practices tailored to their business needs. For instance, a financial services firm will find financial services lens particularly useful for addressing compliance and security requirements unique to the financial sector.

Security pillar

Securing applications and data in the cloud is paramount in the digital era, where data breaches and cyber threats are rampant. AWS provides a robust framework to protect, detect, and respond to security vulnerabilities. The AWS Well-Architected Framework outlines security as a critical pillar, emphasizing protecting information and systems. Key security practices involve encryption, IAM, and meticulous network security configurations.

Ensuring robust protection in cloud environments

Security is a cornerstone of the AWS Well-Architected Framework. As the digital landscape evolves, protecting sensitive data, maintaining system integrity, and ensuring compliance have become paramount. AWS provides a comprehensive suite of tools and best practices to help organizations architect secure, resilient, and compliant cloud solutions.

Key considerations in the security pillar

Security is a foundational pillar of the AWS Well-Architected Framework, emphasizing the importance of implementing robust security measures to protect data, systems, and assets. Key considerations include [3]:

- **IAM**: Implementing IAM policies to control user access to resources, ensuring least privilege principles and **multi-factor authentication** (**MFA**) to enhance security.

- **Data encryption**: Utilizing AWS **Key Management Service (KMS)** to manage encryption keys for data at rest and **Amazon Certificate Manager (ACM)** for encryption in transit, ensuring data confidentiality and integrity.

- **Network security**: Configuring firewalls, security groups, and **network access control lists (NACLs)** to control inbound and outbound traffic. AWS Shield and AWS WAF provide **distributed denial of service (DDoS)** protection and web application security.

- **Monitoring and logging**: AWS CloudTrail and Amazon CloudWatch are essential for tracking activities and monitoring systems. Logging API calls and system actions is vital for auditing and compliance.

Security lens

The security lens of the AWS Well-Architected Framework takes a more granular approach to securing cloud environments. It examines industry-specific and use-case-specific needs in greater detail. This lens helps ensure compliance with stringent *Health Insurance Portability and Accountability Act* (HIPAA), *Payment Card Industry Data Security Standard* (PCI DSS), and *General Data Protection Regulation* (GDPR).

Deepening the focus on protection

The security lens of the AWS Well-Architected Framework focuses on ensuring that cloud architectures are designed to protect data, systems, and assets from potential security threats.

Key concepts in the security lens

The AWS Well-Architected security lens specifically focuses on strengthening the security aspect of cloud deployments. It emphasizes the protection of data, systems, and assets to ensure customer data's **confidentiality, integrity, and availability (CIA)**, particularly in environments requiring rigorous compliance measures.

Key considerations include:

- **IAM**: Ensuring fine-grained access control through IAM roles and policies, while leveraging services like Amazon Cognito for authentication.

- **Data protection**: AWS KMS is crucial for managing and securing encryption keys across various services. AWS also supports secure connections with TLS/SSL protocols to protect data in transit.

- **Detective controls**: Real-time monitoring and logging through AWS CloudTrail and CloudWatch enable initiative-taking threat detection and quick response actions.

- **Incident response**: AWS Lambda is often utilized to automate responses to security incidents, isolate affected resources, and minimize manual intervention.

Security case study

Healthcare application migration to AWS: A healthcare organization must migrate patient data to the cloud while ensuring strict compliance with HIPAA regulations. Using the security lens, the organization utilizes various AWS services to safeguard sensitive data.

Implementation steps:

- **IAM**: The healthcare organization utilizes AWS IAM to manage user access, ensuring the least privilege of access to sensitive health data.

- **Data protection**: They utilize AWS KMS to manage encryption keys and implement encryption in transit using TLS. All patient data stored in Amazon S3 is encrypted at rest, ensuring compliance with HIPAA regulations.

- **Threat detection**: Amazon GuardDuty is deployed for continuous threat detection, with administrators receiving automated alerts about any suspicious activity.

- **Incident response**: AWS CloudTrail records all API calls, and Lambda functions are triggered to isolate compromised resources immediately, preventing further exposure.

Business impact

This healthcare organization successfully migrated to AWS while adhering to HIPAA and other regulatory frameworks. By implementing AWS's security tools and adhering to the security lens best practices, they ensured that their patient data was secure and compliant with industry standards, reducing the risk of data breaches and maintaining patient trust.

Putting the framework into practice

As the case study and lens demonstrated, integrating the AWS Well-Architected Framework's security pillar and security lens is critical to building a resilient and secure cloud environment. Organizations can achieve comprehensive resource protection by combining identity management, encryption, network security, and continuous monitoring.

Moreover, implementing the security lens ensures that industry-specific requirements are met, enhancing compliance and governance frameworks. In the case of the healthcare organization, this holistic approach to security through IAM, data encryption, threat detection, and automated responses allowed the organization to migrate to the cloud confidently, mitigate security risks, and meet regulatory requirements.

On a business scale, the security pillar and security lens serve as a foundation for architecting secure cloud solutions that are adaptable, compliant, and resilient, enabling organizations to navigate the cloud computing landscape confidently.

Reliability pillar

Reliability in cloud architecture ensures that a system consistently performs its intended function correctly and consistently under a defined set of conditions. In the context of AWS, reliability focuses on establishing a cloud environment that can recover quickly from failures, dynamically allocate computing resources to meet demand, and mitigate disruptions such as network issues or faulty hardware.

Building systems that recover and scale

Reliability is a cornerstone of cloud architecture. For cloud environments, ensuring that systems can manage failures, scale dynamically, and continue operating in the face of disruptions is essential for maintaining business continuity. AWS offers a comprehensive set of tools and best practices designed to ensure the reliability of cloud workloads.

Key considerations in the reliability pillar

Reliability ensures systems operate consistently and predictably, even in the face of failures or disruptions.

Key considerations include [4]:

- **Fault-tolrance**: Design systems that can tolerate component failures without affecting overall availability. Using multiple **Availability Zone (AZ)** or multiple region deployments ensures that workloads remain operational even when a failure occurs in one part of the system.
- **Disaster recovery**: Planning and implementing backup strategies using Amazon S3, AWS Backup, and AWS Elastic Disaster Recovery ensures that data is replicated across regions and is recoverable in case of a catastrophic event.
- **Monitoring and remediation**: AWS CloudWatch and AWS Lambda enable real-time system health monitoring. CloudWatch alarms can trigger automated remediation actions, swiftly addressing any issues.

Reliability lens

The AWS Well-Architected reliability lens ensures that cloud architecture is robust enough to operate effectively and consistently, even in the face of system failures or external disruptions. This lens guides organizations through the best practices in building resilient systems that can manage changes in demand and recover quickly from infrastructure disruptions.

Diving deeper into building resilient systems

The reliability lens expands the reliability pillar by offering detailed, industry-specific guidance on designing systems that can operate predictably and consistently in a cloud environment.

By focusing on failure management, disaster recovery, and fault-tolrance, the lens ensures organizations can maintain system reliability during growth and disruptions.

Key concepts in the reliability lens

The reliability lens emphasizes the importance of designing architectures that can operate consistently and predictably, even in the face of failures or disruptions.

Key concepts include:

- **Multiple AZ and multiple region deployments**: Ensuring that workloads are deployed across multiple AZs or regions to avoid single points of failure.

- **Graceful failure handling**: Designing systems to degrade gracefully when a component fails, thereby maintaining critical operations without requiring a total system shutdown.

- **Scalability and elasticity**: Utilizing AWS Auto Scaling, Amazon ECS, and other scalable services enables the dynamic adjustment of resources to meet changing demand, thereby maintaining reliability during fluctuating traffic patterns.

Reliability case study

Online retail platform during peak season: An e-commerce company experiences significant traffic spikes during peak shopping seasons, such as *Black Friday*. The company must ensure that its systems can handle the surge in traffic without downtime or degraded performance. The reliability lens is applied to provide the platform's fault-tolrance and scalability.

Implementation steps:

- **Multiple AZ and multiple region deployments:** The e-commerce company utilizes Amazon EC2 instances across multiple AZs, ensuring high availability during peak traffic periods. The application is also deployed in various regions to minimize latency and increase fault-tolrance.

- **Graceful failure handling**: By utilizing Amazon **Elastic Load Balancer** (**ELB**) and Amazon **Relational Database Service** (**RDS**), Multiple AZ deployments, the platform ensures that if one instance fails, traffic is automatically redirected to healthy instances, maintaining service availability unaffected.

- **AWS Auto Scaling**: The company uses AWS Auto Scaling to add or remove EC2 instances based on traffic patterns during sales events. This dynamic adjustment ensures that the platform can manage spikes in traffic without over-provisioning resources during off-peak times.

- **Disaster recovery**: The platform uses Amazon S3 to store backups of critical data. In the event of failure, the system can quickly restore data from backup, ensuring minimal downtime and data loss.

Business impact

The e-commerce company managed unprecedented traffic spikes during peak shopping seasons without service interruptions by implementing AWS's reliability pillar and reliability lens. Their systems remained available and responsive, maintaining customer satisfaction and maximizing sales. Furthermore, their ability to quickly recover from failures ensured business continuity and mitigated risks during periods of high demand.

Reliability in action

As demonstrated in the case study, implementing both the reliability pillar and the reliability lens enables organizations to construct cloud environments that are resilient and adaptable to changing demands. organizations can ensure their systems remain operational even during high-traffic events or system failures by adopting best practices such as multiple AZ deployments, graceful failure handling, and Auto Scaling.

The combination of the reliability pillar and the reliability lens provides a framework for creating cloud solutions that scale with demand and recover swiftly from failures. This approach maximizes uptime, ensuring that business operations continue smoothly even in the face of unexpected disruptions.

By implementing these practices, organizations can confidently develop systems that meet customer expectations for availability and performance while reducing the risk of costly downtime or service interruptions.

Performance efficiency pillar

The AWS Well-Architected performance efficiency lens is designed to guide organizations in optimizing their cloud resources to deliver the highest efficiency level. This lens helps architects understand how to effectively utilize AWS services to ensure systems are scaled appropriately for performance without unnecessary cost or resource wastage.

Improving resource utilization throughout

The performance efficiency pillar ensures that systems perform optimally by utilizing cloud resources and maximizing throughput. As cloud environments scale and evolve, performance efficiency remains a core requirement for meeting workload demands cost-effectively. AWS offers various services and best practices that enable organizations to achieve optimal performance levels without unnecessary overhead.

Key considerations in the performance efficiency pillar

Performance efficiency aims to optimize resource utilization and maximize system throughput to meet workload demands efficiently.

Key considerations include [5]:

- **Compute optimization**: Selecting the right compute resources, using Auto Scaling to adjust for demand, and optimizing application code to ensure systems meet performance targets.
- **Storage optimization**: Selecting optimal storage classes based on workload access patterns and optimizing data retrieval performance.
- **Database optimization**: Ensuring databases are optimized for scalability, query efficiency, and low-latency in data retrieval.

Performance efficiency lens

The performance efficiency lens focuses on optimizing resource utilization and maximizing system throughput to meet workload demands efficiently.

Key considerations are discussed in the following sections.

Applying efficiency to cloud environments

The performance efficiency lens offers a more in-depth examination of optimizing system performance for specific workloads. By focusing on resource management, performance monitoring, and the evolution of cloud environments, this lens enables organizations to refine their approach to utilizing AWS services for optimal performance.

Key concepts in the performance efficiency lens

The performance efficiency lens focuses on optimizing resource utilization and maximizing system throughput to meet workload demands efficiently. Key concepts include:

- **Compute optimization**: Ensuring that the allocated computing resources are aligned with workload requirements and utilizing Auto Scaling for dynamic resource allocation.
- **Storage optimization**: Identifying optimal storage solutions for various workloads, leveraging AWS services such as Amazon S3 for object storage and Amazon EBS for high-performance block storage.
- **Database optimization**: Using services like Amazon Aurora or Amazon DynamoDB to ensure that databases are appropriately scaled and optimized for specific use cases.

Media streaming service case study

A media streaming service must provide content to a global audience and ensure seamless performance for video playback, even during high-demand periods, such as releasing new content or live events. With a wide range of devices and varying network conditions, achieving optimal performance across regions is critical.

Implementation steps

The implementation steps are as follows:

- **Compute optimization**: The service utilizes AWS Auto Scaling and EC2 Spot Instances to dynamically adjust computed resources based on demand. During peak times (e.g., when new content is released), AWS Auto Scaling adds more EC2 instances, ensuring the system can manage the increased load without compromising performance.

- **Storage optimization**: The streaming platform utilizes Amazon S3 to store video content, providing high durability and scalability. To reduce latency and improve access speeds, the service employs Amazon CloudFront as a **content delivery network (CDN)** to cache and distribute content from edge locations closer to users.

- **Database optimization**: The platform utilizes Amazon RDS with read replicas to ensure rapid access to frequently requested content and minimal user load times. Additionally, they use Amazon ElastiCache to cache content metadata and reduce database load during peak usage times.

Business impact

The streaming service successfully manages global viewership spikes while minimizing latency by implementing the performance efficiency pillar and performance efficiency lens. It achieves a uniform user experience with high-quality streaming, irrespective of location or device, and reduces infrastructure costs by combining EC2 Auto Scaling, Spot Instances, and CloudFront caching. The result is cost optimization, improved user satisfaction, and increased viewership during high-demand events.

Performance efficiency in action

This case study shows how the performance efficiency pillar and performance efficiency lens combine to optimize resource usage while ensuring systems scale efficiently. Organizations can meet performance demands without overspending on unused resources by applying AWS services such as EC2 Auto Scaling, CloudFront, and ElastiCache.

The performance efficiency pillar enables teams to make informed decisions about compute, storage, and database optimization. The performance efficiency lens takes this a step further, offering specific guidance tailored to the unique needs of individual industries and workloads.

Together, these strategies enable organizations to build highly efficient and cost-effective cloud environments that scale seamlessly with demand, ensuring optimal performance at all times.

Cost optimization pillar

Cost optimization in the AWS Well-Architected Framework is essential for managing and reducing expenses without compromising system performance and reliability. This pillar emphasizes the judicious use of resources to achieve the most economical and efficient system operation possible. It involves understanding and controlling where money is spent, selecting the most appropriate and right-sized resources, analyzing overtime expenditures, and scaling to meet business needs without overspending.

Maximizing efficiency without sacrificing performance

The cost optimization pillar in the AWS Well-Architected Framework focuses on ensuring that workloads utilize the minimum resources necessary to meet business objectives while minimizing costs. Organizations must balance performance, scalability, and reliability with the cost of services to ensure their cloud solutions are practical and economical.

Key considerations in the cost optimization pillar

Cost optimization focuses on maximizing resource efficiency and minimizing operational expenses while maintaining performance and reliability. Key considerations include [6]:

- **Right-sizing resources**: Ensuring that the resources allocated to workloads are appropriately scaled to the actual demand. This reduces over-provisioning and the underutilization of cloud services.
- **Purchasing strategies**: Utilizing tools such as Reserved Instances, Savings Plans, and Spot Instances to reduce compute resource costs.
- **Automation**: Leveraging automation to scale, schedule resources, and execute shutdown procedures, thereby avoiding idle resources and optimizing costs to meet the workload needs.

Cost optimization lens

The AWS Well-Architected cost optimization lens provides detailed guidance on achieving the most cost-effective configuration for your cloud environment. This lens enables organizations to navigate the complexities of AWS pricing models and services, optimizing costs without compromising the performance, security, or scalability of their solutions.

Detailed approaches to efficient spending

The cost optimization lens offers additional guidance on maximizing cost efficiency, tailored to the unique requirements of various industries and cloud environments. The lens highlights best practices, tools, and strategies to minimize costs while maintaining the performance and reliability required by each workload.

Key concepts in the cost optimization lens

The cost optimization lens focuses on maximizing resource efficiency and minimizing operational expenses without compromising performance or reliability. Key considerations include:

- **Resource tagging**: Implementing a tagging strategy to categorize AWS resources, allowing organizations to track, manage, and allocate costs efficiently across various departments and projects.

- **Usage analysis**: Continuously monitor usage patterns using tools such as AWS Cost Explorer and AWS Budgets to identify waste areas and optimize resource allocation.

- **Cost-aware architecture design**: Designing architecture that optimizes low-cost services, such as AWS Lambda and Amazon S3 Glacier, to reduce unnecessary infrastructure costs.

Cost optimization case study

A startup company in the data analytics industry has limited resources and needs to ensure that its cloud infrastructure can scale as its operations grow while maintaining cost efficiency. They aim to keep their operating costs low while ensuring their platform remains flexible enough to manage varying workloads.

Implementation steps:

- **Right-sizing resources**: The company regularly reviews its EC2 instance usage using AWS Cost Explorer. They identify underutilized EC2 instances and right-size them, ensuring they pay for only the necessary resources.

- **Purchasing strategies**: The startup utilizes EC2 Spot Instances for non-critical, flexible data processing jobs. This reduces their compute costs by up to 90% compared to on-demand pricing. They also take advantage of Savings Plans to commit to a certain level of compute usage and get further discounts.

- **Automation**: To ensure that resources are only running when necessary, the company implements AWS Lambda for serverless computing tasks and AWS Auto Scaling for its EC2 instances. This ensures that compute resources are dynamically adjusted based on demand, avoiding the cost of running idle infrastructure during low-traffic periods.

- **Resource tagging**: The startup employs a detailed tagging strategy, categorizing resources by team and project. This enables them to track cloud costs efficiently and allocate expenditure accurately across different departments, ensuring better visibility in their spending.

Business impact

By applying the cost optimization pillar and cost optimization lens, the startup effectively maintains low operating expenses while scaling its infrastructure to meet demand. The use of EC2 Spot Instances, Savings Plans, and AWS Lambda ensures that the company only pays for the resources it uses, minimizing waste.

Additionally, with the implementation of AWS Cost Explorer and resource tagging, the company gains granular insights into its usage patterns, enabling it to adjust its spending proactively. This results in more effective budgeting and better financial control, contributing to long-term cost savings.

Cost optimization in action

In this case study, we examine how the cost optimization pillar and cost optimization lens collaborate to enable the startup to manage its cloud costs efficiently. By utilizing EC2 Spot Instances, Savings Plans, and AWS Lambda, the startup reduces costs and builds a scalable and flexible cloud infrastructure that can grow with its business.

The cost optimization lens takes it a step further by emphasizing the importance of resource tagging and usage analysis, which enables the company to make data-driven decisions about resource allocation. By adhering to these principles, the startup maximizes its return on AWS investments and ensures that its cloud resources are utilized as efficiently as possible.

Closing thoughts on cost optimization

The cost optimization pillar and lens work together to ensure that organizations benefit from their AWS resources while maintaining control over costs. Organizations can maintain a crucial efficiency level without compromising performance or reliability by optimizing resource utilization, leveraging cost-saving tools, and continuously analyzing spending patterns. This approach leads to significant cost savings and enables businesses to reinvest those savings into further innovation and growth.

Operational excellence pillar

Operational excellence in the AWS Well-Architected Framework supports effective workload development and management while gaining insight into operations and continuously enhancing supporting processes to deliver business value. AWS emphasizes automation, monitoring, and operational best practices to ensure systems operate efficiently and effectively.

Enabling efficient, secure, and reliable operations

The operational excellence pillar in the AWS Well-Architected Framework focuses on continuously improving processes that support applications and business objectives. This pillar is centered on automation, monitoring, incident management, and fostering a culture of continuous improvement to ensure that systems remain agile, secure, and effective.

Key considerations in the operational excellence pillar

Operational excellence ensures organizations run and manage their workloads efficiently, securely, and reliably. Key considerations include [7]:

- **Automation**: Automating manual processes to reduce human error, speed up deployment, and ensure consistency across environments.

- **Monitoring and logging**: Continuously monitoring systems and applications to identify performance bottlenecks, potential issues, and anomalies.

- **Incident response**: Establishing a well-defined response process to quickly and efficiently address failures and mitigate their impact.

- **Continuous improvement**: Creating a culture of iterative enhancements, conducting post-incident reviews, and adjusting systems and processes based on feedback and lessons learned.

Operational excellence lens

The AWS Well-Architected operational excellence lens enhances an organization's ability to effectively manage and operate its cloud environment. This lens offers detailed guidance on achieving excellence in operations, focusing on automation, monitoring, and responsive processes that ensure applications are efficient, dependable, and continually aligned with business objectives.

Improving processes and delivering business value

The operational excellence lens provides tailored guidance for improving operational workflows in the cloud. It emphasizes automation, monitoring, and performance management to ensure systems run efficiently while minimizing disruptions and risks.

Key concepts in the operational excellence lens

The operational excellence lens focuses on enabling organizations to run and manage their workloads efficiently, securely, and reliably.

Key concepts include:

- **Automation of processes**: Utilizing tools such as AWS CloudFormation, AWS CodePipeline, and AWS Lambda to automate infrastructure provisioning, configuration, and software deployment.

- **Monitoring and observability**: Implementing systems like Amazon CloudWatch and AWS X-Ray to gain real-time insights into system performance, identifying issues before they impact users.

- **Incident response and recovery**: Establish detailed incident response plans, integrate automated remediation, and conduct regular drills to ensure readiness.

- **Feedback loops**: Implementing feedback loops ensures that systems evolve continuously based on performance data, user feedback, and business goals.

Operational excellence case study

A SaaS provider specializing in **customer relationship management** (**CRM**) tools must maintain high availability and reliability while continuously delivering updates and new features to its customers. The provider aims to optimize its operational workflows by adopting the best automation, monitoring, and incident response practices.

Implementation steps:

- **Automation of deployment processes**: The provider uses AWS CodePipeline and AWS CodeDeploy to automate the **continuous integration/continuous deployment** (**CI/CD**) pipeline. This ensures that updates are deployed quickly and consistently across multiple environments without manual intervention.

- **Monitoring and observability**: The company implements Amazon CloudWatch to monitor the health of its applications and infrastructure. They setup custom metrics and alarms to track **key performance indicators** (**KPIs**) and potential issues, such as increased response times or high error rates. They also use AWS X-Ray to trace and debug microservices and ensure optimal application performance.

- **Incident response and recovery**: The provider sets up an automated incident response system using AWS Lambda and Amazon CloudWatch Alarms. When an issue is detected, Lambda functions are triggered to initiate predefined recovery actions, such as restarting instances or scaling up resources, to minimize downtime.

- **Continuous improvement**: The provider conducts regular post-incident reviews, using the insight gained to improve their systems and processes. They also implement a culture of iterative enhancements, continuously improving their product features and operational workflows.

Business impact

The SaaS provider enhances its deployment pipeline by implementing the operational excellence pillar and operational excellence lens, ensuring that updates are delivered quickly and reliably. Automating deployment processes reduces the risk of human error, and continuous monitoring enables the company to identify potential issues before they affect users.

The incident response system ensures that service disruptions are minimized and recovery is swift, leading to higher availability and better customer satisfaction. The CI process enables the company to evolve its systems over time, ensuring its infrastructure and application features remain up-to-date and aligned with customer needs.

Putting operational excellence into practice

The operational excellence pillar and operational excellence lens provide a robust approach to maintaining efficient, secure, and reliable systems. Organizations can achieve operational agility and resilience by automating workflows, monitoring system performance, and establishing incident response processes.

The SaaS provider's approach is a prime example of how the principles from these frameworks can be effectively applied to enhance service delivery and minimize disruptions. With the help of AWS CodePipeline, CloudWatch, and AWS Lambda, the company streamlines its operations, ensuring consistent performance even as the business grows and evolves.

Closing thoughts on operational excellence

Achieving operational excellence in the cloud requires a commitment to continuous improvement, automation, and monitoring. By integrating the operational excellence pillar and operational excellence lens, organizations can develop and sustain agile, reliable systems that align with business objectives, adapt to change, and uphold high service delivery standards.

The combination of automated deployment, real-time monitoring, incident response capabilities, and a culture of continuous improvement ensures that systems remain operationally efficient while driving value for the business and its customers.

Sustainability pillar

Sustainability has become a core principle in cloud architecture, reflecting the growing emphasis on environmental responsibility in the tech industry. AWS supports this shift with tools and practices designed to minimize the environmental impact of cloud computing. These include optimizing resource utilization, utilizing energy-efficient technologies, and enabling customers to reduce their carbon footprint.

Designing eco-friendly cloud solutions

The sustainability pillar of the AWS Well-Architected Framework focuses on designing and operating cloud architectures that minimize environmental impact. It encourages organizations to leverage AWS services and best practices that promote energy-efficiency, reduce waste, and support sustainable practices.

Key considerations in the sustainability pillar

AWS emphasizes sustainability through key practices, such as:

- **Energy-efficiency**: Maximizing the energy-efficiency of cloud infrastructures by utilizing AWS's efficient data centers and selecting the most suitable services for workloads.

- **Sustainable resource usage**: Optimizing resource allocation to ensure minimal environmental impact while maintaining the scalability and performance of cloud solutions.

- **Reducing carbon footprint**: Adopting renewable energy sources, implementing energy-saving strategies, and optimizing workloads to reduce the carbon footprint of cloud deployments.

- **Long-term environmental impact**: Developing architecture that meets current business needs and contributes to the organization's and the environment's long-term sustainability.

Sustainability lens

Sustainability in cloud architecture is not just about reducing costs or improving efficiency; it is about making conscious choices that benefit the environment. AWS provides a robust framework for achieving these goals, allowing organizations to leverage cloud computing to support their sustainability objectives. By implementing AWS's sustainability tools and best practices, companies can significantly lessen their environmental impact while still leveraging cloud computing's scalability, flexibility, and reliability.

Advancing environmental responsibility

The sustainability lens offers targeted guidance on designing cloud architectures that minimize environmental impact. It aligns with the goals of the sustainability pillar, offering best practices to reduce energy consumption and carbon emissions while optimizing the efficiency of cloud workloads.

Key concepts in the sustainability lens

In the sustainability lens, key concepts include:

- **Serverless architecture**: Utilizing serverless services, such as AWS Lambda, to reduce the need for provisioned infrastructure, thereby minimizing idle resources and lowering energy consumption.

- **Resource optimization**: Monitoring and adjusting resource utilization to ensure that only the necessary resources are used, reducing waste, and optimizing operational efficiency.

- **Renewable energy usage**: Selecting AWS Regions powered by renewable energy sources to reduce the carbon footprint of cloud workloads.

- **Carbon footprint measurement**: Utilizing AWS tools, such as the AWS Carbon Footprint Tool, to track the environmental impact of cloud deployments and take steps to minimize carbon emissions.

Sustainability case study

A global retailer with a substantial online presence seeks to minimize its environmental impact while preserving the scalability and performance of its e-commerce platform. The retailer adopts the sustainability pillar and lens to align its infrastructure with ecological goals.

Implementation steps:

- **Adopting serverless architectures**: The retailer moves its back-end processing tasks to AWS Lambda, reducing the need for continuously running EC2 instances. This shift lowers compute costs and decreases the energy consumption of idle servers.

- **Optimizing resource utilization**: The company utilizes AWS Auto Scaling to scale dynamically compute resources in response to demand. The retailer scaling down resources during off-peak hours ensures that it uses only the resources necessary for operational needs, thereby minimizing energy waste.

- **Utilizing renewable energy**: The retailer selects AWS Regions that use 100% renewable energy for their data centers, significantly reducing the carbon footprint of their cloud operations.

- **Tracking carbon footprint**: The company employs the AWS Carbon Footprint Tool to measure and track the carbon emissions associated with its cloud services. This enables it to pinpoint areas for improvement and strive towards achieving its sustainability goals.

Business impact

By implementing the sustainability pillar and sustainability lens, the retailer achieves different key outcomes:

- **Reduced energy consumption**: Shifting to serverless architectures and optimizing resource usage reduces the overall energy consumption of their infrastructure.
- **Lower carbon footprint**: The company successfully reduces its environmental impact by selecting renewable energy-powered AWS Regions and using the Carbon Footprint Tool to track emissions.
- **Operational efficiency**: Utilizing AWS Auto Scaling to match resource allocation with demand ensures that the retailer remains agile while minimizing unnecessary energy usage.

Putting sustainability into practice

The sustainability pillar and sustainability lens work together to enable organizations to reduce their environmental footprint while maintaining efficient, scalable cloud architectures. The global retailer's approach exemplifies how AWS services can achieve sustainability goals without sacrificing performance or scalability.

Organizations can create solutions supporting business success and environmental responsibility by adopting serverless architectures, optimizing resource utilization, and choosing renewable energy-powered regions.

Closing thoughts on sustainability

Sustainability is no longer just an ethical consideration but an essential part of modern cloud architecture. By integrating the sustainability pillar and sustainability lens, organizations can design cloud solutions that minimize energy consumption, reduce waste, and contribute to a cleaner, greener future.

The combination of AWS Lambda, AWS Auto Scaling, and AWS's renewable energy initiatives ensures that businesses can meet their operational and environmental goals cost-effectively and efficiently. By tracking and optimizing their carbon footprint, companies can take meaningful steps toward sustainable growth and environmental stewardship.

Putting the framework into practice

In the final part of this chapter, we will examine how organizations can implement the entire AWS Well-Architected Framework by synthesizing the lessons learned from each of the six pillars and lenses. We will examine how real-world companies have integrated these principles to solve complex problems, optimize infrastructure, and drive business success while maintaining operational excellence and environmental sustainability.

Conclusion

This final chapter brought our AWS cloud computing masterclass to a fitting close by examining the AWS Well-Architected Framework. This foundational model empowers architects and engineers to design resilient, secure, performant, cost-effective, and sustainable cloud solutions. We explored the six pillars of the framework—operational excellence, security, reliability, performance efficiency, cost optimization, and sustainability, each offering actionable guidance for building architectures that meet modern demands while anticipating future growth. This chapter reinforced how the framework transforms abstract cloud principles into structured, reliable, and efficient practice through practical applications, illustrative scenarios, and tool-based support from the AWS Architecture Center.

As we close this journey, we encourage you to carry forward the strategies, tools, and insights gained throughout this book. From the first steps of cloud adoption to advanced architectural governance and innovation, this masterclass was built to serve as your reference point and roadmap in the AWS ecosystem. May it continue to guide your cloud decisions and inspire you to create impactful, scalable, and forward-thinking solutions. The cloud is not a destination but an evolving frontier—and with AWS and the Well-Architected Framework, you are equipped to lead that evolution with vision and purpose.

Join our Discord space

Join our Discord workspace for latest updates, offers, tech happenings around the world, new releases, and sessions with the authors:

https://discord.bpbonline.com

Appendix 1: Smart City Architecture with AWS and the Well-Architected Framework

Introduction

This appendix presents a real-world application of the AWS Well-Architected Framework introduced in *Chapter 14, AWS Well-Architected Framework,* using a comprehensive Smart City deployment as a practical case study. Smart Cities are urban environments that utilize digital technologies and data-driven systems to enhance operations across key sectors, including transportation, energy, public safety, and infrastructure, thereby improving efficiency, sustainability, and the overall quality of life for citizens.

This example was chosen not only for its complexity and relevance but also because of the author's ongoing involvement with Smart City initiatives. It offers an ideal scenario to show how AWS services and the Well-Architected Framework pillars—operational excellence, security, reliability, performance efficiency, and cost optimization—can be used to support a scalable, sustainable, and citizen-focused digital transformation.

This end-to-end case study integrates a wide array of AWS services under a fictional—but realistic scenario in which a government agency issues a public bid to transform a metropolitan area into a Smart City. The resulting system architecture showcases how cloud-native solutions can address modern urban challenges while adhering to architectural best practices.

Structure

The appendix covers the following topics:

- Key features of the Smart City solution
- Revisiting the framework pillars
- AWS cloud computing masterclass
- Implementation scenarios and pillar alignment
- Overview of business problems and objectives
- Smart City solution design with AWS

Objectives

By the end of this appendix, the reader will be able to understand how to apply the AWS Well-Architected Framework to a complex real-world solution and show how AWS services can support urban-scale digital transformations. They will be equipped to evaluate architectural trade-offs across Smart City domains such as energy, transportation, and public safety. They will gain the ability to design scalable, resilient, and cost-effective cloud architectures using AWS-native tools. Finally, readers will learn to translate conceptual cloud principles into concrete architectural blueprints tailored for Smart City applications.

Key features of the Smart City solution

The Smart City envisioned in this architecture is characterized by the seamless integration of technology, data, and urban services to enhance quality of life, improve operational efficiency, and promote sustainable development. The following features are the core components that define its digital infrastructure and intelligent capabilities:

- **Data-driven decision making**: Extensive use of sensors and IoT devices to gather real-time data on traffic, energy consumption, air quality, and more, which is then analyzed to inform better city planning and management decisions.

- **Smart infrastructure**: Connected and optimized infrastructure systems like intelligent streetlights, smart grids for energy distribution, advanced water management systems, and connected waste bins.

- **Smart mobility**: Efficient transportation systems including real-time traffic updates, smart parking, integrated public transport, and promoting alternative modes of transport like cycling.

- **Citizen engagement**: Platforms for citizen feedback, participatory decision-making processes, and access to relevant city data through mobile apps.

- **Sustainability focus**: Initiatives to reduce the carbon footprint through energy-efficient buildings, renewable energy sources, and optimized waste management.

- **Open data policy**: Sharing of city data with developers and citizens to encourage innovation and transparency. Examples of Smart City applications:

  o **Traffic management**: Real-time traffic monitoring and signal adjustments based on congestion levels.

  o **Smart street lighting**: Automated lighting systems adjust brightness based on ambient light and foot traffic.

  o **Energy optimization**: Building energy management systems that monitor and optimize energy consumption.

  o **Waste management**: Optimized waste collection routes based on sensor data from waste bins.

  o **Public safety**: Video surveillance with facial recognition and crime hotspot analysis.

  o **Smart healthcare**: The use of technology to improve healthcare delivery and outcomes, using devices, data, and digital technologies to enhance the efficiency, quality, and accessibility of medical care.

Challenges in developing a Smart City

Innovative city initiatives promise innovation, efficiency, and improved quality of life, but their implementation comes with complex challenges that must be addressed at every stage of planning and deployment. These challenges, from economic and technological limitations, must be understood and mitigated to ensure sustainable and inclusive urban transformation. Key barriers include:

- **High initial investment**: Infrastructure upgrades and IoT deployment incur significant upfront costs.

- **Data privacy and governance**: Citizens' data must be securely collected, stored, and processed.

- **Digital divide**: Ensuring fair access to services across all communities is crucial.

- **Integration complexity**: Legacy systems and vendor-specific technologies can create interoperability roadblocks.

- **Security concerns**: Expanding the digital attack surface requires robust cybersecurity measures.

- **Scalability and reliability**: Systems must perform reliably under varying workloads and fault conditions.

The public bid winners will follow the AWS Well-Architected Framework for a Smart City based on AWS cloud services. The framework focuses on five pillars: operational excellence, security, reliability, performance efficiency, and cost optimization. An overview of what will be included in the project is discussed in the following sections.

Revisiting the framework pillars

The framework's six pillars—operational excellence, security, reliability, performance efficiency, cost optimization, and sustainability—are more than just guidelines; they are the foundational principles that guide architects and engineers in creating optimal cloud solutions that are not only aligned with current technological advances but are also geared towards future scalability and innovations. Refer to the following list:

- **Operational excellence**: This pillar emphasizes the importance of automation, monitoring, and proactive response strategies in maintaining agile and reliable cloud operations.

- **Security**: In an era of increasing cyber threats, this pillar emphasizes a layered security approach to protect data, applications, and infrastructure from unauthorized access and potential breaches.

- **Reliability**: Essential for keeping customer trust, this pillar focuses on creating fault-tolerant systems that assure continuous service availability and swift recovery from disruptions.

- **Performance efficiency**: This involves improving the use of computing resources to meet system demands dynamically and efficiently, ensuring that the solutions are both agile and cost-effective.

- **Cost optimization**: Addressing the strategic need to balance expenditure with performance, this pillar encourages the adoption of cost-effective measures without compromising system capabilities.

- **Sustainability**: Reflecting AWS's commitment to environmental responsibility, this new pillar motivates architects to design eco-friendly systems that contribute to sustainability goals.

Reflecting on insights and applications

Each pillar is explored through various lenses, offering detailed insights into specific applications and industries. This approach enhances understanding and shows the practical application and relevance of each principle across multiple scenarios.

Transformation and innovation

Far from being static, the AWS Well-Architected Framework evolves to integrate emerging technologies and lessons learned. By applying its principles, organizations can better navigate the complexities of cloud computing, accelerate innovation while maintaining governance, performance, and security.

The following illustration presents a practical example of how the AWS Well-Architected Framework is applied in real-world cloud architectures. It outlines the solution components and workflow steps, highlighting how each pillar interconnects to support operational excellence, reliability, security, performance, and cost efficiency throughout the system lifecycle.

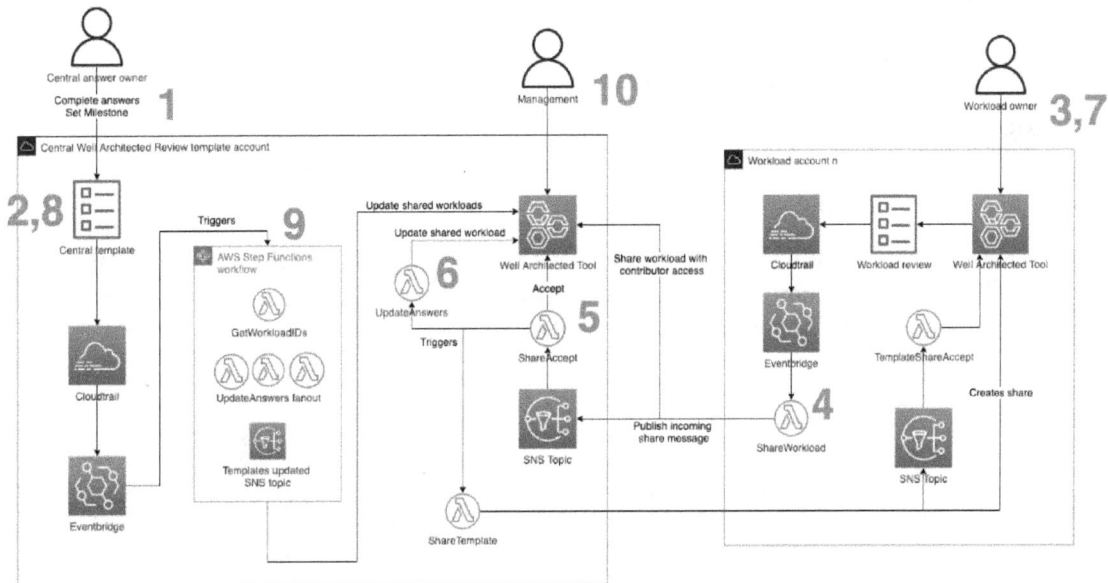

Figure Appendix.1: Solution components and workflow steps

AWS cloud computing masterclass

As we conclude this masterclass, it is valuable to reflect on the journey from foundational cloud principles to the implementation of advanced architecture and migration strategies. This body of work has demonstrated AWS's breadth, from core services, such as compute and storage, to advanced capabilities in networking, databases, and analytics.

Beyond the technical realm, the narrative has consistently returned to best practices— operational excellence, innovation, and continuous improvement. These themes reinforce the idea that cloud maturity is as much about culture and discipline as it is about services and tools.

Embracing the future

Let this guide serve as both a reference and an inspiration for your continued AWS journey. Through real-world scenarios and practical insights, we aim to equip you with the knowledge to engage with the ever-evolving landscape of cloud computing confidently.

In this dynamic space, the AWS Well-Architected Framework stands as a beacon of architectural integrity. May this guide support your ambition to innovate and lead, leveraging AWS's full capabilities to build solutions that are not only functional but transformative.

Together, we can continue to imagine, learn, and shape the future of cloud computing—one architectural decision at a time [1].

AWS Architecture Center

The AWS Architecture Center serves as a centralized resource for architects, developers, and IT professionals. It offers architectural guidance, whitepapers, reference designs, and case studies to help teams build robust and scalable AWS solutions [1].

The following diagram shows how AWS reference architectures can guide common deployment scenarios. It features a recommended architecture for hosting WordPress on AWS, highlighting principles of availability, scalability, and security.

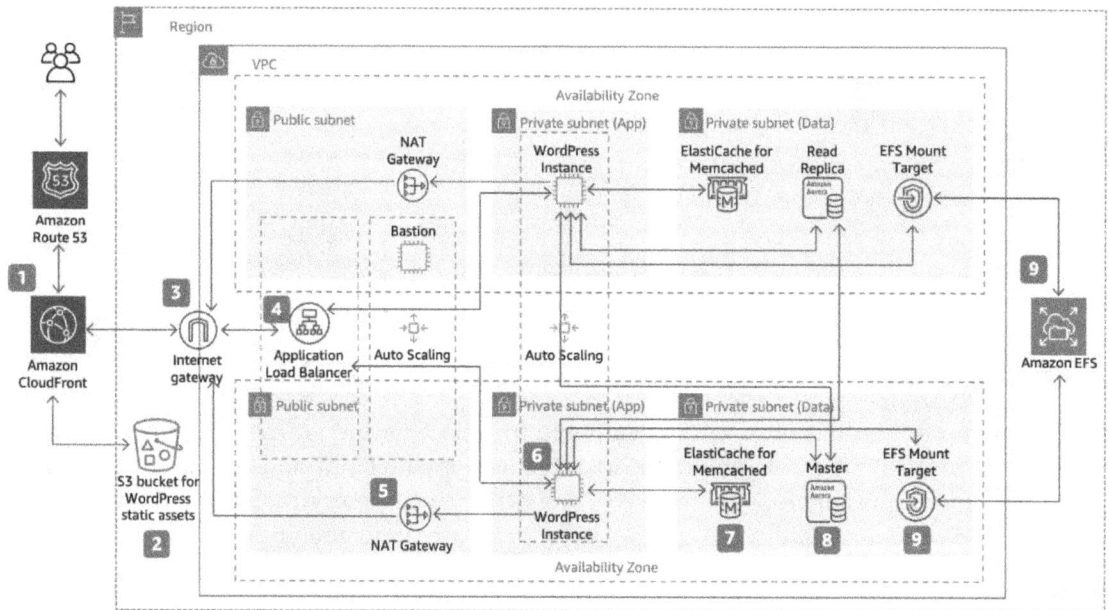

Figure Appendix.2: *Reference architecture for hosting WordPress on AWS*

Implementation scenarios and pillar alignment

Building a Smart City solution requires translating strategic goals into a modular, well-architected implementation. This section outlines how AWS services can be used to develop key components of a Smart City infrastructure. Each subdomain—ranging from public transportation and energy management to data analytics and citizen engagement—is mapped to relevant AWS services and aligned with the AWS Well-Architected Framework to ensure operational excellence, cost efficiency, security, and reliability throughout the system.

IoT for public transportation

Monitoring and managing public transportation infrastructure is a cornerstone of urban mobility. AWS services can enable real-time fleet tracking, data collection, and intelligent routing, as follows:

- **Objective**: Watch and manage public transportation fleets (buses, trains, and other methods of public transportation).

- **AWS services**:
  o **AWS IoT Core**: Collect data from vehicle sensors (location, speed, fuel consumption).
  o **AWS Lambda**: Process incoming data from devices.
  o **Amazon Kinesis**: Stream data to real-time analytics.
  o **Amazon DynamoDB**: Store vehicle data.
  o **Amazon QuickSight**: Visualize performance metrics and route optimization.

Well-Architected pillars

Adhering to the Well-Architected Framework, the following design principles ensure the IoT infrastructure supporting public transportation is scalable, secure, and cost-efficient:

- **Operational excellence**: Use CloudWatch for monitoring and alerts to ensure system health.

- **Security**: Secure data transmission using AWS IoT Device Defender and AWS IoT policies.

- **Performance efficiency**: Utilize Lambda to dynamically manage traffic bursts.

- **Cost optimization**: Optimize Lambda costs using event-driven architecture.

Energy Consumption monitoring for home devices

Smart energy initiatives require robust cloud infrastructure for real-time monitoring, data processing, and predictive analytics. AWS provides a comprehensive toolset to support energy-aware homes and consumers, as follows:

- **Objective**: Enable Smart meters for tracking energy usage in homes and give actionable insights to consumers.

- **AWS services**:

  o **AWS IoT Core**: Connect and manage smart energy meters.

  o **AWS Greengrass**: Edge computing for local device processing and interaction with the cloud.

  o **Amazon S3**: Store large datasets of consumption history.

  o **Amazon SageMaker**: Apply machine learning to predict energy usage trends.

  o **AWS Glue**: ETL for integrating and cleaning data from various sources.

Well-Architected pillars

The success of energy monitoring solutions depends on system reliability, secure handling of household data, and cost-effective long-term storage, all of which are supported by these architectural pillars:

- **Reliability**: Use AWS Backup for data recovery and implement Auto Scaling for IoT services.

- **Cost optimization**: Use S3 for low-cost, long-term storage.

- **Security**: Implement encryption and access control on IoT data with AWS IoT Device Management and **Identity and Access Management (IAM)** roles.

Smart City general platform and services

A unified platform is critical for integrating services across urban sectors. AWS cloud services offer the foundational infrastructure needed for city-wide scalability, automation, and service delivery, as follows:

- **Objective**: Provide a scalable and secure infrastructure for Smart City services, integrating various systems (e.g., traffic management, healthcare, environmental monitoring).

- **AWS services**:

  o **AWS CloudFormation**: Automate the provision of resources.

  o **Amazon RDS**: Centralized relational data storage for city services.

  o **Amazon VPC**: Network isolation to ensure secure connectivity between services.

  o **AWS web application firewall (WAF)**: WAF protects applications from web attacks.

  o **Amazon CloudFront**: Ensures content delivery with low-latency for city-wide services.

Well-Architected pillars

By applying the Well-Architected Framework to the general platform, cities ensure secure operations, cost control, and reliable service performance, as follows:

- **Performance efficiency**: Leverage Auto Scaling to manage variable loads for various services.

- **Cost optimization**: Use Reserved Instances for predictable workloads and Spot Instances for flexible workloads.

- **Security**: Utilize IAM, **Key Management Service** (**KMS**), and VPC security groups to control access and data security.

Data management and analytics

Smart Cities generate massive data volumes. AWS services enable cities to store, process, and visualize diverse datasets, supporting informed decision-making and urban innovation, as follows:

- **Objective**: Aggregate data from various sources (traffic, utility meters, and environmental sensors) and analyze it to gain actionable insights.

- **AWS services**:

  o **Amazon Redshift**: Data warehouse for centralized analytics.

  o **Amazon EMR**: Process large data sets for data transformation.

  o **AWS Lake Formation**: Build a data lake for storage and governance.

  o **Amazon QuickSight**: Visualization of city metrics, trends, and forecasts.

Well-Architected pillars

This architecture uses AWS best practices to ensure data availability, security, and regulatory compliance while supporting real-time analytics at scale, as follows:

- **Operational Excellence**: Implement automation for data pipelines and use monitoring tools, such as CloudWatch, to generate alerts.

- **Reliability**: Store backup copies of critical data in multi-region S3 buckets for disaster recovery.

- **Security**: Ensure compliance with data privacy regulations (e.g., *General Data Protection Regulation (GDPR)*, *Health Insurance Portability and Accountability Act (HIPAA)*) by using AWS Compliance programs and encryption.

Citizen engagement and communication

Effective citizen engagement is fundamental to a Smart City. AWS services support real-time communication, enhance public interaction, and provide scalable infrastructure for citizen-centric applications, as follows:

- **Objective**: Facilitate communication between citizens and city services.

- **AWS services**:

  o **Amazon SNS**: Send push notifications for city alerts, including weather, traffic, and other notable events.

  o **Amazon Chime SDK**: Build a messaging platform for citizen engagement.

  o **Amazon Connect**: Setup a call center for customer support and citizen queries.

Well-Architected pillars

Applying the AWS Well-Architected Framework helps ensure that these communication services are secure, reliable, and optimized for cost and long-term sustainability, as follows:

- **Security**: Secure communication channels and citizen data using encryption.

- **Cost optimization**: Enhance messaging costs by utilizing SNS with message filtering.

- **Reliability**: Use Amazon Connect's built-in redundancy to setup a failover system.

Next steps

The final step after setting up high-level architecture is implementation. The following recommendations provide a structured approach for implementing a Smart City initiative based on AWS best practices and Well-Architected principles:

1. Define a clear architecture diagram for the entire Smart City project.

2. Break down the project into small, actionable milestones, each focusing on implementing one or more aspects.

3. Ensure that you document how each service is being used and why it aligns with the Well-Architected Framework.

Overview of business problems and objectives

To implement an effective Smart City strategy, it is crucial to start with a clear understanding of the city's core challenges and the objectives driving its digital transformation. The following sections outline the business problem and the Smart City initiative's strategic goals.

Business problem

The city aims to enhance urban efficiency and quality of life by implementing a digital strategy integrating various sectors, including transportation, energy, healthcare, and infrastructure. The city aims to use real-time data to make informed decisions, enhance service delivery, and foster a sustainable, interconnected ecosystem for its citizens.

Business objectives

The Smart City initiative outlines the following strategic goals, aligning with the broader vision of becoming a digitally enabled, citizen-centric urban center. These goals reflect a commitment to sustainability, operational efficiency, and public engagement through the intelligent use of technology and data:

- Improve city management and citizen services through data-driven decision-making.

- Improve energy consumption, transportation, and waste management.

- Ensure sustainability through Smart infrastructure and energy-efficient systems.

- Engage citizens in developing Smart City solutions by sharing open data.

- Enable efficient mobility and sustainable development through connected infrastructure and services.

- Promote security through advanced public safety systems.

Core use cases

To meet its goals, the city has shown key cases that are relevant to guiding the implementation of Smart City technologies. These cases represent high-impact domains where AWS cloud services can drive measurable improvements in urban operations and the quality of life for citizens:

- **Smart mobility**: Enhance traffic flow, integrate public transportation, provide real-time traffic updates, and help innovative parking solutions.

- **Energy management**: Enhance energy usage with Smart grids and connected home devices for correct utility measurement.

- **Public infrastructure**: Smart street lighting, waste management, and connected infrastructure for efficient services.

- **Citizen engagement**: Enable participatory decision-making through apps and feedback platforms.

- **Environmental sustainability**: Reduce carbon footprint through the integration of renewable energy and optimized waste management.

Smart City solution design with AWS

Addressing the business requirements for AWS pillars is necessary to effectively implement these core use cases and ensure the smooth functioning of Smart City solutions.

Operational excellence business requirements

To manage a Smart City's evolving infrastructure effectively, it is essential to maintain reliability, automate tasks, and support continuous delivery. The following objectives guide the approach to ensuring operational agility at scale:

- Ensure the city's systems can scale, are easy to manage, and can manage evolving demands while keeping resilience.

- Implement **continuous integration/continuous delivery (CI/CD)** pipelines for rapid deployment and updates.

AWS services to use

AWS provides services that enable proactive monitoring, automation, and control across cloud-based infrastructure. These tools help Smart Cities deliver consistent performance and operational efficiency:

- **Amazon CloudWatch**: This service provides monitoring and alerting for the health of various systems, including traffic lights, energy grids, and waste management sensors. Its goal is to ensure prompt responses to any issues that may arise within these systems.

- **AWS Lambda**: Use Lambda for serverless computing to trigger actions based on events, such as adjusting traffic lights or activating public transport systems based on real-time data.

- **AWS Systems Manager**: Automate tasks such as updating connected devices in infrastructure (including bright lighting, IoT sensors, and other Smart devices) across the city.

- **Amazon CloudTrail**: Track changes to the AWS environment and monitor resource usage for operational audits.

Implementation

A strong operational strategy includes automation, observability, and responsive architecture. Here is how AWS services can be configured to support these goals in real-world Smart City deployments.

Smart Cities are powered by various cloud-native applications that continuously collect, analyze, and act on real-time data. Several designs are implemented using AWS Lambda and an automated CI/CD pipeline built on AWS CodePipeline, ensuring a rapid deployment cycle.

Security business requirement

Smart City infrastructure must manage sensitive citizen data, public utilities, and government services. Security requirements focus on protecting information, adhering to data regulations, and fostering trust through responsible design, as follows:

- Safeguard sensitive data (e.g., citizen information, traffic data, and energy consumption) and follow relevant data privacy regulations, such as the GDPR.

- Secure data in transit and at rest across IoT devices, citizen apps, and city management systems.

AWS services to use

The following AWS services are recommended for implementing strong security controls and protecting critical data assets. They ensure **confidentiality, integrity, and availability (CIA)** across all digital services.

- **AWS IAM**: Define policies to ensure proper access control across all city services, granting only the necessary access to each user, device, or service.

- **AWS KMS**: Secure sensitive data using encryption in transit and at rest.

- **AWS Shield**: This service protects the city's infrastructure from **distributed denial of service (DDoS)** attacks that could disrupt public transport or power distribution.

- **Amazon VPC**: Create isolated networks for different services to ensure network-level security and prevent unauthorized access between systems.

- **AWS WAF**: Protect public-facing applications from common web exploits and keep a secure online interface for citizens.

Implementation

Security implementation spans access control, data encryption, traffic filtering, and threat detection. The strategies outlined below explain how AWS services ensure robust security for Smart cities.

All sensitive data from citizens (e.g., energy usage, transportation habits) is encrypted using AWS KMS. IoT data is securely transmitted using Amazon IoT Core and stored in encrypted databases, such as Amazon **Relational Database Service (RDS)**.

Reliability business requirements

Reliability is a core requirement for mission-critical Smart City systems. These requirements focus on achieving high availability and resilience to infrastructure or application failures.

Ensure the system can recover quickly from failures and scale to manage demand spikes during peak traffic hours or periods of high energy consumption.

AWS services to use

AWS offers various scalable computing and data streaming services that improve application performance and responsiveness. These services adapt in real-time to meet changing infrastructure demands:

- **Amazon S3**: Store backup data and essential city records (e.g., traffic data, historical energy consumption data) with high availability.

- **AWS Elastic Load Balancing (ELB):** This service ensures an even distribution of traffic to microservices and databases, keeping availability during traffic spikes (e.g., traffic updates, citizen engagement platforms).

- **AWS Auto Scaling**: Scale resources automatically to manage large amounts of traffic, especially during peak hours or public events.

Implementation

To keep responsiveness and improve performance, Smart City applications must scale elastically and respond quickly to changes in usage patterns. The following implementations demonstrate this adaptability.

For systems such as real-time traffic monitoring and IoT-based energy meters, use AWS Auto Scaling to automatically manage high request volumes. Amazon RDS and DynamoDB offer universally available fault-tolerant databases for storing data in Smart transportation and energy management systems.

Performance efficiency business requirements

In a Smart City ecosystem, the responsiveness of the system and the scalability of resources are crucial for delivering high-quality public services. The following performance requirements guide the management of dynamically shifting workloads across traffic, utilities, and citizen services:

- Optimize system performance across all services (traffic management, energy consumption, waste management, and other public services) while ensuring systems respond to dynamic city-wide demands.

- Ensure the scalability of IoT devices and connected infrastructure, ensuring data is processed and acted upon quickly and efficiently.

AWS services to use

Smart Cities must rely on services that support real-time analytics, efficient event processing, and scalable compute resources to meet performance goals. The following AWS tools enable consistent, low-latency performance across urban systems:

- **Amazon EC2 and AWS Fargate**: Use these services for containerized and server-based deployments to run city management applications that require efficient scaling. AWS Fargate provides serverless computing for containers, while EC2 instances allow greater flexibility in handling computing-heavy applications like data analytics for traffic prediction.

- **Amazon Kinesis**: Amazon Kinesis is used to ingest and process real-time data from IoT devices, like traffic sensors and Smart meters, enabling immediate insights and actions. This helps process vast amounts of data from Smart devices and sensors deployed in the city.

- **AWS Elastic Beanstalk**: For easy management and deployment of applications related to Smart infrastructure and citizen engagement, AWS Elastic Beanstalk can deploy the required components in the background with minimal configuration.

- **AWS Lambda**: As mentioned earlier, AWS Lambda ensures that lightweight, event-driven workloads (such as activating Smart parking or adjusting energy distribution based on usage) are executed efficiently without the need for dedicated servers.

- **Amazon CloudFront**: To quickly deliver city services to citizens, use CloudFront to cache static content (e.g., traffic updates and city data) and serve it to users with low-latency.

Implementation

By integrating scalable compute services and real-time data pipelines, Smart City infrastructure can adapt to fluctuating demands. The following implementation outlines how AWS supports these adaptive, performance-driven workloads:

- All real-time systems, such as traffic management, energy grids, and citizen engagement platforms, rely on highly scalable services like AWS Kinesis, Lambda, and Fargate to dynamically adjust to traffic or energy usage fluctuations. The system adapts to real-time conditions through autoscaling mechanisms, ensuring the city's infrastructure is responsive under normal and peak conditions.

- For example, if an energy demand surge occurs, the system can scale compute resources dynamically to analyze the data, optimize energy distribution, and relay instructions to smart grids. Similarly, AWS Fargate manages containerized services for real-time transportation updates, adjusting traffic signals as needed.

Cost optimization business requirements

Smart Cities must deliver high-impact services while staying within budget. These requirements focus on minimizing infrastructure costs, reducing idle resources, and implementing pricing strategies that align with service demands:

- Minimize costs while delivering high-quality services for the Smart City.

- Improve AWS resources to avoid over-provisioning and use resources only when necessary.

AWS services to use

AWS offers different tools and pricing models to effectively manage cloud costs, adjusting resource usage, automating cost-saving measures, and ensuring long-term budget efficiency, as follows:

- **AWS Cost Explorer**: This tool tracks usage and cost trends, enabling the city to identify areas for improving its AWS spend. With AWS Cost Explorer, the city can gain detailed insight into its usage patterns and cut unnecessary costs.

- **AWS Auto Scaling**: Automatically scale resources up or down to meet demand, ensuring that the city only pays for the resources needed. For example, Amazon EC2 instances can be scaled based on the workload to match traffic or energy usage demands, ensuring that fewer resources are consumed during off-peak hours.

- **Amazon S3 Intelligent-Tiering**: To manage substantial amounts of data collected from IoT devices, S3 Intelligent-Tiering automatically moves infrequently accessed data to lower-cost storage classes, ensuring cost savings.

- **AWS Savings Plans**: To reduce costs, the city can commit to long-term usage of AWS services, such as EC2 and Lambda, through Savings Plans, which offer significant discounts on on-demand pricing.

- **Amazon Aurora Serverless**: For database needs, Amazon Aurora Serverless can automatically scale compute capacity according to traffic, ensuring the city only pays for database usage when it is needed.

Implementation

Cost-aware architectural planning is crucial in the development of Smart Cities. This implementation demonstrates how AWS services collaborate to minimize operational costs while maintaining optimal performance and scalability:

- The Smart City is built with a heavy focus on cost optimization. For example, AWS Lambda processes data on demand, eliminating the need for server provisioning and ensuring that the city only pays for the compute time it actually uses. This is complemented by Amazon S3 for storing sensor data and historical records, with the intelligent tiering feature ensuring cost-effective data storage.

- For infrastructure and compute resources, AWS Auto Scaling ensures that resources are scaled in line with demand. For instance, during off-peak hours when energy demand is low, the system reduces the number of active compute instances running Smart grid analysis, minimizing operational costs.

- Additionally, the city utilizes Amazon Aurora Serverless for its transactional database, which manages citizen data. This allows the database to scale automatically in response to demand, ensuring no over-provisioning and no idle compute resources.

Integration

Now that we have covered the primary AWS Well-Architected pillars, let us discuss how various components, such as IoT, smart infrastructure, and citizen engagement, integrate into this Smart City solution. To bring the Smart City vision to life, seamless integration of IoT devices, infrastructure components, and citizen services is essential. This section presents how AWS services enable these layers to communicate, interoperate, and function as a cohesive ecosystem.

IoT for Smart City systems

The foundation of Smart City solutions lies in using connected devices that generate real-time data. AWS IoT services provide a secure and scalable framework for deploying and managing these devices across public transportation and home energy systems, as follows:

- **IoT for public transportation**: Use Amazon IoT Core to securely connect IoT devices (e.g., buses, trains, and traffic signals) and enable real-time communication between public transportation systems. This will allow the city to adjust traffic lights dynamically, provide users with real-time information, and track vehicle status in real-time.

- **IoT for home devices (energy monitoring)**: Amazon IoT Core also facilitates the connection of energy meters in homes to monitor consumption. The data can then be processed through AWS Lambda to send notifications to users or trigger energy-saving measures.

Smart Infrastructure

Building resilient and intelligent infrastructure requires continuous monitoring and adaptive systems. The following components outline how AWS supports smart infrastructure, from environmental monitoring to real-time energy optimization:

- **Smart streetlights and environmental sensors**: AWS IoT Core integrates with smart streetlights and environmental sensors to monitor air quality, noise levels, and energy usage of streetlights. The data can be analyzed in real-time using AWS Kinesis and stored in Amazon S3 for long-term analysis.

- **Energy optimization**: The Smart grid system uses AWS IoT Core to manage real-time energy distribution. It is integrated with Amazon DynamoDB to store real-time usage data and Amazon Redshift for historical data analysis and forecasting.

Citizen engagement

A Smart City prioritizes its citizens' involvement. AWS enables the development of applications and platforms that facilitate two-way communication, real-time feedback, and data transparency, thereby enhancing civic participation and trust:

- **Citizen feedback platforms**: The city can develop mobile apps or web-based platforms for citizens to provide feedback, report issues, and access real-time city data. These apps can be built on Amazon API Gateway and AWS Amplify, providing easy access to public data and interactive features.

Implementation

Using Amazon IoT Core, AWS Lambda, and Amazon DynamoDB, all IoT-connected devices in the city are securely connected and interact seamlessly to provide real-time data for analysis and decision-making. Amazon S3 and AWS Redshift store and analyze data, while AWS Amplify supports citizen-facing applications that enable users to interact with city services.

The successful deployment of Smart City services requires a well-orchestrated application of AWS tools across all architectural layers. The implementation strategy ensures real-time responsiveness, secure data flows, and a unified digital environment.

Security business requirement

Security is fundamental to the innovative city framework, particularly when managing personal data, traffic telemetry, and infrastructure controls. The following services protect Smart City systems from internal and external threats.

Ensure data privacy and security for sensitive information like traffic data, energy usage, personal data, and innovative grid configurations. Protect the system from unauthorized access and implement robust measures to ensure compliance with data protection laws, such as the GDPR and the *California Consumer Privacy Act* (*CCPA*).

AWS services to use

To uphold robust cybersecurity and data governance policies, AWS offers various security tools and services tailored for scalable public-sector environments. These services ensure compliance, protection, and integrity across all data layers:

- **AWS IAM**: IAM is used to implement strong access control policies, ensuring that only authorized personnel and systems can access the Smart City's resources.

- **AWS KMS**: Leverage KMS for encrypting sensitive data at rest (e.g., data collected from IoT devices, citizen information, or public infrastructure management data).

- **AWS WAF**: Protect citizen-facing applications and APIs by using WAF to guard against common web exploits, including SQL injection, **cross-site scripting** (**XSS**), and other vulnerabilities.

- **Amazon GuardDuty**: Use GuardDuty to watch suspicious activity and unauthorized access across the AWS infrastructure. This service helps detect malicious behavior in real-time.

- **AWS CloudTrail and AWS Config**: These services enable monitoring and recording of actions taken in the environment, ensuring that governance and compliance standards are met. They can also help track any unauthorized or unexpected actions.

- **AWS Shield**: Use AWS Shield for enhanced protection against DDoS attacks, particularly for public services that may meet high volumes of traffic or targeted attacks.

Implementation

Implementing security effectively across the Smart City requires a layered approach. The following strategies detail how AWS services are configured to maintain privacy, defend against attacks, and ensure accountability:

- IAM roles and policies are defined for different city services (e.g., traffic management, energy optimization, and citizen engagement) to ensure that only authorized systems or users can access sensitive information. Each IoT device or application within Smart City will have its policy specifying the minimum required permissions.

- For example, Amazon KMS encrypts all communication between IoT devices, ensuring the integrity and confidentiality of sensitive data, such as energy consumption or personal information. All encrypted data can then be stored securely in Amazon S3, with IAM policies restricting access to authorized entities.

- AWS WAF will protect the Smart City's public APIs (for example, those used by citizens to view traffic or energy data) from external threats, ensuring that only legitimate requests from verified users or systems can pass through.

- Amazon GuardDuty continuously monitors the Smart City's infrastructure, flagging suspicious activities such as unauthorized access or unusual network traffic patterns. The integration of CloudTrail ensures that all activities are logged and can be reviewed for compliance purposes.

Operational excellence business requirement

Operating a Smart City efficiently requires continuous monitoring, process automation, and real-time feedback mechanisms. This section defines the operational excellence goals and how AWS tools help achieve them. Efficient management and constant improvement of the Smart City's infrastructure, including the ability to monitor, evaluate, and continually improve services.

AWS Services to Use

AWS offers a suite of operational services that empower Smart City administrators to manage large-scale deployments, diagnose performance issues, and proactively maintain system health, as follows:

- **AWS CloudWatch**: CloudWatch monitors the health and performance of innovative city systems. Set alarms for anomalies or performance degradation across services like energy grids, traffic management, or waste collection systems.

- **AWS Systems Manager**: The AWS Systems Manager can automate patching and configuration management for all city infrastructure, thereby automating routine maintenance tasks and improving operational efficiency.

- **AWS Config**: Utilize AWS Config to track configuration changes in the environment, ensuring all resources adhere to the city's policies and governance requirements.

- **AWS X-Ray**: X-Ray debugs and analyzes performance issues in distributed applications. For example, it could trace Smart grid or energy optimization applications to ensure they perform optimally.

- **AWS CloudTrail**: Track all user and system actions on the infrastructure to ensure that only authorized changes are made to the Smart City resources.

Implementation

With AWS, city administrators can automate processes, respond to incidents more quickly, and continuously improve their infrastructure using actionable insights from real-time data, as follows:

- CloudWatch monitors the entire ecosystem of the Smart City's infrastructure and services, including traffic data processing, energy usage, waste management, and citizen engagement. CloudWatch dashboards will enable the operations team to visualize the current health of the services and find potential problems proactively.

- If traffic congestion reaches abnormal levels, CloudWatch can trigger an alarm and prompt the system to scale added compute resources to process traffic data and adjust traffic management systems accordingly.

- With AWS Systems Manager, city administrators can automate systems' patching across different infrastructures. This cuts the need for manual updates, reducing human error and improving efficiency.

- AWS X-Ray will help troubleshoot issues related to system performance bottlenecks. For example, X-Ray can analyze traffic management applications and pinpoint slow database queries or performance issues in communication between different city services.

- AWS CloudTrail will allow the team to keep logs of all changes to infrastructure and policies, which can be reviewed for troubleshooting or audit purposes. For example, if an unauthorized change was made to the traffic management rules, administrators can quickly track the source of the change.

Reliability business requirements

Ensure high availability and resilience for all systems, particularly in critical areas like traffic management, energy optimization, public safety, and healthcare. Reliability ensures that innovative city systems run continuously, even under adverse conditions. This section highlights the AWS-based mechanisms that provide resilience, from failover capabilities to redundant storage.

AWS services to use

AWS services are selected for their ability to maintain high availability, perform consistent backups, and deliver fault-tolerant performance across all Smart City workloads, as follows:

- **AWS Availability Zones (AZs)**: Distribute the Smart City's applications across multiple AZs to increase fault-tolerance and minimize the risk of downtime due to infrastructure failures.

- **Amazon Route 53**: Utilize Route 53 for reliable **domain name system** (**DNS**) routing, directing users to the correct services, particularly during peak traffic periods or when a service is unavailable.

- **Amazon S3 and Glacier**: For long-term data storage, Amazon S3 will manage data from Smart City devices, such as traffic cameras, energy meters, and waste bins, while Glacier will archive data that is infrequently accessed.

- **Amazon RDS Multiple AZ**: Implement Amazon RDS Multiple AZ for critical database instances to automatically replicate data across multiple AZs, ensuring high availability and seamless failover support.

- **AWS ELB**: Ensure that incoming traffic is efficiently distributed across multiple resources to prevent any one system from becoming overloaded.

Implementation

Critical Smart City functions are deployed using redundancy strategies, automated failovers, and intelligent traffic routing—all built on AWS's resilient infrastructure—to guarantee uninterrupted service delivery:

- By deploying the Smart City services across multiple AZs, critical systems like traffic management, energy optimization, and waste management will have failover support. If one AZ experiences downtime, the system automatically switches to another AZ without service disruption.

- Amazon Route 53 will manage DNS requests to ensure users are always directed to healthy services. Route 53 will route the user to an alternative instance to maintain service availability if a particular service or application goes down.

- Amazon RDS Multiple AZ ensures that data for key services, such as traffic flow analysis, citizen engagement platforms, and energy consumption databases, stays available even if an AZ or server fails. This provides continuous availability and reliability.

- With ELB, all incoming traffic to critical applications, such as the smart parking system or public safety services, is balanced to ensure that no single resource is overwhelmed, thereby maintaining optimal performance.

Performance efficiency business requirements

Achieve optimized performance for innovative city systems, ensuring responsive services even with high traffic or complex processing needs. The performance of critical applications, such as real-time traffic management, energy usage optimization, and smart streetlights, must be maintained without bottlenecks or delays.

AWS services to use

To meet the city's performance goals, it is essential to use services that offer elasticity, speed, and scalability. The following AWS solutions provide a robust infrastructure for powering real-time applications, ensuring best resource use and low-latency:

- **Amazon EC2 Auto Scaling**: Utilize EC2 Auto Scaling to dynamically adjust the number of EC2 instances in response to demand, ensuring the infrastructure scales to meet the needs of the Smart City's various applications.

- **AWS Lambda**: Implement Lambda functions to automatically manage events, such as processing traffic updates, without requiring server provisioning. This ensures that the system only uses resources when needed, improving efficiency.

- **Amazon CloudFront**: Utilize CloudFront, AWS's **content delivery network (CDN)**, to expedite the delivery of static content, such as maps, public transportation data, and real-time traffic updates, thereby reducing end-user latency.

- **Amazon Aurora**: For database workloads that require high-performance, use Aurora to manage traffic data, energy consumption data, or other data-intensive applications, ensuring high-throughput and low-latency.

- **AWS Elastic File System (EFS)**: Utilize EFS for shared file storage, allowing multiple systems to access large datasets, such as smart grid data, traffic reports, and video feeds from surveillance cameras, efficiently.

Implementation

These implementations show how AWS performance-focused services ensure responsive, scalable, and efficient city operations—from managing traffic congestion to supporting citizen-facing applications with low-latency data delivery:

- **EC2 Auto Scaling**: Ensures traffic management resources and public transportation systems are automatically adjusted based on demand. For example, more EC2 instances can be provisioned during peak hours to process the influx of real-time traffic data.

- **AWS Lambda**: It can process events generated by Smart devices, such as IoT sensors in Smart parking or home energy meters. Lambda functions can scale up or down as needed based on the number of incoming events.

- **Amazon CloudFront**: Will catch and distribute city-wide data, such as public transportation schedules, air quality indices, and live traffic data, to citizens with minimal latency.

- **Amazon Aurora**: Provides fast, scalable, and cost-efficient data processing for databases managing high-demand workloads. Traffic, energy optimization, and waste management metrics will be stored in Aurora, ensuring quick access to real-time data.

- **Amazon EFS**: Will store and provide shared access to data from multiple Smart City systems, ensuring that resources like real-time traffic reports, camera video data, and energy usage reports are readily accessible by various applications.

Cost optimization business requirements

Manage the **total cost of ownership** (**TCO**) to ensure the Smart City is still financially sustainable. Improve resource use, minimize waste, and align costs with the value generated by each service in the Smart City.

AWS services to use

Maintaining fiscal discipline is crucial to achieving long-term success in Smart cities. The following AWS tools support cost-aware architecture by tracking, analyzing, and improving expenses across all operational components:

- **AWS Cost Explorer**: Use Cost Explorer to analyze cost and usage patterns across the Smart City's services and infrastructure, identifying areas where cost-saving measures can be applied.

- **AWS Trusted Advisor**: Utilize Trusted Advisor to identify opportunities for cost optimization, including rightsizing EC2 instances, reducing unused resources, and consolidating accounts where possible.

- **Amazon S3 Glacier**: S3 Glacier stores data at a much lower cost for long-term archival of infrequently accessed data (e.g., historical traffic data, energy usage statistics).

- **AWS Savings Plans**: For workloads with predictable usage patterns, leverage Savings Plans to commit to consistent usage over one or three years, resulting in significant savings compared to on-demand pricing.

- **AWS Budgets**: Implement AWS Budgets to monitor and alert usage and cost thresholds, ensuring that the Smart City infrastructure stays within the financial plan.

Implementation

With the following implementation strategy, Smart City leverages AWS's cost-saving mechanisms to control cloud expenditure while keeping service quality and infrastructure scalability:

- AWS Cost Explorer will enable competent city administrators to track usage costs across services such as traffic management, public transportation systems, and innovative grid applications. Administrators can adjust resource allocation by analyzing the data to avoid unnecessary expenditures.

- AWS Trusted Advisor offers recommendations for improving resource use. For instance, if an underutilized EC2 instance is running in the Smart City's infrastructure, the Trusted Advisor will suggest downsizing or shutting it down, thereby saving costs.

- For data that does not require instant access, such as archived traffic data or energy reports, S3 Glacier can store it at a fraction of the cost of standard S3 storage, while ensuring that the data can be retrieved when needed.

- AWS Savings Plans can be used for Smart grid and traffic management applications that need consistent compute resources. By committing usage over a period, the city will receive a discount on the EC2 costs associated with these services.

- AWS Budgets enables the city to set financial limits for each department (e.g., transportation, energy, infrastructure) and track progress toward meeting those goals. Administrators are alerted if usage exceeds a predetermined budget, enabling them to adjust and prevent overspending.

Conclusion

The Smart City infrastructure is optimized for performance, reliability, security, and cost-efficiency by following the AWS Well-Architected Framework. These steps ensure that the city's services scale to meet the needs of its citizens while adhering to financial constraints and providing a high-quality user experience.

Each block—security, operational excellence, reliability, performance efficiency, and cost optimization—has been addressed using AWS's best practices and innovative services. these solutions ensure that the Smart City infrastructure is built for future growth, resilience, and long-term sustainability, helping urban areas achieve a more connected, efficient, and sustainable future.

Appendix 2: Bibliography

References

[1]	AWS, *AWS Regional Services List*.
[2]	AWS, *AWS Well-Architected Tool*.
[3]	*H. Saini, R. Saini, and S. Saini, Cloud Computing: A Review on Cloud Security Management, International Journal of Computer Applications, vol. 160, pg. 9–, 2017.*
[4]	*R. Meyer, The Unbelievable Power of Amazon's Cloud, 15 April 2015.* [Online]. Available: **https://www.theatlantic.com/technology/archive/2015/04/the-unbelievable-power-of-amazon-web-services/391281/**.
[5]	*V. Kumar, D. Gupta, and A. Kaur, Cost Optimization in Cloud Computing*.
[6]	*S. Distinguin, Amazon.com: the Hidden Empire*.
[7]	A. W. S. (AWS), *AWS Well-Architected - Security Pillar*, 2024. [Online]. Available: **https://aws.amazon.com/architecture/well-architected/security-pillar/**.
[8]	A. W. S. (AWS), *AWS Well-Architected - Reliability Pillar*, 2024. [Online]. Available: **https://aws.amazon.com/architecture/well-architected/reliability-pillar/**.
[9]	A. W. S. (AWS), *AWS Well-Architected - Performance Efficiency Pillar*, 2024. [Online]. Available: **https://aws.amazon.com/architecture/well-architected/performance-efficiency-pillar/**.

[10]	A. W. S. (AWS), *AWS Well-Architected - Operational Excellence Pillar*. [Online]. Available: **https://aws.amazon.com/architecture/well-architected/operational-excellence-pillar/**.
[11]	A. W. S. (AWS), *AWS Well-Architected - Cost Optimization Pillar*. [Online]. Available: **https://aws.amazon.com/architecture/well-architected/cost-optimization-pillar/**.
[12]	A. W. S. (AWS), *AWS Premium Support Documentation: Trusted Advisor*. [Online]. Available: **https://aws.amazon.com/premiumsupport/technology/trusted-advisor/**.
[13]	A. W. S. (AWS), *AWS Elastic Load Balancing*. [Online]. Available: **https://aws.amazon.com/elasticloadbalancing/**.
[14]	A. W. S. (AWS), *AWS Documentation: Well-Architected Tool*. [Online]. Available: **https://aws.amazon.com/well-architected-tool/**.
[15]	A. W. S. (AWS), *AWS Documentation: WAF*. [Online]. Available: **https://aws.amazon.com/waf/**.
[16]	A. W. S. (AWS), *AWS Documentation: VPC*. [Online]. Available: **https://aws.amazon.com/vpc/**.
[17]	A. W. S. (AWS), *AWS Documentation: S3*. [Online]. Available: **https://aws.amazon.com/s3/**.
[18]	A. W. S. (AWS), *AWS Documentation: Route 53*. [Online]. Available: **https://aws.amazon.com/route53/**.
[19]	A. W. S. (AWS), *AWS Documentation: Machine Learning*. [Online]. Available: **https://aws.amazon.com/machine-learning/**.
[20]	A. W. S. (AWS), *AWS Documentation: Lambda*. [Online]. Available: **https://aws.amazon.com/lambda/**.
[21]	A. W. S. (AWS), *AWS Documentation: IOT Core*. [Online]. Available: **https://aws.amazon.com/iot-core/**.
[22]	A. W. S. (AWS), *AWS Documentation: IAM*. [Online]. Available: **https://aws.amazon.com/iam/**.
[23]	A. W. S. (AWS), *AWS Documentation: Global Infrastructure*. [Online]. Available: **https://aws.amazon.com/about-aws/global-infrastructure/**.
[24]	A. W. S. (AWS), *AWS Documentation: ECS*. [Online]. Available: **https://aws.amazon.com/ecs/**.
[25]	A. W. S. (AWS), *AWS Documentation: EC2*. [Online]. Available: **https://aws.amazon.com/ec2/**.
[26]	A. W. S. (AWS), *AWS Documentation: EBS*. [Online]. Available: **https://aws.amazon.com/ebs/**.
[27]	A. W. S. (AWS), *AWS Documentation: Databases*. [Online]. Available: **https://aws.amazon.com/products/databases/**.
[28]	A. W. S. (AWS), *AWS Documentation: Cost Optimization*. [Online]. Available: **https://aws.amazon.com/cost-optimization/**.

[29]	A. W. S. (AWS), *AWS Documentation: Case Studies*. [Online]. Available: **https://aws.amazon.com/solutions/case-studies/**.
[30]	A. W. S. (AWS), *AWS Documentation: AWS Compute Services*. [Online]. Available: **https://aws.amazon.com/products/compute/**.
[31]	A. W. S. (AWS), *AWS Documentation: AWS Services by Region*. [Online]. Available: **https://aws.amazon.com/about-aws/global-infrastructure/regional-product-services/**.
[32]	A. W. S. (AWS), *AWS Documentation: Auto Scaling*. [Online]. Available: **https://aws.amazon.com/autoscaling/**.
[33]	A. W. S. (AWS), *AWS Documentation - R.D.S.* [Online]. Available: **https://aws.amazon.com/rds/**.
[34]	A. W. S. (AWS), *AWS Cost Allocation and Tagging*. [Online]. Available: **https://aws.amazon.com/aws-cost-management/aws-cost-allocation/**.
[35]	A. W. S. (AWS), *AWS Case Study - GE Healthcare*. [Online]. Available: **https://aws.amazon.com/solutions/case-studies/ge-healthcare/**.
[36]	A. W. S. (AWS), *AWS Case Study - Capital One*. [Online]. Available: **https://aws.amazon.com/solutions/case-studies/capital-one/**.
[37]	Amazon Web Services (AWS), *AWS Direct Connect*. [Online]. Available: **https://aws.amazon.com/directconnect/**.
[38]	Wikipedia contributors, *Amazon Web Services*. [Online]. Available: **https://en.wikipedia.org/w/index.php?title=Amazon_Web_Services&oldid=1241468121**.
[39]	E. Wilson, *Simplify Compliance Audits with AWS Audit Manager*. [Online].
[40]	A. Wilson, *Mastering Network Security with AWS Network Firewall*. [Online].
[41]	F. Williams, R. Services, D. Awasth, Q., S. M. H., and M. P. M., *Effective compliance and audit management using Amazon Web Services (AWS) Audit Manager*. [Online]. Available: h**ttps://www2.deloitte.com/content/dam/Deloitte/us/Documents/risk/us-deloitte-aws-audit-manager-whitepaper-clean.pdf**.
[42]	R. White, *AWS Directory Service: Enterprise Cloud Directory Integration*. [Online].
[43]	M. Turner, *Real-world Applications of AWS Resource Access Manager*. [Online].
[44]	M. Turner, *AWS Security Hub Compliance Standards*. [Online].
[45]	M. Turner, *AWS Case Study: Real-world Applications of AWS Resource Access Manager*. [Online].
[46]	L. Turner, *Real-world Applications of AWS Secrets Manager*. [Online].
[47]	J. Smith, *Securing Your AWS Environment with AWS Firewall Manager*. [Online].
[48]	J. Smith, *Securing Sensitive Data in AWS with Amazon Macie*. [Online].
[49]	J. Smith, *Securing AWS Resources with Amazon Verified Permissions*. [Online].
[50]	J. Smith, *Mastering AWS Identity and Access Management: A Comprehensive Guide*. [Online].
[51]	J. Smith, *Best Practices for AWS Security Hub*. [Online].

[52]	J. Smith, *AWS Resource Access Manager: Best Practices for Secure Resource Sharing*. [Online].
[53]	J. Smith, *AWS Network Firewall: Best for Effective Security Policies*, Practices. [Online].
[54]	J. Smith, *AWS CloudHSM: Security Best Practices*, 2021. [Online].
[55]	J. Smith, *Achieving Compliance at Scale with AWS Audit Manager*. [Online].
[56]	A. Smith, *Securing Your Databases with AWS Secrets Manager*. [Online].
[57]	A. Smith, *Secure Your Web Applications with AWS Certificate Manager*. [Online].
[58]	A. Smith, *Mastering Data Encryption with AWS KMS*. [Online].
[59]	A. Smith, *Getting Started with Amazon Inspector*. [Online].
[60]	A. Smith, *Extending Active Directory to the Cloud with AWS Directory Service*. [Online].
[61]	A. Smith, *Building a Data Lake for Security Data with Amazon Security Lake*. [Online].
[62]	J. W. Rittinghouse and J. F. Ransome, *Cloud Computing: Implementation, Management, and Security*.
[63]	S. Perez, *Navigating Compliance with AWS Artifact* [Online].
[64]	J. Perez, *Protection Strategies Against DDoS Attacks, Journal of Cloud Security*, vol. 8, pg. 113–129.
[65]	J. Monson, *Security and privacy by design: a proactive approach to cybersecurity*. [Online]. Available: **https://www2.deloitte.com/us/en/pages/financial-advisory/articles/resilient-podcast-jacki-monson-security-and-privacy-by-design.html**.
[66]	J. Knight, *Securing Serverless Architectures with Amazon Cognito*. [Online].
[67]	S. Kent, *AWS Identity and Access Management: A Comprehensive Guide*. [Online]. Available: **https://aws.amazon.com/getting-started/hands-on/secure-aws-workloads-with-iam-policy-summarizer/**.
[68]	S. Kent, *Amazon Detective: Investigate Potential Security Issues*. [Online]. Available: **https://aws.amazon.com/getting-started/hands-on/investigate-potential-security-issues-with-amazon-detective/**.
[69]	M. Johnson, *Best Practices for AWS Key Management Service (KMS): A Comprehensive Guide*. [Online].
[70]	L. Johnson and M. Brown, *Leveraging Machine Learning for Data Security with Amazon Macie*. [Online].
[71]	I. Gartner, *Cloud Security Posture Management*. [Online]. Available: **https://www.gartner.com/en/information-technology/glossary/cloud-security-posture-management-cspm**.
[72]	L. Garcia and R. Turner, *Achieving Least Privilege with Amazon Verified Permissions*. [Online].
[73]	M. Davis and E. Wilson, *Using AWS Artifact for Regulatory Compliance*. [Online].
[74]	B. Davis and C. White, *Enhancing Cloud Security with Amazon Security Lake*. [Online].
[75]	R. Brown, *Best Practices for AWS IAM Implementation*. [Online].
[76]	R. Brown, *AWS Firewall Manager: Advanced Security for AWS Environments*. [Online].

[77]	*M. Brown, Securing Your Data with AWS CloudHSM.* [Online].
[78]	*M. Brown, How Amazon GuardDuty Works.* [Online].
[79]	*L. Brown, Managing SSL/TLS Certificates at Scale with AWS Certificate Manager.* [Online].
[80]	*D. Bonilla, AWS Identity and Access Management: Design and Manage Secure and Scalable Permissions.* [Online].
[81]	*AWSm, AWS Firewall Manager.* [Online]. Available: **https://aws.amazon.com/network-firewall**.
[82]	AWS, *AWS Best Practices: AWS WAF.* [Online]. Available: **https://aws.amazon.com/waf/best-practices/**.
[83]	AWS, *Securing Mobile and Serverless Applications with Amazon Cognito.* [Online].
[84]	AWS, *Logging, and Monitoring with AWS WAF.* [Online]. Available: **https://aws.amazon.com/waf/features/logging-monitoring/**.
[85]	Cloud Security Alliance, *Top Threats to Cloud Computing.* [Online]. Available: **https://cloudsecurityalliance.org/research/top-threats/egregious-eleven-deep-dive/**.
[86]	*K.P.M.G., Top Threats and Opportunities in Financial Services.* [Online]. Available: **https://assets.kpmg/content/dam/kpmg/xx/pdf/2019/11/top-threats-and-opportunities-in-financial-services.pdf**.
[87]	AWS Content, *Filtering with AWS WAF.* [Online]. Available: **https://aws.amazon.com/waf/features/filtering/**.
[88]	Amazon Web Services, Inc. (). *Content Filtering with AWS WAF.* [Online]. Available: **https://aws.amazon.com/waf/features/filtering/**.
[89]	AWS, *AWS Whitepapers.* [Online]. Available: **https://aws.amazon.com/whitepapers/**.
[90]	AWS, *AWS WAF.* [Online]. Available: **https://aws.amazon.com/waf/**.
[91]	AWS, *AWS Shield Advanced.* [Online]. Available: **https://aws.amazon.com/shield/advanced/**.
[92]	AWS, *AWS Shield.* [Online]. Available: **https://aws.amazon.com/shield/**.
[93]	AWS, *AWS Security Hub.* [Online]. Available: **https://aws.amazon.com/security-hub/**.
[94]	AWS, *AWS Secrets Manager.* [Online]. Available: **https://aws.amazon.com/secrets-manager/**.
[95]	AWS, *AWS Resource Access Manager (RAM).* [Online].
[96]	AWS, *AWS Network Firewall.* [Online]. Available: **https://aws.amazon.com/network-firewall/**.
[97]	AWS, *AWS Managed Rulesets.* [Online]. Available: **https://aws.amazon.com/waf/managed-rules/**.
[98]	AWS, *AWS Key Management Service.* [Online]. Available: **https://aws.amazon.com/kms/**.
[99]	AWS, *AWS Identity and Access Management (IAM) Identity Center.* [Online].

[100]	AWS, *AWS Identity and Access Management (IAM)*. [Online]. Available: **https://aws.amazon.com/ram/**.
[101]	AWS, *AWS Directory Service*. [Online]. Available: **https://aws.amazon.com/directoryservice/**.
[102]	AWS, *AWS CloudHSM*. [Online]. Available: **https://aws.amazon.com/cloudhsm/**.
[103]	AWS, *AWS Certificate Manager*. [Online]. Available: **https://aws.amazon.com/certificate-manager/**.
[104]	AWS, *AWS Case Study: AWS WAF*. [Online]. Available: **https://aws.amazon.com/waf/use-cases/**.
[105]	AWS, *AWS Audit Manager*. [Online]. Available: **https://aws.amazon.com/audit-manager/**.
[106]	AWS, *AWS Artifact*. [Online]. Available: **https://aws.amazon.com/artifact/**.
[107]	AWS, *API Security with AWS WAF*. [Online]. Available: **https://aws.amazon.com/waf/features/api-security**.
[108]	AWS, *Amazon Verified Permissions*. [Online]. Available: **https://aws.amazon.com/identity/verified-permissions/**.
[109]	AWS, *Amazon Security Lake*. [Online]. Available: **https://aws.amazon.com/security-lake/**.
[110]	AWS, *Amazon Macie*. [Online]. Available: **https://aws.amazon.com/macie/**.
[111]	AWS, *Amazon Inspector*. [Online]. Available: **https://aws.amazon.com/inspector/**.
[112]	AWS, *Amazon GuardDuty*. [Online]. Available: **https://aws.amazon.com/guardduty/**.
[113]	AWS, *Amazon Detective*. [Online]. Available: **https://aws.amazon.com/detective/**.
[114]	AWS, *Amazon Cognito Overview*. [Online]. Available: **https://aws.amazon.com/cognito/**
[115]	IDC, *Optimizing Data Pipelines with AWS Glue and Redshift*.
[277]	L. S. Vygotsky, *Mind in Society: The Development of Higher Psychological Processes*.
[278]	W. Vogels, *AWS Launches Amazon DocumentDB (with MongoDB Compatibility)*.
[279]	D. C. Verma, *Elements of network protocol design*.
[280]	V. Srinivasan, *Mobile DevOps: Deliver Continuous Mobile Apps Faster and More Efficiently*.
[281]	K. Smith, *A Comprehensive Guide to Data Governance Best Practices*.
[282]	J. Smith and A. Jones, *Cloud Computing Advances in Modern Business*.
[283]	A. Smith, *Mastering Data Encryption with AWS KMS*.
[284]	A. Smith and B. Johnson, *Digital Marketing Strategies: An Integrated Approach to Online Marketing*.
[285]	A. Sharma and M. Ganesh, *Internet of Things for Architects: Architecting IoT solutions by implementing sensors, communication infrastructure, edge computing, analytics, and security*.
[286]	J. W. Rittinghouse and J. F. Ransome, *Cloud Computing: Implementation, Management, and Security*.
[287]	R. Raj and A. Breskim, *Hands-On Full Stack Development with AWS AppSync and React*.

[288]	PwC, *Regulatory Compliance in Financial Services File Transfers.*
[289]	PwC, *Financial Industry Cloud Adoption: Cost and Compliance Considerations.*
[290]	*&. G. P. Varghese B., Cloud Native Microservices with AWS: Building, Deploying, and Scaling Microservices in AWS.*
[291]	*M. Murphy, Microservices on AWS.*
[292]	*McKinsey Digital, Optimizing Infrastructure for Digital Transformation.*
[293]	*McKinsey Company, Zero-Downtime Migration Strategies for Enterprise Workloads.*
[294]	*McKinsey Company, Leveraging Automation to Accelerate Mainframe Migration.*
[295]	*McKinsey Company, Improving Security in Cloud-Based File Exchange Systems.*
[296]	*McKinsey and Company, Reducing IT Overhead with Automated Data Transfers.*
[297]	*McKinsey and Company, Predictive Analytics for AWS Migration Cost Management.*
[298]	*D. Loshin, Private Clouds: Selecting the Right Hardware for a Scalable Environment.*
[299]	*D. Loshin, Cloud: Selecting the Right Hardware for a Scalable Environment.*
[300]	*D. S. Linthicum, Cloud Computing and SOA Convergence in Your Enterprise: A Step-by-Step Guide.*
[301]	*Q. Li and J. Hu, A Survey of Virtual Network Embedding Algorithms in Cloud Computing.*
[302]	*R. Lester, B. Carlson, B. Potter, E. Pullen, S. Eliot, N. Besh, J. Steele, R. King, E. Rifkin, M. Ramsay, S. Paddock, and C. Hughes, AWS Well-Architected Framework.*
[303]	*M. Leinhauser, J. Young, S. Bastrakov, R. Widera, R. Chatterjee, and S. Chandrasekaran, Performance Analysis of PIConGPU: Particle-in-Cell on GPUs using NVIDIA's NSight Systems and NSight Compute,* pp. 227-232.
[304]	*a. M. A. S. R. L. Richardson, RESTful Web APIs.*
[305]	*J. F. Kurose and K. W. Ross, Computer networking: Principles, algorithms, and applications.*
[306]	*A. Kapoor, AWS Networking Cookbook.*
[307]	*A. Jones, Mastering AWS Management and Governance.*
[308]	*E. Johnson, Mastering AWS AppSync: Build Scalable and High-Performing GraphQL APIs for Your Applications.*
[309]	*R. Jasek and R. Kokoczka, The Internet of Things in the Modern Business Environment,* pp. 103-120.
[310]	IDC, *Reducing Migration Timelines with AWS Database Migration Service.*
[311]	IDC, *Performance and Scalability of Cloud-Based Database Migration Services.*
[312]	IDC, *Optimizing Data Pipelines with AWS Glue and Redshift.*
[313]	IDC, *Global Retail Cloud Migration Study.*
[314]	IDC, *Cost Reduction in File Transfer Workflows with AWS Transfer Family.*
[315]	IDC, *Cloud Storage Report: Optimizing Large-Scale Data Transfers.*

[316]	IDC, *Cloud Readiness Study: How Enterprises Are Preparing for Migration.*
[317]	IDC, *Cloud Migration Report: Optimizing Workload Transitions to Cloud.*
[318]	G. Hohpe and B. Woolf, *Enterprise Integration Patterns: Designing, Building, and Deploying Messaging Solutions.*
[319]	*Harvard Business Review, The Role of AWS MGN in Digital Transformation.*
[320]	*Harvard Business Review, Maximizing Cloud Migration Success with AWS DMS.*
[321]	*Harvard Business Review, Mapping Application Dependencies Before Cloud Migration.*
[322]	A. Gupta, *Building Scalable Microservices with Amazon SQS, AWS Whitepaper.*
[323]	B. Golden, *Amazon Web Services For Dummies.*
[324]	S. Ghatage and V. Padmanabhan, *Disaster Recovery and Business Continuity with AWS.*
[325]	*Retail Innovation Through Real-Time Data Synchronization.*
[326]	*Enterprise IT Modernization: Challenges and Best Practices.*
[327]	*Cloud Migration Strategy and Risk Management.*
[328]	*Cloud Migration Strategies for Enterprise IT.*
[329]	*Cloud Migration Strategies and Database Modernization Trends.*
[330]	*Cloud Migration Report: Avoiding Pitfalls in Application Modernization.*
[331]	*Cloud File Transfer Strategies and Security Best Practices.*
[332]	*AI-Powered Cloud Migration Planning and Cost Optimization.*
[333]	F. A. Ganz, *The role of partnerships in the development of the Internet of Things (IoT) ecosystem: A global explorative study*, vol. 139, pp. 341-351.
[334]	M. Fowler, *NoSQL Distilled: A Brief Guide to the Emerging World of Polyglot Persistence.*
[335]	*Total Economic Impact Report: Quantifying the Business Value of AWS DMS.*
[336]	*Optimizing Enterprise Migration with AWS Migration Hub.*
[337]	*Improving Cloud TCO with AI-Driven Migration Assessments.*
[338]	*Cloud Migration Trends: The Importance of Pre-Migration Assessment.*
[339]	*Automated File Transfer Modernization Trends.*
[340]	*Accelerating Cloud Migrations with AWS DataSync.*
[341]	Flexera, *State of Cloud Report: Database and Workload Optimization.*
[342]	C. Elachi, *Introduction to the physics and techniques of remote sensing (Vol. 3).*
[343]	D. Doss and A. Wright, *Amazon Web Services in Action.*
[344]	A. Deshpande and V. Thaker, *IoT Data Analytics at the Edge*, pp. 3-25.
[345]	Deloitte, *Financial Services Transformation via AWS Mainframe Modernization.*
[346]	Deloitte, *Enhancing Analytics Workflows with AWS DataSync and Redshift.*
[347]	Deloitte, *E-commerce Scalability and Cloud Optimization.*

[348]	M. Craglia, K. Bie, D. Jackson, M. Pesaresi, and G. Remetey-Fülöpp, *Digital Earth from Vision to Practice: Making Sense of Citizen Observatories.*
[349]	C. Chappell, *Defining Enterprise Risk Management,* pp. 3-6.
[350]	K. Chander, *5G for Business.*
[351]	R. Cattell, *Scalable SQL and NoSQL data stores.*
[352]	R. Buyya, J. Broberg and A. Goscinski, *Cloud Computing: Principles and Paradigms,* A. Goscinski, J. Broberg and R. Buyya, Eds., Hoboken, pp. 74, 82.
[353]	G. C. Buttazzo, *Hard real-time computing systems: predictable scheduling algorithms and applications,* vol. 27.
[354]	M. Brown, *Securing Your Data with AWS CloudHSM.*
[355]	J. Broberg, *Cloud Computing,* First ed., R. Buyya, J. Broberg and A. M. Goscinski, Eds., Hoboken, pp. 511-531.
[356]	R. Brennan, *Full Stack Serverless: Modern Application Development with React, AWS, and GraphQL.*
[357]	*Boston Consulting Group, Accelerating Cloud Migration Through AI-Powered Assessments.*
[358]	*Accenture, Optimizing Multi-Cloud Strategies Using AWS Migration Tools.*

Join our Discord space

Join our Discord workspace for latest updates, offers, tech happenings around the world, new releases, and sessions with the authors:

https://discord.bpbonline.com

Index

www.ingramcontent.com/pod-product-compliance
Lightning Source LLC
Chambersburg PA
CBHW061739210326
41599CB00034B/6727